Out of the many, one,
Out of the din, a hymn,
Out of the anonymous throng, a friend. . . .

SHIFTING BALANCE SHEETS
Women's Stories of Naturalized Citizenship
&
Cultural Attachment

WISING UP ANTHOLOGIES

ILLNESS & GRACE, TERROR & TRANSFORMATION
2007

FAMILIES: THE FRONTLINE OF PLURALISM
2008

LOVE AFTER 70
2008

*DOUBLE LIVES, REINVENTION &
THOSE WE LEAVE BEHIND*
2009

*VIEW FROM THE BED
VIEW FROM THE BEDSIDE*
2010

SHIFTING BALANCE SHEETS
Women's Stories of Naturalized Citizenship
&
Cultural Attachment

Heather Tosteson, Kerry Langan, Charles D. Brockett & Debra Gingerich
Editors

Wising Up Press
Decatur, Georgia

Wising Up Press
P.O. Box 2122
Decatur, GA 30031-2122
www.universaltable.org

Copyright © 2011 by Wising Up Press

All rights reserved. No part of this book may be used or reproduced in any manner whatsoever without written permission, except in the case of brief quotations embodied in critical articles or reviews.

Catalogue-in-Publication data is on file with the Library of Congress.
LCCN: 2011928740

Wising Up ISBN-13: 978-0-9827262-3-5

TABLE OF CONTENTS

I. THE HOLDING ENVIRONMENT

Heather Tosteson
    Invitations & Expectations: Shifting Balance Sheets for All of Us   3
Charles D. Brockett
    Some Facts to Stand on, Some Avenues to Explore   26

II. CHINESE DAUGHTERS: ALL-AMERICAN GIRLS

Kerry Langan
    Introduction   48
Katherine D. Perry
    Song Zi Yang   54
    Are You Her Mother?   56
Linda D'Arcy
    Waiting for Emily   58
Karen Loeb
    Singing Hallelujah   62
    The Children of the White Swan   64
    Someone Told Our Daughter a Story About Ducks   66
    Walking Jiaou-Jiaou with My Daughter   68
    Before Our Daughter Learns English   69
    Customs   72
Diane Raptosh
    The Family Bed   78
    The Mother of Her Second Daughter   79
Kerry Langan
    Double Happiness   80
Madeline Geitz, Anna Anhalt, Alicia Karls
    Chinese Daughters & American Citizens: Q & A, A & Q   98
Jennifer Bao Yu Jue-Steuck
    Goodnight Moon, Goodnight Mom   120

III. NATURAL WOMEN: NATURALIZED CITIZENS

Heather Tosteson
   Introduction: Listening for Cohesion   134

Prelude: A Country of Immigrants

Mariette Landry
   Immigrant Home Movie, 1963   148
John Manesis
   Not Anymore   149
   I Be Millionaire   150
Alexandrina Sergio
   Leaving Bridget   152
   Immigrant   154

What Our Mothers Do For Us

Lisa Chan
   Cheesecake   158
Natalia O. Treviño
   The Naturalization   161
Azadeh Shahshahani
   Reflections   174
Amita Rao
   Re-Creating Her   183

What We Do for Ourselves

Boryana Zeitz
   Running and Crying in America   192
Nikolina Kulidžan
   Becoming American   194
Karen Levy
   Americans   206
   Going Home
Elizabeth Bernays
   Learning with Pollards   214
Weihua Zhang
   Daughter of the Middle Kingdom   223
Maria Shockey
   Oral Histories: Mexican-American Voices   231
Clementina
   I Want to Be One, But I Wonder . . .   247

What Does Marriage Have to Do with It?

Patricia Barone
   The Women Across the Street   260
Cathy Adams
   Chuan   262
Yu-Han Chao
   From French Maid to Chinese Bride   269
Julija Suput
   A Bouquet of Roses   272

Home Is Where . . .

Mariel Coen
   Not from Here, Ni de Alla   284
   Palabras Prohibidas   287
Angelika Quirk
   I Am from the Other Side   290
   My Life   291
   Swearing-in Ceremony   292
   What Is It That's Called Your Country   295
Sandra Soli
   How I Learned Resurrection   297
   Foreigner   299
Sonya Sabanac
   Bilingual   301
   How I Decided to Go a Little Crazy   304
Lourdes Rosales-Guevara
   My Love for the U. S. Came Later   314
Jian Dong Sakakeeny
   Today, I Don't Feel Limited by Any Borders   328
Donna Porter
   It's Only One World. Live It Up!   336

SELECT BIBLIOGRAPHY   347
ACKNOWLEDGEMENTS   349
DISCUSSION GUIDE   351
AUTHORS   359
EDITORS   366

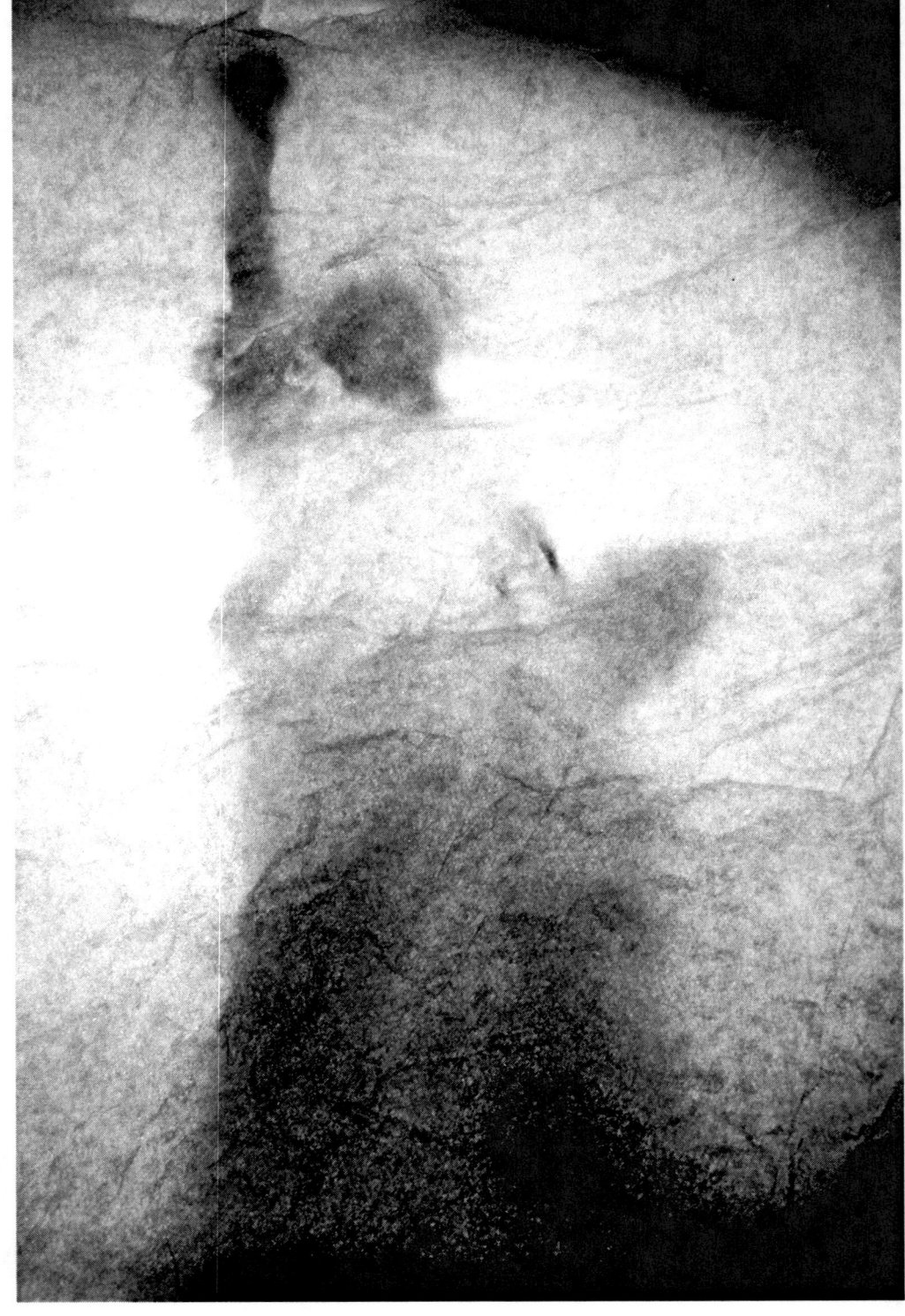

I
THE HOLDING ENVIRONMENT

HEATHER TOSTESON

INVITATIONS AND EXPECTATIONS
Shifting Balance Sheets for All of Us

We assume many of the readers of this anthology will be, like the editors, birthright citizens who have found their own circuitous ways into an understanding of the importance of an open, thoughtful discussion of what citizenship and cultural attachment have come to mean to them—and what rights and responsibilities they see as flowing from this understanding. These experiences of birthright citizens are as crucial to the healthy, full integration of naturalized citizens into neighborhoods, communities and the nation as the experiences of the new citizens themselves, whose stories are at the heart of this book—for they are the holding environment in which these stories of migration and changing allegiances take on new meaning.

I share some of my own journey at the beginning of this collection because it is part of that holding environment and because the issue is personal for everyone involved, the citizen who is naturalized and the often unreflective birthright citizen who is brought into equal relation to her by that oath. What is the nature of that relationship? Who is responsible for it? Who benefits? Where does welcome fit in? Where does respect? Affection? Permanence? I believe we often do our best thinking if it arises from the density, complexity and immediacy of our own experience, that these abstractions—nationality, community, patriotism, democracy—which can arouse such ire and adamancy, mean more and differently when clearly reconnected with their vital and very messy sources in our daily lives.

Often the answers come through most clearly and mysteriously through stories because stories, as Jerome Bruner observes, invite interpretation, expose our normative assumptions and the emotional impact of their breeching, and, through the wholeness of action, transform a multiplicity of perspectives and motivations into one mysteriously meaningful experiential whole. Stories also take two, the teller and the listener—and a bit of enchantment. Whenever we share, however briefly, that near primal quiet that overtakes us when we open to a story (wherever it is found), we may be bringing something new and valuable into being: the feeling of community.

HOW I CAME TO THE QUESTIONS IN CITIZENSHIP

My interest in the related topics of creative acculturation, migration, immigration, and citizenship has as some of its vital and messy sources my profound love and delight in my immigrant Welsh grandmother, my own migratory upbringing (which included many moves inside and outside the U.S. at formative stages in my childhood), my experiences living more voluntarily in other countries as an adult, my friendships with people in these countries and with immigrants and refugees in the United States, my disappointing experiences of good deeds of welcome gone awry, and the social complexity of the unintentionally—and often rawly—pluralistic local community I intentionally live in today.

Immigration

In 1915, my paternal grandmother, Dilys Bodycombe, born and raised in Pontardawe, Wales, sailed from Liverpool on the ship St. Paul and arrived at Ellis Island on November 22nd. She was eleven and accompanied by her mother and father and older sister, Gladys. They were, along with ten more of her siblings, part of the second large wave of European immigrants to come to the States. She was, in a quirky twist, mistakenly listed on the ship's manifest as Lilian, which later would be the name of one of her older son's favorite mistresses. (He would show an over-riding preference for alliances, legitimate and otherwise, with women who were foreign-born.) Dilys was part and parcel of a large, melodiously histrionic family of Welsh coal-miners—who squabbled over cards, serenaded each other with arias, and quoted copiously from their favorite socialist, George Bernard Shaw. They were, like many recent immigrants, very ambitious for their children and saw education as the clearest path to social mobility. On Dilys's part, whose own formal education ended with high school, perhaps this ambition came from the freedom she experienced re-inventing herself in this new world as a woman of the middle class by marrying a graduate of Carnegie Mellon. This re-invention led her to insist after her marriage that she was not the kind of woman who could be expected to do her own laundry, an assumption my college-educated, native-born, and mildly forlorn grandfather seemed to have acceded to without demur even during the Depression, when he lowered his own job expectations considerably. In the same vein, my grandmother imperiously insisted that as a high school student in Wauwatosa, Wisconsin, my father take the College Boards—over the protestations of the principal who said it was a cruelty to my father to suggest he aspire to the Ivy Leagues. They weren't, he insisted, open to residents of Wauwatosa. I assume my grandmother, as was her wont, collapsed in a rage-induced faint and won the argument, for my father took the exams and went to Harvard. Throughout his long life, my father negotiated a complex blend of ambition and feelings of inadequacy and pretense. His mother, however, delighted in his successes as his due—and in her own life happily cultivated a warm and totally artificial British accent for her daily life and an American one for playing Auntie Mame in local theatricals.

On my cherished solo visits to Wauwatosa to visit with her and my grandfather, I found her glamorous and luringly American—something, in those years when my own family shuttled between Denmark, England and the U.S., I was trying to puzzle my way through. American was, I concluded, *joie de vivre*, dramatic accents, silver ballgowns, the red book of famous opera plots, soft Persian rugs, folding TV tables, and television itself—none of which we had in our own houses, whether in Copenhagen, Cambridge, Bethesda, or St. Louis. Snuggling in with my Campbell's soup, watching Porky Pig, America I decided was homecoming, respite from different languages, the precariousness of my parents' marriage, the incessant moves.

Emigration

Perhaps as a response to the baffling time in Europe as a child, the exposure to different cultures, languages, and accents at a stage when I was learning to read, I showed little desire to travel as a young adult. But when my son was thirteen I fell impetuously in love with a Mexican artist and brutally uprooted my son to follow him to Mexico. In part, this act was an expression of my alienation from my own culture at that time. Now, it both horrifies and saddens me that the things I wanted, which seemed absolutely impossible to have in America as I knew it in the mid-80's, were so very simple: more children *and* a life as an artist. The experience of that year and a half in Mexico for both my son and me was extreme, and its effects—both good and bad—permanent. The intensity was heightened because we both felt this was an either-or decision, that we were there, having burned our bridges, without hope of return. For years after, we would say to each other, "Uh-oh. I have that Mexico feeling." It was our code for the kinesthetic flashbacks of PTSD.

I have various scenes that flash before me:

My son saying, white with shame, "I'm not going to school today. They are taking us to the metro so we can see real Mexicans. It's their country and we're supposed to go out and look at them like animals in a zoo." I had recently moved him from a Mexican school (where no effort was made to teach him Spanish) to the American School, an uneasy blend of embassy children whose parents calculated their children's grade average to three places beyond the decimal point and wealthy Mexicans whose bodyguards roughed up the opponents of their charges in the restrooms at lunch. My son couldn't look at Mexicans like exotic creatures. He used the metro daily to get to school. He lived in an area with no Americans. Our own resident Mexican had recently moved out. We didn't have the luxury of that distance—the bars.

"Here in this culture you are totally helpless," a woman named Milagros said to me with a smile I could not pretend was friendly. "You are like an infant. Speechless. Dependent. It was the same for me in France. I had no control. It was their world. It was up to *me* to adapt."

I remember practicing saying the word *socorro*—help—over and over as I came home on the metro late at night. I needed to believe that if, assaulted on those five dark blocks back to the apartment, I cried out loudly enough, clearly enough, someone would come to my aid. I needed to believe—and I couldn't in a country where a pharmacist would overcharge me for a band-aid to cover an openly bleeding hand.

I can remember my son, desperate to protect us, turning to me and saying, "You're too trusting. It's time you started treating Mexicans the way they treat each other. You have to think blood. Your blood is more important than theirs."

I can also remember great kindnesses and genuine affection. My lover's father saying happily, "Ah, you are not like the other Americans I have met. You are intelligent and also passionate. You are warm." I can remember the genuine hopes he and his wife held for us, the pain they felt at the obvious pain my son and I were experiencing.

I can also remember, a year later, back in the States, watching myself with astonishment waiting at the bus stop in Watertown, Massachusetts. I, who before our time in Mexico had always found casual interchanges difficult if not impossible, was the one who was smiling, chattering on about the weather, the bus schedule. I observed this new social self with bemused pleasure. It didn't matter to me if people responded. *I* knew, whether or not they did, that however different they thought we were, *I* knew that I still had more in common with them than I did with anyone else in the world. For the first time, I truly felt as American as the next man or woman in line: *enfranchised*.

Culture Shock and Creative Acculturation

Out of these experiences, in my professional life I developed a profound and expanding interest in the pervasive effects of culture shock—the traumatic destruction of belief systems—an interest that has informed much of my professional work: including the role of contradictory belief systems (and dismantled and reconstructed ones) in the psychological and social effects of environmental exposures, questions of credibility across intellectual disciplines, social trust between scientists and the public, the development of our spiritual life, the experience of illness. Most importantly, I became interested in the role of narrative in developing social trust by providing us with a way to talk about what basic assumptions, what basic social contracts (so deep they may never have been voiced or seen) had been broken, what we understood to be the consequences of those ruptures, what could, or had already, come to take the place of those early beliefs.

At a purely personal level, I found by circumstance and interest that many of my closest friendships and my choice of volunteer activities involved helping recent immigrants feel more at home here in the States. This wasn't purely or even primarily altruistic. *I* felt most at home in these relationships. Not because we had so much in common—rather because we knew we didn't. But out of our different lives, we had this core experience of culture shock in common, an experience that shaped our thinking, our assumptions and our expectations in large and small ways, that helped us affectively experience systems of thought as delicate and interdependent living organisms. But also as distinct from ourselves. We had, obviously, not died from moving from one system to another. We were, weren't we, here to tell the tale?

I was especially interested in the importance of friendship in helping us negotiate these seismic changes—how having one person in the new culture who saw us as a whole person, profoundly equal, could affect our resilience and our responsiveness. This awareness, if effective, moved both ways. I remember two interactions with a Somali friend in Watertown that demonstrated this process.

Karima was a bright, beautiful, Europe-raised, American-educated daughter of a liberal Somali diplomat who now lived in exile in Saudi Arabia. Karima had worked all her professional life for UNICEF and had spent much of that time in Bangladesh. She had recently married and was now living in Watertown. We met on a train from Boston to New York—and talked intently the whole way, happily comparing cross-cultural observations. She was warm, inclusive, and extremely comfortable in every situation I saw her in. I remember calling her once after attending an African-American Episcopal church in Cambridge, where I was warmly greeted, made astonishingly at home (one woman deciding to share with me an envelope of photographs of a recent family gathering as the minister—"Oh, that's just Cecil, don't worry about him, we grew up together."—delivered a long sermon). I was very grateful and also acutely aware that I was the only white person there. "This must happen to you so often," I said to Karima after I finished describing the experience, my mélange of feelings. "Hmm," she agreed, "you can call it exceptionalism if that makes you feel better."

The other occasion was when I met Karima and her sister for lunch. Karima's sister, a Williams' graduate and now a diversity trainer in Washington, D.C., talked about how very tired she had been of being so exceptional at Williams, the relief she felt in Washington where her skin color was unremarkable. She also talked about her grief when her secretary, a white woman old enough to be her mother, had recently died of cancer.

"When she died, I cried," Karima's sister said. "I didn't realize how close she had become to me. It was the first time I have ever cried for a *gaal*."

"What is a *gaal?*" I asked.

Karima looked very uncomfortable. I looked back and forth at the sisters.

"An infidel," her sister said.
"An outsider," Karima corrected.
"In our language, there is no difference," her sister said.

The Full Cost of Acculturation
Another friendship of longer duration has had a more direct influence on how this anthology, and its focus on women, finally came to be. I have known Saana for fifteen years, since her early twenties when she first came to the United States with her family as a refugee from the Middle East. I have been able to observe at closer or more distant perspectives over the years the complexities of the process of acculturation for her—how she and her sisters and sisters-in-law (no mothers accompanied them here) have helped each other decide what they should adopt from American culture, what they desire to but don't dare, what they reject outright, what dimensions of their original culture and religion they have claimed more determinedly here than they did before they came because of responses they have encountered here in the U.S., especially after 9/11.

What I have been struck by, not just with her but with all my immigrant friends, is how invisible the very high levels of thought, will, wisdom, courage and constraint required to change cultures are to others who have not had the experience. Saana and her sisters have never veiled and have an open and direct demeanor. They dress so stylishly that you might not notice that they are carefully covered to observe Muslim expectations. You would not know how much went into their decision to shake hands with men at work or in social situations, a gesture they now make without any observable hesitation. You might not understand that the one thing about her experience in the States that Saana feels would be impossible to share with relatives back in her country of origin is how very much she enjoys her freedom here. "They would call me a bad woman," she explains.

In the past five years, I have watched Saana negotiate alone another set of questions crucial to her own life. I have seen what it means for her to be the only unmarried daughter in her family system, to desire an independent life organized around her own professional development and to find this desire unspeakable, more than that, potentially dangerous. I have also seen that at times I am a help to her, that the differences in our basic assumptions, my ability to articulate her individual right to equality and the pursuit of her own happiness, is sometimes a support and often an unbearable contradiction to the world she experiences as most real.

One spring when Saana and I together conducted focus groups with immigrant women concerning the physical impact of exclusion (something people who are second language speakers are quick to notice), the conversations naturally moved to different cultural ways to express welcome and rejection. I noticed that when Saana used the phrase, "They would say you are a bad woman," which she did recurrently, there was always a powerful charge to it. I thought of how many of my own friends were probably 'bad girls' but great women. I began to explore what this meant to her, being called a 'bad woman.'

As a feminist, a professional woman, a friend and a mother figure, I could not bear the idea that by cultural convention, this wonderfully competent young woman who clearly thrived and excelled in her work would become the unpaid maid to her married sisters and because she was not married, indeed seemed to have no desire to marry, all forms of individual accomplishment were going to be limited for her—that she would repeatedly keep putting her own professional aspirations on hold for others. Was her rebellion at this what she thought of as being a 'bad woman'? What was it that she most wanted at this point in her own life I asked her? It turned out that she wanted what she knew was more impossible even than a fully absorbing career. She wanted an apartment of her own.

I invited her to begin writing about this desire. What would happen, I asked her, if you just said to your father and brothers that you wanted an apartment of your own? She began her essay this way: *If I were to say I wanted to live by myself, my oldest brother would kill me—except he does not live here in this country. My father's heart would break because he would be so afraid for me, afraid for what people would say.* Out of this came several devastating stories, one about the total social ostracism a set of first cousins, all girls, experienced in their home country because they dared to wear pants, and even exchanged words with neighbors who were not their brothers. It didn't matter that they were at the top of their classes in high school and college. This stigma, Saana assured me, would last at least until the fourth generation. She still admired her cousins, however. She recognized that their own father never lost his pride in them. But the other constraint was the one she referred to in the story, the persistent physical abuse by her oldest brother that began as soon as she was pubescent. "He beat me because I was stronger than my sisters. He beat me because he could not beat his mother or his father."

I was heart sore as I heard this, for you must understand that this was a very moderate family, Saana's father was a kind man of great spiritual integrity, dedicated (as Karima's father had also been) to providing his daughters with educational opportunities not allowed their mother. Saana's favorite brother was remarkably supportive of his wife and his sisters, attending his own children's births and telling me many years later, "In my culture it is still a shocking thing for me to have done this, but in this case American culture is better. She was afraid, all alone in this country. She needed me there. She needed not to be alone." Saana's stability, support, motivation, and encouragement all come from her family—as do these damaging constraints.

As I listened to my young friend describing what opened up when she even thought about saying that she would like to have a room of her own, I thought, who of us here would have the courage to do something like this if we felt that death would be the result? Who would even know, looking at this elegant, apparently fully acculturated young woman, what force fields she threaded daily. Suddenly I said, "Saana, you were trained as a lawyer. If an uneducated woman came to you, another refugee who like you is now an American citizen, and told you her husband or her brother was beating her, what would you tell her her rights were as an American citizen?" A light went on in Saana. It was astonishing. The fear disappeared. "I would tell her it was against the law, that he could be prosecuted."

It was as if there were two realities for Saana and, like a revolving theatrical set, they were invisible to each other. "We are Middle Eastern inside the house," her sister-in-law once said with a laugh. "American when we step outside. It is easier that way."

But at what cost? This was when I began to think about how women as carriers of culture can both imprison and transform themselves and others. Since Saana thought differently when she thought for others and when she thought for herself, I began to ask her, "What from your culture would you like to pass on to your niece, or to a daughter, because it would make *her* life richer here? What is the *more* you would like for her—as your mother wanted education for you?"

I found myself in these conversations falling back on core American ideals—those simple ones that we are constantly being invited back to: equality, justice, the blessings of liberty for ourselves and our posterity. I began to think about how deeply engrained they were in me—and how they were both the sweetest freedom and an unbearable taunt and temptation for Saana. *And no one could see.* What does it mean to claim even the *dream* of a room of one's own, or a child of one's own, if for the first twenty years of your life for someone to even *think* you thought of them held the threat of death, whether or not a dictator was in power? And that no one, inside your family or outside it, would put up a hand to stop him? What do these ideals of ours that we ask people to swear allegiance to without any mental reservation mean in such a situation?

Saana often said to me, "This is not about religion, this is about culture." And soul, selfhood, human community at the most fundamental levels. I grieved for the gifts she couldn't realize, for the loss that was to this society she had so eagerly chosen to be part of. Gifts that would be used without acknowledgment, perhaps even without awareness, within her family circle.

I began to think that the constructive conversation that needed to take place, not only with Saana and her sisters and sisters-in-law and cousins but also with her brothers and father, could take place only after each of them, individually, had made a conscious commitment to upholding these American values—whatever culture shock that might entail. I also realized that it might be a conversation that was safer to conduct through the mysterious mediation of a book, through many stories both similar and dissimilar, many invitations to interpretation, many moments of identification from the wholeness of our own experience.

Good Deeds Gone Awry

About two years ago we were in the early stages of developing a writers collective as part of our press and were talking to writers we had published in different anthologies who seemed to be particularly open to our approach. One was a young man, an ambitious aspiring writer who had emigrated in his teens from an Eastern European country in the former communist block. I had liked his work, whose subject matter was the strains of acculturation, the tensions between his loyalty to his family and his overwhelming desire to do well in this country, both to make up for his parents fall in status and to ensure his integration.

He, however, was hot on the possibility of getting us to publish an anthology on the fall of communism in his birth country. We were hesitant, I in particular. "I don't want to support anything that just helps displaced elites feel self-important," I told him bluntly. "*Your* story interests me—the sense you are trying to make of your history, the costs and rewards for your parents of immigrating, the choices these pose for you here. Our audience is American—the issues raised need to be ones that directly affect people here, that let your neighbors *here* understand what you and your history brings to *them*."

"Yes, yes," he said eagerly. "Just write it out and I will include it." A remarkably enthusiastic and entrepreneurial young man, he persuaded his university department to provide money to cover printing costs. I felt hedged in.

My ambivalence increased as we proceeded. The manuscript we received was organized according to the priorities we had feared, a conversation between Eastern European writers about the (self)importance of their own experience. We reorganized it to follow the emotional trajectory of immigration and acculturation that would be more meaningful to American readers. "Whatever," said our young writer busy with a hundred job applications. The editing was intense because most of the contributors weren't native speakers. "Oh well, thought we did a good job," the young writer said. My doubts intensified. I could see how this was a good experience for him—it gave him a publication, it allowed him to make points with his compatriots, might help with his job applications. I could see how it might be good for the contributors. But for us, a tiny, U.S.-based small press with a commitment to inclusion? But I had a liking for this young man. I identified with his desire to belong. The job market *was* terrible. He could use some help. So I went along.

During this period, we had been given by a compatriot of our busy young writer a shrink-wrapped copy of a substantial volume of an obscure literary magazine dedicated to Native Americans that he had recently guest-edited. I put it on a shelf. That ill-considered anthology still needed revisions. I finally tore open the shrink wrap and opened the book-length magazine the day I released the anthology to our printer. I was breathstruck. It bore the same title as the book we'd just sent in, the contributors were nearly identical, and it had been published just two months earlier. Without a word from our ambitious young man. Not a peep. What on earth was he thinking? *What were we?*

A mitzvah, I kept muttering to myself. I did it as a mitzvah? For heaven's sake why? I thought about all the work our assiduous young intern, also an aspiring writer, had put into the book. All the editing we had done. I thought of having a book on our list for years that symbolized such a misuse of my desire to welcome.

"No," I said to my husband and co-publisher. "I will not support behavior like that in any way. It is against everything we stand for. We acted in good faith. He *used* us."

"You will destroy his academic career," my husband, an academic, worried. "This has serious consequences that even he may not be aware of."

"Exactly," I said. "Better he learn here. We'll absorb the cost, take the responsibility for cancelling. He can try to publish it elsewhere. But I cannot *help* him take advantage. It's bad for his character. It's bad for his future."

I consulted with members of the Collective. "Of course he can't be a member," they said. "Who could ever trust him after this?"

We called our printer and cancelled.

The repercussions were fascinating. The ambitious young writer, who obviously knew what he had been doing, first tried to persuade us that he had respected the letter of his contract, that the writers might be almost identical, the title the same, the topic the same, but the works included different. We should, he said, publish it because this would be a *book*, not a volume in an obscure literary journal funded by a major U.S. foundation to provide an outlet for Native American writing. A book, he said, would be more prestigious for them. All he was concerned about was disappointing his compatriots. "Their voices deserve to be heard," he said. "It is my job to help this happen." He sounded selfless. Almost devout.

What fascinated—and shocked—us was how virulent the responses were from those compatriots, especially from middle-aged men with substantial professional careers. We received threats of law suits—and worse, often using their institutional affiliations. One man, a dean at a law school, told us we reminded him of the communist censorship committees of his youth. Another had more physical threats: "I hope you realize now that you never mess with Eastern Europeans." There was, in all this, a raw rage and an even more shocking sense of entitlement. *Over such small stakes.* Ten pages, at most, in a publication from a very small press. Why, I wondered, knowing what we know about them now, would we ever want to help their voices be heard?

I ended up with a reluctant admiration for the ambitious young writer, who, like an alley cat, kept focused on landing on his feet. I haven't checked it out, but I assume he did. Only one contributor—and the dean of his university—suggested that we might have felt betrayed by his behavior.

"If you *ever* think that behavior like that is acceptable academically—" I said sternly to our intern.

"No, m'am," he said in his south Georgia accent. *"No, m'am."*

"Or necessary," I added. For that was also what I couldn't understand.

We spent a week decompressing at the beach. I wrote and wrote. Wept. All those threats. All our good intentions. It was on one of our walks that this citizenship project emerged.

"There are two grievances that are the heart of this," I said. "One of them is mine: How can you misuse our good will, and our limited means, in this way? All you want are our goods, not our values! And on the other side, it is: All you want is what I can do for you. But whatever I do and whatever you say, I will never be truly equal. You will never see my *intrinsic* value. I will never belong." For these professional men, there was added to this their fury at relinquished privilege, for the truth is they were far more important in their small, totalitarian pond than they ever can be in this tumultuous sea we call the United States, which I insist on believing is as communitarian as it is individualistic and capitalist.

"Everyone comes in trailing their own original system. That is the lens they see everything through. That is just the way the world is. They really believe this, and recreate it. That is why citizenship is so important," I added. "It names them both—the rights and the responsibilities. We *all* need to think about this. Both grievances are real."

My husband, our resident political scientist, started musing about the implications of this. "I believe this might be a place where liberals and conservatives can meet, where a constructive conversation might begin—" And we were off, shock, anger and disappointment transformed, having found, once again, the *We in Them, the Us in You.*

"But I'm sticking with women," I insisted. "They rarely make death threats."

(I want to point out this volume does include a number of contributions, some brilliant, all moving, by women from Eastern European, formerly communist countries.)

LIVING INTO OUR QUESTIONS, LIVING INTO OUR ANSWERS

Continuous Conversations

Since our ocean walk a year ago, the general furor about immigration —especially illegal immigration—has increased remarkably. But it should not drown out this very necessary conversation about welcome, mutual respect, and creative collaboration. This conversation is especially important given the dramatic increase in immigration in the last thirty years, particularly from countries whose political systems and cultural assumptions, particularly about gender equality, are very different from the ones that are now our own.

So that is what we want this anthology to do—serve as a catalyst for conversations that are bounded by some clear values we can all appeal to, ones that we as a society and a nation have appealed to from our conception. These are the numinous ones found in the Declaration of Independence—*We hold these truths to be self-evident, that all men <u>and women</u> are created equal, that they are endowed by their Creator with certain unalienable rights*—and in the Preamble to the Constitution, and in the naturalized citizenship oath. We are certainly not saying that as a country *we* have not had a long journey, do not still have a long journey before us, to realize those ideals. But they are our shared pole star. For those who make an intentional commitment to become a citizen, we *can* ask whether a cultural pattern they bring with them is congruent with these ideals and if it is not, ask that the incongruence be resolved in favor of these ideals. And for those who have not had to make the long journey required of people who are naturalized citizens, who were born privileged by these assumptions of equality, we can ask that they enter into the radical reciprocity that these values imply.

For a commitment to the equality of all is, ultimately, about full inclusion—on both sides. It is a big thing we are all promising each other and it is more than just tolerating each other's existence. It is about admitting someone quite different from you into your qualitative universe and asking them to do the same of you, it is acknowledging their blood is as red as your own, their experience as valuable. To do this requires tolerating very different views of ourselves and assuming responsibility, on both sides, for our power to include and the need to use it in ways that honor that ideal of fundamental equality. Discovering and sharing stories—personal ones, passionate ones, honest ones—and accepting their invitations to interpretation is a very good way not only to begin but to continue.

Why and why now?

Why do we feel this conversation is important to have right now? I don't know about others, but I am personally so tired of opening up the paper and seeing the increasing rigidity in our political parties, both established and insurgent, tired of the assumption that there isn't honor in someone who does not share our views, that difference of opinion is unpatriotic. I would say that, in this far from perfect union, the inability to both respect difference of opinion and honor the necessity, the self-evident truth, of common ground is unpatriotic. I felt I saw that acknowledgment of common ground, if only for a second, when President Obama at the close of this year's State of the Union message remarked that however contentious our politics, there is no place on this earth any of us would rather be.

But we do need to act as if this is the case. My husband retired recently and, given his personal respect for difference of opinion, it felt very appropriate that the past students who were invited to give guest lectures were a leading Republican political consultant, active since the Reagan years, and a rising Democratic one, active in Obama's campaign. At a dinner following, the charming Republican consultant responded to my question about whether increasingly virulent negative campaigning was contributing to intolerance and ungovernability, "If you look at our political parties, compared to those in other countries, the policy differences between them are really very very small." The Democratic consultant nodded.

But what, I wondered aloud later, does it mean in our common politics when we treat our differences as if they are matters of life and death, as if those differences are questions of absolute good and absolute evil. We respond that way long enough and that *is* what they become.

We respond differently and that is what they stop being. We face such difficult issues now as a nation—intractable recession, formidable debt, increasing income inequality, education, health—we can't afford to magnify what divides us. We all have a right to our differences—but that right is only meaningful as it is grounded in our common, and communally constructed, good.

What helps us respond differently? What ways of talking, listening, and acting make it safe for us to open to someone else's experience and be faithful to our own? This isn't, for me, as this essay shows, an abstract question. It's one I live out, as I think we all do, in small ways every day. One of these is how we handle immigration.

By choice we live now in an unincorporated area of DeKalb County, part of the large Atlanta sprawl, in an area that has, over the last twenty years, become one of the major refugee resettlement areas in the country. It is also on the black-white fault line of the county, which means it is one of the few places in Atlanta, or the South, where multiple levels of integration are both real and, perhaps permanently, raw. Some days, it fits us like a glove. Some days not. Here are a few vignettes.

Welcome

One thing that fills me with an irreducible and intense pleasure is to make someone feel seen, welcome, especially someone who doesn't yet feel completely at home in this country. In part, I do this because it meant so much to me in the various countries we've lived over the past dozen years to have someone see me, smile at me, respond to my game but insufficient Spanish or Portuguese. In part it is because it delights me that my country is home to the world—it appeals to my imagination and to something more primal, the world *I* need. I love when the Ethiopian clerk at the grocery store looks up from bagging my groceries beaming as I say his name, or when an Indian woman rubs the leaves of my spring fern that cascade over the edges of my shopping cart, and then rubs my poncho in the same way and asks, "Spanish?" I think she is talking about me and say, "No. American. Are you Spanish?" (I'm so into the moment I forget the poncho I'm wearing is Mexican.) She shakes her head, "No. From India. Nanny. No English." "Oh yes you do," I say encouragingly. "And every day there will be more. But it's hard." I love the way the cashier shows her which of the coins that she has poured into his hand she can leave with him, which are hers to keep. I also love being greeted with the same warmth by our Nigerian pharmacists, our Ethiopian librarian. Belonging. It's irresistible—and not something I ever take for granted.

Safety

I have other responses as well. The particular small neighborhood I live in was originally white, built in the 1950s just outside the beltway by AT& T engineers who favored solid brick ranch houses and large lots now densely shaded by mammoth, precariously rooted pines, tulip poplars and magnolias. In the 1960s, the neighborhood integrated, so the oldest white residents here are the ones who had the flexibility, inclusiveness, and proprietariness to stay put. With the refugee influx in the 1970s and on, the neighborhood also became home to various new immigrant families—for example our dear Vietnamese neighbors, Mr. Ngo and Mrs. Truong. There is a long running civic association in the neighborhood. Its major focus is vigilance against the opportunistic crime that is common in the area and its major activities seem to be tending the local garden spots and sending high priority emails about suspicious looking black men in the neighborhood. There is a hyperbolic quality to these emails which my friend and neighbor Honey, an African-American lawyer, has kindly cautioned against, but which reflects the fact that many of the writers are elderly and knew a time when their neighborhood was safer.

I was driven to share my reservations about the civic association in an odd way. Our neighbor Mr. Ngo came over to see us one morning. We had seen him and his son talking with the police the day before. He came over to tell us that he had been mugged the morning before as he pulled into his driveway. (He works at night, as he has for thirty years, bagging newspapers for the *Atlanta Journal Constitution*.) The mugger, when Mr. Ngo refused to get out of his car, had pulled him out. Mr. Ngo re-enacted for us how the mugger had dragged him, sliding off his chair onto the floor, his hands outstretched as if still gripping the wheel, a look of shock and horror on his face. Mr. Ngo, in his early seventies, weighs about a hundred pounds at most. He is also very stubborn and energetic, and promptly called out to his son, who was visiting, to come and help him give chase to his attackers. He had two concerns. One was that the robbers may have found in his wallet information about the CD he was amassing to help with the education of his two children (who were either completing or contemplating medical school). His wife had assured him that they could not access the CD. So, it was the other concern that he was coming to share with us—in the form of a request.

"My son go now. My English no vey good. If I cah you and say 'Hep me'—" He gestured as if he were picking up a phone and repeated,

"I say, 'Hep me,' you cah nah won won foh me? I fray I cah and they no unuhstan."

Of course I agreed, and also went out and bought him mace and a piercing whistle. For the next few weeks, my husband arranged to be at the window when he drove up in the morning. Joining him there the first morning, I registered Mr. Ngo's other response to the robbery. He had pulled out the American flag he usually flew only on holidays like the Fourth of July so that it would welcome him home each morning.

What I did *not* do was report the incident to our civic association because I felt they would exacerbate the trauma he was experiencing. They saw threat everywhere. Instead of sending a barrage of cautionary emails, wouldn't it be a better use of our time to introduce ourselves to our neighbors and learn enough of each other's language that we can recognize all our cries for help? So that if we cry "*socorro*" or "hep me," we can be sure someone will respond? It is hard for me to imagine any genuine civic life that doesn't have at its central focus this common commitment and reassurance.

Exclusion

This attitude of welcome isn't always shared, of course—and in ways that sometimes bring me up short. One day, I was at our local library talking with my friend Shiferaw, one of the librarians, about how we might publicize our call for interviews. He offered to distribute flyers at his church. As I was leaving, I looked out across the fence in the parking lot to the local soccer field and saw some foreign flags hung on fences and what looked like an international fair being set up there. What a perfect place to share some flyers, I thought. So I drove over and walked down to where the booths were being set up. Only women were there. What could be more perfect? *Not.* It turned out it was an exclusively Ethiopian fair. When I showed our flyers and tried to explain the project, women looked away, backed off, ushered me on to someone else. I came away with a very uncomfortable feeling. Why was I trying to foster more understanding and appreciation for the experiences and contributions of immigrants when they were so obviously dismissive of me? Whose country *is* this anyway?, I wondered. Whatever the answer, the truth was that at that moment I felt, and was meant to feel, like the intruder, the outsider.

Freedom of Expression

I have an even more complex set of responses to my recent visit to the little shopping plaza up the street that is the major gathering place for all the Somali taxi drivers in the area. All the stores and the local pizza parlor are halal. The Somali market, where we occasionally go to buy bananas, cardamom, Bosnian and Ethiopian bread, sells camel meat as well. The clothing stores feature lovely long flared skirts and ornate caftans and abayahs. The mannequins all wear colorful hijab. It is not a place where a woman, and certainly not one who doesn't wear hijab, feels particularly welcome.

What bothers me most, however, are not the men with their askance glances, their slightly aggressive postures, but the young women who come into the small but well-stocked and busy market wearing the longest and fullest and blackest of abayahs and also face-obscuring niqaab. When I hear them talking I feel anger. From their speech, these are U.S. born, middle-class African Americans. They giggle, scold their children. Under the veils and the abayahs, I glimpse equally theatrical dresses. But this is all their choice. Nothing will happen to them if they strip down right there among the cardamom and fufu. I realize my anger comes because of what I know about the valiant struggles of my friend Saana to live into her unaccustomed freedoms. But when I make the connection, that only makes my response more intense. So, instead I make myself think of the only other person I've seen recently wearing a face veil—a light floral one made of a worn sheet. She is a gentle, psychotic bag lady who frequents the library. The veil is attached with a frayed, dingy white string. It helps with the pollution, she says. Her slightest breath sets it fluttering wildly. The librarians smile, make eye contact when the fabric falls, check out her books, unfailingly polite.

Community

But enough of that. I want to close with an image that feels very promising to me which involves my friend and neighbor Betty Hasan-Amin and her husband Ronnie Amin. At some point as we were compiling the anthology, I realized that we had received no submissions at all from women from Africa—an absence that felt particularly striking to us given that the area where we live is so dense with refugee and immigrant populations from a number of African countries, especially Somalia, Burundi, Sudan, and

Ethiopia. I decided that we would try to augment the collection with some interviews, and when none of my contacts with the various refugee agencies identified women interested in participating, I called Sister Betty because I knew that with her own fascination with people from other countries and cultures she would be interested in the project. Many of her nursing aides were from Africa and I knew that she and her husband had opened up their backyard the previous summer so a family of Bhutanese refugees could plant a garden there. Sister Betty is an African-American Muslim who was paralyzed in an accident at seventeen and has spent over forty years in a wheelchair. She is a strong advocate for people with disabilities both in the African-American community and more recently with refugees and immigrants. When asked, she promptly made up a list of people for me to contact.

I stopped by Sister Betty's house one day to conduct an interview with one of her contacts. As I began to walk up the drive, I was over-taken by a young Pakistani man in a wheelchair. "You can help push me," he said with a laugh as his chair stalled a little on the inclined driveway. "Just kidding," he said as soon as he saw me begin to respond. I recognized him then as the young man we had met once fearlessly wheeling his chair on the side of the heavily trafficked main street in the area because, he explained, the sidewalks were so broken they were impassible. We'd talked about citizenship then, and the robbery at the convenience store where he worked, in which he was shot and paralyzed. He'd seen my camera and asked me to take photos of the sidewalks and send them to our state representative. This afternoon, after acknowledging the acquaintance, he asked with curiosity, "You know Sister Betty?" He stopped to talk with Sister Betty's husband Ronnie who was arranging items for one of their frequent yard sales.

It turned out there was some confusion about the date and time of the interview, so I chatted with Sister Betty instead, who told me about the letter she had recently written to Attorney General Eric Holder asking what he could do about the great racial inequality in charging and sentencing young black men, and the nearly insuperable challenges these young men had to face, even after serving their sentences. "Where is the forgiveness?" she asked. "You do your time, you take responsibility for the mistakes you made—non-violent ones, usually—and you still can't find housing, apply for a scholarship, get a job. They talk about rehabilitation, but I don't see it. You are taking away all their alternatives."

By this time, the house was heady with spices and the smell of frying onions and meat. Ahmed, who had come over to make a proper Pakistani dinner for Sister Betty and Ronnie, was wheeling seamlessly back and forth in the kitchen. He chimed in, "Yeah, you go bankrupt, they forgive you after awhile. Five years, I think, and you can start again. But a felony, it's with you all your life. Why can't they say, after five years or ten with a perfect record, you don't have to carry the blame no more?"

As I'm leaving, Ahmed and I chat briefly about whether he'd like to be interviewed about citizenship. "You know I only have my green card. I can apply for citizenship next year. I only got my green card because I got shot and paralyzed. I'm going to become a citizen as soon as I can. That was always my plan. From the time I came here, even though I was illegal, I always paid taxes. People asked me why, and I said because I might need that help later."

As I left, Sister Betty told me that she and Ronnie would be moving to a local apartment complex. "You know I find suburbs lonely. People don't drop by. The only people who do are our Vietnamese neighbors. I'm a little worried about the safety, but I'm going to love the mix of cultures." Most of the many apartment complexes in the area are filled with recently arrived refugees and immigrants. I can see Sister Betty holding a permanent open house.

Outside I sat with Ronnie on the sofa in the garage. The Vietnamese neighbors came over, a grandmother and her ten-year-old grandson on a skateboard and her seven-year-old granddaughter on foot. She was looking for some sandals for her youngest grandson. She was also helping out her neighbors, for she knew that Ronnie has been out of work for eighteen months now. She waved a pair of small, sturdy black plastic sandals at Ronnie. "One dollar," he said. She nodded. Handed him the dollar. Left.

Ronnie told me about the futility of his job search, how it was weighing on his spirits. He also described how, after all these months of job seeking, at sixty-two he had reluctantly applied for Social Security—and as soon as he had received it, Sister Betty's disability benefits were cut. He shook his head. "How can anyone live on that?" However you moved them, the numbers wouldn't add up. "If you don't have a good moral training," he said, "I could see how you could get desperate, do things that were wrong."

He went on to tell me that he was trying to focus on the things that matter to him. He had gone to a lecture at the nearby community college and ended up in conversation with the professor, who told him about a program for seniors to go back to school. "What do you think?" he asked me.

"I think it's a wonderful idea. What do you want to study?"

"I thought about religion," he said, "But they told me that's not one of their majors. So I thought social work. I'd like to do some counseling. There's a lot of young men out there that could use some help."

"And you'd be good at it. You've gone through it all with your own sons. You think about these things and discuss them at the masjid."

He sat there thinking, then shook his head. "I'm not sure. Some days, you know, the only thought I have that is clear is, *Be the change you want to see.*"

What is the change we are invited to be as U.S. citizens at this time in our history? What small acts—of perception, interpretation, giving and receiving—make that change a living, breathing reality? That is what we invite everyone, ourselves included, to think about as we read the stories shared here, as we share our own responses to them with one another, as we revisit our own experiences and discover new patterns, find cohering balances of invitation and expectation, rights and responsibilities, astonishing gifts, challenges, and opportunities. Together.

The stories included here are true but when necessary names, locations, and other important identifiers have been changed to protect the privacy of the individuals involved.

CHARLES D. BROCKETT

SOME FACTS TO STAND ON, SOME AVENUES TO EXPLORE

The purpose of this essay is to provide the reader with context for this volume's personal accounts of immigration, acculturation, and naturalization. It will cover, admittedly in brief fashion, the following: historical overview, U.S. distinctiveness, current immigration demographics, the naturalization process, acculturation and identity, and the situation of immigrant women.

Overview

We often say in the United States that we are a nation of immigrants, taking pride in the Statue of Liberty's welcome to the "tired . . . poor . . . [the] huddled masses yearning to breathe free." Yet at other times it sounds instead like many of us wish to replace Emma Lazarus's poem with a 'no vacancy' sign. Immigration controversy is not new—it has ignited intermittently for more than a century and a half.

The Know Nothing movement opposed the growing Catholic population prior to the Civil War, Exclusion Acts later in the nineteenth century targeted first the Chinese and later all Asians, and historic laws in 1921 and 1924 greatly curbed all immigration, especially from outside of Europe. Conversely, an equally significant immigration reform in 1965 removed legal discrimination against non-Europeans and opened the door for greatly expanded immigration from all over the world, thereby setting the scene for the immigration debate of recent years.

Consensus and controversy: Although it is widely acknowledged across the political spectrum that the U.S. is greatly in need of another fundamental reform in immigration policy, we are so divided over the issue the Congress has been unable to legislate successfully. A major study was commissioned by

Congress in 1990 to examine the issue and suggest appropriate reforms. The Jordan Commission did just so in its outstanding report in 1997 (and prior preliminary reports) but Congress did not act.(1) A broad bipartisan coalition for reform did emerge in the second term of President George W. Bush and for a while it looked like it might succeed; however, the effort collapsed in 2007 under withering attack from the right.

Throughout these controversies, most U.S. citizens have been clear that as a country we have benefitted from the continuing flow of immigrants joining our society. We certainly agree, and the contributions to this anthology demonstrate why. However, contemporary survey data also show majority dissatisfaction not just with current policy but also with current levels of immigration. Although some scholars and activists argue for the free movement of labor across open borders paralleling that of capital, this is an infrequently held position.(2) Most U.S. citizens are unwilling to allow all hardworking people of good moral character who would like to immigrate to the United States to do so. Because there are so many who would like to come, we agree. There are limits to how many newcomers can be incorporated successfully into a community as part of a continuing flow. The harder questions are what is the desired level for the U.S. population of foreign compared to native born and what criteria should be given priority in determining who is permitted to immigrate.

Historically the United States has been among the most permissive countries in its immigration policy (except for 1924-1965) as well as in allowing for naturalization. An important way of understanding U.S. history is the expansion of who we allow to join us by becoming U.S. citizens, from only whites in the beginning to no restrictions for the last half century on who you are in terms of race, religion, gender, or nation of origin. Alongside all of the country's defects, this must be recognized for the extraordinary achievement that it is, creating a diverse population of citizens unmatched except perhaps by Canada.

Citizenship and Community: But what do we mean in the U.S. by the 'citizenship' that we offer to those who wish to join us? Some might be comfortable with a minimal expectation, perhaps not much more than an instrumental relationship in the marketplace. Others might have broader expectations of agreement on core values and the full acceptance of the responsibilities of membership in a *community*. When the immigration level reached its peak in the early twentieth century, a strong Americanization movement emerged that at its best aimed at facilitating the assimilation of immigrants into the existing community. At the time immigrants were seen as often coming from backgrounds radically different from those of the native born. Yet at that time they were almost all Europeans.

Today where I live on the outskirts of Atlanta our immediate area features not only sizeable numbers of native-born blacks and whites but also significant groupings of Afro-Caribbeans, Bhutanese, Bosnians, Burmese, Eritreans, Ethiopians, Indians, Liberians, Mexicans, Nigerians, Pakistanis, Somalis, and Vietnamese. Given the great increase in the level of immigration in recent decades and its broad expansion of U.S. diversity, the Jordan Commission called for renewed attention to Americanization, which it identified as: "a set of expectations that the United States, which chooses to invite legal immigrants, legitimately has of newcomers. It applies equally to the expectations immigrants legitimately have of their new home."(3) We agree—with both parts of the statement.

Immigration Policy: Cycle of Permissiveness and Constraint

In the early days: At the point of its independence the United States was overwhelmingly populated by Protestants from the British Isles along with a smaller number of Protestants from continental Northern Europe. Forcefully marginalized from this society, of course, were the Native Americans and African Americans. Citizenship itself was offered only to free white persons by law in 1790. Through the first three decades of the republic, immigration flows were minor with immigrants constituting less than one percent of the population. Unrestricted immigration, a non-controversial policy under such conditions, grew more controversial with the rapid expansion of both the number of immigrants in the decades up to the civil war and with its diversification as large numbers of Catholics entered the country, beginning first from Germany in the 1830s and then from Ireland in the 1840s. This intensifying conflict, however, was overwhelmed by the even more divisive set of issues that culminated in the Civil War. Immigration itself diminished as well with both the war and the years of economic difficulty that followed.(4)

Immigration expands: As U.S industrialization accelerated later in the century, though, so too did immigration once again. Not only did the U.S. become more of a magnet but multiple socio-political changes in Europe led many from Central, Eastern, and Southern Europe to seek a better fate across the Atlantic. Many were single males, many eventually returned home. Nonetheless, for the five decades beginning in 1880, the U.S. welcomed some 30 million immigrants; during the first decade of the new century this represented about 40% of the country's total population growth. The immigration level peaked in both the decades of the 1890s and 1910s at 15% of the population.(5) In the industrial cities of the North the rate was probably closer to 20%.

And contracts: Many of the immigration controversies of today would be familiar to the protagonists of this earlier period. Movements to restrict immigration levels appeared alongside its expansion, culminating in the Quota Acts of 1921 and 1924. The resulting sharp fall of immigration to the U.S., especially from outside Western and Northern Europe, had been preceded some decades earlier in the western states where the major immigrant flow had been from Asia. Economic and cultural concerns, as well as racism, led to a series of exclusion acts. First targeted were Chinese laborers in laws passed by Congress in 1882, 1884, 1886, 1888, and 1902. Diplomacy culminating with the Gentlemen's Agreement of 1908 greatly curtailed immigration from Japan. South Asians were excluded in 1917 and most remaining Asians by the 1924 law.(6) Removal of these restrictions in the 1940s and 1950s then led the way (although the relevant country quotas were miniscule) to opening immigration altogether in 1965.

Current situation: The foundational law governing policy now is the Immigration and Naturalization Act passed in 1952 and amended repeatedly since. The landmark legislation of 1965 removed the country quota system established in the early 1920s, instead establishing separate ceilings for the two hemispheres; this division itself was removed in 1978. Priority under the law is given to family reunification, critical employee skills, and artistic excellence. Refugees were originally included as a priority category but were removed in 1980 and since then have been treated separately.

Although the precise number has varied, until 1990 the overall annual ceiling was less than 300,000 legal immigrants. In 1990 it was more than doubled. For the decade through 2009 it climbed again, hitting just over one million immigrants in most years.(7) These changes are reflected in the percentage of foreign-born residents in the overall population. From the high of 15% early in the twentieth century the rate dropped steadily down to its lowest point since data was collected of only 5% in 1970. Under the impact of the 1965 law, immigration (legal and otherwise) then began growing faster than the overall population with the increase of the last four decades just as steady as the decline of the prior period.(8) By 2009 the foreign born had climbed back up to 12.5% of the total population.(9)

The U.S. Experience Compared

Anglo-settler colonies: The immigration debate is not unique to the United States as similar conflicts have flared up throughout Western Europe in recent years. However, the controversy does have unique qualities here. The countries most like us—Australia, Canada, New Zealand—remained relatively homogeneous societies based on a shared British cultural heritage much longer than the United States (or in the Canadian case, bifurcated between English and French-speaking regions). These Anglo-settler colonies had no equivalent of the great waves of Catholic or Jewish immigrants coming to the U.S. in the nineteenth and early twentieth centuries from all over Europe—such as Ireland, Germany, Poland, Russia, and Italy—and recreating the U.S. as a far more diverse society.

U.S. Slavery: Neither did these cousin countries have an archaic plantation system based on African slave labor dominating a substantial portion of their country. Slavery's legacy for the U.S. has been complex. For the immigration debate it includes a large portion of the native-born population that was often excluded from mainstream society for a century after slavery's end and for whom a disproportionate number continue as poor and marginalized. To the extent immigration is a cost to society through competition for scarce jobs, that cost is borne disproportionately by African Americans. To the extent immigration is beneficial, for example, through cheap domestic help and the many positive manifestations of cultural diversity, those benefits are more likely to accrue to the affluent, who are disproportionately not African American.

Western Europe today: In recent decades the other former Anglo-settler colonies have grown more heterogeneous by opening their immigration policies, most notably so in Canada.(10) The same is true for the 'old' countries of Western Europe. Once the ports of departure, they are now points of destination. In the economic boom following World War II reconstruction, large numbers of immigrants came seeking better lives in the more prosperous north—for example, coming from the Asian subcontinent to Britain, from North Africa to France, from Turkey to Germany, and from Latin America and Northern Africa to Spain. As their numbers have increased, especially with second and third generation residents, so have the conflicts—which should be familiar to us in the U.S.—related to cultural difference, assimilation and multiculturalism.

Border with Mexico: There are other countries that have at least as high a percentage of immigrants as part of their total population or even higher than the United States (notably Australia and Canada) but none share the feature that dominates discussion in the U.S. Nowhere else in the world is found the porous border between a wealthy country and a much poorer one like the two-thousand-miles division between the U.S. and Mexico. Opportunity's pull is an irresistible attraction for many Mexicans, their cheap labor yet willingness to work hard and well is too irresistible for many U.S. employers (and consumers), and the border is too long and often too remote to adequately guard.

Public Opinion

In recent decades the immigration debate in the U.S. has largely concerned the vast numbers of illegal/undocumented/unauthorized immigrants living and working among us. Given the rapid increase of the undocumented numbers until the economic crisis beginning in late 2007 this is not surprising, especially because their numbers had exploded throughout the country in many communities previously untouched by the phenomenon. This controversy looms so large in our society that it inevitably colors how many native born respond to any issue related to immigration. Say 'immigrant' and people often immediately think 'illegal.' This unfortunate and unfair connection needs to be broken; indeed, that is one of the motivations for this anthology. How best to handle the situation of the estimated 11.2 million illegal immigrants living in the U.S. (as of March 2010)(11) is not the subject here but is instead explored in our forthcoming companion volume *Complex Allegiances.*

U.S. residents on the whole view immigration as a positive force for the country, even with the complicating impact of attitudes about illegal immigration. When asked at three different points across the last decade, "In general, do you think immigrants who come to the United States today help the country and make it a better place to live or hurt the country and make it a worse place to live?," pluralities consistently selected "better" over "hurt" with an average spread of nine points.(12) Nonetheless, respondents are not in favor of increasing legal immigration. The results vary with the survey and precise question wording—sometimes the plurality sides with keeping present levels, sometimes with decreasing the level. However, increasing the level of legal immigration does not place first. This is true also among Hispanics, with one survey showing 57% of Hispanic respondents selecting "left the same" and only a quarter supporting an increase.

Scholars find these patterns to be true for at least the last sixty years.(13) Yet, at the same time the pace of both legal and illegal immigration has continued to grow. Immigrants and their U.S.-born children account for 55% of the growth of the total U.S. population during essentially this same period (i.e., between 1966 and 2008).(14) Whether one disagrees with public opinion or not, this ongoing disjuncture in a democracy between public opinion and policy is undoubtedly a major source of the intensity of the controversy surrounding this issue. During times of economic distress, public concern tends to be all the greater.(15)

Foreign-Born Residents

Immigration growth: There have been two big changes in recent decades in the size and spread of the foreign-born population in the U.S. that help us to understand the intensity of the current *nationwide* immigration debate. First, the ratio of the foreign-born population continues to grow, constituting 12.5% of the country's total in 2009, up from 11.1% at the start of the decade.(16) If current trends continue, the previous record of 15% from a century ago will be passed in a little over a decade. If these trends were then to still continue, the ratio would hit 19% by about 2050.(17)

The largest state concentrations, both in absolute numbers of foreign-born residents and their percentage among the total population, are California and then New York—26.9% of California's population is now foreign born. In numbers these two states are followed by Texas, Florida, New Jersey and Illinois; Nevada and Hawaii are added to these top states when looking at percentages.

Growth in new areas: Second, for growth across the last decade, new states now appear at the top of the list when understood in terms of percentage growth: South Carolina (76.6%) and Kentucky (73.9), followed by Montana, Wisconsin, and Georgia. As the following map indicates, in

2006 there were twenty-one states with faster growth in their foreign-born population than the six traditional immigration 'gateway' states. Leading the way in percentages are Delaware and South Carolina. Perhaps more significant, though, is Georgia where the immigrant population has grown so rapidly in recent years that the state is now posed to surpass Arizona and Massachusetts in absolute numbers of its foreign born and to be ranked seventh nationally.

Immigrant categories: It is important to note that overwhelmingly the foreign born in the United States are here legally. Indeed, there are substantially more naturalized citizens among the foreign born than there are illegal immigrants. As of March 2010, naturalized citizens were 37% of all foreign-born residents, permanent residents 31%, the undocumented 28%, and legal temporary migrants 4%.(18)

A slight majority of the foreign born have come from all parts of Latin America and the Caribbean (53%) with almost another quarter from South and East Asia (24.1%). The leading sending country, of course, is Mexico (29.9%) with no other country representing over 5% of the total. In order, the most important are: Philippines, India, China, El Salvador, Vietnam, Korea, Cuba, and Canada.

Immigrant success: If immigration is motivated by a desire for better opportunities to make a good life for oneself and one's family, then as a group even first generation immigrants are successful at doing so. However, there are pronounced differences between region of origin for both education and earnings. Immigrants born in Asia and the Middle East are more successful than the native born while those from Mexico are substantially less successful.

Education: Current U.S. residents born in South and East Asia are much more likely to be at least college graduates (48.9%) than the native born (28.1%), as are those who come from the Middle East (44.6%), while those arriving from South America are at about the same level (27.4%) as the native born. In contrast, more foreign-born residents have less than a ninth grade education (20.7%) than do the native born (3.5%), with Mexican immigrants having the highest percentage (41.6%) among those with data provided.

Income: Not surprisingly, the same trends hold for earnings. Immigrants from Asia and the Middle East are more likely than the native born to place in the highest category (over $50,000 annually): 37.4% and 36.5% compared to 27.8% respectively. Conversely, among all of the regional groups, those born in Mexico are substantially more likely than the native

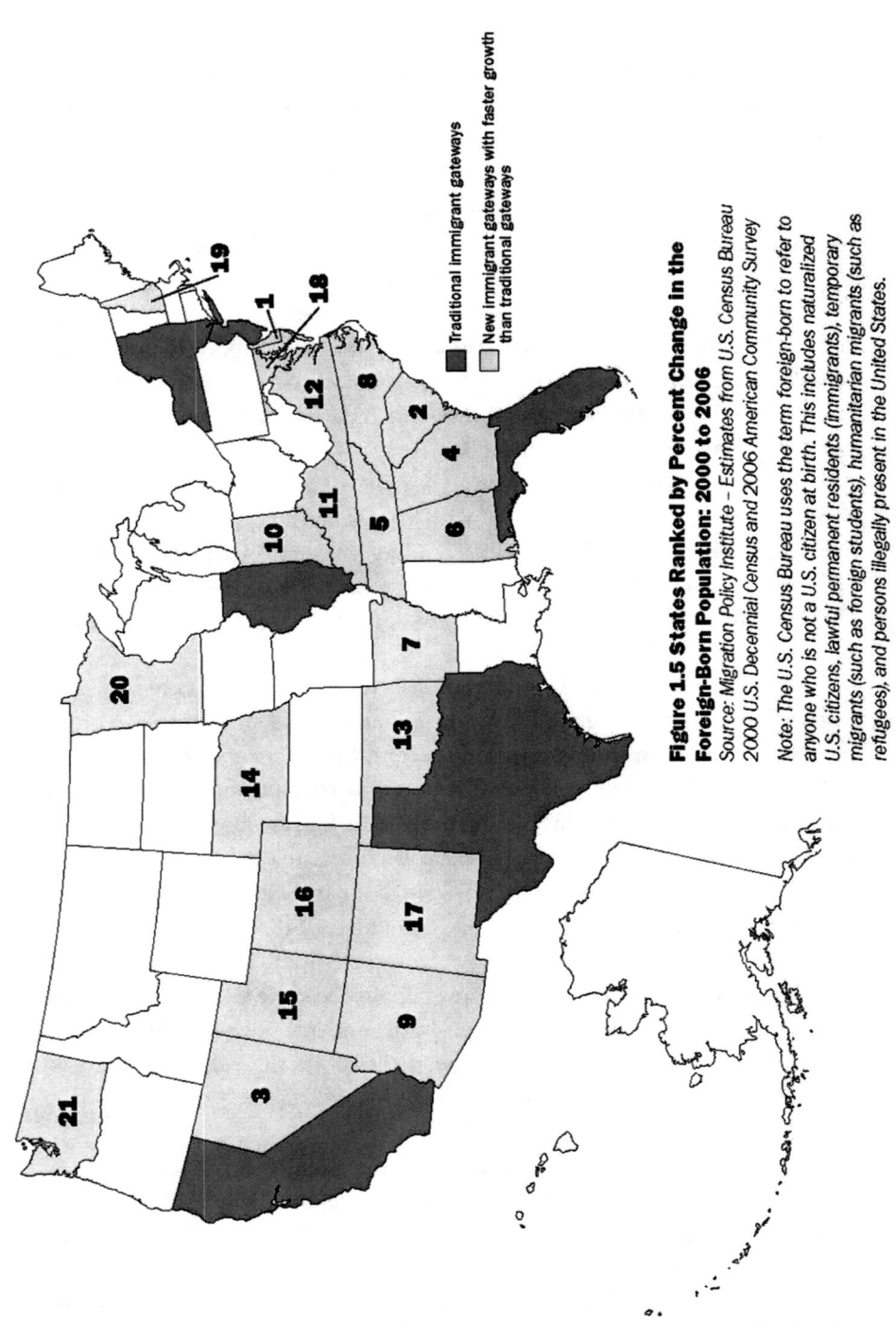

Figure 1.5 States Ranked by Percent Change in the Foreign-Born Population: 2000 to 2006

Source: Migration Policy Institute – Estimates from U.S. Census Bureau 2000 U.S. Decennial Census and 2006 American Community Survey

Note: The U.S. Census Bureau uses the term foreign-born to refer to anyone who is not a U.S. citizen at birth. This includes naturalized U.S. citizens, lawful permanent residents (immigrants), temporary migrants (such as foreign students), humanitarian migrants (such as refugees), and persons illegally present in the United States.

U.S. Task Force on New Americans. Building an Americanization Movement for the Twenty-First Century. Washington, D.C.: U.S. Depearmtent of Homeland Security, 2008: p. 9.

born to earn under $20,000 annually—51.9% compared to 35.3%. Similarly for total household income, immigrants from South and East Asia are 4.6 times more likely than their counterparts from Mexico to place in the top quintile (about $102,000). The median household income of Asians is $68,000, almost double that of Mexicans ($35,400). The comparable figure for the native born is $50,700.

Becoming a Citizen

Requirements: For the foreign born to become a citizen of the United States they must be at least eighteen years old.(19) They first must live under 'permanent resident' status for a minimum of five years (three years if married throughout that time to a U.S. citizen) and have been continuously in the country for at least the prior thirty months. Often referred to as the 'green card,' a permanent resident card authorizes the recipient to live and work legally in the country on a permanent basis.(20) There are multiple paths to a green card but two are the most common. Current citizens and permanent residents can sponsor immediate family members (and some others) for a green card, as can employers who can certify that this would not displace other workers. Also of importance are green cards for refugees and asylum recipients. Refugees are required to apply for a green card one year after they are admitted to the country; those receiving asylum are encouraged to do so but are not required.

Process: Once these requirements are met, the permanent resident is free to apply for citizenship. Along with the appropriate paper work, the applicant must pay a non-refundable fee, now $675. Eventually (depending on the backlog in one's area) the immigration interview will be scheduled. At this time the applicant is required to show the requisite understanding of U.S. history and civics, along with the ability to speak, read, and write basic English, such as handling the interview itself.(21)

Language mastery: For many potential citizens sufficient mastery of English is the primary barrier to actually naturalizing. Indeed, about half of legal residents are estimated to need English instruction before they can pass the test.(22) English is "spoken less than very well" in 30.5% of the homes of the foreign born, with Mexico as the region with the highest score at 38.5%.(23) Although the U.S. government encourages the foreign born to seek English language classes and contributes monies to these state and local efforts, many of the interested are frustrated by insufficient classes and the resulting waiting lists. In Phoenix, for example, Arizona's largest English as a Second Language (ESL) provider had a waiting list of over 1,000 people when interviewed in 2006, with a waiting time of up to 18 months for its highest demand evening classes. Even worse, in New York City most ESL providers were so overwhelmed that they discontinued waiting lists and moved to a lottery system.(24)

Insufficient English skills on the part of the foreign born is often of concern in the U.S. to the native born. A helpful comparison is a study of U.S.-born immigrants to Mexico—"shockingly few" could speak Spanish, even among those who had lived for a decade or more in the two towns studied. Nor did the researcher meet any who had obtained Mexican citizenship or were in the process of trying. Typical instead was the response: "Well I guess I'm an American living in Mexico."(25)

Who naturalizes: In 2009, only 44% of the foreign born were naturalized citizens, down significantly from 64% in 1970.(26) Still, the 2009 figure is higher than at the decade's beginning (40%) and consequently the share of naturalized citizens in the overall U.S. population increased to 5.5% in 2009 from 4.5% in 2000.

There is substantial variation in naturalized citizenship between the sending regions, probably related at least in part to composition of older and newer immigrant groups. Over 55% of foreign born from Europe, Asia, and the Caribbean are now citizens. The comparable figure for Latin America is much lower at 32%. However, other forces are undoubtedly at work as well. Naturalization for those from South America runs at about 46% whereas the comparable figure for Mexico is only about 24%. Of course, over half of the Mexicans are undocumented and therefore not eligible for citizenship.

State comparisons: There are also substantial differences among the individual states. California, with the most foreign-born residents, features both the highest percentage of naturalized citizens (12.3%) as well as non-citizens (14.6%) as part of its total population. The other states with at least 10% of their population naturalized citizens are, in order, New York, New Jersey, and Hawaii. Generally, the highest proportions of naturalized citizens among the foreign born are found in the northeastern states, the lowest in the southern states. The comparable state rankings for foreign-born residents who are not citizens are Nevada, Texas, New York, and New Jersey.

Immigration and Identity

The practical side: People immigrate for opportunity, they come to improve their lives. To some extent the decision whether to naturalize is one of material self-interest, of straightforward cost-benefit analysis. However, over the years both legislative and judicial action have opened many of the benefits of living in the U.S. to non-citizens and even to illegal immigrants. Still, there are important benefits that accrue only to citizens. Furthermore, legislative proposals at both the national and state levels would make this all the more so if passed, as is probable for at least some of them.

Attachment and identity: But human beings are much more than rational calculators of material self-interest. Attachments and identity matter too. For many of us they matter greatly. Although the material advantage of naturalization is often clear, for many foreign born taking that step comes at an emotional cost and for some it is so great that the step cannot be taken. I have a friend, for example, who has been here for some three and a half decades as a political exile. His wife and his children are U.S. citizens. But he cannot bring himself to break his affiliation with his homeland, an idea he experiences as a fundamental betrayal.

Assimilation: This tension pervades many of the stories in this anthology and for me is much of what provides its richness. I appreciate the insights these stories give me into an experience so different from my own as a native-born citizen with multiple ancestral lines straight back to pre-revolutionary days. As we think through the many complex issues raised in this area an important distinction to keep in mind is one that guided the Task Force on New Americans. Its 2008 report emphasizes the difference between cultural and political assimilation, pointing out that in the United States, "The cultural sphere—traditions, religion—is up to the individual."(27) Immigrants are free to hold onto cherished traditions of their birthland as long as they wish, even as they become citizens. Indeed, it is this resulting multiculturalism that for many of us is one of the great benefits of the broadening diversity brought by the immigration boom of recent decades.

Political integration: At the same time, *Building an Americanization Movement for the Twenty-first Century* maintains that political integration (assimilation) is a reasonable expectation, indeed a necessary one in order to "bind together immigrants and citizens from different cultures." The core components identified by the report are "embracing the principles of American democracy, identifying with U.S. history, and communicating in English." It is this political integration that protects the basic U.S. commitment to "diversity with unity."(28)

Traditions and rights: Even with this distinction in place, of course, hard questions remain. Indeed, this is precisely a primary motivator of this anthology. Some traditions are antithetical to American democracy and its core principle of inalienable rights. The contemporary tension probably receiving the most attention is our subject: the equal natural rights of all people, not just men. It has taken us most of our history as a nation to get here but the principle is now fundamental: women have the same unalienable rights to life, liberty, and the pursuit of happiness as men—regardless of what one's birthland customs might say to the contrary.

Significantly, the language of the *New Americans* report does not specify "knowing" principles and history but instead "embracing" and "identifying with." Following a number of researchers, the report emphasizes, "Citizenship is an identity and not simply a benefit," adding that "Feeling and being perceived as part of the political community is an important indicator of a person's integration into a society." That developing such feelings and identifications might take years—and perhaps even more than a generation—should not surprise or alarm us. These are, after all, very primordial issues for many people. But neither should the length or ambivalence of that process diminish the importance of the expectation itself.

The Oath of Allegiance taken as the culmination of the naturalization process by which the immigrant becomes a U.S citizen is archaic in its language. It remains with us because reform efforts have always been stymied by disagreement about what should be pledged in its place. Even if archaic in language, the Oath is very clear in its essence: choosing to become a U.S. citizen requires no renunciation of cultural traditions but it does ask explicitly and clearly that new citizens shift their allegiance and identification to the political community of the United States of America. The Oath states:

> *I hereby declare, on oath, that I absolutely and entirely renounce and abjure all allegiance and fidelity to any foreign prince, potentate, state, or sovereignty of whom or which I have heretofore been a subject or citizen; that I will support and defend the Constitution and laws of the United States of America against all enemies, foreign and domestic; that I will bear true faith and allegiance to the same; that I will bear arms on behalf of the United States when required by the law; that I will perform noncombatant service in the Armed Forces of the United*

States when required by the law; that I will perform work of national importance under civilian direction when required by the law; and that I take this obligation freely without any mental reservation or purpose of evasion; so help me God.

Gender

Who immigrates: As in so many areas of life, until the feminist revolution hit several decades ago, women were only minor subjects in the literature on immigration; instead, migrants were "usually conceived of as males or genderless."(29) Yet, women have migrated more frequently than have men to the U.S. since 1930 and today a slight majority of all foreign born in the United States are female. Once again region matters: women substantially outnumber men coming from Africa, Canada, and Europe while men by a lesser margin outnumber women coming from Central America and Mexico. Some women migrate to the U.S. to join husbands already here but many others come responding to the traditional lure of the United States: greater economic opportunity and personal freedom.

Employment: Female immigrants often find their first employment in the low-wage sector. This often includes even those arriving with substantial education and even from elite backgrounds—going "from mistress to servant," as characterized by one researcher.(30) Demand for this type of female employment has expanded dramatically in recent decades as native-born women have entered the paid work force and turned to others for help with childcare, housework, and meal preparation. Females are also in demand in many low-skilled, labor-intensive industries. One study, for example, quotes a white male boss in a California assembly shop: "Just three things I look for in hiring: . . . small, foreign, and female. You find those three things and you're pretty much automatically guaranteed the right kind of workforce."(31)

However, it is important to realize that many other well-educated immigrant women do find professional employment and we now have a long history of their distinguished accomplishments. By the early 1990s, professionals represented more than a quarter of all female immigrants. Compared to native-born women they were also "significantly overrepresented in professional positions."(32) Many excellent examples of such women are found among the contributors to this anthology.

Freedom: Even when greater personal freedom was not an original motivation for migration, it often is embraced as one of the great benefits of life in the United States. This is especially true of expanding gender roles within the family and community beyond those of the birth culture—a significant theme running throughout many of this anthology's contributions. Research indicates that these gains in gender equality reinforce many foreign-born women's desire to remain in the U.S. whereas men, who are more likely to experience a deterioration in their status and privilege with immigration, are more likely than women to wish to return to their birth country. This can lead to interesting dynamics, as one scholar explains: "I have documented the tendency of many Dominican women to spend large amounts of money on expensive durable goods . . . which serve to root the family more securely in the United States and deplete the funds necessary to orchestrate a successful reentry back into Dominican society."(33)

Family life: Families are complex, though, and so are migration dynamics, making generalizations difficult. As an example, compare gender relations between immigrants coming to the U.S. from Mexico. If the man precedes the woman for several years, when she joins him in the U.S. "the husbands proved more amenable to assisting their wives in the domestic tasks they had mastered in their wives' absence." In contrast, "when spouses and children migrated together . . . patriarchal patterns were more likely to be maintained, even when women worked outside the home."(34)

Patriarchy: Generally, patriarchal patterns do erode over time among immigrants but the pace varies by family, original culture, education, economic opportunity, and existance of a relatively homogeneous immigrant enclave. Still, researchers who have pioneered in studying these issues have been surprised by patriarchy's persistence. As one concludes, "The dilemma confronting many immigrant women, it would seem, is to defend and hold together the family while attempting to reform the norms and practices that subordinate them."(35)

Conclusion

In 2006 President George Bush appointed the Task Force on New Americans, following in the footsteps of the 1997 report of the U.S. Commission on Immigration Reform. Two years later the new task force issued its own report, titled *Building an Americanization Movement for the Twenty-first Century*. On its first page the task force affirmed the historical and continuing contributions of immigrants to the United States—as we do in this anthology and as survey data show so too do most citizens. The Task Force states:

> The United States has been since its founding, and continues to be, a nation of immigrants. Immigrants have been drawn for centuries to America's promise of liberty and justice for all. Their quest for freedom helped define the founding chapters of America's story, and their hope, courage, and ambition continue to strengthen this nation. Immigrants are great assets to America, bringing vitality and optimism to our economy and society. They build, renew, and enrich this great nation and our national character.(36)

"Diversity makes America strong, but unity keeps America successful," the Task Force emphasizes.(37) As the percentage of foreign born continues to climb in the U.S., we hope that our new immigrants will understand the importance of their contribution to building that unity. And we hope that those of us already here will continue to see how much our society and our own lives are enhanced by that diversity. We believe that the contributions in this anthology will help us all to appreciate how diversity and unity can continue in the United States to live together, even when in creative tension, and enrich us all.

Endnotes

(1) U.S. Commission 1997. The commission was chaired by former Congresswoman Barbara Jordan until her death in 1996.
(2) As examples, from the right, see Riley 2008; from the left, Chomsky 2007.
(3) U.S. Commission 1997, p. 27.
(4) Unless otherwise indicated, sources for this section were Graham 2004 and Schuck 1998, 2003.
(5) Bloemraad 2006, p. 27.
(6) Lowe 1996, pp. 180-181, n. 14.
(7) Department of Homeland Security.
(8) Bloemraad 2006, p. 27.
(9) Pew Hispanic Center.
(10) For an insightful comparison of contemporary immigration policies in Canada and the U.S., see Bloemraad 2006.
(11) Passel and Cohn 2011.
(12) The source for all survey responses reported in this paragraph is http://www.pollingreport.com/immigration.htm.
(13) Schuck 1998, p. 10.
(14) U.S. Task Force 2008, p. 3.
(15) Espenshade and Hempstead 1996.
(16) Unless otherwise indicated, the source for this section is Pew Hispanic Center.
(17) U.S. Task Force, p. 4.
(18) Passel and Cohn 2011, p. 9.
(19) U.S. Citizenship and Immigration Services, "A Guide to Naturalization." Web.
(20) http://www.uscis.gov/greencard
(21) Information on the test and study materials is available at www.uscis.gov/citizenshiptest
(22) U.S. Task Force 2008, p. 24.
(23) Pew Hispanic Center.
(24) Tucker 2006, pp. 1-3.
(25) Croucher 2009, p. 64, 142.
(26) Gryn and Larsen 2010.
(27) U.S. Task Force 2008, p. 2.
(28) U.S. Task Force 2008, pp. ix, 2.
(29) Pessar 1999, p. 53. Other sources for this paragraph: Loucky 133-136;

Pew Hispanic Center; and for this section, Berger 2004.
(30) Maxine L. Margolis as quoted by Gabaccia 1994, p. 97.
(31) Pessar 1999, p. 63.
(32) Gabaccia 1994, pp. xv, 95.
(33) Pessar 1999, p. 65.
(34) Cited by Pessar 1999, p. 61.
(35) Pessar 1999, p. 67.
(36) U.S. Task Force 2008, p. 1.
(37) U.S. Task Force 2008, p. 44.

References

Berger, Roni. *Immigrant Women Tell Their Stories.* New York: Haworth 2004.
Bloemraad, Irene. *Becoming a Citizen: Incorporating Immigrants and Refugees in the United States and Canada.* Berkeley: University of California Press, 2006.
Chomsky, Aviva. *"They Take Our Jobs!" And 20 Other Myths About Immigration.* Boston: Beacon Press, 2007.
Croucher, Sheila L. *The Other Side of the Fence: American Migrants in Mexico.* Austin: University of Texas Press, 2009.
Department of Homeland Security, "Persons Obtaining Legal Residence Status 1820-2009." Web. 25 Feb. 2011.
Espenshade, Thomas J., and Katherine Hempstead. "Contemporary Attitudes toward U.S. Immigration." *Internatonal Migration Review* 30.2 (1996): 535-70.
Gabaccia, Donna R. *From the Other Side: Women, Gender, and Immigrant Life in the U.S., 1820-1990.* Bloomington: Indiana University Press, 1994.
Graham Jr., Otis L. *Unguarded Gates: A History of America's Immigration Crisis.* Lanham, MD: Rowman & Littlefield, 2004.
Gryn, Thomas A. and Luke J. Larsen, "Nativity Status and Citizenship in the United States: 2009." Washington, D.C.: U.S. Census Bureau, October 2010. Web. 7 Apr. 2011.
Loucky, James, Jeanne Armstrong, and Larry J. Estrada, eds. *Immigration in America Today: An Encyclopedia.* Westport, Ct: Greenwood Press, 2006.

Lowe, Lisa. *Immigrant Acts: On Asian American Cultural Politics*. Durham: Duke University Press, 1996.

Passel, Jeffrey S. and D'Vera Cohn. "Unauthorized Immigrant Population: National and State Trends, 2010." Washington, DC: Pew Hispanic Center (Feb. 1, 2011). Web. 19 Feb. 2011.

Pessar, Patricia R. "The Role of Gender, Households, and Social Networks in the Migration Process: A Review and Appraisal." *The Handbook of International Migration: The American Experience*. Eds. Charles Hirschman, Philip Kasinitz and Josh DeWind. New York: Russell Sage Foundation, 1999. 53-70.

Pew Hispanic Center, "Statistical Portrait of the Foreign-Born Population in the United States, 2009." Web. 19 Feb. 2011.

Riley, Jason L. *Let Them In: The Case for Open Borders*. New York: Gotham Books, 2008.

Schuck, Peter H. *Citizens, Strangers, and in-Betweens: Essays on Immigration and Citizenship*. Boulder: Westview Press, 1998.

———. *Diversity in America: Keeping Government at a Safe Distance*. Cambridge: Harvard University Press, 2003.

Tucker, James Thomas. *The ESL Logjam: Waiting Times for Adult ESL Classes and the Impact on English Learners*. Los Angeles: National Association of Latino Elected and Appointed Officials, 2006. Web. 4 Apr. 2011.

U. S. Commission on Immigration Reform. "Becoming an American: Immigrant and Immigration Policy." 1997. Web. 3 Apr. 2011.

U.S. Task Force on New Americans. *Building an Americanization Movement for the Twenty-First Century*. Washington, DC: U.S. Department of Homeland Security, 2008.

irit and prin-
ng has gone
of the popu-
e increasing
roblem be-
on on the
nigrants.
xcellent
nothing
he law

struct

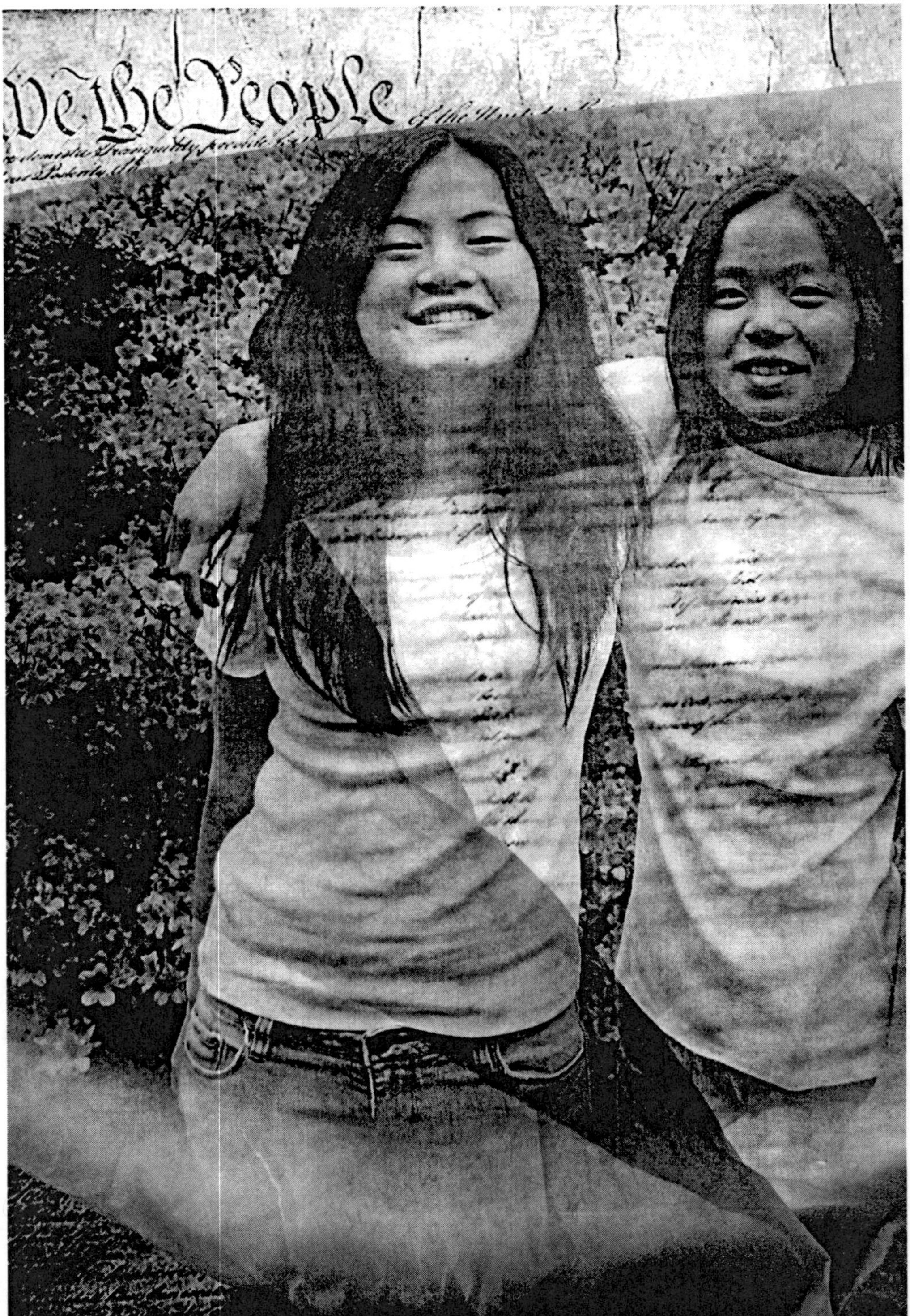
We the People

II

CHINESE DAUGHTERS: ALL-AMERICAN GIRLS

KERRY LANGAN

INTRODUCTION

China has long fascinated me. With four thousand years of history, the Chinese have given the world one of its major civilizations. Five years ago, I stood on the Great Wall and marveled at this triumphant feat of engineering, a precise assemblage of earth and stones that rises from the hills in a massive show of strength and beauty for 5,500 miles. Each small section of the wall is impressive, but my eye couldn't help but travel its visible distance, tracing the endless castle wall, with its fortress watchtowers placed at exact intervals, as it winds on and on through the countryside, as seemingly long as Chinese civilization itself.

The wall was built to keep invaders out of a country that preferred to be left alone. For the vast majority of its history, China was her own world, a self-sufficient land that sent no envoys abroad. To learn China's secrets, traders had to make the arduous journey to Asia, but they were well rewarded for their efforts. The Land of the Dragon is credited with an impressive list of the world's inventions including paper, gunpowder, the compass, print and moveable type, India ink, porcelain, silk, steel, kites, and on and on.

In the past two decades, China has given the world her most unique gift, her daughters. From behind the Great Wall, China has sent forth thousands of tiny female ambassadors. In 1991, the U.S. State Department reported that American families and single parents adopted 61 Chinese infants and toddlers. Word quickly spread that healthy infant girls (and a few boys) were available for adoption, and the United States soon led the world in Chinese adoptions. At its height, in 2005, 7,906 American adoptions of Chinese females took place. Overall, approximately 150,000 babies and toddlers were adopted from China in the last twenty years, with roughly half now living in the United States.

Most are familiar with China's one-child policy, implemented in 1979, to arrest overpopulation. During the twentieth century, China endured disastrous famine and poverty. During the Great Leap Forward, *thirty million people starved to death*. It's a statistic I can't completely comprehend: it's simply too large. This era of starvation devastated China. To feed all of her people, China had to drastically reduce her population.

Boys carry the bloodline and family name in China. Sons take in their aged parents while daughters care for their in-laws. Without a son, aged Chinese parents risk becoming destitute and homeless. If only allowed to have one child, survival and cultural preference dictate that it must be a son. Those couples that dare defy the policy by having more than one child suffer reprisals such as loss of jobs and homes. Hence, 150,000 Chinese girls growing up around the globe, in the United States, Ireland, England, France, Australia, Spain, the Netherlands and elsewhere. China's daughters are living in twenty-six countries worldwide, a global expatriate community comprised of members who did not choose to leave their homeland.

Of course, now China is realizing how valuable girls are. Who will the sons marry? There must be grandchildren to carry on the family name and honor the ancestors. The one-child policy is loosening; couples in some areas are allowed to pay a variable fee to have a second child. Most significant, China's tenacious attitude regarding gender inequality is at long last losing its grip. Many urban couples desire, even prefer, girls, citing the loyalty of daughters. Modern China is experiencing phenomenal development and has a great need for employees, men and women, to replace her aging workforce. In the current economy, daughters can provide for a family just as well as sons. There has also been an increase in domestic adoptions since the growing middle class is able to afford adoption fees and the costs of pediatric care. Some have speculated that the one-child policy may be completely dissolved sometime in the next decade.

Not surprisingly, the number of Chinese babies eligible for international adoption is diminishing. In 2009, Americans adopted 3,001 babies from China, a decrease of 66% since 2005. The wait for a baby, at one time less than a year, is now several years, causing couples to have to update expensive adoption dossiers. As a result, couples and single parents are looking to other countries for more rapid adoptions.

Still, approximately 75,000 adopted Chinese children, more than 95% of them girls, are now naturalized American citizens. Roughly 15,000, a full 20% of the adoptees, are growing up in a two-mile radius on the upper west side of Manhattan. The rest are coming of age in other cities, college towns, small towns, and rural communities across the United States. The oldest of the girls are now college women. Because of the decreased adoptions and longer wait periods, the majority of the youngest are toddlers and small children, rather than babies.

Not surprisingly, many books have been published about America's Chinese daughters. Whenever I'm with a group of fellow adoptive moms, many sentences begin, "Oh, have you read . . . ?" and then we compare and contrast notes on non-fiction books such as: *Baby, We Were Meant For Each Other* by journalist Scott Simon, or *Lucky Girl* by Mei-Ling Hopgood, Xinran's *Message From An Unknown Chinese Mother*, *The Lost Daughters of China* by Karin Evans, *The Waiting Child* by Cindy Champnella, and a host of others. During this last year, *The Red Thread*, a novel by Ann Hood, was a popular read. And, of course, we can't help comparing our parenting styles to Amy Chua's, described in her controversial book, *Battle Hymn of the Tiger Mother*.

There are beautiful books about adopted Chinese daughters written for children, but there's a strong need for books with Chinese-American girls that don't discuss adoption. The girls are so much more than their adoption experiences and they need to see themselves reflected in literature as typical American children. Of course, every Chinese daughter I know, including my own, has a personal library of picture books telling the stories of girls like them who came to America as babies. *I Love You Like Crazy Cakes* by Rose A. Lewis has vivid illustrations and exuberant text. A personal favorite of mine is Stephen Molnar-Fenton's *An Mei's Strange and Wondrous Journey*, with its quiet mood and almost reverential text. Our daughters greatly appreciated *Kids Like Me In China* by Ying Ying Fry and *When You Were Born in China*. We were fortunate to meet the author and photographer of the latter title at a conference and have the book inscribed. Author Sara Dorow wrote to our older daughter: "Madeline, May you continue to grow and learn your story in great ways." The photographer Stephen Wunrow wrote, "Madeline, Treasure your heritage and your own special story of your beginnings." Each time I open the cover of this book and read these words, I thank Dorow and Wunrow for reminding me that each adopted Chinese daughter shares a common heritage, but she also has an original and individual story. This duality is at the heart of the Chinese adoption experience.

International adoption is not new in America. Children born in parts of Asia, Central and Southern America, and Africa have come to the

United States for decades. The Chinese adoption experience, however, is unique because almost all of the adoptees are female with no knowledge of their birth parents. They grow up with explanations of the one-child policy and a description of their "abandonment" site. Their numbers also reflect a chronological generation, a community of 75,000 females who arrived in the United States over an approximate twenty-year period. They represent a cultural sorority, one whose exclusivity was determined by the nation that relinquished her tiniest citizens to America. Each girl, however, is living an individual life with her own thoughts and feelings on her adoption. What has influenced her opinions? What has she been told about her birth, and how does that affect her sense of self? What does she know of Chinese history and culture? Does she simply identify as American or as American Chinese?

We invited submissions from those involved in all aspects of Chinese adoption to address the balance between "natural" and "naturalized" and were delighted to receive so many reflective, poignant, and triumphant replies. Not surprisingly, and perhaps most fitting, all of our contributors are female, grateful mothers of daughters born in China and the daughters themselves. As a group, the submissions represent a kaleidoscope of memoirs, fiction, poetry, and self-interviews, all attesting to the wonder of the experience.

Many adoptive parents remark that the moment the adoption process became 'real' was that remarkable day when their daughter's photo arrived in the mail. Katherine D. Perry evokes that moment in her poem, "Song Zi Yang," in which a mother introduces herself to the photo of a baby designated to be her daughter. Perry reaches out to the Chinese mother of her daughter in "Are You Her Mother?" and finds, despite their differences, they ultimately share a love for the same baby.

In "Waiting for Emily," Linda D'Arcy tells the story of waiting in a beautiful Chinese hotel for her daughter to arrive from a rural orphanage. The mother of three biological children, she reflects upon the long journey, physical and emotional, that has led to this moment. Her experience has been lived by thousands of American mothers, those emotional, endless moments just before cradling a new daughter for the very first time.

Karen Loeb's sweet and funny poems share moments from an American couple's ecstatic first days with their bright and happy three-year-old daughter. They have much to learn from each other. What does "hoi moon" mean? How does one walk "jiao-jiao"? What clues are there to the first three years of her little girl's life? Loeb's short story "Customs" deals with what is seen, but not necessarily with what is known. The story is an absorbing account of the assumptions people make based upon appearances, familiar and otherwise, alone.

Diane Raptosh's poems, "The Family Bed" and "The Mother of Her Second Daughter," acknowledge the presence, sometimes dreamy and soft, other times loud and intrusive, of unknown relatives on the other side of the world. Exploring the definition of 'family,' she makes room for those members not visible but reflected in her daughter's face.

In "Double Happiness" I tell my own story. My husband and I are the proud and ever-grateful parents of two precious teenage daughters born in China. After vowing to myself to never publicly share our experiences, I underwent a huge change of mind and heart and committed our story to paper. My memoir reflects upon what brought about that change.

Most joyous are the submissions from American-Chinese teenagers, those girls about whom so much has been said and written. At long last, the girls speak for themselves. Three young women, Anna Anhalt, Madeline Geitz, and Alicia Karls, generously share their views and opinions about the gamut of their experiences as daughters transported from China to America. Their intelligence, confidence, and humor are evidence, I believe, of their natural gifts rather than their naturalized experiences. I'm certain these young women would have lived incredible lives regardless of the country they called home, but I'm truly grateful as an American to know they are my fellow citizens. Hopefully, the world will hear from more and more of these young women as they continue the journeys they began in China years ago.

Finally, Jennifer Bao Yu Jue-Steuck, author of "Goodnight Moon, Goodnight Mom," writes of the heartbreaking death of her American mother and how her grief summoned fresh acknowledgement of the loss of her Chinese mother many years earlier. Her desire to connect with adopted Chinese daughters around the globe motivated her to found Chinese Adoptee Links International (CAL), "the first global group created by and for the more than 150,000 Chinese adoptees and friends in twenty-six countries." The story of our Chinese daughters literally spans the globe.

阳春市人民医院

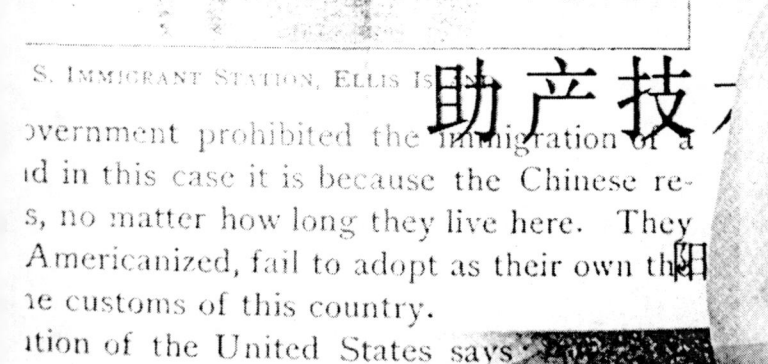

人民共和国卫生部

助产技

S. IMMIGRANT STATION, ELLIS IS

overnment prohibited the immigration of a
d in this case it is because the Chinese re-
s, no matter how long they live here. They
Americanized, fail to adopt as their own th
e customs of this country.
tion of the United States says
aturalized in the United S

KATHERINE D. PERRY

SONG ZI YANG
    —February 1, 2010

I am six days short of your seven months,
and you will not know me for many more weeks.
But I study the pictures sent to me by people in power
who make these decisions for us.
Your body dressed in pink frills and stitched flowers,
your smile only half given to the photographer
who entreats you to smile for the Americans.

You can smile when you feel like smiling, Zi.
Do not pretend for me or for the camera men
that will follow you from here on out.
But when you do feel like it, never hold it back . . .
give the world everything it can hold.

I see the shortness of your hair, cut for the picture,
the slight crossing of your eyes in the face of flashbulbs
and fuss you do not understand, with or without a smile.

You have been chosen for me. I have been chosen for you.
And the single vision of the photograph allows me to see
what cannot be reciprocal for months. Let me introduce
myself to you.

I am your mother.

I will be the only mother you ever know.

You have another somewhere there in Guangdong.
Someone who could not keep you. A woman frozen,
no, petrified, by the constraints of her time and place.

But I am awaiting you: smiling.

ARE YOU HER MOTHER?

Searching faces on airplanes,
on sidewalks, in restaurants, in packed
Forbidden City
for her jawbone, the gentle flare
of her nose, the curve of her brow bone,
I explore the chocolate eyes for despair
or regret, a woman who is missing something:
a tiny human in her arms.
Candidates are fewer than I imagined
in this abundant city, noses are too long,
cheeks too sunken, eyes too sure of the next
movement. But you could be anywhere,
maybe not in the tourist places, and maybe
not in Beijing, but you are here in China,
and you would not know me
and you would not think to see
in me the part of you that I carry
because she is not in my arms either.

And should you see us together,
as we tour the orphanage, as we walk together
through the zoo, the grocery, the streets
of Guangzhou, you will not speak,
but I will search you, search for you:
you, the mother of my child,
you, who have severed strings for reasons
clear to you in this world where we must push
our way through; we strain to make places
workable for ourselves.

I hope that you wanted her to find
an American, America, my education obsessions
as you placed her on the college steps.
I hope that you wanted her to move
away from here, you wanted her to have
many children, to keep her daughters,
to learn English.
I hope that my desperate desire to love
her somehow fills the hole
left by your desperate desire to survive.

We are alike, you and I.
We love her more than the world.

LINDA D'ARCY

WAITING FOR EMILY

The Grand Hotel in Nanchang, China makes a perfect postcard. It is a gleaming twenty-story hotel on a peaceful, swan-filled lake set back a mile from the main road. The contrast to the poor, industrial city is staggering. The white swans, and the clean, white building are a hidden oasis from the gray, dirty landscape of the city and the poverty of the countryside. Most of the hotel's patrons are businessmen who expect a four-star experience to make their time away from their comfortable lives back home more bearable.

Beyond the windowed entry, sliding glass doors open to a spacious lobby with polished, black granite floors. Silk upholstered sofas and mahogany coffee tables are carefully placed. The requisite hotel gift shop sells everything from toothbrushes to $5,000 jade necklaces. In the rear of the lobby is an enormous restaurant that boasts a "full American breakfast," as well as "dim sum all day."

Twelve years ago I spent a week at the Grand Hotel. I sat in this lobby one afternoon for six hours, just waiting, alternating between the comfortable couches and pacing the shiny floor as I kept peeking out the windows. My husband, Sean, and I waited with four other couples for the van to bring our babies from the orphanage.

The Leping Social Welfare Institute was only seventy miles away, but the trip took five hours because of the poor road conditions in the rural areas leading to the city. It was a sticky, hot July day. As we sat in a cool, almost frigid lobby, we were all conscious that the van was not air-conditioned and the trip over the bumpy, rutted roads would be sweaty and difficult. Foreigners were not allowed at this orphanage. I knew from our adoption agency that my baby was living with one hundred other infant girls who slept two to a crib, lined up row after row in a cinder block building with no heat in the winter, or running water. I was spared the trauma of seeing the other babies who would be left behind.

The stress was rising on everyone in our group. Would our children be healthy? How would they bond with us, complete strangers? Were we naïve to think that we were up to this challenge? It was the first time in my life that I connected so quickly and deeply with other people. None of us had met before we arrived in China, and now we would be sharing the most intimate family experience—the arrival of a child. Adopting was more emotional for me than giving birth to my three children. I waited so much longer than nine months for this day. There were more unknowns. I could never relax because I was fearful that the adoption wouldn't take place. I was sure that one document would be missing from my meticulously organized paperwork, that this would end the whole process and I wouldn't get to take my baby home. I was nervous being an American in a Communist country that might not understand my motives.

I chose to adopt from China because I was upset after reading an article in 1995 about the country's one-child policy to curb over-population and about the abandonment of baby girls: The cultural importance of having a son created a situation where, possibly, there were more than one million baby girls in orphanages. It was a beautifully written, moving story about a woman who went to China to adopt a baby girl. She was presented with two babies when she arrived at the orphanage. One was gray, sickly, and pale. The other was plump, pink, and healthy. She chose the sick baby. One year later, when she wrote the article, the baby was toddling around her apartment in perfect health. I never forgot her words: "I made the right choice."

What convinced Sean, who wanted more biological kids, was my answer when he asked me: "Are you telling me that this is the only way we can have more children?" My emphatic "yes" was all that it took. I made plans to sell my restaurant, which I had owned for the past twelve years, so I could dedicate time to the adoption process, and adjust to my new career of being a stay-at-home mom. I wanted to be home with my adopted daughter because I felt that she would need me full-time, more than my others ever did. This was my mission—to make up for the love my new daughter missed because she was abandoned on the day she was born: left on the side of a road, or a bus station, although I was never told where, and spent the next six months in an orphanage. If I devoted myself to her, then I could make it all right.

Once Sean and I decided to adopt, we had many obstacles to overcome. First, because we already were the parents of biological children, we were put in a "special needs" category (This no longer applies to current adoptions). We had to be willing to adopt a child with a minor, correctable medical condition. This could have meant a hair-lip, missing digit, or a clubbed foot. Some were listed as having a heart condition, which we were told was a code word that nothing was really wrong, but a way to make more babies adoptable. Our facilitator assured us that most likely we would get a healthy baby, and I was confident. I diligently worked on the paperwork, which took months to assemble: a home study from a social worker, fingerprints, police reports, immigration approval, notarized letters, and state documents.

Six months into the endless paperwork I received a call from our caseworker at the adoption agency saying, "Linda, I'm sorry to tell you this, but China has put a hold on all adoptions for couples with biological children. We don't know when, or if it will open up." I was devastated. She went on to say, "Why don't you consider adopting from Vietnam or Russia?" She knew that I only had daughters, and continued excitedly, "You could get a boy from Vietnam!" A voice screamed in my head, "I don't want a boy, I want a girl from China!" I called her back two days later and said that we would wait it out until the government changed its mind. Six more long months later, China reversed its policy. Our status now shifted to an official "waiting family."

One more, agonizing year later, we got the call from our caseworker: "Your baby's name is Le Yuan. She's five months old and living in an orphanage in Leping City." Our daughter's picture arrived a few days later. I shook as the Federal Express man pulled up to the house. I ripped open the envelope and staring back at me in a grainy digital picture was a beautiful baby girl. Her head was shaved and bare, and her round, chubby face with its little red mouth and full, rosebud bottom lip was perfect. She wore a white, quilted onesie with a blue duck appliqué that was two sizes too big, but it was her deep, brown expressive eyes that became my focus. Her powerful gaze went through the camera, past the photographer, onto the paper, and traveled 7,000 miles to reach me and make me fall in love. It was as if she knew her eyes could speak and say, "Mommy, please come get me."

I wanted to hold my new daughter, but it would be three more weeks before Sean and I would be allowed to travel to China. My daughters named their sister Emily, even though I chose Anna. I wanted them to love everything about her, so Emily she would be. My friend Mimi threw together a hasty baby shower, and I packed up my child's essential new Baby Gap wardrobe, along with medicines, formula, diapers, and toys. My dream was finally becoming reality, and I couldn't wait to begin this journey after two long years of waiting.

We arrived in Beijing, and then flew to Nanchang to meet Emily. There had been devastating floods from the swollen Yangtze River before we arrived, and the view from our taxi window on the way to the hotel was of the poor, ravaged countryside. We passed soaked rice fields and crude two-story houses where people put all of their possessions on their roofs to save them from the damaging water. Some sat perched on top of their house as if waiting for something better to happen. I was now seeing Emily's China. These were the same rice fields where she would have grown up to work. The toothless old man squatting in front of the makeshift shop selling tin pots could have been her grandfather.

Waiting in the hotel lobby for what now seemed to be days, we at last saw a van pull into the circular drive outside the glass windows. We ran to the door and feverishly flashed our eyes over the five orphanage caregivers, each holding a baby. The women, who had been surrogate mothers on their orphanage shifts, were curious about us, and repeated two of the few English words they knew: "Lucky Baby. Lucky Baby." We could tell that these babies were loved by the way these women doted over each one. Our Chinese facilitator nervously handled the paperwork and began to call out each mother's name to come and be given her baby.

She placed in my arms a tiny eighteen month-old baby. I was so caught up in the emotions of the moment that I never realized it wasn't Emily. Sean was obsessed with videotaping every second of our first meeting, and I gushed in front of his camera, "Oh, Emily, we've waited so long for you—" Just then, the facilitator came over to me and said, "We make terrible mistake. This not your baby." She quickly swapped the babies, and I started again for the camera, with just as much emotion, "Oh, Emily, we've waited so long for you. . . ."

Everything that I said and felt, both times, came pouring out of me in ways I never expected. She was a perfectly healthy baby who smiled and kissed us with her small, round open mouth the minute we held her. The waiting was over. Her "medical condition" was listed as heart disease. I was relieved because I was sure that there was nothing wrong with her heart. It was a hidden condition that put her in a category to be adopted by me. The condition of my heart, which was filled with instant, unconditional love for my new daughter, was changed forever.

KAREN LOEB

SINGING HALLELUJAH

I'm not a musical person. A friend
assures me everyone is musical. But
I'm the kid who mouthed the words
when everyone else was singing. That's why
it's such a surprise when hours after
we meet our daughter in a Chinese hotel
"Twinkle Twinkle" rushes out of my mouth.
In between trips to government offices,
signing adoption papers, we walk around town
and sing. It seems to comfort us, a three-year
old with new parents or a man and woman with a
new daughter.
For some reason a song from a Spike Lee movie
jumps into my husband's mind
and he isn't shy about singing it.
> *One, two, three/the devil's after me,*
> *Four, five, six/he's always throwing sticks,*
> *Seven, eight, nine/he misses every time*
> *Hallelujah, Hallelujah.*

When "hallelujahs" appear, we raise our arms,
our hands shiver and shake. We make
the most of it. Our daughter can't pick up the song.
English is months away for her
but she gets the hallelujah part just fine.
Think how hard it is to say if you've been
speaking English your whole life. Imagine a little
girl whose tongue and throat have only
had Chinese travel through, imagine her belting out

"Hallelujah" punching her arms in the air
on a bus of American families going to
a celebration dinner
one of the Chinese guides, her voice crowded
with wonder,
saying, "Did you hear that? I can't say it.
How can she say that?"

THE CHILDREN OF THE WHITE SWAN

The children of the White Swan parade
through halls and lobbies held in their
parents' arms or pushed in strollers.
Every few days the guest list changes
but new children always appear—

a contingent just in from Nanning or
Wuhan, Yangjiang or Shanghai.
Alongside these children leaders of the
world book a room. Queen Elizabeth has
stayed here—now we have too—my daughter,
my husband and I—for twelve days.

The children of the White Swan are mostly
girls. No one knows why—everyone knows
why—a hush hush topic that sizzles with
the word *abandonment.* Who counts the
cost in tears to the parents who left her?
Who tallies the cost to the baby who lay
on a street near a police station by a gate?

Our daughter is both unlucky and lucky. She
was left near a restaurant—four days old.
It's impossible not to imagine that she lay
there screaming for long hours. The terror that
she had then is posted somewhere
in her still. She was taken to an orphanage
which is where her luck began.

The children of the White Swan come and
go—poised to make a brave journey across
oceans across cultures. Some say they
are the fortunate ones—the ones who are
ferried to America or Europe. Our daughter
will decide that for herself, girl of the White Swan
with sisters everywhere.

(The White Swan Hotel in Guangzhou is where many families stay during the adoption process.)

SOMEONE TOLD OUR DAUGHTER A STORY ABOUT DUCKS

Every night we show her books, talk through
stories, point at images. *Goodnight, Gorilla,
Goodnight, Moon.*
Often we make animal sounds
of whatever is there. My husband
does horses and cows. I do pigs and lions.
Our daughter laughs
but gives us no impression she has seen
illustrations of these animals before.

So it's a big surprise when a duck appears,
and before my quacking voice emerges
she points to the picture, says *coin-coin*
with a perfect French accent.
Sitting on the floor we look at her
pleased and overwhelmed.
Someone in China
told her a story about ducks,
showed her drawings, made the sound
using French—a mystery to us even now.

Many families can spiral backwards
remembering first day, first hour
the very moment of celebration:
it's a girl! We have none of that,
only the way our daughter holds
a spoon so deftly betraying the love
it took to teach her, and the words *coin-coin*—
sounds of a storyteller
brought from China
echoing in our house.

WALKING JIAOU-JIAOU WITH MY DAUGHTER

Home in Wisconsin one Friday
afternoon I choose a chilly walk
the wind not minding its own business,
nosing its way past our coat collars.
"Maybe we can make it all the way
to the Halloween house," I say.
"*Kokunay?*" my daughter asks, not quite catching
all the English words.
"Too cold," she says after one block.
Her white hat and purple jacket
aren't enough.
She does a one-eighty twirl, saying *jiaou-jiaou*
striding backwards toward our house.
It's so nippy I find myself walking backwards too
giving the north wind and blowing
leaves a cold shoulder.

Now I'm walking *jiaou-jiaou* with my daughter.
She turns her head to see if I'm still backwards.
Laughter rolls out of us.
I walk *jiaou-jiaou*
the whole long block home,
she does too,
seems like miles,
our faces twinged with cold,
aching with smiles.

(The word jiaou-jiaou sounds a bit like "jow-jow" in English.)

BEFORE OUR DAUGHTER LEARNS ENGLISH

Before she learns English
she proclaims "*Hoi moon*" waving her
arm like a flag over the dining room
table. Could she be talking about
the moon? my husband and I marvel.
Rising from dinner
we rush to the window
push aside the sheers,
our three-year-old daughter
pressing between us

all of us gazing upward
at a sprinkling of silver coins in the night sky
but no moon.
Our daughter smiles slyly.
"*Hoi moon,*" she says in a soft voice.
"*Hoi moon.*"
We point to things—
a potted plant
the rocking chair
a broom
the black and white cat,
ask, "*Hoi moon?*

"Noooo," she says, frowning
shaking her head,
but she won't show us
won't go up to whatever it is
and say, "*Hoi moon.*"
Months pass. She learns some English.
Still she announces "*hoi moon*" at odd times
in the bathtub
doing flashcards
going outside.

One afternoon the three of us
walk in our neighborhood
of houses and churches.
My mother might say a bee got in my bonnet.
I start chanting "*hoi moon*" to
bushes, a tricycle
a man digging a pond.
"*Hoi moon?*" I ask. Is that
"*Hoi moon?*"
"No," she says. "No."
I rush up to someone's house, tap

the mailbox.
"*Hoi moon?*" I ask.
She shakes her head.
I lean down, tickle the neck
of a ceramic frog guarding the entrance.
"*Hoi moon?*" I dare to ask.
"No," she says, laughing at me, her face
lit with amazement that a grown-up doesn't know,
her soft black hair swinging in denial.

I point to the front door.
"*Hoi moon?*" I ask again.
She rolls her eyes.
"Yes," she says.
"*Hoi moon,*" her voice flooded
with relief that we finally get it.
My husband and I can't believe it.
We've won the lottery
hit a home run

done triple somersault flips,
landed on our feet.
I realize I'm on someone's property,
dash to the sidewalk
sprint across the street
motioning my family to follow.
I climb the cement steps
of First Lutheran Church—
its three red doors beckoning me.
I tap one of them. "*Hoi moon?*"
"Yes," she says. "*Hoi moon.*" Her voice
is astonished that I would even ask.

(Hoi moon is a word from the Gaoyang dialect of Cantonese in Southern China.)

CUSTOMS

They are lined up in the "nothing to declare line"—Rachel, her husband Sam and their daughter Jade, ten and a half, with her two ponytails flattened from twenty hours of travel. It's their second trip to China. On the earlier trip, Rachel and Sam traveled to southern China to meet their daughter for the first time. She was three years old when they became a family.

Rachel thinks of all the dried fruit and the protein bars that are in their luggage, not to mention the vitamins and herbs, and wonders if they should have gone way across the room—the place with problems and inspections and questions. She hopes the DVDs and books which you're specifically not supposed to bring with you won't be spotted. She has the passports and she's in front of her family. It's not very crowded—after all, it's close to midnight, but still, there are two lines of people in the "nothing to declare" section wanting to get through the gate and, finally, into Guangzhou. She looks around and sees that all airports look the same—that is, they could be anywhere in the world in this big hall of a place. There is nothing that marks their location. The people who built this probably wouldn't like these thoughts—it's a new and improved version of an airport since they were last here in 2001.

"Mom, I can't stand up another second." Jade bumps her forehead on her back.

"You're too tall and old to carry," Rachel says, turning to brush away some hair from her daughter's face.

"I'm hungry too," Jade declares.

"It's just a few more minutes," Sam says. He looks as bedraggled as Rachel feels, with his sandy red hair poking up, beard stubble showing and his thick-lensed glasses that he put on halfway through the trip when his contacts felt like sandpaper.

It seems to be true that the wait is over. They're next. In a nearby lane, a man with a crew cut and black glasses is also poised to be next in his line. She wonders if he's from the U.S. and why he's going to China.

"How you doing, honey?" Sam asks.

She smiles back at him. "My head's buzzing, and if I close my eyes, I'm sure I'll fall asleep standing up." In a desperate attempt to hide the ravages of travel, she's pulled her graying brown hair into a ponytail, using one of Jade's bands, a bright chartreuse number, as wide as a silver dollar, with a rash of polka dots.

They move up in line, and she slides the passports and entry cards through an opening in the glass. A clerk, a young man who doesn't look more than fifteen, glances at her. She knows he has to be older, and because she's much older, she realizes that this is just another example of people in their twenties and thirties looking younger to her. Sam also has this happen to him on a regular basis. They were shocked to find out that their mail carrier at home was forty. Forty. They could have sworn she was twenty-five. She once again makes a note that she would do a dismal job selling alcohol or tobacco in a store, not being able to judge age.

The clerk is shuffling through their documents. Any minute, Rachel expects him to say they have to have their bags searched—that they're in the wrong line. Her face feels flushed—maybe he'll read this as a guilty look.

"What is this?" the teenage-looking clerk asks.

Now her face is definitely flushed. Another clerk, a young woman, is standing next to him. How did this crowd scene occur? Rachel hadn't noticed anyone come over. They're both peering out at her. The clerk waves something at her from behind the glass, and again asks, "What is this?"

She wants to explain that they very carefully got their passports, going all the way to Minneapolis, not trusting their local P.O. with something this important. There can't be anything wrong. Could he be talking about how her current ponytail makes her appear completely different than the pageboy in the photo?

"Answer him," Sam suggests in a soft voice.

Rachel looks more carefully at what the clerk is holding. She leans closer to the glass. "It's a driver's license," she says. "It's from Kentucky." What on earth are they showing her? She looks to her left and sees the man with the glasses watching her. It's his face on the license.

"What's Kentucky?" the clerk asks, looking at the other clerk. They both wait for the answer.

"It's a state in the U.S., below Illinois. You know, a province, like

Guangdong."

"But why is it a Kentucky license?" he asks.

"Because he's from Kentucky," she says. She looks over at the man, who's listening intently. She wants to ask him if he's really from Kentucky. Instead she explains that each state issues its own license. She has one from Wisconsin.

"In China, just one license," he says. "From Beijing."

"It's different in the U.S.," she says.

"What's happening, Mom?" Jade asks.

"It's okay," Rachel says, not knowing if it is. She's being asked to verify this man—she doesn't know him, and she hasn't even been admitted to the country yet.

"Okay," the clerk says, handing the license back to the other clerk. The man from Kentucky nods at Rachel. An idea begins to squirm around in her brain that maybe she shouldn't have been so fast and loose with the Good Housekeeping seal of approval on this guy.

Now their clerk is actually checking their passports. He examines one and then looks up, scanning their faces. Finally he says, "Who is she to you?"

Rachel feels something lurch inside her chest. "Sorry?" she says. "Excuse me?"

"Who is SHE to you?" he repeats, pointing at Jade.

"Daughter. She's our daughter." She wants to run very far away, in the other direction, grabbing her daughter and husband, telling them that this was a big mistake. But the other direction is the tarmac and then a whole lot of water.

"But she is Chinese," he says, waiting for Rachel's reaction.

"Yes, she is," Rachel agrees. She no longer wants to be helpful, to verify and assure.

"You are not Chinese," he says, with a half-smile on his face.

"No," she says. "We're not Chinese."

"I'm completely starved," Jade wails behind her.

"You're white," he announces, with triumph in his voice. "So how can you be her mother?"

"I COULD EAT A RHINOCEROS," Jade hollers in what is, charitably, an outdoor voice.

"Adoption," Rachel explains.

The clerk frowns. "What is it?" he asks.

"We adopted her—from an orphan . . . a social welfare institute. She is our adopted daughter." The words *adopted daughter* stick in her throat. Jade is someone she and her husband would lay down their lives for, someone they love without preconditions or limits. Now someone who doesn't know them is making trouble.

"I have never heard of this," the clerk says.

"Well, it's done all the time," Rachel says, hearing exasperation tangled in her voice. She knows Sam is tense too, that he's also remembering the eighteen long months the adoption process took, and the trip to Milwaukee to have a government clerk not unlike this one smear black ink over their palms and fingers for official prints of the entire hand.

Their clerk of the moment gives another glimpse at their documents. "Okay," he says.

Just like that? It's okay. But then he asks another question:

"So what are you going to do in China?"

It's midnight now. She hopes this will end soon, that the person meeting them will be on the other side of the wall. "We're teaching." She names the university, and the clerk nods, sliding their passports back to her. "Good for six months," he says. "Enjoy your stay in China."

"Is it okay, Mom?" Jade asks.

"I think so."

"Awesome." She's dug into a suitcase and found a granola bar that she's munching on.

Rachel looks over at Sam. "You did good," he says.

"I hope so," she says. "I hope the guy from Kentucky wasn't a terrorist or smuggler or something."

"It's their lookout," he says. "They shouldn't have asked you in the first place."

The very man they're wondering about is far ahead of them now. Sam nudges Rachel's arm. Through the glass doors they can see the blond head disappearing inside a taxi.

Weeks later, riding the Metro in Guangzhou, on the way to Hai Zhu to buy toys for Jade's orphanage that they'll be visiting, Rachel's sure she spots the man from Kentucky. At least she notices a man with thick black glasses and a blond crew cut. When she lifts up her hand to wave, she's positive the man at the other end of the car sees her do this. It's too crowded to attempt to go over to him. At the next stop, she watches him quickly hustle off the train and briefly look around before she loses sight of him in the throng moving up the escalator.

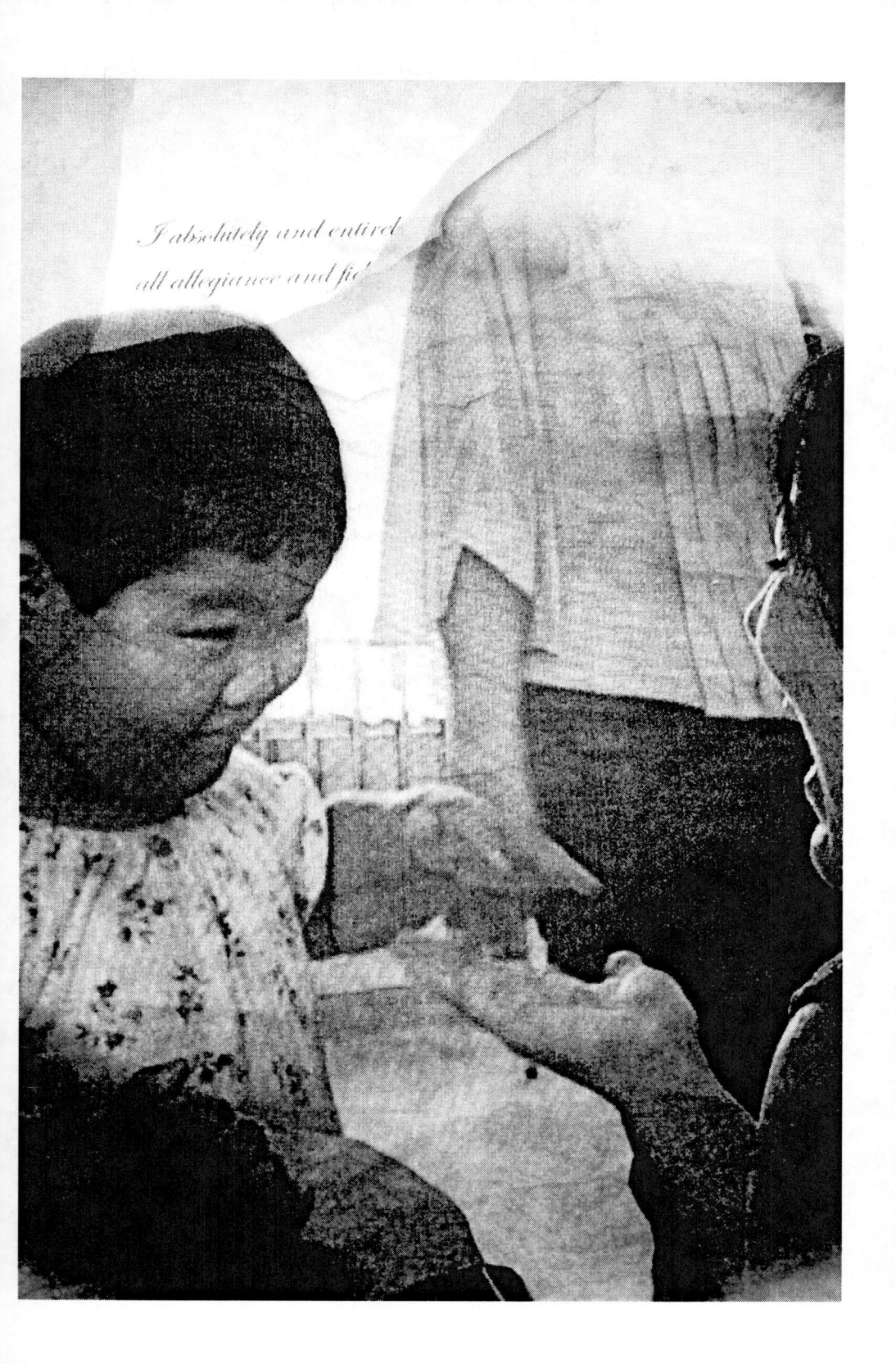

I absolutely and entirely
all allegiance and fid

DIANE RAPTOSH

THE FAMILY BED

Great Aunt Josephine and Uncle Vince stretch and shift. Arranged in fan shape at the mom's right hip are all the men she's ever been with, washed in by the years. The youngest daughter, eyes wide beneath closed lids, has three fathers: the mother's ex, whose eyebrows twitch as he blinks off a dream, the mom's current husband as stepdad. The youngest girl's birth parents hail from the northeast lip of Nanjing city. They lie here every night, quiet as air, one hand gripping the mattress rim, another hand fluting the skin on the waters of Xuanwu Lake, near the foot of the far blue bed of Mount Jiuhua.

THE MOTHER OF HER SECOND DAUGHTER

This woman takes up a place in their house as huge and baffling as the bass sax. Secure as a foghorn, off and on. Think of the bronze-winged jacana, that tropical water bird whose fingerlike toes walk across floating live stems. Sometimes she is so calm light fears the lay and weight of its very shadow; sometimes she enters the room as simply an isosceles triangle—the rough molecular shape of the smell of mint—or sometimes open at one angle, in the form of the percussion instrument. She is both shout and the susurrus used to converse with a wild cat. Hers is the in-house stature of a power forward in the NBA, the gentleness of an elephant nosing for pungencies. Listen to that smell!—this other woman on a continent half the world away shushing and tisking her sole daughter, whose lower lip and jaw jut at precisely the same angle.

KERRY LANGAN

DOUBLE HAPPINESS

When we first returned home from China with our daughter, Madeline, in 1995, we faced so many questions: How would we reverse our days and nights to get back on Eastern Standard Time? How quickly could we have our eight month old examined by a doctor? Would we have her re-immunized? Should we switch to a soy formula? How long should we wait before taking her to visit relatives in other parts of the country? I was certain of only one thing: I would never write about any of this.

Why? Madeline, and everything about her, was too precious to discuss with mere words. The joyful experience of coming together as a family was beyond sacred to her father and me. I'd never be able to adequately write about the bittersweet moment she was first placed in my arms, my heart expanding with the universe, Madeline breaking into wails and reaching for her caretaker. Nor could I explain the deep attachment we felt to the other eleven families in our adoption group who were mirroring our experience, immediately head over heels in love with their new daughters. Some miraculous great fortune had matched us with the child who was *meant* to be ours. Holding Madeline in those first moments, taking in her little turquoise outfit and the scratch on her nose, I wanted to convey love and safety to her. At that moment, I was a stranger to her, but I was also her mother. I was trembling, thinking, "Please, let me be worthy of this baby."

We toured the cities of Hefei and Guangzhou in a blissful, sleep-deprived state, marveling that our most cherished dream had actually come true. In the market, Chinese merchants and shoppers rubbed the babies' heads in hopes that the good luck of infants going to wealthy America would rub off on them. In my right mind, I would have felt disconcerted about the implications of the gesture, of their mistaking me as wealthy because of my race and because I was holding a Chinese baby whose future had been determined by her gender. In my newly maternal state, however, I could only focus on the discomfort Madeline felt when strangers approached her. Her life had been turned upside down in a moment, and she was right on developmental schedule for stranger anxiety. In our first days of family life, Madeline had become trusting of Bob and me, her reliable source of food, but we sensed her fear that we might place her in the arms of a stranger. When going out in public, Bob carried Madeline and I walked alongside. We had noticed that the Chinese were less inclined to approach a tall man with facial hair than a diminutive, dark-haired woman dressed in Chinese clothes (to appear more familiar to Madeline, I had ransacked local shops to find the same dress worn by her orphanage caretaker). From a distance, I might've passed as a Chinese woman. I knew, Bob knew, all of the parents knew that we were the lucky ones. With everything that was wrong in the world, it was still possible for something beyond wonderful to happen; we had been given a child! And not just any child, but Madeline, our precious, precious girl.

How had we ever existed without her? I just wanted to look at her forever, to absorb her every expression and emotion, to assure her that I would always be there for her. When you fall in love that fast, your body undergoes an ecstatic shock. I wondered if I could possibly be experiencing the same hormonal surge of mothers who have just given birth. Bob was reduced to an amusing puddle of paternal love. Madeline threw anything she could get her hands on down on the floor and laughed when her father stooped his large frame to pick up toys, spoons, cups, napkins. If his baby wanted to play "Daddy fetch," Bob was not going to disappoint her. He had very little previous experience with babies, but Madeline was *his* baby. She entered our lives on the ten-year anniversary of Bob's and my first date. As I watched my husband dote on our daughter those first days, I laughed and said, "Well, I was the woman of your life for ten years, but there's a new girl in town."

We were in our daughter's native country, the country we would come to think of as our second home. We promised ourselves that we would learn Mandarin (we now know the few phrases we learned from *Big Bird in China*) and that we would return to China when Madeline was old enough to store memories. We filmed the journey on our camcorder and shot a ridiculous number of rolls of film. Still, during those first days as we explored China and exulted at the sights and landscape, we couldn't wait to get Madeline 'home,' to Oberlin, Ohio, where we could really settle into family life. Madeline was our life; she was all we would ever need. I knew that within moments of holding her that first time. Write about any of that? Impossible.

Once home, I filled private journals with observations about Madeline's every moment ("She loves her little jean jacket! She is pointing at everything! Her doctor says she is 'besting American standards' in terms of physical and cognitive development!"). Every morning, I ran to her crib, clasping her to me and kissing her smooth cheeks over and over. Her shiny, almond-shaped eyes gleamed with recognition. She said "Baba," Chinese for "Daddy," before she said, "Mama," and put the biggest smile on Bob's face. As he entered the house after work, Madeline would clap and grin, proudly displaying her four baby teeth. I'd relate to Bob how Madeline and I had spent the day traveling through the house with a basket of infant toys and books, following the sun as it traveled from window to window. In no time at all, she seemed to understand everything I said and would repeat sounds back to me. Someone at Madeline's orphanage had taught her to raise her tiny fists in weight-lifter fashion, a straining, hilarious expression on her face. Bob and I would call out in unison, "Super Baby!" and Madeline would giggle. She was a super baby, able to fill our hearts with every smile and break them when she woke up with nightmares, which was often. Those were the nights when my heart broke and I wondered if she were crying for what she left behind or out of terror that we would leave her. Bob and I would rock her, walk her, and sing to her for hours. In the morning, she'd be smiling again and we were exhausted but happily relieved.

Madeline started walking at ten months and started reading three and four-letter words at sixteen months. Her orphanage caretakers had named her 'Wandao,' Chinese for 'scholar,' and it certainly seemed an apt name. She was robust and healthy, always eager to eat. In restaurants, we learned to position her high chair so she couldn't reach other tables and merrily swipe a bagel or a muffin from a shocked diner. People stopped and chatted with us everywhere we went. Bob and I forgot Madeline didn't resemble us; she was our daughter, simple as that. We assumed people approached us on the street because she was cute. Babies can't help being irresistable; they draw crowds. But then, at a local store, a new salesclerk stopped me when I started to introduce myself, saying, "Everyone in this store knows you're Madeline's mother." Oh. How does everyone know my daughter's name? The clerk continued, "You are Madeline's mother, right? The Chinese baby?" There were other Asian babies in town; Madeline certainly wasn't an anomaly. She was, however, the first Chinese baby adopted by American parents in Oberlin. I realized that even in our racially diverse town, Madeline stood out because she didn't look like her father and mother. I had thought long and hard about racial issues when completing the adoption paperwork, but once Madeline was with us, I could only think of her as my daughter, of me as her mother. The rest of the world, however, saw two races, two cultures, and I knew this would be pointed out to Madeline as soon as her playmates became verbal and articulate. I often wondered how I would answer her first questions about our differences. I knew that we'd have that conversation many times, that the nature of it would become more complicated as Madeline grew older. And I assumed those conversations would forever remain private.

Five months after returning from China, Bob and I took Madeline to her immigration hearing. Often parents dress their children in red, white, and blue outfits for the event, a fashion declaration to celebrate becoming an American citizen. I, however, disregarded color and simply dressed Madeline in her warmest clothing to withstand the chilly January weather. Bob and I felt conflicted about the hearing. We wished Madeline could have been eligible for dual citizenship. Becoming an American citizen meant she was no longer a Chinese citizen, at least on paper. We felt we were losing a part of her heritage and that saddened us. In a U.S. Immigration official's office, we were instructed to raise our right hands and swear that Madeline was willing to take up arms on behalf of her country. My jaw dropped. Bob and I turned our heads to make eye contact with each other, to confirm that we hadn't misheard what we were supposed to pledge. Madeline had only recently turned one and I wasn't comfortable with the idea of her as a soldier, to say the least. It seemed unfair that we had to make such a declaration because I hadn't given birth to her. If I protested, would she be denied citizenship? Did other nations insist on such pledge from their prospective citizens? Madeline squirmed on my lap, restless and eager to move about, and I repeated the words as instructed. When the official said, "Madeline is now a citizen," however, I was happy to know that my daughter now had the full rights of an American and the protection that entails. The proposed Equal Rights Amendment had never passed, but on that day, I was fairly certain greater opportunities awaited Madeline in the United States than she would have had in China. Because she was born in another country, she cannot become president of the United States, but other than that, she has full privileges of citizenship.

There was another family with a Chinese child outside the Cleveland immigration office that day. Their baby, also a toddler, was adorable and male.

His mother laughed, saying, "We just checked both boxes, boy and girl, and lo and behold!" she gestured to her son. She told me how funny it was to attend area FCC (Families With Chinese Children) events because it was always "a ton of little girls and Jason." That day, Madeline and Jason stood side by side as we took their picture and then raced up and down the hallway. They had no idea that they had just become American citizens.

Madeline grew up so quickly. When she was two, she exuberantly ran ahead of us as we chased her. She was experiencing life as an individual, proclaiming her independence. We moved to London for a time, where people often asked me if I was Madeline's nanny. I would laugh and say, "No, she's mine." I had met many nannies, almost always women of color caring for a white child. Everyone seemed intrigued that a child of color had a white mother. I barely had time to register their interest, however, because keeping up with Madeline took every ounce of my energy. She was involved in lots of pre-school activities held at gyms, libraries, and museums where she occasionally met other little girls born in China. Our American daughter was intrigued with the little girls who looked like her but spoke with a British accent.

Bob and I were very happy watching Madeline out in the world, but we also swallowed the lumps in our throats. Our arms were aching to hold another baby. We completed more paperwork, underwent another home study, took the requisite medical tests, and underwent the police checks required to adopt again. We returned to Oberlin, and eight months later, in August of 1998, Bob traveled to China and brought home Anna, our beautiful, round, bald, 'Buddha baby.' In the years since Madeline's naturalization, the immigration law had changed. Anna's adoption had been finalized overseas which meant she became an American citizen upon entering the United States the first time. We had to file additional paperwork to obtain proof of citizenship, but an immigration hearing was not required. Bob and I decided to take the additional step of 're-adoption' in the state of Ohio. Doing so meant the girls would be given English language birth certificates issued by the state. Their original birth certificates are in Chinese, of course, and indecipherable to most Americans. Part of our motivation to re-adopt was hearing of a family that was detained at the Canadian border because officials thought the parents might have abducted the Korean-born adolescent in their car. The child was their legally adopted son, a member of the family since infancy. To ensure that we'd never find ourselves in that situation, we opted for compiling as much documentation as possible. Although I grew up in Buffalo, close to the Canadian border, we never ventured into Canada with our daughters until they had their Ohio birth certificates. We would have been outraged and heartsick if officials detained us and questioned the girls as to who their "real" parents were. Fortunately, we've never had any difficulty traveling with our daughters, including a return trip we made to China in 2005 with ten of the twelve families from Madeline's adoption group.

Anna. Where to begin? Again, I experienced love at first sight and it was clear that Bob was equally besotted. We weren't sure of her exact age; she had been given the birth date of December 26, 1997 at the orphanage, but everyone seemed to think she was younger. A baby has to be in a Chinese orphanage a minimum of three months before entering the adoption pipeline, so birthdays are often backdated to help the baby join a family as soon as possible. December 26th is Mao's birthday, and the date is given as many children's birth date. We celebrate Christmas, and it seemed unfair that Anna's birthday would be overshadowed by the holiday. I had kept a journal during the adoption process and had had a very strong feeling on January 14, 1998 that Anna was born, and we celebrate her birthday on that day, but would happily celebrate in December should that ever be her preference. In any event, we assumed our new baby was seven months when she joined us and her pediatrician concurred with the estimate.

One thing was very clear; Anna had no stranger anxiety. Madeline had been very guarded around people, but Anna loved attention and beamed at strangers. Whereas Madeline had been determined to express her independence, Anna loved to be cuddled and carried everywhere. Bob and I were the recipients of that Chinese fortune, double happiness, as we reveled in baby bliss again. Anna filled our hearts to the brim, and I filled journals writing about our new daughter who was "the epitome of all things soft and sweet." When her hair came in, it was very fine and pale brown, standing straight up on her head. It was so soft I couldn't resist fluffing it with my fingers all day long. My father called her "Spike," and we sometimes referred to her as our "punk rocker baby."

Madeline was bursting with happiness. When I wheeled the girls around town in a double stroller, Madeline would lean forward and place her hands protectively on Anna's shoulders when anyone approached us. She instructed her baby sister, "Just close your eyes and pretend you're asleep if you don't want to talk to them." We were fortunate that many of Madeline's friends became big siblings about the same time, Madeline so proud to be a member of the club and wearing an "I'm a Big Sister!" pin on every outfit. I couldn't imagine anything more wonderful than being a mom to a beautiful little girl and equally beautiful infant. Our family was now complete, and I thanked all the guiding forces in the universe that I never had gotten pregnant. If I had, we wouldn't have Madeline and Anna, and they are equal parts of my heart and soul. They are quite a team, best friends from the moment Madeline planted the first kiss on her baby sister's bald head. Anna's arrival brought a new wave of questions from people who approached us on the street. They asked, "Are they sisters?" and I would respond, "Of course." They persisted, "No, really? Are they *really* sisters?" I smiled and answered, "In every way possible except biological." I never doubted that family meant more, much more, than DNA.

I was fortunate to learn that before becoming a mother. Bob's mother was an incredibly kind woman who treated me as a daughter. We were very close and became even closer after her husband died. During her last days, when she was very frail, Bob and I told her that we were adopting a Chinese baby whom we would name "Madeline" in her honor. It was the most fitting name because my mother-in-law, not a blood relative, had taught me so much about motherhood. Although she was already in death's shadow when we told her about our Chinese baby, our last moments with her were joyous because she was delighted to know another grandchild was on the way. Later, Bob and I would learn that Madeline had been born a couple days after her funeral.

My experience with non-biological family, however, goes back even further. On the first day of kindergarten, I met my oldest and dearest friend, Maria, whose family became my second family. At a difficult time in my life, when my own mother was emotionally unavailable, her mother, Theresa, whom I address as "Mom," opened her house and her heart to me. I could not love her more and Bob sings her praises. Theresa has been there for every milestone of my life and, of course, she is "Nonny" to Madeline and Anna, no ifs, ands, or buts. The girls couldn't be more proud of their beloved Italian-American grandmother who's so cool she wears skinny jeans and pink high tops. At four-feet, nine-inches tall, Theresa is the matriarch of our family, and the girls are currently campaigning to have her move in with us. Mom spoils the girls, I protest, and she pulls rank. I find myself saying things to her like, "Madeline and Anna get their stubborness from you," and she happily concurs. Biology may not have put us in these familiar family roles, but we inhabit them no less completely. Love can bind you every bit as tightly as blood. It was no big deal that our daughters happened to be born on the other side of the world; I would have gone to the moon to bring Madeline and Anna home.

Of course, Bob and I feel enormous gratitude to China for making our family possible. I often think of the girls' birth mothers, women forced to give up their baby daughters because of complicated, intersecting reasons: the one-child policy, the ancient and persisting gender preference for boys, exclusively male ownership of property in many parts of China, and the harsh reality of poverty. I imagine a woman in China with Madeline's classic Han features, her luminous, full moon face, her incredibly thick dark hair and glistening eyes. Madeline was born in Hefei, an area in central China known for poverty and attractive women. She had been "discovered" on a busy street, and on our return trip to China, we found the street and walked a good portion of it. My heart thrashed in my chest as I pictured my daughter as a bundled newborn on the sidewalk or a bench. I imagined her birth mother as working in one of the shops we had visited, or perhaps she had traveled from the countryside into the city. I worried how Madeline would feel upon visiting the site, whether it would be overly emotional. Bob and I had agreed in advance that should she show any sign of distress, we'd simply turn around and return to the hotel. As it turned out, the oppressive heat was the only thing our daughters discussed that day. We heard the, "Are we there yet?" line over and over. Madeline dutifully posed for a few photos on a very noisy block with lots of construction taking place, and then said, "Can we go back now?" Clearly, she wasn't upset, and I was relieved, though I wondered if she would someday come back to this spot on her own, if the passing years and her changing sense of self would lead her back to the spot that initiated her journey to America.

Anna, our Cantonese beauty, is from Yangchun in southern China, "The City of Eternal Spring." The name given to her at the orphanage, "Chun Hua," is literally translated as "China Flower," but is read as "Springtime in China." Anna was seven when we visited Yangchun, and there I looked about the streets for a woman with round brown eyes, medium-brown hair, an oval-shaped face and long legs. Or maybe I'd spot a brother, the coveted son, or the older sister, the child born within the confines of the one-child policy. With the advances of DNA technology, I sometimes allow myself to daydream that we will one day meet the women who gave Bob and me our daughters, our lives.

It has been fifteen years since our first daughter's adoption and, after promising myself never to write about it, I now sit at my laptop spilling my mind and my heart into these pages. What changed? The simple answer is: so much. I am no longer the mother of infants, toddlers, or young girls. Madeline just turned sixteen and Anna is thirteen. The girls are no longer living completely in our domestic sphere. They are out in the world handling all the trials and tribulations that adolescents and teenagers go through, their responses shaped by who they are. And who are they? They are bright, curious girls who started their lives halfway around the world. In the U. S. since infancy, their experiences are almost completely American experiences. But Americans look at them, at their dark brown eyes, their straight dark hair, their tawny skin, and know that they do not carry my or my husband's genes.

Now I discuss anything and everything with the two amazing girls who, along with the clothes on their backs, carried their keen intelligence from their homeland. People ask them questions that they share with me. Despite the presence of so many adopted Chinese girls currently in the United States, blunt ignorance on many aspects of Chinese adoptions abounds. I haven't always been the most polite mother when approached by strangers wanting to share their opinions on international adoption with me. Most commonly, people are eager to make disparaging remarks about the Chinese people instead of the Chinese government's one-child policy and largely male right to property. I generally remind people that American women only received the right to vote a century ago and, of course, one hundred years is a blink of the eye when you're considering four thousand years of Chinese history. I talk about the poverty, of the *thirty million* Chinese people who starved to death during the Great Leap Forward, of the scarcity of food to feed an outsized populace. And I always speak of the enormous risk Chinese mothers take to place their babies in plain sight before making what must be a heartbreaking exit.

Our immediate environment is usually very comfortable for a mixed race family. We live in a college town where the population is wonderfully diverse. Although Oberlin only has some eight thousand residents, our racial demographics are more akin to that of an urban environment. Key nineteenth-century abolitionists lived in Oberlin, and our African-American population includes many descendants of the courageous travelers of the Underground Railroad. Buffalo soldiers are buried in our cemetery. Biracial families are common and multiracial families are not uncommon. Students from all over the world, including China, attend Oberlin College and the Oberlin Conservatory. As a result of all these factors, Oberlin has gained a reputation as a supportive and friendly place for families with internationally adopted children. Madeline's first playgroup included another girl born in China, a boy born in Russia, and a girl born in India. They had all been adopted as infants or toddlers. As a little girl, Madeline loved to spin a globe and point out where she and her playmates had been born.

So, yes, people such as the sales clerk might know I am Madeline's mother, but I never sensed judgment in that knowledge. When our daughters are out with their friends, I doubt anyone gives them a second glance. Outside the lovely bubble of our town, however, the girls are stared at, sometimes whispered about. At a gas station in rural Indiana, a man with a brusque manner shouted at me, "Hey! You adopted those two, didn't ya?" I got the girls back into our car before turning to him and saying calmly, "No, I just ate a lot of rice when I was pregnant." I drove off knowing that I should have been a better ambassador for adoption, for China, but, frankly, sometimes I'd rather not be bothered. A friend of mine was once at a playground with his biracial daughters when he was accosted by a stranger who demanded to know, "How'd that happen?" I liked my friend's answer: "I broke a chain letter." I heard of a woman who, when asked about her daughter's origins, handed the inquirer a small card printed with the words, "Forgive me for not answering and I'll forgive you for asking." Some find this rude, but I understand her desire to go about normal activities with her young daughter without being expected to answer a stranger's questions in front of her daughter.

Adoptive mothers know the shorthand when approaching one another: "Hi, your daughter is beautiful. I have two girls who were born in China." Then the excited conversation: "Where in China is your daughter from? What adoption agency did you use? How old was she when you got her? Are you sending her to Chinese school?" I walk away feeling as if my extended family has grown. I'm generally a sucker when it comes to children, but when I spot a baby girl with Chinese features, my maternal heartstrings are plucked loudly. I 'recognize' her in a way I don't other infants. I feel as if the baby is related to my daughters, to my husband and me, and I realize once again that I identify with China as much as I do America. My Chinese daughters are American girls, and I seem to have dual maternal citizenship.

There was a time in this country when adoption was shrouded in secrecy, files sealed, people lied to about their biological relatives. As Caucasian parents of Chinese daughters, we could never have engaged in such subterfuge, even if we had wanted to. We want to empower our daughters by giving them as much information as possible so no question will catch them off guard, intimidate them, or make them uncomfortable. After vowing to never write about our adoption experience, I wish now that I could speak to any and every person who might approach our daughters in the future. I would implore them to treat Madeline and Anna with respect, to not make assumptions about their origins, to understand if they don't want to converse about their heritage at that given moment, to honor the right to privacy they gained when they became American citizens.

But if I am completely honest, I have to admit I have made assumptions myself. Perhaps 'assumptions' is not the appropriate term for the details I have told my daughters about their infancies. I have *hopes* for the what, why, when, and how things happened during the very first days of their lives, and I have shared these hopes. Like many parents of children whose origins are largely unknown, I may be wearing rose-colored glasses, and I am more than a little hesitant to remove them.

A few months before going to China to bring Madeline home, I saw the Woody Allen film *Mighty Aphrodite*. Despite the typical Allen humor, the film drove something home to me that I think about often. The main character, Lenny, is a loving father who can't help being enormously proud of his adopted son's profound intelligence. He's confident that his child's birth mother must be a genius, and he sets out to find her. Linda is definitely not the Mensa mom Lenny had assumed she must be. No, she's a sweet but hapless prostitute, and Lenny can't resist trying to introduce conventionality and respectability into her life. As an adoptive mother, I can relate to Lenny's wish to better her life. We don't know who our daughters' birth mothers are. Yes, we guess at their maternal situation, but we don't actually know anything about their personalities, their work, their families, or how they feel about their lost daughters. Like Lenny, we're hoping for the best possible scenario, but we can't alter previous events.

On our reunion trip back to China, our family spent a delightful afternoon with the director of our younger daughter's orphanage. Throughout the hours together, the director, an incredibly kind, enthusiastic woman, kept gathering Anna up into her arms and joyfully swinging her around. She was ecstatic that a family had journeyed back to the orphanage. We felt such warmth in her presence; the visit felt like the happiest of family reunions. She took us to the hospital where Anna had been found, showing us the exact spot at the entrance gate where our baby was first spotted. Although thrilled to have this information, I asked the interpreter to say "discovery" site instead of "abandonment" site. The interpreter turned to the director and translated my request into Chinese. The director looked puzzled but immediately offered an apology. I wondered if the Chinese word for "abandonment" sounded as harsh to her ear as the translation did to my own. I tried to convey that I did not want Anna to hear the term, that we had never used that word when discussing her story. I had always presented the most positive scenario of being placed at the gates of an infants' hospital to my daughter. Through the translator, I tried to explain that 'discovery' was a better word. Better. As if I could change anything about an event that had taken place seven years earlier in a foreign country. I had also hoped, naively, that I could impact how Chinese adoptions are discussed, to 'better' that discussion. Maybe the word 'discovered' could forever replace the word 'abandoned' in the adoption dialogue, or maybe I was as naïve as Lenny. If I ever met Anna's birth mother and her story was not the one I'd told for so many years, I might be tempted to do all that I could to assist or influence her so I wouldn't have to alter the loving story I'd told my daughter of her first days. But would that be right? Would that be fair to Anna?

When children are young, we tell them fairy tales and reassure them with the 'happily ever after' endings. As the parents of Chinese daughters, we don't know the 'before' story. So many things happened to the girls before we appeared on the scene. Each was conceived by parents we don't know, born in a place we don't know, left in a public area, found, brought to an orphanage where each was cared for by people who are strangers to us, likely shared a crib with a baby about the same age, and, through a major miracle involving a mountain of paperwork, was placed in their adoptive parents' arms. Those are the bare bones of the matter; we don't have a lot to work with. We tell the 'Everybaby' story and we tell it in the best possible light. Yes, your birth mother so wanted to keep you. She was forced by family and tradition to give you up. When she placed you in a public place, she watched from a distance to make sure you were found immediately. You are always in her thoughts. Yes, this is undoubtedly the story of many Chinese daughters, but we don't know if it is truly Madeline's or Anna's story.

Our daughters, however, are more than old enough to question what Bob and I have told them. Of course, we've never been untruthful, but we've painted the picture of their first days with a gentle brush and in soft, soothing pastels. Once while sipping hot chocolate with Madeline after a fun night of ice skating, I said to her, "I wish your Chinese parents could know how wonderful you are. I wish they could know that you're so kind and smart, and such a wonderful big sister." My four-year-old responded, "I think Anna's and my parents have a *loooong* telescope they can see us through, and they know we're okay." She curled her fingers into a circle and looked at me through the round hole. Her tone was very reassuring, and I was happy that she could so comfortably and creatively respond. At that moment, I wished she could always carry her sweet little story about the telescope with her. Even today, it is difficult to tell our daughters that there are girls in China given nicknames that, translated, mean 'No more girls' and 'Wish for boys.'

Gender inequality is what is known about the situation, but it's undoubtedly more complex. To deem all the women virtuous and suffering and all the men entitled and arrogant brings us back to the polar opposites presented in fairy tales. Two images stand out strongly in my mind from our return trip to China. On a beastly hot day in late July, a group of us went shopping in a large department store in Hefei. The store was air-conditioned and moms and daughters were happy to browse rack after rack of clothing, calling out to one another when we found an exceptionally attractive item or a great bargain. The girls were ten years of age, giddy and chatty. Store staff and shoppers noticed us, western mothers with Chinese daughters, all of us speaking English. At first, a few Chinese women stood twenty yards or so away from us, observing us as we sorted through the apparel. More people joined the group and soon there was a small crowd of Chinese women huddled together, whispering and glancing surreptitiously at us. I tried to read their expressions. Surprised? Definitely. Happy? I didn't see a single smile. Angry? No one shouted at us, but, of course, no one would have. Scared? I'm afraid they were. One of the girls asked, "Why is everyone looking at us?" Her mother answered, "Because you're all so cute."

Later, we mothers contemplated more difficult answers: Because they never expected you to come back. Because you are a secret that haunts them. Because they think you may be trying to find your birth mothers and if you are successful, they will go to jail. Because it's not fair that their initial grief over losing you should be compounded by not knowing if one of you may be one of their daughters. This last answer is the one that slays me, and I can't help but believe it is the true answer. Or am I as naïve as Lenny?

The second incident struck me just as deeply. Anna and I were on an elevator in a lovely hotel in Beijing. She was holding a small panda that traveled with her wherever we went. With us on the elevator was an elderly Chinese man, not much taller than I am. He looked at Anna intently, heartbreak in his slight smile, his eyes gentle and moist. There was a dynasty of loss in his face and I was not surprised when he held his hand out to cradle my daughter's cheek. Anna, then seven and very shy, was not frightened. The three of us were quiet as we rode up floor after floor, his hand on her face. I so wanted to talk to him, but I know hardly any Chinese. Also, he had no interest in me; his gaze never left Anna's face. The elevator stopped and he withdrew his hand, leaving us in the small compartment. The doors closed and Anna said to me, "He was like Grampa." I nodded, blinking rapidly to halt the tears.

My father had died ten months earlier, having lived his last three years with us. Anna was his youngest grandchild and his constant companion, the two of them thick as thieves, eating candy behind my back (and hiding the wrappers) while Anna explained the latest happenings on *Rugrats* and *Sponge Bob* to him. Anna was named for my father's mother, a woman who had left Ireland when she was sixteen for the chance of a better life in America. My father couldn't have been happier that his Chinese granddaughters had crossed an ocean for the same reason as his mother.

On the elevator that day, I looked at my Anna and said, "I'm sure that man has a granddaughter just as wonderful as you." I know many adoptive moms like myself who often think of our daughters' birth mothers with sadness and gratitude. This experience on the elevator, it shames me to admit, was one of the first times that I considered the grieving men in China. Nothing was more precious to my father than children. The father of three daughters, he maintained, "The only thing better than boys are girls." Having grown up with only female siblings was one of the early reasons I became interested in the plight of the baby girls in China. If one of us had somehow been whisked to another country, my father would have spent every moment of his life tracking us down. Like the gentleman on the elevator, he'd be looking for us in the face of every child.

    Generally, American parents of daughters born in China are eager to provide ready access to their heritage. If anything, we go overboard. I've heard of many parents purchasing sixteen gifts while in China to parcel out to their daughters on their first sixteen birthdays. New moms learn how to prepare congee for their babies' breakfasts; recipes are readily available on the Internet. Many girls attend Saturday lessons at Chinese language schools. I don't know a single mother of a daughter born in China who doesn't have the China Sprout catalog at the ready. We order Chinese-themed books, games, jewelry, clothing, and music. Tour the bedroom of any of our daughters and count the stuffed pandas. If there's another Chinese daughter in the vicinity, the families know each other. We send donations to Half the Sky, an organization active in improving the welfare of babies and children in Chinese orphanages. During Chinese New Year, we put up displays in our daughters' schools and pass out red envelopes filled with chocolate coins wrapped in gold foil. We keep in touch with orphanage staff, sending them pictures and letters. And, of course, many of us have taken our daughters back to China for extended visits.

    In our multicultural town, having parents who go a bit crazy over your heritage is okay most of the time. We have friends, however, whose daughters are the only students of Asian heritage in their class or even their school. There are times when these girls do not want to be singled out as a representative for an entire culture. Standing out during adolescence is not always easy, and differences of any kind are generally not cool. It's not surprising that some Chinese daughters have turned to their American parents who are so ready to affirm their heritage and said, "Enough. Stop. Back off."

    I understand. I remember the look of disappointment on my own mother's face when I told her I wanted to quit Irish dance lessons. We lived in a heavily Irish-Catholic neighborhood, but I decided I wanted to be just American, not Irish American. Today, I love to visit my beautiful childhood neighborhood and have written about it in my fiction. My husband and I honeymooned in Ireland and I cried when it was time to leave. I can't get enough of Irish music and literature. Still, when I was eleven, any heritage would have hindered the individual identity I was trying to forge. It's a common story often told by children and grandchildren of immigrants in the United States. The new generation relates more to its current country than the heritage of its ancestors. I know there have been times when Madeline and Anna felt that I was acting like an overzealous convert, an American mother embracing all things Chinese so they would never feel deprived of their birth culture. My children are certainly not afraid to tease me about it, and I've learned to say, "Okay, message received."

Madeline's and Anna's feelings about their heritage will no doubt also be influenced by other Chinese daughters. The infant girls who came from China in the first wave of adoptions in the early 1990s are in college, and enrollment numbers will swell in coming years. It's certainly not hard to imagine them exchanging information and sharing confidences in classrooms and dorm rooms. Some of these young women will likely meet young men from China, the 'little emperors' so desired by their culture that their sisters were placed in front of hospitals, in crowded train stations, or left in busy outdoor markets.

Imagine this encounter: relinquished, American-Chinese daughter meets adored Chinese son. Of course, the situation with girls in China is not the fault of its boys or young men. Our daughters may meet male students whose families mourn the loss of daughters, sisters, granddaughters, cousins, and nieces. Some of these young men may wish they had the opportunity to grow up in the United States. Undoubtedly, friendships between some of our daughters and Chinese sons will take root, adding yet another chapter to the ongoing identity story. It's certainly not beyond comprehension to predict some romantic liaisons forming (and the inevitable conversations: "Where were you abandoned? Is there any chance we could be related?"). Some of the adopted daughters may journey back to their first homeland to meet their husbands' families or even to live. And what type of reception will they receive? Will they be perceived as American women or as returned Chinese daughters? While growing up in America, a girl's appearance identified her Chinese heritage. In China, her years and experiences in the United States will identify her as American. But to what extent? Will one side of her heritage outweigh the other? Chinese daughters will make that decision for themselves, and we will have to wait and see how uniform their response is. So much of their lives were pre-determined, their preferences and opinions not considered, but, at long last, the girls will speak for themselves.

...ned lightning, and her na...

...of Eile...

MADELINE GEITZ
ANNA MAE ANHALT
ALICIA KARLS

CHINESE DAUGHTERS & AMERICAN CITIZENS Q & A, A & Q

Madeline:

Anna, Alicia, and I live in Wisconsin, Minnesota, and Ohio, respectively, but in some ways we feel closer than any other group of three could. We were adopted from the same orphanage in central China in July of 1995. Our birthdays are a few weeks apart—it's even possible we could have shared a crib at our orphanage. We, along with several other girls in our adoption group, have gathered at annual reunions in Chicago, a central meeting point. We also took a return trip to China together in the summer of 2005. All of us have asked, and been asked, similar questions regarding our adoption experiences. This collaborative self-interview provides answers to those often asked questions. Our editor, Heather Tosteson, asked us to consider additional questions regarding naturalization and citizenship. You'll see that the three of us are in agreement on many points but also have a variety of opinions on others. It is evident, however, that we share deep pride in being the unique Chinese daughters that we are.

How has being adopted affected your life?

Anna:

Oh goodness, where to start. Quite honestly being adopted has affected my life of course, but from the every day-to-day life of mine I rarely am reminded of it or think about it.

I mean when I do think about it, yes of course—if I wasn't adopted the language I would speak would be different, my culture would be different, who I hang out with, my life experiences, my opportunities—all different.

I am a person who does believe that everything happens for a reason. I don't think my adoption was an accident, I don't think where I am today was an accident and I KNOW that wherever life happens to take me in the future won't be by accident either. Being adopted doesn't define me, it's just a part of my life that has helped bring me to where I am today.

Alicia:

Being adopted is one of the biggest things that define who I am. I'm here because of adoption; I have a mom because of adoption; I have an amazing life because of adoption. I *definitely* wouldn't be the same person without being adopted. I don't mean to say that everything I do is based on adoption; it's just a really big part of who I am. I don't go around saying I'm adopted, but I sure am proud if I get asked. I don't think of my mom as my adoptive mom (yes I've been asked), I think of her as my mom, as anyone else would think of their parent. I also hate answering the question "if your real parents ever wanted you back would you leave your fake mom?" First of all, she's not my "fake" mom. Second of all, no, because I love my life right now; my birth parents had to make a choice and it must have been for a reason. I'm never going to be ashamed that I got adopted, that would be like being ashamed of being myself.

Madeline:

It's rare that I think of myself as adopted, or factor in my adoption to who I am as a person. 'Adopted' isn't some sort of state that I think of myself to be in—I was adopted at eight months old and, in my lifetime, I'd rank it as about as notable an event as losing my fifth tooth, or getting my seventeenth haircut. Now, this is not to say I'm ungrateful in the slightest about being adopted by such a loving family—my luck in receiving such a perfect life was one in a million—but my adoption is not what makes me Madeline, or the only thing that makes me who I am. I am the combined result of everything in my life—every birthday, every crush, every pair of jeans, every song I sang in the shower, every font I used in a school report, every CD I put on my Christmas wishlist, every math equation I ever solved, and every color I ever painted my toenails—not just the event of my adoption.

Have you ever returned to China?

Madeline:
    We often had reunions with the families in Chicago, and for our tenth reunion we planned this trip to China. We started out in Beijing, then moved on to visit Hefei, Guangzhou, Yangchun, and Shanghai.

Anna:
    Yes, it was during the summer of 2005, I had just finished fifth grade and was going into sixth grade. My parents and I and all of the other girls who were adopted along with me and their families all flew out to spend two amazing weeks in China. In those two weeks, we managed to hit five major cities, one of them being my hometown, Hefei.

Alicia:
    It was really emotional and *definitely* a once in a lifetime experience. We all got to see which orphanage we came from, where we were found, where our parents had stayed to get us, we saw everything and more. We all traveled to the Great Wall, Beijing where they were to hold the 2008 Olympics, and to see the Terracotta Warriors and so many cool places. All of us girls had planned to take our parents back for the fifteen-year anniversary in 2010, but sadly we didn't get a chance to do that.

What was it like going to China and not being able to speak Chinese?

Anna:
    It was definitely interesting. So many times people would come up to me and start speaking in Chinese to me. I only looked at them apologetically and tried to explain that I did not understand. Having that language barrier was a situation I had never been in before. It was challenging, frustrating at times, but at the same time it really made me want to learn the language.

Alicia:
    It wasn't as hard as I thought it would be. I think most of the natives in China had a sixth sense and were able to tell that we were not Chinese speakers although we looked Chinese. Having a translator for a guide was extremely helpful. When we would go to a restaurant, our tour guide would

just order us all food and then we'd get to experiment, so it was kind of fun not being able to tell what we would get. Of course when we stopped at the McDonald's all of us just showed five fingers for the number five meal. It honestly wasn't that bad.

Madeline:

At several points during my family's trip to China, women or men would come up to me and speak Chinese. Admittedly, I felt some guilt. My schooling never provided me with the opportunity to learn Chinese, and when given the opportunity at a young age, I didn't take it seriously. Now I was in a position where people made assumptions about me based on my appearance—in China of all places!

In my high school, you have one of two language options: French or Spanish. If given the opportunity, like several of my adopted friends, I would have taken Chinese. I take French, a subject you can't take lightly—you have to memorize all the vocabulary, study the conjugations, and understand which tense to use—and that's not even considering pronunciation. Just taking French makes me imagine how difficult learning Chinese would be—the writing would be next-to-impossible to memorize and the speaking would involve a series of difficult tones. I admire those students who are committed to taking it.

People didn't make assumptions based on your appearance before?!

Anna:

Well, that's kind of funny. Ever since I've been in school, I've always been known as the Asian nerd. School, learning, all of that academic stuff came so naturally to me. Lol. My friends blamed it on the Asian in me. I'd just laugh and shrug it off. It's funny because I don't even know why I'm good at school, I mean I do like it, but why does it have to be because I'm Asian? Haha. I'm like the definition of the stereotypical Asian student. But I don't mind. The funniest part about it though, I think I push myself harder than my parents do. Once I grounded myself for getting a B+ on a report card in fourth grade. Lol.

Madeline:

I got some mild teasing about being Chinese in second grade, but

I had a terrific teacher, Mrs. Peters, who not only helped me stand up for myself, but also taught the whole class how insensitive comments can hurt.

Other than that, not really. I mean, the assumptions they would make would have to be true—what kind of Asian would I be if I wasn't an intelligent over-achiever with overbearing parents?

Wait, that sounds a bit racist!

To the 'unOberlin-ized' ear, my constant jokes involving race could be taken offensively. I answer calls from my Asian-American friend, Hannah, for instance with "herro?" and constantly joke about squinty eyes' correlation with intelligence. This carefree and silly attitude isn't only towards Asian cultures, however—you can also find my group of close-knit friends joking about white supremacy or being 'incredibly gangster.' While we certainly use outdated stereotypes, we do it with no harm intended. That's what is so great about Oberlin, Ohio, my hometown. In a high school of less than three hundred people, we're a mixing pot of races, social classes, and interests. People come to the football games not only to watch our football team play, but also to support our marching band. The academic challenge team, drama club, and art club are just as active and have as much pride as the volleyball team or the cheerleading squad. Teachers make just as many Oberlin jokes as the students.

I learned it was really different outside Oberlin.

When I was thirteen, I attended a 'leadership camp' near Sandusky, Ohio. Being one of four non-Caucasian campers, I was often asked if I could speak Chinese. My dry sense of humor was misunderstood, and although everyone had good intentions, the lack of diversity made me uncomfortable. My vegetarianism at the time, readily accepted as 'the norm' in Oberlin, was unaccepted. In fact, the group I was in wrote a skit that referred to vegetarians as 'veggie huggers' and 'weak.' That weekend, I gained a new appreciation for where I live.

Why were you adopted?

Anna:

Well, I was adopted when I was only seven months old. I honestly don't remember anything. I was found on the side of a street near a bus stop in February of 1995, I was adopted a few months later in July.

Alicia:
No one really knows the full reason why I was adopted. The orphanage never got a reason, they can only make assumptions: war, poverty, the law of only male children, or death. All they know is that I was left outside of a police station between December and May. It may not sit well with some people that I'm really not bothered with this information, but it's because I'm fine with it, like I said earlier, it must have been for a reason. And it was for a reason that I was adopted.

Madeline:
My birth mother gave birth to me and then left me on a busy street in Hefei, a city about 300 miles west of Shanghai, where the police found me and then took me to an orphanage.

Being left?! How does that make you feel?

Anna:
I wouldn't say I was 'left'—I'm a very positive person and I'd like to think that whatever the reason my mother had to give me up, it was a very good one. Was it because I wasn't a boy? Was I one child too many? Was my mother too poor to take care of me and wanted me to have an opportunity for a better life? I will never know. . . .

What I do know is that I have what is called a 'Chinese tattoo.' It's not a real tattoo, like what we think with the ink and whatever, it's merely five needle pokes in my left arm. Supposedly my birth mother gave it to me, each needle mark is supposed to represent her love for me that will stay with me forever; that's what my mother who adopted me told me. I've never learned much more about it—I rarely think about it. It's visible, it's like a scar—but friends at school when they first notice it are always so curious about it. I've never met anyone else who has it. None of my Chinese sisters have it.

Madeline:
My mother, during the return trip to China, was incredibly adamant about using the phrase 'discovery place' rather than 'abandonment place' (the usual term) when referring to the spot in Hefei where my birth mother left me. Frankly, I didn't care at the time and still don't care now. It was where I

was left, and the name shouldn't matter.

What's your family like? How did they tell you that you were adopted?

Anna:

I love my family. It's not perfect, but what family is? My mother adopted me when she was single. It's crazy to think that my mom came all the way to China to get me all by herself. She's very independent and I love that about her. When I turned three, she married and that's when my father adopted me also. I have two older sisters from my dad's previous marriage. It's funny because they are both over the age of thirty, and I'm TALLER than both of them; I tease them all of the time. They both have their own families now. My sister Crystal is married and has three wonderful children. My sister Jessica just had her first baby February 16th!

I don't exactly remember how or when my parents told me I was adopted, I'm pretty positive they told me somewhere around kindergarten or first grade. I do remember I would have these spells and get really upset, crying because I missed my mom—the mom I had no recollection or memory of.

Alicia:

My family is the best, biggest, most important thing to me in the entire world. It may sound cheesy, but it's true. It's just me and my mom in our house, but I love her more than words could explain and I don't know what I'd do without her. My cousins and aunts and uncles and my grandma all treat me as if I were flesh-and-blood related. For a class in high school this year we're required to make a Family History Project; it includes a family tree, a biography of someone living, a biography of someone who's passed away, a ton of things and then some that we're allowed to make up on our own. At first I started to get a little worried, I didn't know anything about my family tree let alone my family. But of course I had my mom and her heritage. That made it even more clear that that is my true family. It really doesn't have to be birth related to be considered kin. My family project (almost complete) has a large chunk of my mom's family background and as much as I could find on my own family. The latter part doesn't consist of too much, but just enough to make me feel unique.

Madeline:

My adoption was never a secret—journals, videos, and reunions document the adoption.

One of my mother's favorite anecdotes is an incident that occurred when I was two years old. We were driving in the car when she heard me say from the back seat, "I want to be a whi-gir like mommy." She immediately pulled over the car and climbed into the back seat to tell me that all races are beautiful and I should be proud of my heritage.

I was rather preoccupied, staring out the window. I repeated myself: "I want to be a wri-tuh like mommy." She blinked. Writer!

In kindergarten, a similar situation happened. I came home from school sobbing one day.

"What's wrong?!" my mom asked in horror.

"At school I was called a name!" I wailed.

My mom's mind raced to the worst—had I been made fun of for my Chinese descent? Had I been called a 'chink'? Already halfway to the phone to call the school I cried out what, to me, was one of the worst things I could have ever been called:

"THEY CALLED ME 'FLOWERPANTS'!"

Yes, yes. That day at school I had worn a pair of floral-print sweatpants and had been called the horrific name 'Flowerpants.' While I'm sure that most would be scarred to this day with that kind of treatment, I have forgiven the perpetrator of such foul language.

My mother has a million stories to tell about my sister and me. While I occasionally get frustrated over the fact that she's protective, she has also put up with all my temper tantrums, worries, and irrational fears. She supports me in everything I do. We have a very loving relationship. :)

My father is a professor at Oberlin College. He is an incredible father. He's genuinely one of the nicest people you'll meet; he comes to all of my school related functions, and is a fantastic cook. I called him 'Baba' when I was a baby.

My younger sister, Anna, was also born in China. I make fun of her for being a 'typical teenager,' with a strong interest in appearance, name-brand clothing, and eyeliner. Although we're very different on almost all fronts (music, size and type of friend circles, beauty regimen) we get along incredibly well. Having a sister means so much to me. Occasionally, we're asked if we're 'real' sisters. "Not biological," I reply, "does that make us unreal?"

A very special member of the family is our "Nonny." Despite technically being my mother's best friend's mom, I consider her my grandmother. Our family is not defined by biology, but by love, which is definitely shared between us. My nonny talks with me about literature, music, life, and everyday annoyances—especially the word 'boyfriend.' Every kid should be fortunate enough to have a grandmother like Nonny.

Have you ever had access to your birth culture?

Anna:

My parents have always wanted me to embrace my Chinese culture. When I was younger, I would take all of my possessions from China to school, sort of like a show-and-tell and teach my class about China, and where I came from. They would ask me questions, get a chance to look at my things and I'd have a blast. It was fun for my classmates and me; I probably did this every other year from second grade to sixth grade.

And of course at home, we have Chinese for dinner at least once or twice a week. Haha, sometimes I ask myself if it wasn't for me would my parents eat Chinese food as often as we do. We have little Chinese artifacts laying around the house too, like our book all about China, a jade globe we bought on our trip to China and this Asian tea-table that my dad bought off of a Chinese restaurant called 'Golden Gate' haha.

Madeline:

My parents exposed me to a lot of Chinese culture when I was young. They tried to get me started on learning Chinese, bought me book after book on Chinese adoption, and emphasized my Chinese heritage, occasionally to an extent I viewed as extreme.

I think my mother feels more like the mother of a Chinese daughter than I feel like a Chinese daughter. She pushes incredibly hard for a certain environment around me. When I mention a new student who happens to be Asian, my mom's first instinct is to ask if we've become close friends with them and if she can invite him or her to dinner. When I told her that I wished I was white so I could have red hair, she immediately emphasized my dark-haired beauty. I sometimes joke she has an Asian fetish. She sometimes jokes there's probably a dead body hidden among the mess in my room.

Have you talked to your American parents about your Chinese parents?

Anna:

I don't as much as I used to. Sometimes the subject comes up, but never really goes into too much depth. Actually, it came up somehow a few weeks back during dinner with my dad, and it actually got my dad choked up and crying. I didn't find it all too awkward because it shows how much my dad loves me, but at the same time I don't think it'll be another main dinner convo in the near future.

Alicia:

Certainly. I never lied about my curiosity. If I had a question about my heritage when I was younger, I would just come out and say it. But for a while I had always wondered if it hurt my mom's feelings in any way for me to talk about my Chinese family to her. Finally I brought it up and we had a conversation about how she wasn't getting her feelings hurt, but she wanted to make sure I knew that she was my family now.

Madeline:

"Mom?" I asked one day, "What would we do if we found my birthparents?"

"I would lay at their feet and thank them," my mom replied.

I curled my seven-year-old features into a look of disgust. "Gross! But would I go back to live with them?"

"I would invite them to come live with us," she replied.

"How do you think my mom and I will get along? Won't the whole language thing be a problem?"

"We'd learn. We'd all learn from each other."

What are your earliest memories?

Anna:

My mom has so many pictures, as much as she doesn't like her picture being taken now, she has hundredssssss from when she first got me. There's a picture she has framed of me as a baby, it's what the agency sent to her and told her that this is what her baby girl looked like. I hate that picture, haha. I was chubby baby, and she for the longest time called me her 'Buddha Baby.' It was sooooooo embarrassing. But you gotta love my mom(: haha.

Madeline:

My earliest memories are my mother telling me my 'adoption story' and how she held me in her arms for the first time.

"You were drinking green tea when I first saw you," she always recalls. "You were the most beautiful baby I'd ever seen."

"Mo-om," I'd always respond. "You're embarrassing me!"

My mom kept a journal describing everything from my first words to my art work to the poetry I dictated to her as I was growing up. I can look into this journal and see what my favorite book was when I was two, my first words, and what the tooth fairy brought me when I lost my front teeth.

What was it like being at an orphanage?

Anna:

Well, since I was only a few months old when I was in the orphanage I really don't remember what it was like or how I acted when I was there at the orphanage. I will always remember what it was like going back to visit though.

Alicia:

I was only seven months old so I don't remember anything at all. When we went back ten years later, they said it hadn't changed much. When we were walking around, we saw babies through the windows in their cribs. Some were alone in their crib, but there were many who had a friend with them. My mom and I had wondered if Ellie and I were friends in the same crib. (Ellie and I have the same estimated birthday and we call each other twins.)

Madeline:

I don't remember. I was eight months old when I was adopted. However, on our return trip I remember being really apprehensive about going back to the orphanage. What happens to the kids who weren't adopted? What are the conditions like?

What was it like visiting your orphanage?

Anna:

Oh goodness, I remember riding our big coach bus to the orphanage. All of the parents were talking amongst themselves, and all of us girls sat in the back of the bus giggling like we usually do. When we got there, I remember being really anxious, not in a scared way, but more curious. I had no idea what to expect.

The orphanage was sort of divided into different sections, almost like villages. The baby rooms were set up like a three-story motel. A bunch of rooms with maybe four to six cribs in each. There were little babies crying, sleeping, and eating everywhere. What amazed me the most were the women who attended all the babies. They had so many to take care of and the number of women to the number of babies to attend to was crazy.

I also remember going to another part of the orphanage, it was sort of set up like an apartment. We visited one little 'home' and there were four or five kids living there, with a caretaker of course. They were all between the ages of five to thirteen I believe. They were so sweet and innocent, playing and watching TV and looking at me and all of my Chinese sisters who were also staring back at them. The sad story, though, was that the chance of these children being adopted was slim to none. Parents always want the babies, you know. Rarely do adoptive parents want children who are reaching their teenage years.

It's sad but true.

Madeline:

My parents had bought me a long black skirt and silk top to wear to visit the orphanage. On the day of the visit, the parents had us line up in front of the orphanage sign—a sign surrounded by a fence. In an attempt to get in front of the sign I jumped down off the fence, only to slip into a puddle of mud and sliced my hand open. To everyone's surprise, I laughed. It helped to relieve the tension.

After cleaning off at a nearby water spigot, I took the picture with the rest of the girls, and we finally entered the orphanage.

I had made the assumption the orphanage would be one large building, but instead it was several buildings. In a conference room we met with the current orphanage director as well as the former director of the orphanage who had been there when we were infants. We received gift bags at the orphanage that contained a beautiful picture of a tree that stood outside our first home. The orphanage director showed us some of the orphanage's files—pictures our families had sent them of us over the years.

The staff was excited to see all of us. The previous orphanage director said, "When these girls were babies, they were my family. Now you bring them back to us ten years later, so healthy, so beautiful. Now we are all family."

We toured the buildings, including one that was designed specifically for infants, and another that resembled a preschool. I had been particularly worried about seeing older children at the orphanage, girls my age who for some reason had not been adopted. They may have arrived at the orphanage as toddlers or older children. To my relief, the older children lived in 'apartments' with a 'mother' and a 'father.' Everything was clean and comfortable.

My sister's orphanage was different. Her orphanage is a single new building (it had been a few separate ones when she was there) and has fewer children. Her city of Yangchun has a population of around sixteen thousand, as opposed to Hefei's almost five million. At her orphanage, we visited an infant room where my mom proceeded to fawn over every baby. The orphanage director, ecstatic to see my sister Anna, took our family out to lunch in celebration.

What does it mean to be an 'All-American Girl'?

Anna:

I remember a few times when I was younger, when I started to like boys and I'd notice how often my girlfriends with their long flowing blonde hair and blue eyes always seemed to get the attention. I wanted to be like them. I'd watch TV and wish I were those girls in the movies; of course they were white. Whenever I'd look in the mirror I'd be reminded of my appearance, my small eyes, and jet-black hair.

As I got older though, I luckily was able to not only accept who I was, but also absolutely LOVE myself. Haha. I know that sounds a little weird, but I just love who I am and I love that I'm an Asian girl. I get compliments on my long dark hair all the time, and I'm told by my family and my mother's co-workers and friends what a beautiful girl I am.

I don't know what it means to be an 'All-American girl'—to be honest, America has become, and still is in the process of being so diversified and so many different cultures that I don't think there's really a certain look, or personality that makes a girl 'All American.' I know who I am, and that's really all that matters.

It's so funny, if you were to ask my mom what I spend the most time doing now-a-days, she'd say, "Oh goodness, you'll find my daughter looking at herself in the mirror or taking pictures of herself." Haha. I tell myself I can't help that my self-esteem sits on the top of Mount Everest(:

Alicia:

I honestly don't think there is such a thing. Everyone can be All-American if they want to be, or they could choose not to. There are a million different definitions and there are absolutely none. All-American could mean the stereotypical blonde-haired, blue-eyed babe in every TV show out there; or it could mean the adopted Chinese girl who's not perfect by any means but lives her life the way she wants to. It could mean whatever you want to think it means.

Madeline:

I have no idea what 'All-American' is supposed to mean. Literally, I would assume the only 'All-American' people are descendants from Native Americans. I'm an American citizen, but so much more than that. I'm an older sister, a daughter, a niece, a grandchild, a student, a musician, a team player, a teenager with too much on her mind, a writer, an artist, a best friend, an aspiring computational biologist, no, history professor, no, photographer.

I am Madeline Wei Langan Geitz. I was born in Hefei, China on November 19, 1994 and adopted by Kerry Langan and Robert Geitz July 25, 1995. I am the older sister of Anna Chunhua Langan Geitz. I am anything I could want ever to be—a million different futures lie ahead.

Well, except President.

What does it make you feel like to know you can't become president in the only country you can remember?

Anna:

I remember when I was younger how badly I wanted to become president. I've always been the girl to TAKE CHARGE, wanting to be a leader and if I couldn't be queen, president was the next best thing. Haha(:

But quite honestly the more I learn about politics, I call myself crazy for ever wanting to put myself in that zoo of a place.(:

Alicia:
    Personally, I don't want to be the president; don't get me wrong, I want to make change, that's for sure. But I have no desire to become the president of the United States. However; that doesn't mean that I agree with that law, or limitation. What's the difference of the seven months of my life that was spent in China? I have no memory of China; it's not like if I did become the president that I would put Chinese government ideas into the United States. I would have the same mind and ideas as if I were born here in the U.S. because I don't remember anything about China.

Madeline:
    While I have no interest in becoming president (it's really just a figurehead position, in my opinion), I feel the principle is outdated. It's not necessarily a pressing matter, though. I haven't really heard of any political candidates born outside of the U.S. interested in running for the position of president.

Do you feel loyalty toward China—cultural or political?

Anna:
    Well just because I'm Chinese, it doesn't make me subject to or responsible for standing up for a country that I was born in but never really LIVED in. I'm 100% Chinese, and 100% a citizen of America.

Alicia:
    I feel culturally loyal but not politically. Probably because I don't want to forget my heritage, not because it's a requirement or obligation. It's just a preference.

Madeline:
    I don't know anyone in China personally; I know far more about the United States. I identify myself as an 'American citizen,' not as a Chinese citizen, so I don't feel any cultural or political 'loyalty' towards China.

When you vote in two years, will your attitudes toward China influence how you vote?

Anna:
    I'm not really the kind of person who allows others to influence the choices I make. And considering I don't really have one point of view or angle as to how I feel about China and its people, I don't think it'll influence my vote at all.

Alicia:
    No, I don't think they will.

Madeline:
    Technically speaking, I won't be able to vote in two years—I have a mid-November birthday. However, the issues that attract me the most are healthcare and education. While issues involving foreign policy, naturalization, and citizenship are of interest to me, they won't necessarily sway my vote.

Have you been politically active? If so, what have you done to participate in the political process? What issues have attracted you? What activities have made you feel most fully a U.S. citizen?

Anna:
    Quite honestly as far as being politically active—I'm a political couch potato. I have never personally participated in anything related to politics except for maybe a few class discussions and debates in a history class here and there. I do find elections and current events, issues and controversies interesting though.
    There's not really anything in particular that makes me feel MOST like a U.S. citizen. I'm a U.S. citizen every day, whether I'm going to my U.S. history class third hour, staying home from school because I got strep throat, online shopping or going to my local public library. I'm a U.S. citizen. End of Story.

Alicia:
    I keep up with what's going on in the news, but I'm in no way 'politically active.'

Madeline:
I volunteered some time for data entry and phone calls during the 2008 Obama presidential campaign. This was an experience that opened me up to learn about the American political system and how I could be a part of it, even though I can't vote.

To be honest, I don't feel 'American' like one feels 'blonde' or 'tall' or 'overweight.' The times I consider myself American are when I'm registering an account for a website and select 'USA' as my country, traveling with a U.S. passport, or taking ' U.S. History and Government.'

I hope to travel more outside of the United States, or to participate in a study abroad or foreign exchange program. I imagine going to other countries would make me 'feel' American. As of now, I was born in China, but have been living in the United States almost my entire life, so I don't have a point of comparison.

You are part of an interesting cultural phenomenon of the last twenty years, the foreign adoption of Chinese babies, almost all of them female. These babies are now girls coming to adulthood and developing ideas of their own about the reasons for and the personal impact of this phenomenon.

How do you understand the causes of this phenomenon? Do you think this preference for male children and disproportionate abandonment or relinquishing of females was determined primarily by the Chinese government's top-down one-child-per-family policy, by the larger historical depreciation of women in China, or by an intersection of the two?

Anna:
Well I think in the 90s when I was adopted, it was a mixture of the two: the Chinese government ordering only one child per family and the fact that Chinese culture says that the son is in charge of taking care of his parents as they age. But now, as time goes on, I think that the world is constantly changing and evolving. I believe that the idea that daughters/girls are less than or unequal to sons/boys is slowly disappearing.

Alicia:
I'd say it was a mix between the two. The government probably wouldn't have had the one-child rule (choosing the female over male) if not

for the point of view about women.

Madeline:
I think that the family name and the greater earning potential of males are the chief factors. China is changing, though, and people are realizing the value of girls.

Do you feel that your own birth mother had a choice when she left you? Do you think she should or could have stood up against her culture's clear preference for boys?

Anna:
Well seeing as how I don't know the reason for my mother having to give me up, I can't really say. Yes, maybe my mother gave me up because I was just one child too many, or I was one child too many and the only reason she would've kept me was if I was a boy. I will never know. I believe that whatever the reason, I'm sure it was very difficult for her, but she felt that it was the right thing to do at the time.

Alicia:
If it was the law, I don't think that she had a choice to leave me. I also don't think she would have stood up against society. I have a feeling that it would have been really hard to give up a child in the first place, and probably even harder to go against the form of government and society. I honestly haven't given much thought about it though because I believe everything happens for a reason; she left me there, and that led to my adoption. It doesn't matter why she left me there, I'm here now and I can't do anything about it.

Madeline:
I don't know if my mother had a choice, or if she would have been the type of woman to stand up to this idea. It's not my concern, though—I've been adopted and there's no use in looking back.

Has this phenomenon affected your own valuation of women? Has it made you a feminist? Will it affect what issues you choose to vote on when you are able to vote? How?

Anna:

My adoption has never, and I don't believe will ever, sway my opinion and views on other women. I'm not a feminist—I'm not a 'label'. I'm just me. When I vote, I will vote for what I think is right, what I believe will be the best for myself, my family, and my country, as well as the rest of the world.

Alicia:

It probably has some impact on how I value being a woman. But I think that I would have been more outspoken about sexist issues anyway. It hasn't made me a feminist, but I won't settle for sexist remarks by any means.

Madeline:

I never consider 'fighting' for women's rights, but for equal rights. In American today, women are attending colleges, law school, and medical school in growing numbers. Though I'm happy women are doing so well, I would never champion them over men—inequality of any kind is unfair.

How does the good luck of your own positive experience with adoption factor into your understanding of the importance of the foreign adoption of Chinese girls? Do you feel that you personally are better off than you would have been if you had been raised in China?

Anna:

Well honestly I think the idea of adoption anywhere is important and such a wonderful thing. Whether it's in China, Africa, Indonesia, or even here in America. My aunt is a social worker and is helping parents adopt children here in the U.S. every year. My grade-school gym teacher adopted his kids from Ethiopia when I was in fifth grade, and my sixth grade teacher adopted a baby girl from Vietnam the summer before I started middle school. Anyone who chooses to adopt and give a child an opportunity to love them and care for them is a truly whole-hearted person.

I can't say that if I wasn't adopted my life would be less than what it is today. It would just be different. Am I better off here, yes that may be true. But I think I'd still be a great person regardless of where I was raised.

Alicia:

    I believe I had a second chance being adopted. I'm really religious, and like I said earlier, I believe everything happens for a reason. I believe that it was in God's plan for me to be left and then adopted. It makes me want to give another baby a chance at something that I got to receive. And yes, I know I am better off being raised in the U.S. When we went back to China after ten years, we saw how and what the girls did who were still at the adoption agency. They seemed like that had a nice life; they had food, shelter, clothes. But I'm eternally grateful for what I have here because I was adopted.

Madeline:

    I don't think either life would have been 'better,' just different. It's difficult trying to imagine a different life than the one I have now. I don't know who would've come into and shaped my life had I never been adopted.

Chinese daughters are a phenomenon not only in the U.S., but also in other developed countries such as the Netherlands, France, Sweden, Spain. Do you think these children feel as All-Dutch or All-French as you feel All-American?

Anna:

    Yes, I think that any person who is born in one country and raised in another will feel most like where they were raised.

    I started a fashion blog last year. Through this blog I've managed to meet and learn about so many other girls around the world. I've talked to girls from Spain, India, Great Britain, Canada, Germany . . . you name it. Some of them I have learned are adopted just like me.

    One thing we all have in common is that we know who we are, where we are from and the life we live in the country we're currently residing in.

Alicia:

    I have no idea, because I'm not them.

Madeline:

    I think that other Chinese daughters feel similar to me—when your home country is the only place you can remember, you feel most connected to that country.

In all these countries, do you think these girls and women will influence attitudes toward China? How? Do you think they will influence views on naturalized citizenship in these countries? Global citizenship? How?

Anna:

I can't really speak for others. I mean we are all individuals; some may feel the need to influence attitudes towards China, while others like me don't really feel the need to do so. Every person, and every girl has her own opinion on how to view her surroundings, ideas and thoughts; this includes views on naturalized citizenship and countries.

I love the fact that I can say I was born in another country, adopted by a loving family and live a wonderful life with no regrets. I also love talking with other girls just like me, girls who were born in one country and adopted into another, any chance I get. But quite honestly I'm just like everybody else. There's no special treatment or sticker on my forehead that says I'm different because of my situation. I'm just another person on the outside looking in when it comes to half of these global situations.

Madeline:

I don't think adopted Chinese daughters can influence attitudes towards China or naturalized citizenship by themselves. Our attitudes towards China are generated by what we can personally associate with—with the American economy in the hole, several Americans look jealously towards China at the moment for their cheap labor, high population of workers, and growing economy, while they are unemployed. I'm unsure how many citizens can relate to the idea of being adopted from a country because their gender is 'less desirable.'

While it's great to be a part of a world community of ambassadors, we can't, and shouldn't, represent China because we haven't lived our lives there! I'm no more of an expert on China than I am on Belgium or Gambia. Perhaps in the future adopted Chinese girls will have global conferences and discuss what it means to look like a person of one country and identify with the people of another.

I absolutely and

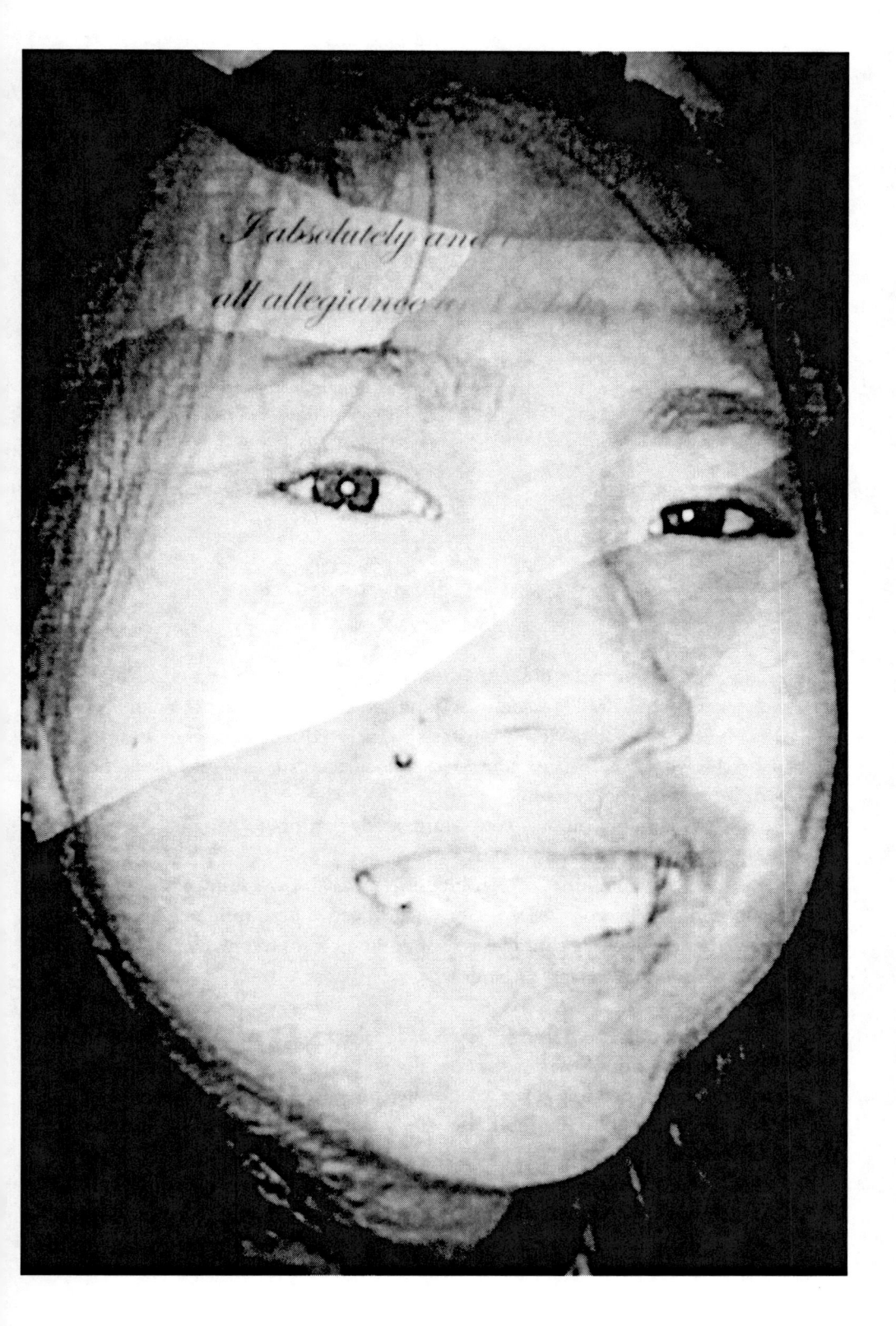

all allegiance

JENNIFER BAO YU JUE-STEUCK

GOODNIGHT MOON, GOODNIGHT MOM

> *We stand*
> *all of us drawn here*
> *by an invisible cord eons long*
> *awaiting the start of a ritual*
> *removed from its womb*
> *by distance and by hope. . .*
> —Janet Jue
>
> *Writing is an act of hope.*
> —Isabel Allende

She is four years old. Mom reads her all-time favorite picture book, *Goodnight Moon*. Nestled under her Winnie-the-Pooh covers, her small head is sandwiched between Mom's outstretched arms, the book directly in front of her brown eyes. The green-and-red-colored pictures leap out, filling her with wonder and appreciation.

"Goodnight moon," coos Mom, softly petting her long brown hair. Goodnight Mom. Goodnight stars.

"Goodnight kittens," continues Mom, kissing the shiny wisps on her small head. She is nearly asleep. Her small fingers on her mother's firm arm detach, her eyes wilting shut like a flower folding from too much sun.

"Goodnight stars. Goodnight air." Mom's voice is softer now. Quiet.

"Goodnight, Mommy," says a half-asleep four year old as she yawns and Mom slips out of the covers, carefully and lovingly tucking them round her little frame, bending down to kiss her forehead. Strings of dark brown hair stick fuzzily above her head, defying gravity, on her faded Winnie-the-Pooh pillow.

Her miniature stomach rises and falls slowly with warm puffs of air. The light fades. The door creaks to its nearly closed position. A soft glow from the hallway falls into her room, warning monsters to stay far, far away. The light leads to safety—like runway lights that guide airplanes back to earth in pitch-black, stormy nights. Straight to the 24/7 haven of Mom's protective embrace.

Goodnight, Jen. See you in the morning.

Goodnight, Mommy. Goodbye.

Mom tiptoes away, her figure a small blip in the dark.

Then one morning, a hospice care worker arrives at the house just before dawn, just before two strange, scary men in black suits roll Mom out our front door, down our driveway, down the majestic mountain where our home kisses the California sky, down the long stretch of Highway 1 that cradles the coast and nearly dips into the deep blue of the Pacific, down and away . . . until nothing is left but the smell of Mom's perfume, a fog of memories, and the whisper of her voice reverberating in my heart.

My name is Jennifer *Bao Yu* "Precious Jade" Jue-Steuck. I am thirty years old. My birthmother is from Jiangsu province, China. In 1979, when I was nearly two years old, I was adopted privately by an American couple from California, at a time when adoption of Chinese children was almost unheard of. It was a complex affair. Paperwork for my adoption was issued through Hong Kong and Taiwan, where my birthmother lived when I was born. My first tongue was Mandarin, followed by English (post-adoption), Cantonese (at Chinese school in California), French (from age seven at school), and a sprinkling of Californian Spanish.

During my childhood, I never gave much thought to being adopted—I was far too busy with homework, cross-country running, dance team, cello, and piano. But when my American mother died from the 'silent cancer' (ovarian) in 1999, I felt a *double loss* and experienced a *double mourning*: the loss of my mom, to whom I was very close and, to my astonishment, a second loss that sprang out of the blue, lurking in a place so deep and layered I didn't even know of its existence—the loss of my birthmother, the mother I never knew, yet whose breath, blood, and spirit make these words possible.

I think of both mothers now, listening to the roar of engines as our plane takes off from Hong Kong, China bound for London's Heathrow Airport. I am returning West from my first trip to China since my adoption twenty-eight years ago. . . .

The momentous occasion for my inaugural return to China is Hong Kong's First Adoption Festival. The three-week-long series of educational talks, interviews, workshops, film screenings, and press meetings—hosted by the nonprofit organization Mother's Choice (Hong Kong) in November 2008—includes fellow guest speakers Dr. Amanda Baden, Jessica Emmett, Adam Pertman, and Nancy Thomas.

During the festival, we meet hundreds of adoptive families in Hong Kong. It seems that at least half of them belong to expat communities. As a co-founder of Chinese Adoptee Links (CAL) International—an all-volunteer group with the mission of creating a multigenerational social network for the 150,000+ Chinese adoptees living in twenty-six countries—I've had the privilege of meeting adoption communities in eight countries. This is by far the most diverse group of parents I've met in a single locale. One night, after the festival screening of the newly released feature film, *The Ticket* (based on a true-life Chinese adoption tale), a parent raises her hand and asks, "Jennifer, why did you set up CAL International?"

"Well . . ." I pause, wondering how to explain the serendipitous series of events and 'chance encounters' spread over thirty years. "You see," I say, as my mind travels back, "it all started with a pen pal."

"A pen pal?"

"Yes, a pen pal. In Paris."

We were nine years old. Her name was Valérie, and we only exchanged three letters. But ten years later—at the age of nineteen—I was a sophomore university student studying abroad in Paris.

I didn't know a soul in France.

But I had something special in my pocket from America: Valérie's letters. The letters she had mailed ten years before (when I was the new kid in fourth grade) to my house in Laguna Beach (Orange County), California. Valérie loved to draw, and I remember a large envelope included one of her creations—a fantastic cartoon caricature on the back flap. How I loved looking at the soft brown envelope with its peculiar French stamps. It was large and luminous, and unlike anything I had ever seen before. The cartoon etched into its silky soft skin looked so beautiful—indeed, to my eyes, *magical*—especially since I couldn't draw at all!

I remember receiving the letter one day after school. It was my first year as a new student at Laguna Beach's Top of the World Elementary School, and I was having a hard time adjusting to my very Euro-American school. For the first time in my life, America's deep-seated racial tensions were being thrust into my face right on the playground. I felt sad. Confused. And, at its worst, humiliated and ashamed. But of what? Of being Chinese? Of being adopted? Of being different? Probably all of these. I begged my mom to send me back to my old school. How comforting it was to know that I had a friend halfway across the world, a friend who seemed to appreciate, and actually delight in, my difference.

As I nervously clutched an enormous encyclopedia-sized telephone book in Paris (they still had telephone books in 1999), I sucked in a deep breath and watched its pages fly. *Don't worry,* I chatted to the butterflies in my stomach, *she's probably moved.*

But as I flipped through, my eyes fell on her very name and number! My heart skipped a beat.

I dialed and said, "Bonjour."

It turned out we were neighbors! We met in person for the first time and Valérie showed me her apartment, and even treated me to a delicious meal at her parents' gorgeous restaurant in the *Sixième arrondissement*. She lent me some much-needed student supplies (like a Walkman, a radio, some fun books), and shared a bit of *her* City of Light, as only a lifetime resident of Paris could.

Nearly a decade later—at the age of twenty-eight—I found myself wandering the streets of Barcelona, Spain. I was there for dissertation research as a Ph.D. student at the University of California, Berkeley. To my surprise, I continually bumped into Chinese adoptees. In the grocery store. At the library. Strolling down streets arm-in-arm with their Spanish parents. My heart warmed at the sight of so many adopted girls, and fond thoughts of my own childhood surfaced from shadows of memories long forgotten.

But there was one little girl in particular I will never forget. It was a beautiful afternoon, and as I turned a corner onto a busy Barcelona side street, two little brown eyes bored a hole into mine.

The intense eyes belonged to an adopted Asian girl walking towards me on the street with her mother. She kept staring at me in such a haunted way that her gaze sent chills down my spine. As we passed one another, it was as if our spirits touched, awakened in a flash of mutual recognition. Her eyes, flushed with longing, held onto mine until she could no longer see me and the cord was cut. *What was that all about?* I wondered as I shook a ghostly shadow from my shoulders. *She looked at me as if . . . as if I could be . . . her birthmom.* I fought back tears.

I couldn't believe how many Chinese adoptees there were in Europe. In Cork, Dublin, London, Paris, Barcelona. It seemed like they were everywhere. Later that summer, I was privileged to meet Chinese adoptees in Ireland. We were excited to connect. One little girl in particular, named Maeve, reached for my hand as we crossed a street in southern Ireland and wouldn't let go. Her mom, Mary D. Healy, looked surprised. "Maeve normally doesn't take to new people." Another little girl embraced me and asked if she could go home with me.

As I spoke with several families in the Emerald Isle, we wondered how we might be able to create a global community. There was just one obstacle: the Atlantic Ocean. How could we possibly bridge the 'pond'? On the plane ride home to California, I thought of little Maeve, and the girl with haunting eyes in the streets of Barcelona. They tugged at my heart. What could I do for them? Was it possible that there might be a special connection between adoptees that I had never—in my entire life—known? Or was it merely coincidence that we seemed to share a special bond?

Back in California, I had a thought. I remembered Valérie, my pen pal in Paris. I asked Mary D. Healy of the Irish Chinese Contact Group (a Families with Children from China branch of Ireland) if we might be able to start a transatlantic pen pal program. If I could find participants in the U.S, I thought, the pen pal program could connect Chinese adoptees in America to Chinese adoptees in Ireland.

As Siobhan Hegarty, a volunteer parent in Dublin, matched Irish-Chinese adoptee pen pals to teens in the FCC Northern California chapter, I began to wonder, Why haven't I ever met a Chinese adoptee *my own age*? Were there others like me? If so, where were they? And what were their perspectives on life as adopted people?

I went online and searched. *Nada.*

I couldn't find a single group that I—a young adult Chinese

adoptee—could join. My heart sank. From DESIS United (for adoptees from India) to VAN (Vietnamese Adoptee Network) to FAN (Filipino Adoptee Network), I didn't seem to "belong" anywhere. Families with Children from China seemed a tad closer (at least I was Chinese!), but I wasn't yet a "family" and I certainly didn't have any children, let alone children from China. What could I do?

Since I didn't know any other adult Chinese adoptees, I decided to find them by starting my own organization. I wrote to Ruthanne Lum McCunn, author of *Thousand Pieces of Gold*, one of my favorite childhood books, who had kindly responded years before to a letter I had sent to her for a sixth-grade English project. I asked if she might be willing to serve on the CAL Board of Advisors, and she said yes.

That encouragement led to a series of letters sent round the world and the ensuing discovery of fellow adult Chinese adoptees who called places like Israel, England, Italy, New Zealand, New York City, and Hong Kong home. Slowly, one letter at a time, CAL International—the first global group created by and for the more than 150,000 Chinese adoptees and friends in twenty-six countries—was formed. Our website, *Book of Dreams*, launched on Valentine's Day 2006.

This summer we returned from our second all-volunteer CAL G2 "Global Girls" Ambassadors Teen Trip to Europe, and Maeve (the girl who held my hand in Ireland two years ago and wouldn't let go) hugged me at the end and said, "Jennifer, I'll miss you until I see you again." My heart melted. And I thought, *I'll miss you, too, Maeve.*

When Mom was first diagnosed with ovarian cancer (Stage III C), she went in for emergency surgery on Christmas Eve. I was nineteen. A fighter to the end, she baffled all her doctors and beat the odds (of living only three to six months longer). She slipped away quietly two years later, sometime between skylight and twilight, sleeping beside me under our living room Christmas tree. The holiday lights blinked on and off as I whispered in her ear, endlessly repeating the names of people who loved her: "Popo (grandmother) loves you. Dad loves you. I love you. Chris loves you. Auntie Suzie loves you. Di Yee (first aunt) loves you. Mitsuye loves you. *I love you, Mom. . . .*"

When two men in black suits came to our house, the younger one stole a glance at me and whispered, "Is that your mom?" staring at the lifeless body beside me.

My voice wouldn't come. Couldn't come.

All I could do was nod. Just once. Just in time to bury my face and swallow an ocean of tears. "Yes," I had wanted to say, "that's my mom. That . . . *was* . . . my mom. My hero."

But the words evaporated on my tongue as my heart quietly shattered into a million pieces. We had had so many dreams together. *How am I supposed to do this without you, Mom? This was our dream together. How am I supposed to go on without you?*

The death of a parent is symbolically a closing of one's adoption story, since our adoption narratives, or origin stories, often begin with them and their heroic journeys to travel halfway around the world to connect with us. To find us. It is difficult to describe what it feels like to lose a parent when you are adopted, and how many feelings—often deeply layered—this can trigger about one's adoption. There are no instruction manuals, and often few (if any) mentors to offer guidance when parents die. How can anyone be prepared for death, adopted or not?

The first trip back can also be a symbolic closing and re-opening of one's adoption story. (In my case, it is the story of twenty-eight years. The story of my lifetime "abroad" and the events that helped shape my search for identity.) But it is a route we know by heart. For we have traveled it before. Just in the opposite direction. For some, it can unearth a host of questions and memories. For others, it might not.

On the flight home from Hong Kong's First Adoption Festival, I feel a deep sense of gratitude to Mother's Choice for hosting this historic event. I thank Mother's Choice for the opportunity to return to China, to meet the adoption communities in Hong Kong, to exchange stories, to share CAL's story, and most importantly, to listen and to learn from one another with compassion, dignity, and grace.

Two festival events, in particular, comprise "firsts" for me. One, meeting a group of prospective birthmothers at the Mother's Choice Pregnant Girl's Home, is a special gift. With the help of Cantonese translators, the pregnant girls (ages thirteen to twenty-four) ask their most pressing questions: "Do you miss your birthmother? Are you angry at her? Have you had a good life with your adoptive family?" Dr. Amanda Baden, Jessica Emmett, and I share our adoption stories, our feelings about our birthmothers. I'm the last person to speak: "I have to be honest," I say. "There have been times in my life when I felt angry towards my birthmom." A few of the girls recoil, holding their swollen bellies. "But I understand that she did the best she could and I am grateful to her." Their eyes soften. "Even if I never meet her in my entire life, she will always be a part of me. I will always be extremely proud of her."

Suddenly, we all burst into tears—the circle of young birthmoms-to-be, the adult adoptees, the translators, and the organizers. One pregnant girl wipes away a tear and says, "Before meeting you today, I thought that I would place my baby for adoption. But now," she adds, tears streaming down her cheeks, "now I'm not so sure." She hugs her baby by wrapping her arms around her tummy.

My heart beams a ray of compassion to this young girl, no more than sixteen years old, who faces such a tough decision. *She's just a girl*, I think to myself. *Practically a child herself. I am nearly twice her age, and yet . . . I have no concept of her experience, except that she is the same age my birthmother was when I was born. This girl, this young woman,* the realization sinks in, *could be my birthmom*. I look into her eyes softly. At that moment, an interior clap of thunder sends my eyes scanning the horizon, *Where are you, birthmom? Where are you today? Could you be here in Hong Kong even, your spirit roaming this very mountain?*

Little did I know that a few days later, I would actually bump into *another* birthmom—Dr. Amanda Baden's birthmother. In the flesh! Dr. Baden gently nudges me after one of her talks and says, "Jennifer, I want you to meet my birthmom." My gaze follows hers and—lo and behold—I see the most radiant, gorgeous fifty-something woman standing at a distance in one of Hong Kong's most elegant shopping malls, chatting in Cantonese to a friend. Seeing someone's birthmom is like seeing a film celebrity you've admired—for years—for the very first time in real life. Suddenly, they don't seem so *superhuman*, so mysterious, anymore. And yet their magical aura is very real. "Does she speak English?" I ask.

"No. Not really." Amanda smiles, waving to her birthmom.

"Do *you* speak Cantonese?"

"No. Not really." Amanda smiles again, this time looking at me. "But somehow," her eyes sparkle, "we manage."

I keep staring at them (I know I shouldn't, but they both look so beautiful), going down the escalators of the mall with the festival organizers.

And then I realize why I keep staring, *I've never seen a birthmother and daughter together before. It looks so ordinary and so extraordinary at the same time.*

My last glimpse of them—Amanda and her birthmom—is in that chic mall, standing side by side, chatting like old friends.

Without the warm welcoming embrace of Mary Child, David Youtz, the wonderful Mother's Choice family, and fellow guest speakers Dr. Amanda Baden, Jessica Emmett, Adam Pertman, and Nancy Thomas, I think the 'return' trip would have hardly been a return at all. For what is a *home*land trip? What does it really mean to go home? To me, home is neither a place nor a country (for nations' appellations and borders can and *do* change over time), nor even necessarily the land that rests beneath our feet. Today, China may be my 'home.' Tomorrow it might not. Today, America *and* China may be my home. Tomorrow, they might not.

To go home, 'to return,' is—at its core—more about people (including the ghosts of our pasts, presents, and futures), community, and a sense of continuity, belonging, legacy, and pride: ***ADOPTION PRIDE.*** As adopted people and global citizens, we may find ourselves cloaked in several identities during the course of our lives. To have a community of role models, friends, peers, and families—who support us throughout our lives as we travel back, sway East, sway West, lose our parents, travel forward, raise our own children, forge unique paths, and continue to remember and to re-remember, to explore, to mourn our loss, to appreciate our gifts, to embrace our challenges, to connect and reconnect with our birth countries, our passions, and perhaps, one day, our birth families—is the home that may have no particular name or distinguished slot in Greenwich Mean Time or identifiable plot on the crisscrossed lines of latitude and longitude. Rather, the *home*land trip is—in essence—a lifetime journey, one that varies as much as the vicissitudes and veracities of each individual human spirit.

What I know for sure is this: There is no such thing as perfect parents. Losing a parent ultimately makes you appreciate what you have *all the more*. No one can ever replace your parents, *adopted or not*. My mind drifts to a dream as our plane turns, casts a shadow over Hong Kong, and veers towards London. Returning once more to the memories of the person whose heart will always be my home. *Home*, as they say, *is where the heart is*. . . .

A little girl, Jennifer Precious Jade, and her adoptive mom, Janet Jue, descend from the plane. "This is *Bao Yu* (Precious Jade)," beams Janet proudly, "my daughter," to a crowd of aunties and uncles—and then under her breath she whispers, "My baby, my Precious Jade, this is your new home now. In America all of the dreams of your teen-aged mom and all of the dreams of the mothers before will be realized. I will love you forever. I will protect you forever."

Precious Jade sinks deeper into her mother's arms, and hides her dark brown eyes behind her mother's shoulders, safe from the onslaught of curious eyes. . . .

"Mommy, did you know that there are thousands of us now?"

She could not have known. She could not have known when she picked the little girl up all by herself, when she flew to Hong Kong and the Republic of China all by herself, speaking Spanish sprinkled with perfect American English and creative Cantonese—'Canglish' to Mandarin translators—that twenty years later there would be so many Chinese girls adopted throughout the world.

"I am not lost, Mommy. Not in any sense of the word that English can express. There may be some things that I do not know, like my first words and the first day I learned to walk and to speak in Mandarin, but these things are lost *to* me; it is *not me* who is lost. The word *lost* implies having a ghostly owner, and I am no possession," Precious Jade says to the sky, who nods and winks.

Mommy nods, relief flooding her face. Her voice travels across ghostly lands and ghostly galaxies and seven high seas, soaring over tall mountains that tickle the blue belly of the sky with their rounded tips.

I forgot to give you this. I come from ghostly lands to bring you this gift—the gift of my living words. It may come in memories of dreams of sleepless nights and salty tears, but in it lies all of my hopes that you will write every day of your life as your truest self. You are capable of things that I could only dream of, because you are overcoming challenges that I could not. Inside of you is not just my courage and strength, but also an alchemy of authenticity and ability from your birthmother, and from her mother and from me, from my mother, and from all our great grandmothers before us, an endless cord eons long . . . awaiting the start of a ritual—that ritual is the gift of you. With every breath you take, our collective hope herein lies. You are authentic, powerful, lovable, beautiful, kind, worthy, creative, and capable. Both of our families—by birth and by love—are so proud of you. Go forth with these gifts, removed from our wombs by distance—and by hope—but connected by our words, our breath stitched onto this very sheet of paper by ink, sewed to an invisible live cord eons long, by the geometry of our greatest gifts, our collective sorrows, and the mystical mana of our mothers' enduring love. Remember—

> *We stand*
> *all of us drawn here*
> *by an invisible cord eons long*
> *awaiting the start of a ritual*
> *removed from its womb*
> *by distance and by hope. . .**
> This ritual is the *Gift of You.*

"Goodnight moon," coos Mom, softly petting her daughter's long brown hair. "Goodnight stars. Goodnight air." Mom's voice is softer now. Quiet.

"Goodnight, Mommy," says a half-asleep four year old. Her miniature stomach rises and falls slowly with warm puffs of air. A soft glow from the hallway falls into her room, warning monsters to stay far, far away. The light leads to safety—like runway lights that guide airplanes back to earth in pitch-black, stormy nights. Straight to the 24/7 haven of Mom's protective embrace.

Goodnight, Jen. See you in the morning.
Goodnight, Mommy. Goodbye.
Mom tiptoes away, her figure a small blip in the dark.

I love you, Mom.

---

*This passage is an excerpt from "Poon," a poem by Janet Jue (1941–1999), published in *Sowing Ti Leaves: Writings by Multicultural Women* (eds. Sarie Sachie Hylkema and Mitsuye Yamada, Irvine, California: MCWW Press, 2nd edition, 1990).

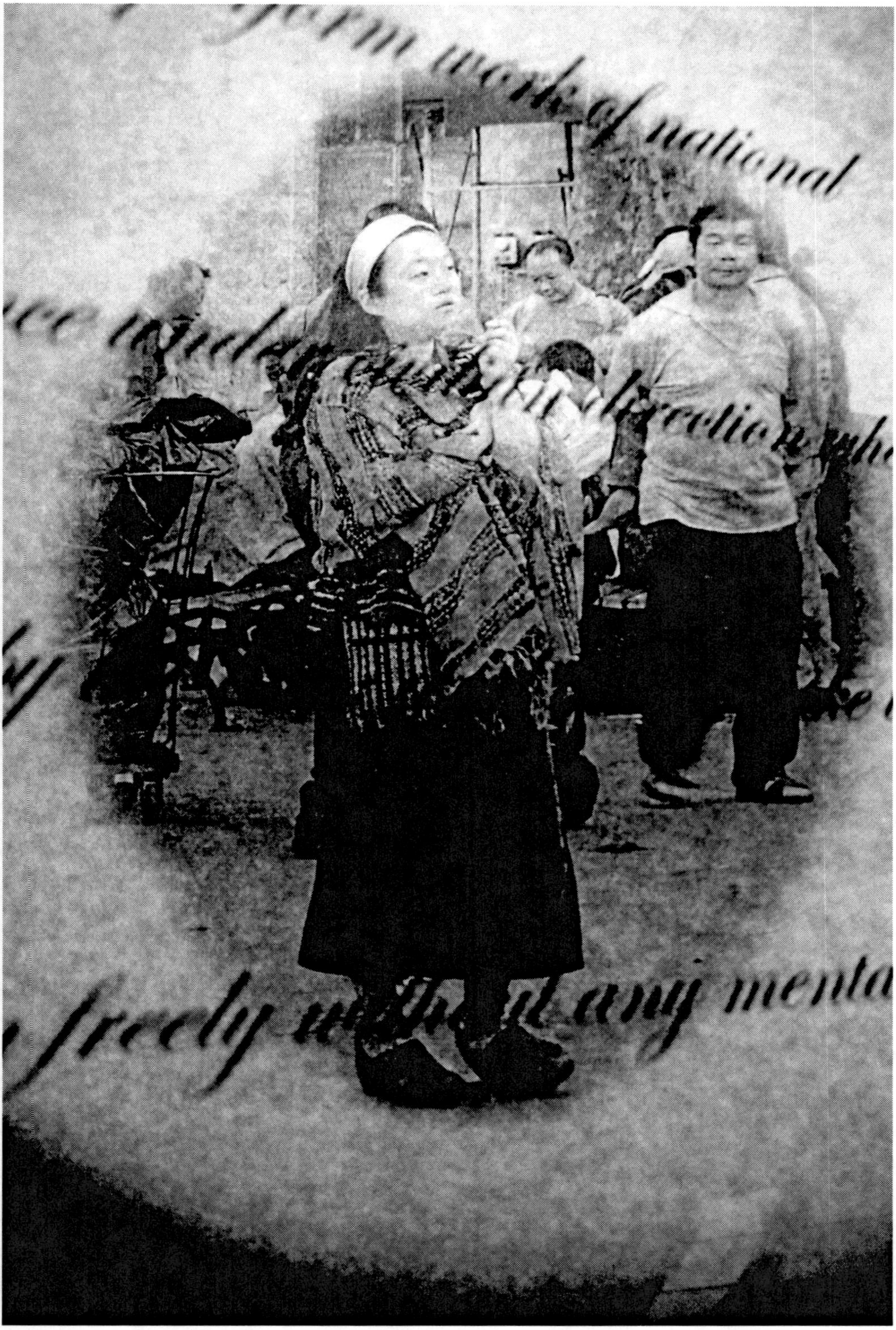

the Government

ments does the Constitution have?

tion of Independence to

our ind... Brita

independ... ain

nited Sta... Brita

the Declaration of ...ence?

III

NATURAL WOMEN: NATURALIZED CITIZENS

HEATHER TOSTESON

LISTENING FOR COHESION
Out of the many, one; out of the din, a hymn;
out of the anonymous throng, a friend.

Assimilation and integration constitute a two-way street. Those who want to join America must be received and welcomed by those who already think they own America. . . . The burden to make this a united country lies more with the complacent majority than the beleaguered minorities.
Arthur Schlesinger, The Disuniting of America

People are not likely to find in political principles the deep emotional content and meaning provided by kith and kin, blood and belonging, culture and nationality.
    Samuel Huntington, *Who Are We? The Challenges to America's National Identity*

Remember, remember always, that all of us, and you and I especially, are descended from immigrants and revolutionists.
    Franklin D. Roosevelt, to Daughters of the American Revolution, April 21, 1938

Not like the brazen giant of Greek fame/ With conquering limbs astride from land to land;/ Here at our sea-washed, sunset gates shall stand/ A mighty woman with a torch, whose flame/ Is the imprisoned lightning, and her name/ Mother of Exiles.
Emma Lazarus, "The New Colossus"

   In our country, we don't have a good *language* for interdependency that balances our strong emphasis on intentionality and individuality with our equally strong commitment to creating care, a state of genuine social attachment that protects that far from invincible individuality—and calls it continually to align with something larger than itself. We can't bring that community into being by ourselves however much we may wish it, so our individual commitment, unmet, is powerless. But that community cannot exist for us without our full participation, and we can't receive its gifts without accepting at the same time our profound interdependence. So, it would be helpful to have some language that lifts up those individual choices through which something more and qualitatively different from any of us—community, country—comes into being.

Martin Luther King's 'blessed community' comes far closer to evoking that community than 'Land of the Free, Home of the Brave.' For me, it is the corollary of that radical statement, "We hold these truths to be self-evident, that all humans are created equal, that they are endowed by their creator with certain unalienable rights. . . ." What moves *me* each time I hear these words is the profound universality of the *We*—and the image of community that flows from it. What do relationships based on that assumption of essential equality look like, feel like, *lead* to? Where do the large variations in our abilities and our circumstances fit into this commitment? Where does *care* fit in this conversation about truths, unalienable rights, individual liberties?

These questions arise anew for me as I read the fascinating stories here, each one absolutely unique, each of them, when read in relation to the others, creating something more—and different—from what any one of them alone can do. But these questions also rise when reading women's stories in general because the assumption of equal intrinsic value for women has been one of the most difficult of truths for most cultures, religions, and nations to align themselves with—in deed as much or more than in words. This commitment to the intrinsic equality of women is often resisted because it is perceived as the most fundamental assault on community. If *everyone* is free to pursue their own happiness, who will hold the whole? Who will do the welcoming? Who will do the nurturing so essential for a species that has such a long developmental period outside the womb that our most basic survival requires family, community—and minds that can conceive of them?

I think we're all a little wary of attachments that are purely voluntary. We experience them as more fragile than blood bonds, or ones cultivated, contained by social force. But what happens to anyone when we take choice away from them? What relationships come into being then? I am going to suggest that one of the most important questions about immigration—what defines the concerns on both sides—is attachment and interdependence, that our challenge is how well we can hold the intrinsic equal worth of each other in consciousness—aware that doing so, on both sides, it is a choice, an *affective* choice.

Other countries are often referred to as the motherland or fatherland. This is rare to non-existent in the U.S.—and for good reason. Our country, in its essential premise, is not based on the value of an inherited, unquestioned allegiance, rather on a consciously chosen one. In other words, in our relation with our country, we are not children, we are adults responsible for ourselves and the world we are making and remaking. We are not being invited to be passive subjects but discerning, intentional, and *passionately attached* participants.

The radical nature of this intentionality is played out in naturalized citizenship. Each naturalized citizen comes from someplace where their inclusion was assumed. They are now being asked, and asking themselves, to transfer their primary loyalty, emotional, political, and civic, to another 'person' in an active, mutually influencing relationship. Perhaps the best metaphor for this is marriage. The choice is voluntary, adult—much of its contract explicit—but underneath there is an assumption that from it something mysterious, cohering, transforming and emergent will come: Family in the case of marriage. Nationality in the case of citizenship.

In some ways, whether or not we say it, many birthright citizens expect of naturalized citizens the kind of attachment associated with childhood—not the conscious mutuality of marriage. My own question is whether that kind of unconscious unquestioned attachment is healthy for any of us as citizens, or whether the kinds of attachments we read about here—dynamic, complex, bittersweet, intensely aware of the element of choice—may be the ones that we all need to make to sustain us through recession grown thick and triumphal exceptionalism grown thin, that these intentional commitments are what are needed to help us realize, yet again, the unfulfilled promise of that *We* that is the constantly corrective heart of our country.

There are many themes in this fascinating series of poems, memoirs, fiction, reflections, and oral histories, but I would invite us to listen especially for the complex dynamics of cohesion, or, more exactly, to listen for cohering, a drawing together out of great difference. For belonging *is* a pervasive theme here. What does it mean in a new country? What did it mean to us before we knew there were alternatives? How does knowing there are alternatives change our understanding of belonging, looking forward *or* back?

The title of this section—*Natural Women, Naturalized Citizens*—was the original inspiration for the whole anthology. In particular, we wanted to focus on what happens when something as deeply engrained as gender role and expectations, something we grow up feeling is so natural it feels intrinsic, comes into direct conversation with other values that may not be congruent, like intentional citizenship in a country that posits the equality of all as its central tenet. The contributors to this section are all, in one way or another, exploring the dynamic between individual liberty and community, both past and nascent. But gender is rarely the explicit theme, which is in itself interesting.

The relation of gender and this American promise of equality, is, however, a central question for birthright citizens who are imagining their way into the experiences of immigrants—whether their own ancestors or their immigrant neighbors as we find in the first section: *Prelude*. To stand in someone else's shoes, we need to be in touch, consciously or not, with that in our own experience that makes that momentary identification possible. Mariette Landry hears the underlying fear in the immigrant experience. John Manesis revisits the constraints women immigrating early in the twentieth century experienced, exploring what it is like to hear their stories now, to count a cost almost invisible then. The subject of Manesis' poem "Not Anymore" says: "Anonymous? Not anymore./Let all your readers know/who I am and where I've been./ Don't leave out a thing." Alexandrina Sergio ponders, in both her poems, what the cost has been, especially for women, to be asked to leave their essential identity behind, and in "Leaving Bridget" contrasts her mother's and her daughter's choices, one more self-negating, the other more assertive, than she feels capable of herself.

In the second section, *What Our Mother's Do for Us*, we hear women in their twenties and thirties describe their mothers' journeys to citizenship—a major motivation for which was their desire to enhance their children's educational opportunities. Sometimes, as in Lisa Chan's "Cheesecake," this is an instrumental decision driven primarily by family loyalties—the desire to improve children's eligibility for scholarships and the ability to travel more easily to care for an aging mother. In Natalia Treviño's funny account of how her mother passed her citizenship exam, we also see how the author's own understanding of her mother and her mother's choices influences her understanding of the meaning of citizenship for herself at fifteen, moves it from something purely instrumental to something more profound: "I have been pledging my allegiance like this every day at school, with my hand over my heart. But I don't mean it. This pin, this oath means I am not Mexican anymore and my mother is a soldier." It also means, she is told, that this is the day she can change her name to anything she wants. Suddenly her own participation is intentional. What is wonderful in this account, speaks so powerfully of another kind of freedom, is how her parents respond: "There are no suggestions. No opposition." She is the one who decides to reorder, however slightly, her allegiances, aware now of the implications of such a change.

Azadeh Shashahani's memoir describes her experience immigrating with her family from Iran at sixteen. She talks about her fondness for her accent, which brings her back to this charged period of transition—when her assumptions about herself and her family, about what was normal, what was privilege, were challenged, revised. This was the moment when she began to participate consciously in the making of her adult self, a time when her preferences and those of her parents did not necessarily coincide—either in Iran or in the U.S. Her physician father's choice to return to Iran, to the professional life available to him there, acknowledges the profound, sometimes intolerable, losses that immigration requires. However, his choice to live where he could make the biggest difference reflects a social commitment that informs his daughter's own career in the U.S. as a civil liberties lawyer—a career that was made possible by his own decision to come to the States.

In an attempt to understand herself, Amita Rao tries to understand her mother's adventurous early years, the determination and courage that inspired her to leave rural India, seek higher education despite her brothers' resistance, and then to leave India entirely for Kuwait and then for the United States, ultimately becoming a naturalized citizen. Rao's own journey, in the reverse direction, leads her finally to U.S. citizenship as well: "In a roundabout way, tracing my mother's footsteps back, I came to the same conclusion my mother had come to: once you leave home, returning is never the same so it's best to just keep moving forward. But, unlike my mother's practicality, mine was spurred by the emotional nature of wanting to belong, to feel an unquestionable right to home somewhere."

In the third and largest section, *What We Do for Ourselves*, we hear from women from Bulgaria, Serbia, Israel, Australia, China, Mexico and Sierra Leone, most of whom came to the States voluntarily and independently in early adulthood. In most cases, their choices to become citizens were inspired directly by their own relationships with the United States. Both Boryana Zeitz and Nikolina Kulidžan were sent in their late teens to the United States to study, with the tacit understanding that they would do everything they could to stay. It is hard to imagine the pressure to achieve this expectation put on these highly accomplished young women. Zeitz locates her own experience of migration inside her father and grandfather's histories of migration; it unites rather than separates her from them. However, her insistence on voting comes from her history in a totalitarian state: "I tell them, having lived through the opposite, that being part of a democracy is both an incredible privilege and incredible responsibility and that we deserve the governments we tolerate."

Nikolina Kulidžan, in her beautifully written memoir, says she wishes that instead of answering multiple choice questions for their citizenship exam, aspiring citizens were required to write an essay "about what it is we love about America and what makes us American." She writes with a keen eye for the tensions and ironies of her experience in the United States, especially in relation to Serbia. Kulidžan also describes those relations that have made the difference for her, for example, the people in Utah who collected money for a college scholarship for her at the time the U.S. was bombing Kosovo: "You want to spend *your* time asking other people for *their* money to send *me* to college?" Her own workplace in the U.S. Army, a highly diverse group of multicultural people, many foreign-born, comes to represent what membership in the U.S. might mean for her: "We do our jobs, we are nice to each other, and we tolerate the differences even when we don't like them. It's pluralism at its best. It's what I love about this country when it works, and what I want to change about it when it fails."

She also describes vividly the roil of emotions she feels as she is given a flag whose origin most perfectly sums up her ambivalence—and the gesture that also sums up her attachment to her new country: "The two men standing sternly in front of me just gave me something from their hearts. And when I accept the flag from Eddie I accept it with my heart."

Karen Levy in her memoirs explores a life lived in transit between two countries, Israel and the U.S., and how the tensions of divided loyalty within her family intersect, sometimes explosively, with those of national attachment. As with Treviño, choices made for her by her mother need to be re-enacted to become fully her own: "I was still searching, for the land that would feel like home, for the people who remember what had been before it all changed, for the voice in which to say it all."

Elizabeth Bernays and Weihua Zhang, one from Australia and one from China, came to the U.S. later in their lives and for professional reasons. The changes they are invited to are starkly different. Bernays, who emigrated as a mid-career entomologist, describes with candor, edge, and acceptance the sense of betrayal she felt moving from the collaborative and bureaucratic structure of British science to the intensely competitive, entrepreneurial structure of U.S. science. She is given tenure at U.C. Berkeley, but little money to start a lab. She feels betrayed at having to develop such an instrumental relationship with colleagues and country: "It was a brand new culture and I was a novice. No longer did an appointment automatically mean the provision of the wherewithal to do the work." This complaint could be echoed by many immigrants and refugees. The edge of bitterness has to do with the tension between the invitation and the welcome. Bernays herself moves back and forth in her responses to the changes demanded of her: "I became broader in my thinking, more flexible in my intellectual pursuits. I had to learn the rigors of writing convincing research grants and explaining why the work was important, a process that involved self-advertisement that had always been anathema to me but ended up making me feel that I had a distinct place in the scientific world."

Weihua Zhang, on the other hand, had no idea of staying when she came to the U.S. in 1989 to spend a semester at Swarthmore. With the help of an African-American professor, she finds her way into American culture and values through folklore and the writing of African-American women—which becomes the subject of her doctoral dissertation. After twenty years as a resident, her decision to become a citizen is, like many mothers, related to improving her daughter's educational prospects. Her own attachment to this country, interestingly, comes not through words but through images. It seems that standing shoulder to shoulder with a native-born American audience looking back with them, sharing perspective on both images of earlier Chinese immigrants to Savannah (the city she now calls home) and at her own images of modern China is what finally makes her feel she has a home here.

In the oral histories that complete this section, seven Mexican-born women, interviewed by Maria Shockey, share what assimilation and cultural identity mean to them individually, definitions that develop from the necessities and rewards of their own direct experiences. "I'm not from here or there. It's just a constant, stressful situation. It's like a state of limbo," one woman says, while another says, "I speak Spanish and live in the U.S. I chose my identity from the categories that were offered me." Another says, "We have to make ourselves a complete person . . . a person of two cultures." She adds, "We, my husband and I, have to follow the ways of the United States . . . or we lose our kids. Understanding this is a form of assimilating."

Clementina, a refugee from Sierra Leone, shares the tumultuous path that brought her here and her clarity about wanting to be a citizen: "Immediately I got here, I was open—there were many things I saw you have to be a citizen to do, so that helps me make up my mind." "But sometimes," she adds, "you do have a home fever."

The next section, *What Does Marriage Have to Do with It?*, explores more intentionally a theme that fascinates birthright Americans. The difference in their approaches and interpretations and that of women more directly engaged in these decisions is interesting. The immigration scholar Donna Gabaccia in her book on women and immigration, *From the Other Side: Women, Gender, and Immigrant Life in the U.S., 1820-1990*, makes the observation that throughout U.S. history, Americans have focused on the status of married immigrant women and the need to protect them from the domination of their husbands, while immigrant communities have often focused on the need to protect immigrant women from the dissolution of American culture. One is able here to see a similar difference in tone between the American-born and foreign-born writers—and in the questions they raise. In Patricia Barone's poem, "The Women Across the Street," which is concerned with mail-order brides, the poet says, "I could have offered/ something . . . but I kept myself/ to myself." The question raised for her is whether she is doing enough as a neighbor. In Cathy Adams's story, "Chuan," the subject is also the oppression of a mail-order bride, however the bride is the protagonist of the story, so we enter her sensibility, rather than see her from afar, as she stumbles out of a limiting marriage. The tone is poignant and the social isolation of Chuan intense. In both Barone and Adams, the men are portrayed without complexity—their motive for domination having to do with their desire to escape the greater equality of American women.

However, the tones of Chao's "From French Maid to Chinese Bride" and Julija Suput's "A Bouquet of Roses" are more inflected, the women's professional skills well integrated, their social circles expanding and engaged. They are far more concerned with the workings of the labyrinthine and inflexible immigration system than gender relations, other than how they may influence that process. Chao's story is interesting because, raised in the U.S. from ages five to nine, she so identified with the U.S. that she constructed much of her identity around her intention to return. The difficulty of gaining permanent residency status triggers anger that she must prove her fitness to immigrate to the U.S. when it is obvious to her (and to her family back in Taiwan) that she has been permanently shaped by her early identification with U.S. values and way of life. It will be through marriage to a Mexican-American, whose cultural identity formation may well be far more ambivalent, that Chao will become a citizen.

Julija Suput's memoir of how she came to the U.S. with her two teenage sons, enticed by her romance with an American and the opportunity this might provide her sons, includes many of the elements found in Adams's story. But Suput's memoir is, like Bernay's and Zhang's, ultimately a story as much about professional fulfillment as it is about romance, for although she came because of opportunities for her boys, she stays because of the opportunities she finds here for herself.

In the final section, *Home Is Where. . .*, we find women finding their preferred location between the poles of nostalgia and full attachment. Mariel Coen embraces the full length of her tightrope—and uses all the languages at her disposal to balance and express herself: "I can sway my demeanor, my diction and conduct/depending on the meal set before me/the shoes of my audience/the tone of your voice."

Angelika Quirk's poems express a beautiful, dense nostalgia for the physical reality of both sides of her life: "I pledge allegiance to two countries,/ and when I travel across the ocean/I yearn for the other side." Sandra Soli's poems celebrate both the optimism of the U.S.—"These new lives/ that always come to save us."—and the xenophobia that is also part of many immigrants' reception.

Sonya Sabanac's work, like many others, expresses the conflict of being stretched between two worlds, two longings: "My two languages live like step-brothers." Her memoir ,"How I Decided to Go a Little Crazy," brings together several themes we hear throughout—the bitterness of immigrants who felt no one reached out to them, and also the radical revising of their own gender expectations to thrive in a more assertive culture. Bernays learns to self-advertise; Sabanac learns to go a little crazy.

In the oral histories that close the collection, we have three quite different forms of attachment to the U.S., all strong. Lourdes Rosales-Guevara, a Cuban émigré, talks about her identification with her grandfather and aunt, who did not emigrate with her and her family—and also the strong sense of belonging to the U.S. that developed over time and allowed her, when the situation required, to exercise her full rights as a citizen: "This is one of the wonders of this country. You can sue for your job. This was also the loneliest part of my life."

Jian Dong Sakakeeny, who came from China around the same time as Weihua Zhang, felt from an early age she would emigrate—an interesting decision for a child of her background. However, when she describes why her parents' lack of education was the central gift of her upbringing, we begin to feel why she felt a natural affinity for the U.S.—and why facing the cultural challenges most immigrants face, she would find her footing rather quickly:

> I have always felt that I am a world citizen. I knew the path to travel was education, and I pushed myself to study hard, especially English. My parents were uneducated and that was a blessing in disguise. They didn't know about the typical mores and customs of raising children, how they should and shouldn't behave . . . . I had the chance to figure everything out for myself instead of being told what to believe . . . . I learned to rely on myself, to find inner strength. As a child and young adult, I chose to study very hard. My parents were very proud of me, but they didn't push me. That was my choice and I became a lifelong learner.

It is also interesting to note that the experience of all the women raised in China, whether mainland China or Taiwan, is devoid of discussions of gender inequality. Sakakeeny explicitly rejects its significance in her own upbringing.

Sakakeeny also feels herself more a citizen of the world than the U.S.—her naturalized citizenship is more a response to family pressure, a desire to bring her mother to the States, than a growing attachment to the U.S. specifically. Donna Porter, who also clearly feels herself to be a citizen of the world, has a far more specific attachment to the U.S. A native of Zambia, she first lived in the U.S. as an elementary school student. The effect of this exposure was as identity forming for her and her siblings as it was for Yu-Han Chao. Porter's determination to return to the U.S.—and the widely varied worlds she navigates—makes for a fascinating story. From a life of privilege and wealth in Zambia to work-study at Berea College in Kentucky, to marriage to an Atlantan with a ninth-grade education, she finds herself at home: "It's only one world," she says. "Live it up."

Home for each of these women, as for all of us, is where we experience our most profound needs met. Sometimes it comes by developing, like Coen, a fluid sense of self, or several selves, that expand into the specificity of our present condition; or, like Quirk, developing a nostalgia that nurtures, makes us complete by creating a continuum between our earliest selves and the one we are now; sometimes, like Levy or Suput, it is by making an exclusive choice, casting our vote, rolling up our tightrope.

Throughout this wonderful collection, I am struck by how resilient and resourceful, talented and self-actualizing these women are—how they make full use of the increased liberty they may experience here. There is no doubt, as well, what they add to the resources of our country. Another observation that feels significant to me, given the importance of emotional attachment in fostering a sense of shared nationality, is how different the acculturation experience is, indeed *what* the individual acculturates to, if they experience support, feel, as Kulidžan does, that someone who is a citizen—foreign or native born—has given something of their heart to them. The distinction is important for in many of these accounts there is little energy or interest in civic return, having something to give back to U.S. society *as a society*. It is hard to do so unless we feel we have received—and it is here that the paucity of our language for community and care is most obvious. The U.S. government immigration site lists as the most important reasons to consider U.S. citizenship: the right to vote, a chance to reunite families, a way to protect your children's right to remain in the U.S., protection in cases involving illegal activity, and international travel made easier. It is hard to see here where belonging and real social participation within the U.S. community fit in—or how, on either side, these can be talked about as an orienting desire.

The citizenship ceremony itself provides, for many, a vision of the beloved community. People are able to see, in all these people from around the world who are now reciting an oath with them, who have traveled the same difficult journey of acculturation and made the same intentional commitment to help create a society in which they too are equal, the beginning of a new *We the People of the United States*.

It is as much up to those of us who have not had to make that journey to citizenship as it is up to those who have to continue to expand that *We* by insisting that it include us all, birthright and naturalized. Americanization moves in two directions, a mutually influencing conversation, a continuous exercise in inclusion. So, read on. When you're done, find someone whose journey to full, engaged citizenship is rather different from your own. If you're foreign born, find someone native born. Listen. Listen as if that person is saying, *We*. Imagine walking in their shoes, seeing through their eyes. Ask the same of them, and see how your story, too, changes with that hearing.

First

...ington on Monday, the nineteenth day of May,
...nine hundred and nineteen.

RESOLUTION

...Constitution extending the right of suffrage
...to women.

...House of Representatives of the United States
...thirds of each House concurring therein,
... an amendment to the Constitution,
...purposes as part of the Constitution
... of the several States.
... shall not be

PRELUDE:
A COUNTRY OF IMMIGRANTS

MARIETTE LANDRY

IMMIGRANT HOME MOVIE, 1963

Without sound
there is no thunder to send her
crouching on the cellar step,
no broken English, no curse or prayer
in Italian, no husband calling her
crazy, or worse, trying to
pinpoint the storm's distance
by counting seconds
between lightning and thunder,
while her son pans through the house
with his instruction book, tripod,
and new 8-millimeter Bell and Howell,
checking the light as he shoots her
from behind, shadowy, slightly
out of focus, the zipper of her black dress
glinting, the apron knotted at her neck,
his presence uncalled-for as she turns,
stunned, into the close-up,
her face overexposed,
her lips voicelessly moving.

JOHN MANESIS

NOT ANYMORE

The editor, preparing a book
about Greek-American experience,
telephoned a widowed writer,
Athens born, raised in Minneapolis.

Her parents had urged three sons
to pursue professional careers,
advising her to marry young
and raise "a nice Greek family."

She did not disappoint,
produced five children in six years,
and later tended to her ailing spouse,
a pharmacist with a failing heart

who often commanded her,
"Annio, amesos!"—"Anna, at once!"
For three decades she also endured
her mother-in-law's barbs.

At the end of the interview,
lowering his voice, the editor asked
if she wished to "remain anonymous,"
lest she offend a relative.

"Anonymous? Not anymore.
Let all your readers know
who I am and where I've been.
Don't leave out a thing!"

I BE MILLIONAIRE

I was sixteen in 1922
when Papa sent me to America
to live with his sister, Thea Maria.
I thought I'd go to school
to teach myself, to learn things,
but no, after I got here
she show my picture to Christo,
35 years old man who work for railroad,
saved money, wanted young Greek wife.

When he come to Thea Maria's house,
I know he like me right away.
He says he wants to marry me
and didn't ask for *preika*—
what you call it, dowry?
When he left, I told her, no,
he was too old for me.
She said I have to, that Mama and Papa
had money for only one-way ticket
and made agreement with her,
just like I was *katsiki*, goat,
somebody sold from farm.

So Christo married me,
I had three boys, break my back
in the garden full of rocks,
bake 10 loaves of bread a week,
wash and sew clothes, fix all the food,
and you know something,
he thought it was onions
I cut that make me cry.

He was foreman on railroad,
want nothing more than that,
gone most of the time,
and when he gets home,
he doesn't understand why
I won't jump in bed right away
and spread my legs for him.
Up to day he died, he said,
"Be like me, happy go lucky."
I cannot lie—he was good family man,
never swore at me or raised his hand.

See the picture on the table?
That's the one Papa took
before they put me on the boat.
Look how beautiful I was—
even old Panayiotis, one time a priest,
always watch me when I walk by.
Not just beautiful but smart, too.
I tell you God's truth, if I was a man,
I be millionaire.

ALEXANDRINA SERGIO

LEAVING BRIDGET

I was such a small girl
barely able to see over the table top
in that jostling place
where a man took their hands
first my mother's, then my father's,
pressed each finger to the inkpad
then onto a paper form.
Fingerprints were required for citizenship,
promises to foreswear all that had been home,
oaths of allegiance to the new country.

Why did you come all the way to America, Daddy?
Because this is a better place.

Everyone we knew then came from somewhere else.
The Irish girls mostly hired on as domestics
and were lumped together as The Bridgets.
Others—each one an Other—were
Wops, Polacks, Frogs, Kikes, Micks.

Intelligent, dignified, light skinned—
no one dared insult my stern handsome Daddy,
and my Mother—
five feet tall, not to be trifled with,
attitude burnished early on by
membership in the Cumann na mBan—
Mother was never a Mick.
But just to be sure, she ironed flat her brogue and
armed with barely creased papers
went to court and changed her name to Patricia.

Mommy, why does Uncle Owen call you Bridie?
Oh, that's just a little-girl name. My name is Patricia.

With a smoothed brogue, a changed name
the lucky could get their baggage unpacked sooner.

I think it's done differently now.
My daughter—an Other—slaps the label on herself.
I'm here. I'm queer.

I cringe.

Mom, if I take their weapon and make it mine
they can't use it against me.

If only The Bridgets could have dared that.
If only my mother hadn't to trade her lovely name
for downpayment on a Better Place.

Note: *Cumann na mBan* ("The League of Women") was organized in 1914 as an auxiliary corps to the Irish Volunteers. The Irish Volunteers mounted the 1916 Easter Uprising, the opening act in the Irish War of Independence.

IMMIGRANT

"In Bulgaria I'm a different person."

The houses and birdbaths,
the trees, the people,
are all images on boards.
Menace stirs behind every stage-scene fence.
I am ecstatic when the dog proves tied.

The sun's scorch blinds me to the road.
I tread like someone with a dropped foot,
grazing down to detect ruts and stones.

The men, the women, the children . . .
(Such straight teeth! Such magazine clothes!)
I capture and tame the words they sing.
Their tunes and rhythms escape.
My lyrics clash with the music,
halt the room like an elbow on piano keys.

The mirrored face is vaguely familiar
I've become a slice of me.
I'm not sure which slice it is.

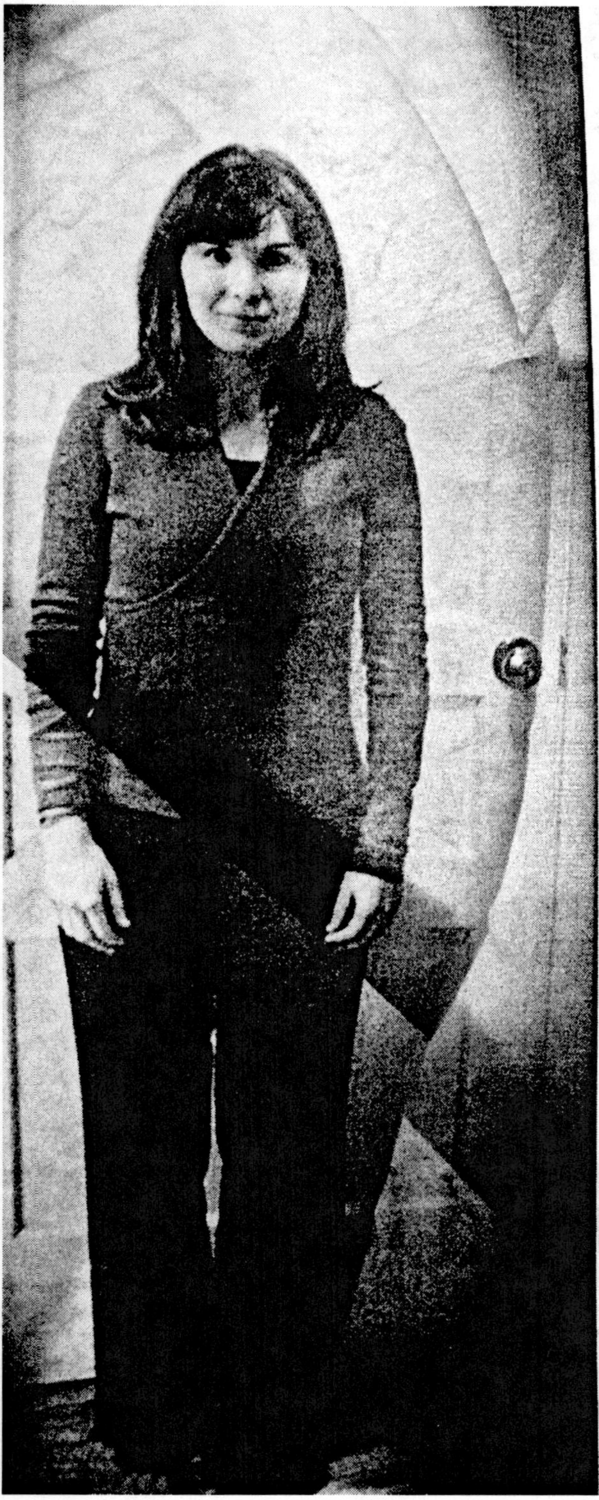

ur
olds us
ties

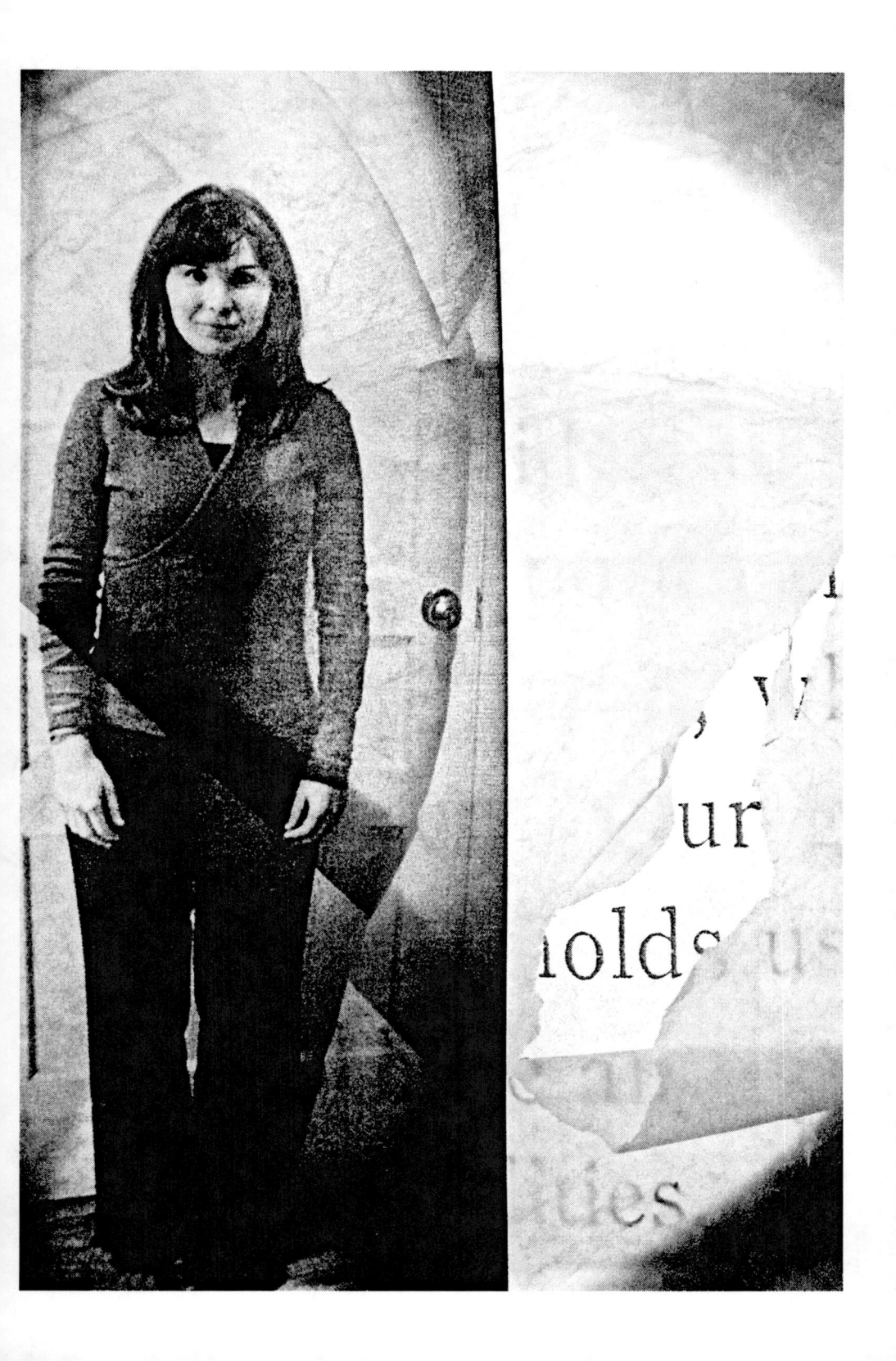

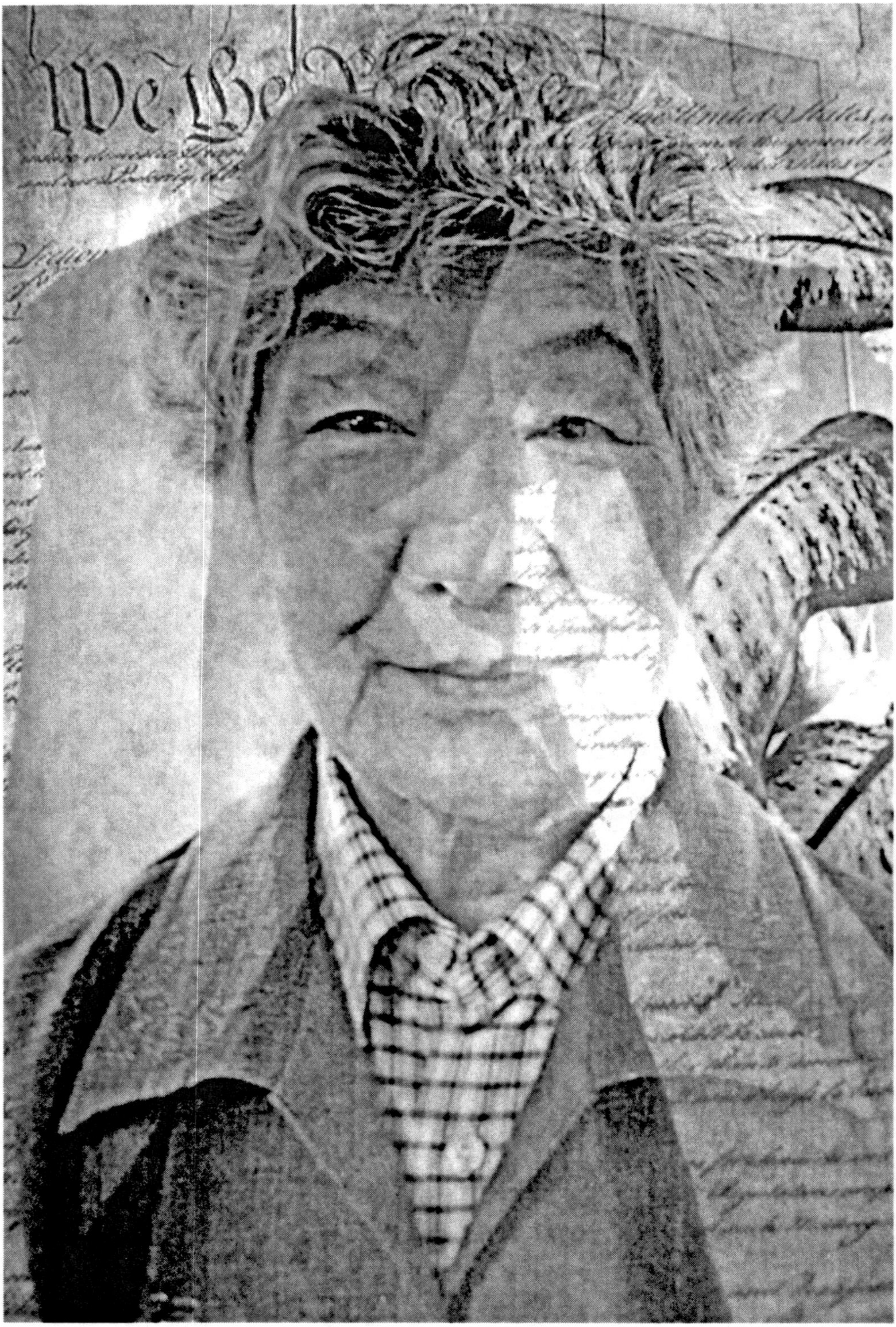

WHAT OUR MOTHERS DO FOR US

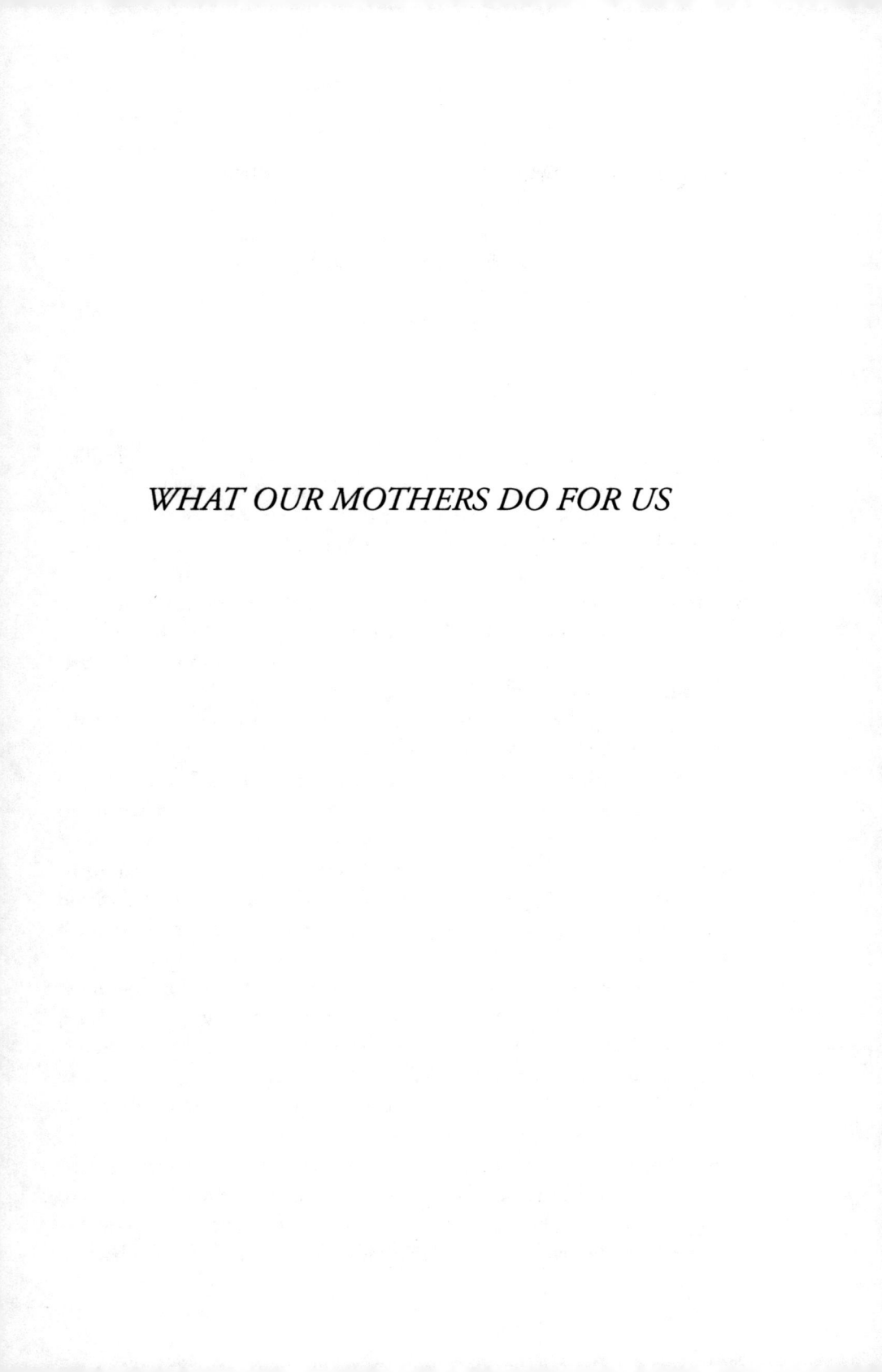

LISA CHAN

CHEESECAKE

She drops the cubed chicken into the wok, and the kitchen is filled with its sizzling and crackling. Next, a splash of soy sauce sends a plume of fragrant steam into her face. The whir of the hood fan and the scrape of her metal spade temporarily drown out the sounds of her children playing in the backyard under the hot South Carolina sun. They will turn as brown as chocolate if they stay out there too long. She is reminded of her own youth and days of tropical Hong Kong heat. The sun was something that got into her eyes and burned her neck as she ran to work or rushed to school. It was never something she played in like her children did today.

Today is an irregular break from her daily routine of working at the Chinese restaurant she and her husband had started. They had arrived in the United States with only the idea that hard work in the U.S.A. could lead somewhere better. Hard work in Hong Kong wasn't leading anywhere, so she and her husband thought they may as well try working in a new country. Finally, twenty years later, today is the day she and her husband are to be naturalized citizens. The official ceremony that they are required to attend offers them the rare opportunity to stay home in the afternoon and eat lunch with the kids.

Even with the day off, she is still cooking in the kitchen, cleaning, and fixing up the yard. They are never aware of words like: *work-life balance*, or *rest and relaxation*. The word *weekend* means busier days and longer hours. *Monday* means food deliveries. *Tuesday* is the day they roll egg rolls. Every day is filled with organized tasks, and the years slip by, marked only by to-do lists and a few extra gray hairs. She had thought that as long as she followed the rules and laws of this country, she would be safe, but three years ago she had tried to go on a cruise as a first-time family vacation. It had been a circus getting the proper paperwork and visa prepared for herself. This scared her because her mother was aging and she knew she would have to go back to

Hong Kong soon. The idea of holding a U.S. passport was something that made sense. Slowly, throughout the years, she started to hear new words like: *Medicare, Social Security,* and *retirement.* These things were still foreign to her, even after all these years of paying taxes and running a business, but there was a fear that these things would remain out of her reach unless she did something about it. Becoming a naturalized citizen felt like the next step for a better future.

Her husband enters the kitchen and starts setting the table. The bowls and the chopsticks clatter on the table. These sounds of family life make her happy. She feels complete, even though the business worries her and she still wonders about how she will pay for the college education of her three children. Three children in college one day! The thought of it fills her with motivation.

The last two decades of hard work are paying off. Her children look happy and healthy. She has a business, a car, a home with air-conditioning, and a husband who truly is her partner. Back home, the men were always gambling and did not respect a hard-working woman. Here in the States, women and men are more like equals. She watches her husband go out into the backyard to call the kids in for lunch. *"Sihk faaan!"* he calls. They scramble out of the pool and he helps to towel them dry. She watches with affection and feels like she has everything she ever wanted, even a country that matches her own ideals.

"Mom, are you turning American today?" her son asks.

"No. I'm Chinese. And so are you. Don't hold your chopsticks like that."

They hold bowls of rice to their mouths. Usually they eat oranges after their meals, but today a cheesecake dessert is waiting for them in the refrigerator.

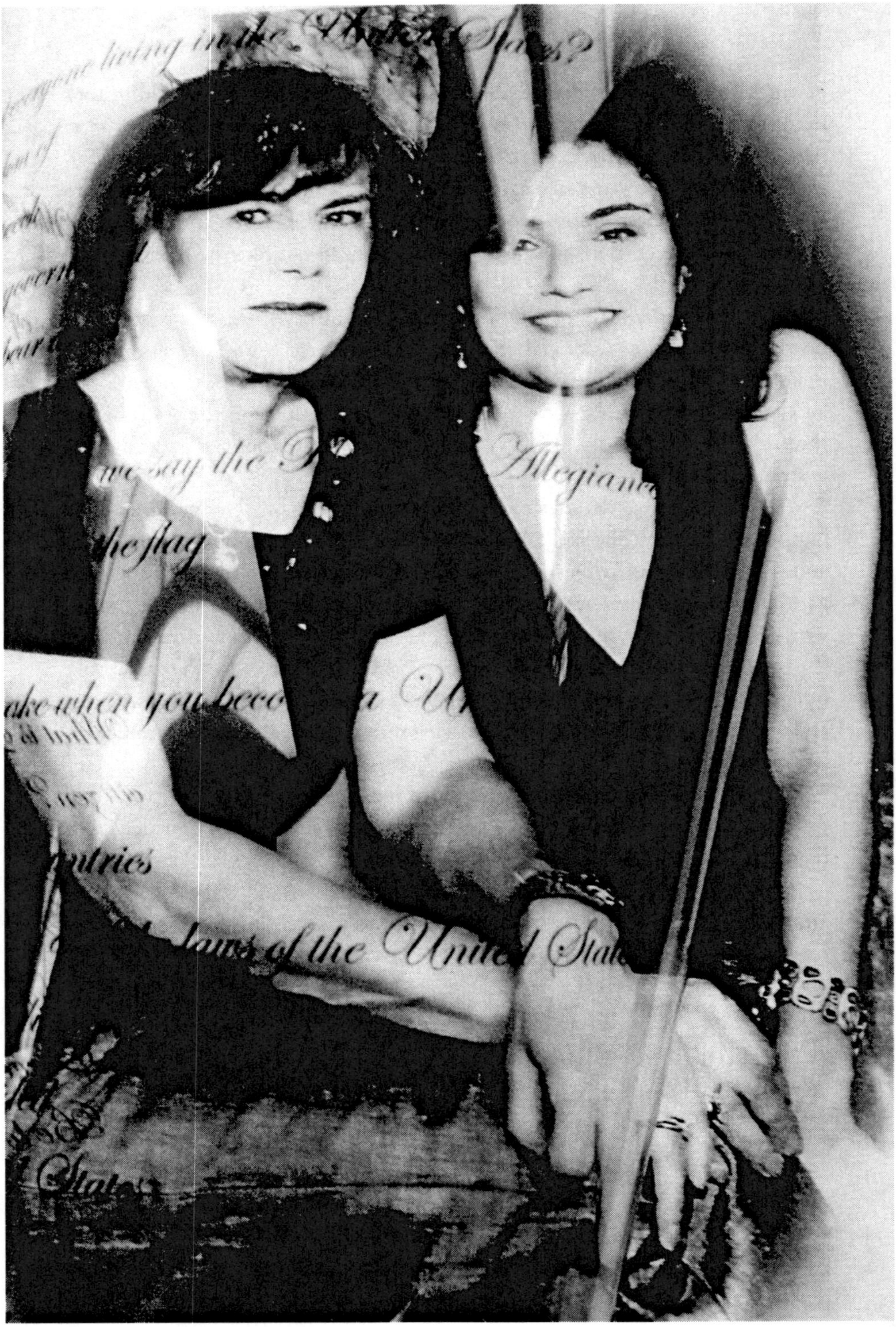
we say the
the flag
laws of the

NATALIA O. TREVIÑO

THE NATURALIZATION

It is November, and I have been Mexican all my life. My cousins say we are all *norte americanos* because we are all born on the same continent. I imagine saying this to Rosy and Greta down the street. They will roll their eyes.

It is cold in the house this morning. Dad likes to keep the temperature as close to nature as possible, so my skin is unable to imagine crawling out from the covers. I dress like it's winter, but by the afternoon bus ride, we are sweating. I never get the clothes right in this kind of weather.

Mom has a strange look on her face when I get home, her eyebrows raised and looking down at her skillet, like a glass elevator is taking her way up. The cooking smells pour out from her narrow kitchen. Salted meat sizzling with onions. Small cubes of fried potatoes set aside, their grease sinking into the white paper towel below them. I give my mom an absent kiss on the cheek, put my books on the table instead of going straight to my room. I want to know what scared her.

She adds the tomato sauce to her already sizzling skillet, and there is the sudden cymbal sound of frying liquid. The aroma of *picadillo* lifts from the pan.

"*Ay mi'jita.*" Her cigarette is resting on her old brass ashtray, growing a long, gray speckled tube that is about to crumble. She is stirring the tomato sauce while it bubbles. She lets out a long breath that hisses in unison with the sauce. "I hefto take a test."

"What? Why?" My mom does not take tests. Except I remember her getting ready for her driving test when I was in third grade. My stomach curls a little.

"I have to become a seetizen."

"What? You've never wanted to become a citizen." We've asked her about this. Lots of times.

"I hefto. Or Javi kennot go to school."

"What school?" My brother is already in school. I can't put together what she is saying.

"The yuniversity!"

"What does that have to do with it?" This has to be a mistake. It feels wrong, so it must be. She takes a last, deep puff of her cigarette, her whole face puckered to take it all in. She blows the smoke out into the vent above the stove. She punches the white tube into the ash tray.

"Or they will charge too much. They will charge ten times more if he's not Americano! *Así son las escuelas aquí.*" She's smashing her cigarette into dust.

The last thing my brother wants after he graduates is to go to college.

"So this is the only way we can go to college?" My life might be over. All my good grades down the tube.

"But Dad is a citizen? That should be enough!"

Her hands are covering her face. She sucks in a breath through her teeth, and she begins laughing, her neck deepening into a rose color. She covered her face like this when I was twelve and told her I started my period. She held her head in her hands like she had to recover from being kicked in the chest. This test is not good. It's like my period.

Dad comes out of his bedroom looking happy after work while mom is already heating the tortillas directly on the flames. He puts the news on. Zinging music followed by Chris Marrou with his plastered hair, and blaring lights stream through the house.

We all sit down to start dinner, and I am worried. Mom can read English even though she talks to me in Spanish. I know she can read it. I think she can. She reads the paper every day. She tells me the news stories, the gossip from *The Star*. She thinks the stars and the politicians are all trashy people—*gente corriente*. But I don't think she can write it. No chance of that. The only thing I see her write are letters to my 'Uelita in Mexico, and those letters are in Spanish. She never lets me read them. I don't know how to read in Spanish anyway.

The only things she writes out in English are the numbers on her checks when we go to the grocery store. She has had the same cheat sheet in her checkbook from I don't know when—on the back of the register pages behind the calendar in bright blue longhand, her letters gliding and ignoring the lines. It's the same cheat sheet I've seen since I was in elementary. You can see the numbers, four, eight, twelve, fourteen, fifteen, all the way to one hundred, pages of numbers written in English. You can smell the aroma of her perfume, mixed with her smokey Salems. She needs this list, even after twelve years of living here, and when she asks the clerk to sound out the amount, she is looking down her list: "Feefty. Okhay, feefty, what? Ah. Feefty three. *A ver.*" And she finds the words. Four and fourteen always give her trouble. But not even my friends get those right, they take out the u in fourteen.

On my plate, Mom's beans and rice swim in the *picadillo* juices. The peas and peppers almost float in the clear, brown juice. All the liquids exchange each other's flavors in the swollen bellies of the plain rice. She is standing at the stove turning new tortillas over the flames for us, her fingers touching the fire with each turn.

I start to think about scholarships, but I cannot say this out loud. So I say, "Mom has to take a test?" And we are all chewing.

Dad likes his tortillas charred. He tears off a piece of one and nods.

"Dad, this has to be wrong. What kind of test? You're already a citizen, right? Can't we apply for that ourselves when we go to college?" I do not want her to fail. My mother only finished third grade in Mexico, and that was so long ago. She told me her father did not see why she should go to school with four little brothers to look after. She had to stay home, help my grandmother, take heads off of chickens for the stew, sew up their little school uniforms, wash their diapers by hand. Start the rice before they came home from school hungry for their sopa and warm tortillas. Raul loved his a little burnt at the edges like my dad. Armando loved his soft and not too hot. The little one wanted his tacos empty just soaked in the juices.

"They sent a book for her to study. She has to know the history. Some facts." Mom stands up again to heat more tortillas, laying two tortillas at a time directly on the fire. With one hand, she lifts the dish towel on our table, and with the other slips the hot tortillas in a folded towel that waits warm by my dad's plate. He grabs the newest, hottest one and tears off a piece to help him scoop up all the juiciness on this plate. The other tortillas stay just warm enough, coaxing heat from each other under their blanket.

I start to think that maybe this test will be the beginning of that life

I want for her. Her accent is thick, sure, but she is beautiful too, and I start to dream. She can be more than a housewife. She can work at a department store selling jewelry or make-up. We could go to the mall together with her discount. Greta's mom works at a department store, and once I told her how cool I thought it was that her mother works.

"Don't be an idiot. You don't want that. You have it all. Your mother waits on you hand and foot." I did not know what she meant by hand and foot. I know English, but waits on you hand and foot? I had heard of a disease that sounded like that. It all sounded like an insult.

"What do you mean?"

"Hand and foot! Gives you everything, expects nothing! You have no idea how lucky you are! She does your wash. She makes your bed. Cleans your bathroom. Makes you breakfast. Drives you to school. I have to do all my own laundry. My mom makes me do everything myself. Sucks."

I didn't think of her as waiting on me, that I needed someone to wait on me like my dad did. Like her little brothers. But I am fifteen and I have no idea how to do laundry. I've never ironed a shirt. She won't let me.

So my mom and I start to pick up the table, and I ask, "Well, can we help you study?"

She answers without looking at me. "I started today."

"Really?" I wipe the crumbs from the table with the wet paper towel she has squeezed out for me. She does not want any smears left after I wipe.

She nods while she takes in her cigarette. "Just a leettle beet." I figure I can practice with her. It can't be that hard if they want real immigrants to take it, like people who just arrived here. We've lived here almost my whole life.

But it is a test. It might be hard.

She hands me the Study Guide. There is a brief history of the United States in the front. A table of contents, an index. It is about twenty-five pages long. The sample test is in the back. "Come on. Let's do this," I say. We sit at the clean table. Now the national news is blaring from the television. Tom Brokaw and his bad bad news about everything. I start with the first page. "Who was the first president?"

"George Wachington."

"Good! But you already knew that I bet." She smiles and inhales her smoke deeply. She starts to laugh and choke a little.

"What?" She is breaking up.

"Bolo, Bolo, remember George Wachington in Nueva York?"

Dad turns around from his recliner, his pipe resting on his lips. He takes it out and starts pursing his lips to hold back a laugh. He lets the laugh out as he remembers. "Your mother and I were in line at the airport in New York." He is getting those dancing eyes telling me. "And she nudged me." He's turning red and enjoying this. "She nudged me in the ribs." He struggles, and a high laughter comes out of him. My mother has her head down and is crumbling into hysterics. Both of them are.

"And I tell your father, look, Bolo, look." And she bursts. "Look!" And she points at the TV like she's recreating the moment. And she cries, "It is George Wachington!" And they both burst out again, their laughter louder than the new improved Tide commercial.

Dad takes a breath. "And I said, 'What? *Pues que te pasa?* George Washington is dead!" And he's bent over, unable to speak he is laughing so hard. Tears are falling from his eyes. He catches his breath. "I told her, 'He was a president!' But there he was, there was George Hamilton!" And now they rupture into flaming *carcajadas*, singing in unison.

"The movie star? Mom! George Washington? Oh my God, Mom!"

"*Ya! Ya! Déjanme estudiar! Aver, síguele, mi'jita,*" she motions as she collects her breath.

I stop chortling. And I hear the names rhyming in my head, Washington, Hamilton. "Okay." Both named George. "Now when did the U.S. become independent?"

"Ahhhmmm. Sebenteen, sebenteen," She starts crunching her breath again in a laugh, her hands over face, her deep breaths puffing out clear air. "I doan' know." I release my breath while she inhales the smoke.

"How can you not know? You do know! Just think! You've heard it a million times! We all have!"

"Whait a minot! Sebenteen." She lights another cigarette, still chortling, searching her memory, ashamed like she's had a second glass of wine at Christmas. "I know. I know thees!"

"This is the second question, Mom. We need to study a lot."

She holds back her laugh, then breaks out, "*Ya párale*! You are making me nervous!"

"Mom." She is making me nervous. "It's 1776, see? Right here. You knew that, right? When is this test?"

My brother comes out of his room carrying his rifle. "Don't worry, Mom. I don't even want to go to college." He heard everything while he was cleaning it, getting ready to kill birds in the backyard.

"Don't be an idiot," I say. "You have to go to college. Mom is just nervous. This is easy, Mom. Everyone knows 1776. You'll remember that."

But I wonder where I learned it. First grade. I was coloring a flag. "Okay, what are the three branches of government?" I am sure I cannot name them.

"Eh-ummm. *Executivo, Legisletivo, y—espérate, espérate!*" She is thinking hard lowering her black eyebrows trying to remember. She takes in a drag from her cigarette. "*Judicio. YA! Déjenme sola!* I can du-et!"

"I'm outta here." My brother leaves, his rifle held upright the way Dad showed us. I liked how she got it. This would work.

"Mom, let's do it another way, okay?" I start the next question.

"*Déjame!* I will do it." I put the book down. *Jeopardy* is on television. I lie down to watch. The pipe smoke is stronger than her cigarette smoke. I want to bury my nose in my shirt. A faint haze where the smokes combine floats over my head, taking the color out of the paneled walls. She holds the cigarette tilted back like a movie star while she mumbles names and dates to herself, forgetting to smoke, the ash burning up into the cloud around her. Her eyebrows are lifted again in that elevator look.

On the day of her test, Mom is already dressed up and she is frying our eggs, her hair fixed up, her make-up is complete with lipstick, her clothes extra dressy, the cigarette sitting in its brass cradle. She's wearing the nice wool pants and the taffeta blouse we got on sale. I cannot stand eating eggs in the morning, and it is especially gross to see my brother eating them, the drippy cloudy gooey whites. I cannot even look at him while he chews. My mom eats a piece of toast. I dip my buttered toast in the egg yolk, the only part I can swallow.

"I been studying. *A ver que pasa,*" she says. Her face reminds me of my grandfather's as she says this, twisted in a little serious frown. And we all know he had bad luck. Lost the tips of his fingers in an accident at that garage. She wipes crumbs off of her blouse and skirt, and as she walks to her bedroom, her heels sink quietly into the carpet. I slide my sickening egg whites into the trash and I wonder if she will pass the test by the time I want to go to college.

Her make-up faded by the afternoon and she is back in her regular clothes and smiling into the spaghetti sauce on the stove. I still have my books in my hand. She sees me and says, "I deed it!"

"You passed? You did it! What grade did you make?" I feel a little bad asking, but I want a number.

I wonder why she is cooking. On a day like this.

She looks sheepish, "Not that good."

"What? Mom! But you passed! Did they give you a grade?"

Our voices have traveled into the hallway to the bedroom. Javi comes out of his room with a dirty rag wiping his rifle. "You took the test today?"

"Javi! Didn't you see her all dressed up this morning?"

"No."

"You are so blind! I don't know how you shoot anything."

"I deed it. Ya!"

"But what was the grade?" My brother is licking the side of his lower lip, which is a bit puffed with snuff. God, he's disgusting. I can tell she does not want us to know, but it comes out of her. "Sebenty-six." And she is really smiling.

I sink. That is almost not passing. But she did it. I know I could have helped her make an A. How hard could it have been with questions like who was Ben Franklin? This is a C, but it's like an A. She is no *burra* like she always says. She only took the test once. She told us she might have to take it twice. It must have been a hard test.

She continues to stir the meat for the sauce.

"So what was it like? What did you miss?"

She looks up and starts look embarrassed. Her fingers immediately cover her eyes, holding the bridge of her nose like she got water up her nose in a swimming pool. "You are not going to belevit. How many stars are—"

She is smiling like a kid in trouble. We are waiting, picturing stars, and then it hits my brother. "On the flag?"

She lets a laugh burst out. I hear a "jes."

"Mom! What? What did you put? This had to be the easiest question on the test! The easiest answer! Everyone knows this. Everyone!"

"I put thirty-seex." And she is laughing with her head down.

"I thought there were thirty-six states. I read it in the book."

"She's right," my brother says. "There were thirty-six states, stars on the flag, a long time ago."

"Thirty-six?! But mom! God! There are fifty! Fifty states, fifty stars! You know that!" Her cigarette's ash is growing long. It is okay for us to laugh because she is laughing too. We are all in hysterics, tears streaming from our eyes, our laughter rising to the ceiling with her smoke.

"I know! I know! Ay," and she gasps and finally breaths in deeply. *"Ya, ya no me digan nada!* I am done with eet!"

We have been laughing at her for years, in the car at the Dairy Queen drive-through when she repeatedly tries to say the impossible "hembergher," and clerk asks her over and over, "What was that, Ma'am?" Her English so thick and muddled, so hoarse and Mexican, impossible to understand over a microphone, especially once she starts cracking up.

When my grandmother laughs at my Spanish it is the same. I'll be talking. I'll make it up a little because my Spanish cannot catch up to my English, so I guess all the time. I know I've guessed wrong when her face starts to struggle. I try again, and then she busts into deep, heaving smoker's sigh, like an engine that cannot start, and then she gasps to repeat it the way I do, hoarse, unable to get it out, and there are tears leaking from her eyes. When I hear the correct word through her breaking breath, I hear my mutilation of it, and my body starts to shake with laughter. We wipe the trickles of salty tears from our faces.

I look at my mom. "At least we could have gone out for dinner, Mom! Don't you want to celebrate?"

She frowns at me like it is no big accomplishment. *"Nombre, pues qué tienes?"* It's like she's standing there and she just filled ten buckets of water, and is about to carry them all, and she is telling me it's no big deal. It's like that.

I try to fall asleep. I start to wonder when and where would she have heard about the fifty stars? How many times did I have to color the flag in? The map of this country. How many times was I told what the stars were for?

I smell her food. It is in my sheets. She says she hates cooking, but does not let me learn. I want to cook something, anything, but she shoos me away. I remember asking her if I can chop the celery for her on Thanksgiving.

I like the way it sounds, the crunching. "No, no, no. Go do your homework. Study, *niña*, study. Do you want to be a donkey like me? *Soy una burra*. Don't be like me. *Applícate a la escuela*. I don't want you in the kitchen your whole life." She is angry when she says this. But I have cousins who aren't even allowed to speak English to their mother like I do, and they do good in school and cook. I want to chop onions, sauté them with tomatoes, be in charge of frozen ground beef like Greta: turn it slowly over on a hot, oily skillet until it thaws and crumbles. I cannot even heat a tortilla without her yelling at me to get out of the way. I asked her once if I can boil eggs and she said, "Why? You hate eggs."

My brother and I have to miss school. We're all going downtown to the courthouse where she's gonna swear in to become American. Once she does, it is automatic for us. We'll be Americans too. I like it for her but not for me. It seems wrong. We sign and that's it. I don't even see why I have to go. My friends do not know about any of this American citizenship business. Not the test. Not college tuition prices. They don't have these problems. They never had to do this because they were born here. They remind me constantly. They are White as far as they are concerned even though they are browner than me. I'm a wetback. They don't care if I have papers.

Mom is extra dressed up, wearing one of those wool skirts we bought during the devaluation. It is cream-colored with a silk lining. Silk! And it drapes over her small hips and flat stomach. Fifteen dollars. I got two of them as well, but they are too grown up for me. They are super rich looking like the clothes in the magazines. She is wearing a light plum-colored sweater. It has a bow attached to the neck, and is tied in a wavy swooshy kind of way. I want to swim in it. She is wearing her wedding rings, which she never wears unless she's going somewhere special. Diamonds that interlock with other diamonds. None of my friends' moms have anything like it.

Her perfume rests on all of our clothing as we drive the long way downtown. I look out the window and start to dream. I dream about visiting Africa or Australia or the moon, or to live like a monkey, drink from waterfalls, study and eat plants and roots, tell time by animal movements, bug paths, or stars. I begin to remember my newt I found in the front yard, his sweet, impossibly small face. I had to let him go after two days since I didn't know what to feed him. If I had been a botanist, I would I have known what to feed him, but then I think I would rather be an astronaut. I love math, which is weird I know for a girl. Such a waste of time to love all these opposite things. Just like Mom's expensive perfume seems wasted for this day. It's the perfume Dad brought back from his trip to Paris before they were married. It is so old, but strong. It should only be used for a special dance or something.

We arrive at the room where she will be sworn in. There are at least seventy others. Mostly Mexican, but some Chinese, some Black. There are the American and Texan flags draping down like elegant dresses at the front, gold-trimmed. Each of us gets a little gold flag pin. I kind of hate the tacky thing. I hold it, and it makes my hands sweat so I put it away.

A man begins the oath, asking everyone to lift their hands and repeat. There is a Bible. I can hear my mother's voice among the others as she renounces allegiance to any other country. Any foreign prince. Mexico. My stomach is angry. That she will bear arms in a state of war. My mother will bear arms? Have no allegiance to Mexico? So help her God?

My mother's hand is raised and her lips are flat as they speak these strange new words, words tumbling into a room of accents, coughs, and trembling voices. Her eyes are distant and steady, but her eyebrows curl with wonder as if she is falling.

I have been pledging my allegiance like this every day at school, with my hand over my heart. But I don't mean it. This pin, this oath means I am not Mexican anymore and my mother is a soldier.

An hour later, I am standing in another government building at the immigration officer's cluttered desk. "Sign your name here, above your face." There is a picture of me already glued to a thick paper, crisp and tan colored, the one where I become a citizen. It has those constitution letters like they had in the old days. Mom and my brother have already signed theirs. The officer points, creating an arc with his finger, touching where I should sign.

So I begin to sign carefully in my twisted cursive, hoping my whole name fits in the tiny space with a deep purple marker, its tip thick for my letters. But I curve my whole name over the top of my head in the photo, my name, Natalia Treviño Ortegon.

The officer looks at my name and the lines of disappoint bend on his forehead. "This is not the name on the form. Do you want Ortegon to be your new last name?"

"My new last name? Treviño is my last name. Ortegon goes after it—that's how it is on my birth certificate."

"You can change your name today to anything you want. Right now. Kathleen. Suzy. Lots of people do it. Candy. This is the one time you can change your name forever." I think of Asian girls I know named with their American nicknames. I think of teachers who can never say my name on the first day of school.

"You mean, if I don't change it, I'll have a new last name?" My chest is pinched. Why would I have to change it? I like my name. I think I like it. No one told me. I imagine people making fun of my new name at school. Who is named Ortegon? Treviño is bad enough.

"Here, just erase it." I look at him, see the hurry in the little puffs he lets out of his flaring nose.

He offers his pencil. I have never erased marker in my life. I've never written on a photograph or erased something on it either. This man is crazy.

But the name smudges off. Part of the photo smudges along with it. The official photo has a new, white arc above my head. I do not know what I will put.

My chest is cracking open, and I am about to split in half. I do not want to write Ortegon on my school papers, on my report card, but I think of my grandfather—just dropping him like that. This is my mother's last name. This is my name. My grandfather would kill me for this—even though he is dead.

My parents do not speak. They are waiting. There are no suggestions. No opposition.

Sometimes you are outside when it happens. You are outside on a hot day with your friends. You are sweaty between your legs and under your pits, and your friends are laughing about how you fell at the four-square game at lunch, and how you always sucked at it, you wetback, and you're sitting right on the ground on the driveway because no dad is coming home yet from work, and driveways belong to the kids 'til then. And the heat of the day is peaking, but there is a new wind that comes from down the street, and it is cool and Alaskan and immediate in its swoosh. It sweeps up the leaves that have fallen, the leaves that were burnt to death that October. And a lake of coolness washes over your sweaty body right there, right where you were sitting in the sun just a second before, joking and shining and needing a shower. And then it is all a darkening shade above you, a drop in the temperature and a gust as sharp as a cool drink on your dry tongue. And that is how it happened with me.

"Can I put it as my middle name?"

He frowns a little. "Sure, if you want to. Any name you want." He's thinking I'll regret this. He is hurrying me. And I sign my new name in the whiteness.

My mother's last name sitting—not where it belongs, at the end of my name, but in front of my father's last name. No longer a ribbon at the end of a kite's point to honor her. Mexican women never erase their names when they marry, but add a new strand to their name and fly it on their children's name too.

And I look at the newly tied ribbons on this photograph, in those letters written over letters, twisted and poorly attached to one another, writing Ortegon over Treviño, and Treviño over Ortegon, so both names are on top of each other, the photo marred forever by this mess of smearing, erasing, and rewriting, this twisting of coiled of o's twisting over curly r's, so many letters interlaced and blurred in a fuzzy filigree, this name doubled on itself. Ghosts hovering in a whitened space above my head.

life, liberty, and
to secure
nstituted an
iving their just
bowers fro
governed
hat w

AZADEH SHAHSHAHANI

REFLECTIONS

If there is one thing that will always raise curiosity about my origins, it is my accent. It has indeed turned into such an inseparable part of my identity that I am reluctant to lose it. It often takes me back through time, to when I was sixteen and had just arrived from Iran. Having to master a new language was no more difficult than adjusting to a strange environment with people who looked different and dressed differently from me. Indeed, my black hair and light brown eyes seemed far out of place in the private high school in Memphis in which I was first enrolled. If it were only for such superficial differences as appearance, however, I would have undoubtedly had a much easier transition. It was, rather, the strikingly different culture. I remember that I was shocked seeing fifteen-year-old girls not only wear make-up, but also drink and smoke.

It was my parents' aspirations for their children to benefit from a better education and opportunities in life that brought me here. They had lived in the United States in the mid to late seventies, when my father, having obtained his medical degree from Iran, went through his residency training and my mother obtained her nutrition degree. After spending seven years in the U.S., they went back with my five-year-old sister, hoping to make a difference in their homeland with their newly acquired expertise. After two years, exactly four days after the revolution, I was born. My name, Azadeh, means "free-spirited," signifying the great hopes that my parents and the many other parents who named their daughters Azadeh that year bore for the revolution. Their hopes were soon dashed, however, as the oppressive regime of the shah was replaced by a theocracy in which there are rules governing every aspect of people's lives in public, and even private, spaces. In this system, one's advancement in professional and especially official ranks depends in part on the extent to which one chooses to profess one's religiosity, as defined in a regime-dictated manner.

Fifteen years later my parents decided to move back to the United States. They were disillusioned by the failure of the new regime to bring any meaningful liberty to its people, rather imposing its own system of oppression under a different guise; by the long war with Iraq, which had drained them emotionally; and frustrated by the lack of opportunities for themselves and their children. It was especially the latter that had infuriated my parents, as despite his high level of knowledge and years of experience, my father was replaced as the head of a medical institute by one of his trainees who enjoyed better connections with government officials.

There was also the lack of meaningful educational prospects for me and my sister, as the sole criterion for gaining acceptance to the university was the entrance exam which was only administered once a year and was accompanied with exceedingly high levels of competition. Had it been only the exam, however, my parents might have had a less difficult time imagining a bright future for their daughters. But the examination was also accompanied by a test of one's Islamic background, which was ultimately meant to ensure availability of spots for associates of the regime and weed out those seen as holding potentially 'dangerous' ideas, even if intellectually far surpassing the others. And as one advanced in the academic curriculum, the religious fitness criteria became more stringent. The ones placed at the top in any field were more often than not relatives of a government minister, or otherwise those making a point of displaying their adherence to Islamic norms as defined by the authorities.

This was the context that persuaded my parents to make the move and in my father's words, "rescue [their] children from this hopeless situation before it gets too late."

It was in summer of 1993 when my parents and sister ventured to the U.S. for a brief visit, leaving me behind. (My parents had indeed obtained permanent residency during their stay in the U.S. through my father's work. At one point, my father had apparently wanted to throw out the green cards, deeming them useless as my family did not contemplate any thoughts of ever coming back to the U.S. on a permanent basis).

This trip was only the first in a series of four or five visits over the next year, during which my mother took the naturalization exam and became a citizen, thus enabling her to apply for permanent residency for me as an immediate relative, and my father got a job in his old hospital. With each visit, the level of admiration for the U.S. in their tone increased and their determination for departing to this land of opportunity became firmer. This was while they tried their best to keep this hidden from me, the sole opponent of departing our birthplace with which I felt such intimate and strong attachment. The image that I had from the U.S. at this time was one of corruption, crime, and the loss of cultural identity. I was steadfast in preventing this voyage from taking place, crying over every piece of furniture that was sold and arguing furiously with my sister, who was in fact, based on her fond childhood experience, highly desirous of going to the U.S. The hardest moment for me was when we sold our house. This had been my home ever since I was five years old and it harbored a host of memories . . . of the old willow tree and the quiet nights in the garden. To this day, whenever I go back to Iran, one of the first things that I do is to go back to our old valley and look over our house—all whose ivies have been ripped from its walls and replaced by an ugly dark brown color. I still feel a great bond to it, stronger than any I have ever felt for another abode.

It was the summer of 1994 when my father and sister left for the U.S., leaving my mother and me behind to wait for my green card to arrive by the end of the summer. As time passed, I felt less bitter towards the U.S. What led to my change of heart was mostly conversations with my friends who all envied the great opportunity that had befallen me and compared it to their own situation, as they had already begun preparing for the dreaded entrance exam. In fact, when my father, distressed by the loss of his social status as an esteemed doctor in Iran and by separation from my mother and me, told me that he was thinking of coming back, I pleaded with him to stay put, consoling him that my green card would soon be ready and we would join him and my sister.

My green card however did not arrive by the end of the summer; neither was it ready in September or October. By that time, school had already started and my classmates were well on their way into the second year in high school. The wait was becoming intolerable for me, especially since I had decided not to register in school that year, thinking that my green card would be ready by mid to late summer. So I was afraid that I would fall a year behind. It was becoming increasingly harder for my family to tolerate the separation and the feeling of uncertainty.

Finally, in late November, we got a notice that my green card was ready to be picked up at the American consulate in Abu Dhabi. After a brief trip to Abu Dhabi, I finally had my green card in hand, and we ventured on the trip to join my father and sister in Memphis, Tennessee. The trip was fairly eventless, except for an incident at the Tehran airport, where an official mistakenly thought that we did not have all the necessary documents to exit the country and nearly gave my mother and me a heart attack.

So on December 20, 1994, roughly sixteen years ago, I arrived in the United States. After the initial settling in, my parents started looking around for a school to enroll me in, a private school that is. Any remote thoughts that they might have harbored about the possibility of enrolling me in a public school vanished immediately after my mother briefly visited a public school nearby and was appalled by the sight of students my age smoking and what she perceived as the intimidating posture of some of my prospective male classmates.

So they finally chose a private all-girl high school in Memphis designed for the daughters of the select wealthy and famous in the city. A factor aside from the good education provided in the school was its sex-segregated nature. As I had spent my elementary and secondary education in a sex-segregated school system similar to other school children in Iran, my parents presumed that the setting of the new school would make me more at ease. Little did my parents know that the high tuition that they were paying for that semester in a high-class school did little to make me feel at home.

Even though there were efforts by the school administrators and students to make me feel comfortable, I had an intense sense of nostalgia for my intimate group of childhood friends. I had dreams each night that I had gone back to Iran and was chatting with my two closest friends. But alas, I would wake up in the morning, and not only was there no sight of my friends, but I had to go to school, feeling isolated and depressed. In fact, many a time during our breaks, before I knew it, everyone had departed, and I sought refuge in the bathroom, crying and remembering the good times in Iran where during our school breaks, I was always surrounded by friends, longing for a quiet moment for myself.

It was partly the language barrier that had led to my sense of isolation. Even though I could read and comprehend most everything, I had a hard time communicating. It took me another year to become proficient in everyday conversation, and another three years to become familiar with the various slangs used commonly by teenagers. I remember getting frustrated over the meaning of 'cool,' having heard it so often that I finally had to ask my classmates to explain the significance of this mysterious word to me. They tried hard, but failed to make me fully grasp the meaning.

The language barrier was further compounded by the cultural one. One day, a handful of my classmates and I were sitting around and they all started talking about their boyfriends. Not only did I not have any boyfriends at that time, or in fact, for a long time after that, I found the concept of a girl my age going out with boys a bit unusual and unacceptable.

It was furthermore a challenge for my classmates to accept me, as many of them were not used to seeing foreigners around. They had grown up and studied in a fairly homogenous community. The occasional exchange student who they encountered was from western Europe and therefore much less strange looking and behaving than someone arriving from some far away place named Iran, practicing a scarcely known religion called Islam, and writing in such funny looking characters that bore more resemblance to drawings than to regular alphabet.

And there was, furthermore, the socio-economic gap. The first day that I arrived, the school administrators assigned two of my classmates to be my companions so that I would not be totally alone. During the first class period, Algebra I, one of them was standing by the door waiting for me to get out so that she could introduce herself. My classmates later told me that looking at her from a distance, they thought that she was a guard for the newly arrived foreign princess. They were talking about me! Being from extremely wealthy families, my classmates could not even imagine that a girl from an ordinary family newly arrived in the country whose only means of livelihood was her father's salary (which provided for an adequate, but by no means luxurious, life) could accompany them at that school. She had to be a princess or otherwise someone who could afford a guard.

The gap in our families' wealth was in fact one of the factors that made me most uncomfortable at school. This was best illustrated by the striking difference in our clothing. In Iran, during elementary and secondary school we were all assigned uniforms consisting of pants, long coats, and scarves, all the same color. We would wear this uniform every day, accompanied by warm sweaters underneath, and jackets and hats in the wintertime. Never did I have to worry about what to wear to school or exhibit excessive concern about the way I looked. Nothing could be more different than the norm in my new school. Not only did I not enjoy the comforts of a uniform anymore, but I also had to worry constantly about what I would wear to school. Jeans were not allowed and dressing up was in fact encouraged. There was no need for official sanctioning of elegant clothing however, as the norms of fashion observed religiously by all my classmates did the job adequately. They mostly wore chic expensive-looking skirts and dresses all throughout the week. The most distressing fact at that time for me was that none of them seemed to wear the same outfit twice. It took me a long while before I felt confident strolling around in whatever I had on on a particular day, choosing to neglect the probing glances of my classmates trying to figure out where I had bought my outfits from and possibly how much I had paid for them.

I also scarcely felt comfortable as the only Muslim in the school, and the only Iranian no less. Our history teacher had a map hanging on the wall of the classroom where Iran had been pinpointed as a state supporter of terrorism, making me feel most unwelcome, even though I as an individual Iranian, a teenager much less, had little to do with whatever policies the Iranian government pursued.

It was three months into my arrival when the news of the Oklahoma City bombing broke. I was most apprehensive, as speculations immediately began flowing that the perpetrator could be from Iran or Iraq. I was most relieved when it was revealed that the perpetrator of this crime was not a Muslim.

Compounded with all these difficulties was the lack of the warm familial network. Not only were there no more of the weekend visits to the grandparents' house where I was surrounded by aunts, uncles, and cousins, but the usual sense of warmth at home that I had grown up with was lacking as well. The move had proved especially hard on my father. He had enjoyed especially high status and prestige in Iran as one of the most well-known specialists in the whole country and an associate professor at a well-known university. Now he had been demoted to the status of a chief resident, having to take orders from his previous companions who had now risen to the level of department chiefs in the hospital. He was used to the respect that patients pay to physicians in Iran, as something that they feel is naturally owed to them, and was shocked by what he deemed as rude patient behavior. Neither was he used to the pager system and having heard so many horror stories about patients who would resort to ruthless lawyers at the first opportunity to make poor doctors go bankrupt, he was scared of making the slightest mistake. He was also stressed about earning enough money to feed his family, something that he was scarcely ever worried about before in Iran.

In fact, scarcity of economic means was something that my family and especially the two of us sisters were not used to. Instead of enjoying annual trips to Europe and spending our holidays at our villa by the seaside on the north of Iran, we all of a sudden had to worry about how much money we spent at the grocery store and whether the clothes we bought were on clearance.

To this day, I cringe whenever I think of those first months. The culture clash and extreme sense of nostalgia for home made the early months far from pleasant for me. This feeling of unfitness and longing to go back did not last too long however. My father got a better job opportunity in Michigan and we moved to Troy, a suburb of Detroit, at the beginning of my junior year. In many ways, this was a haven for me. I enrolled in a public school where there were many others who looked different and spoke various languages at home. The average student did not come from an exceptionally wealthy family, rather a normal one, just like mine. I was still occasionally and sometimes ruthlessly teased about my foreign looks and behavior and had to spend many a lonesome lunch period at the student cafeteria, as nobody would sit with me. But gradually I made friends and started to feel more at home.

In my senior year in high school, my father decided to go back to Iran to practice medicine in his old office. The pressures of the U.S. system had proved too much for him to adapt to at his age. Even though suffering from loneliness and being separated from his family, I could feel that his sense of pride was restored as he spoke of how, on his first day back, there were about a hundred patients at his office, many having brought flowers and sweets and thanking him for having come back.

After having spent four years in college in Ann Arbor and three years in law school, here I am, an Iranian-American lawyer. I now enjoy a fair number of friendships and do not feel the tendency to go to the bathroom during the breaks at work to cry any more. I occasionally do have dreams about my old friends in Iran (many of them have also left Iran), but have managed to keep in touch with most through email and Facebook. I never managed to resume the old family gatherings—not even when I go back to Iran, as most of my family members have left—but I cherish different family bonds now as I am an aunt myself and have an Iranian spouse. I cherish the vast opportunities for learning and academic progress and the relative freedom to state my opinion I have here; things that I would have never dreamt of if I still lived in Iran.

One of the freedoms that is most appealing to me about living in the U.S. is the right, free from governmental interference, to practice one's religion, or no religion at all. As an ACLU lawyer, I now get to defend this and other fundamental guarantees contained in the Bill of Rights. As I watch with interest and apprehension the movement reverberating in my birthplace over the past two years and cries of "Azadi" by the people who poured out in the tens of thousands into the streets to demand greater freedom, I am reminded of the importance of these rights. We cannot afford to lose any of these fundamental freedoms, as evidenced by the willingness of people in my birthplace to risk their lives to secure them.

uralized
njoy almost
Zen
Aliens
live
move freely a
they are entit
nd to s
dom

AMITA RAO

RE-CREATING HER

With surgeon-like precision, I pried, my questions like tweezers, trying to pull out the thorn stuck under my mother's skin.

"No, wait, wait—hang on! You worked in a jewelry store while you studied for your exam? How?"

"What do you mean how? I worked—that's how," Amma's exasperated voice traveled down the phone line between New York City and Atlanta.

Amma doesn't quite understand my fascination with the woman she used to be. As far as she's concerned, she, an Indian immigrant now living in the city of immigrants, had done what she had to do. The woman I knew growing up in that yellow house with the red roof in the heart of immigrant Queens, the one who did what was expected, worked, cooked, followed society's customs and who urged her daughter to follow them, was the one whose phone calls I ignored. The woman my mother had been before I came into existence, the one who stormed out of her farm-life in India and hitch-hiked to the big city against her family's wishes, that was the one who enthralled me, who I idolized. After twenty-eight years of marriage however, I would only catch glimpses of this woman when Amma would casually mention, "I remember Italy. It was beautiful . . . remember Kamala Aunty? She and I did a two-month tour of Europe when we were working in Kuwait." It was in her stories of a time, of a place that I can barely imagine that I could finally see how I was my mother's daughter, so I kept prodding.

When Amma took her United States citizenship exam in a nondescript Homeland Security office in New York City, I was a month into my own journey of discovery in the land of her birth, attempting to find answers to questions of belonging in my own life. After fifteen years of living in the land of the free and the home of the brave, I was still coasting on my permanent resident card. In high school, when I became eligible to apply for that coveted Unites States citizenship, I had been too obsessed with attempting perfection as a student to recognize my privileged status. After that, there were always work, money and time—a life that kept happening—as excuses for why applying for my U.S. citizenship wasn't a priority. But when those excuses ceased to exist, I confronted the real reason for my procrastination: in English accented with an American tongue and none of the lyrical quality of my mother's, when my binational identity was questioned, I could retort that I still carried an Indian passport.

Growing up in an immigrant household in Queens, I became an expert at being Indian on one side of the front door and American on the other. My mother had left India in the mid-seventies, in her own mid-twenties, seeking her refuge. I first asked about her journey when I was a teen, managing to somehow look past my own teenage life. Her words made me look at her with new eyes, allowed respect to tinge my gaze on the woman whose backbone I had always scoffingly questioned. "I left," she stated with finality, having looked directly into my teenage eyes as we sat at the kitchen table. She drew a deep breath, almost as if for fortification to travel back to what she had escaped, and then, staring into her coffee cup, continued, "Your uncles didn't want me to go to college. There would have been no one left on the farm to cook and clean if they let me go to college."

My mother grew up in a small town in southern India, in a farming family. I had grown up on the stories of my mother waking up early to cook for the family and farmhands before racing off to school; she came back home during her lunch to serve the farmhands their lunch and sweep and wash the front yard before once more heading off over the hill to school. Her education, in a rural farm in 1950s and 1960s southern India, was a privilege, not a right. Her guarantee was that she would cook, clean and eventually be married off to do the same for her husband's family. As the youngest of seven, by the time her turn for college came around, her older sisters had already made good their escape, leaving their youngest sister to hold the fort. On the verge of losing the last of their caretakers, my mother's elder brothers put their foot down, pulling the no-money card on my mother when she brought up the subject of going to college.

In the face of her brothers' resistance, my mother did something

I wonder if I ever would have had the courage to do. "I left," Amma had stated, "I packed a bag and I walked to the bus stop." Anger took her up the hill but the bench at the bus stop took the wind out of her sails. She had no money for the bus to Bangalore, where her sisters were studying, an overnight journey on a bus through the mountainous Indian Ghats. As she told me how she sat crying on that bench, amazement began to fill her tone as she continued.

"Some guy sat down next to me and asked me why I was crying. When I told him I wanted to go to Bangalore to study but had no money for the bus, he gave me two-hundred rupees. That was a lot of money at that time. I don't know why he gave it to me, but I was grateful. I took his name and address down and promised him that I would return the money—and I did. I sent him the money later, but I don't know what happened to him, if he ever received it." Her head tilted, shook, as she said, "Can you believe it? He actually gave me the money."

Amma got up from the kitchen table and went to the sink to wash out her coffee mug. With her back to me, she concluded, "After that, I got to Bangalore and joined your aunts. I stayed with them in their hostel and went to college." "But," I interrupted, unwilling for this story to be over, "how did you pay for it?" My mother turned her head back to me, her lips quirked, something not quite amounting to cynicism tinting her brown eyes, and uttered, "Your uncles paid for it."

This is where she always used to end her story when I asked her to tell me how she left India. This overthrow of family expectations is what she associates with leaving. It took me until I was twenty-seven to ask my mother how she ended up in Kuwait, working as a nurse, how she met my father there and decided to marry him, to learn what she had to do to create a life for her husband and two children in the United States.

After getting a degree in nursing in college, Amma got a job in Bangalore. When she saw an ad a few months later asking for nurses to come to Kuwait, she was the only one in her all-male crew of nursing friends to apply. Once her acceptance came through, she finally, physically, left India. For Amma, that pivotal moment was when she walked off that farm and to that bus stop, determined to claim her life for herself.

When I finally, years after I first heard her story, questioned how she felt when she left, Amma's laughter filled the phone lines spanning the distance now between the two of us, exclaiming, "I was young and I just wanted to leave! To leave all those expectations." She left India, flew to Kuwait, lived in a hostel with other nurses from India at night and worked at a hospital during the day. "We went to class too," she added, "to learn Arabic. It didn't take long. After that, it was fun. I worked, was able to buy things for the family in India, went on a European tour with friends—it was fun!"

This was a side of my mother that she had never let me see before; I wondered who the practical woman I grew up with was, because this woman, the one who tossed off expectations and kept walking with a smile on her lips, that was my mother. I finally understood why Amma never argued against me leaving her home for a college dorm four hours away; why, when I lost my job at the start of the recession, she didn't blink twice when I said I was going to India for two months instead of starting the job search; why, she hugged me tight when I told her, at twenty-six, that I was moving 850 miles away from her, and said, "Good, if that's what makes you happy." She understood the desire to leave to find oneself.

The difference between Amma and me, however, is that she did come back to tradition. She allowed herself to be talked into a marriage with my father. "I left, but I kept coming back to India, to my family. It was home, what I grew up with," she elaborated over tea the last time I was back visiting in NYC, "my friends in Kuwait cared about me and wanted me to be happy. For them, that meant marriage and, finally, I gave in. I agreed to meet your father, to get married." Tears choked her voice as she whispered, "I lost myself."

When I asked her to describe how our family got to New York City, her tone shifted, dropped. "That's a long story," she sighed. "I've got time," I replied, prodding at her to open old wounds in an effort to soothe some of my own, to finally understand the dichotomy I saw my mother as. After getting married, she had allowed my father to take on the stereotypical head-of-household role, relegating herself to the background. When I grew up and came into my own feminism as a teenager in the late '90s, I struggled to make sense of the woman I had heard stories of, unable to reconcile them with the woman I lived with.

"You know the war had happened. We had nothing. I had to create a new life for us." Amma was speaking about Desert Storm. After watching the apartment building across the street from us in Kuwait go up in flames while soldiers marched the street with guns the size of a school-going child, my parents joined their friends in a midnight journey across the Kuwait border into Baghdad, turning us from middle-class, well-to-do NRI status to refugees. What half-truths they had to tell to accomplish this, I still don't know. After somehow ensuring we got to safety in my father's brother's house in India, my parents hatched a plan to rebuild their lives.

Most people would have remained at home, rebuilt their lives among family. Many of my parents' friends from Kuwait did do just that. But, my mother had left once and though she may have come back to tradition, she was determined to leave again. I was eight at that time. I cried when Amma left for the airport to go to New York. Eventually, though, my tears dried up and I went back to playing tag with my cousins. For two years, while she studied for her RN exam, got a job, created a new life for us, I wrote her one-page long letters every weekend in my precise, cursive writing, overseen by my father, and spoke to her on the phone. Idyllically, I believed what I was told, that she was studying. It was only when I decided to apply for my U.S. citizenship at twenty-seven years of age that I reflected on my mother's story, of her unintentional road to American citizenship.

When I called my mother to tell her I was applying for my citizenship, she snatched the conversation out of my hands. "Oh, good, finally! I've been telling you for years to do it. It's really easy. You have to go get finger-printed and take the exam and . . . ," my mother continued, zooming off into her version of being helpful. Eventually, I interrupted.

"How did you feel when you got your U.S. citizenship?"

"What do you mean? How I felt? I felt fine!" she retorted quickly. I laughed. "No, I meant, what were you thinking? Why did you decide to apply for citizenship then? How did it feel to give up your Indian citizenship?"

"Oh, honey. I left India in the seventies. It was a long time ago. And I wanted the benefits of being a citizen, for Social Security and what not. We've worked here all this time. It doesn't make sense to not get the benefits too." Unlike the identity crisis taking place in my head at the thought of giving up my Indian citizenship despite having grown up in New York City, practicality ruled the day with my mother as it has done since the day I was born. Her

U.S. citizenship was just one of those things that had to get done.

After all these years of conversations with my mother, I had learned that the question I asked her was important. She answered things at face-value. Asking her how she left home got me a story on exactly that—how she left home. A question on how she got to Kuwait resulted in the steps preceding the event with no elaboration on the actual experience of being in Kuwait. So, I finally asked her the question that I knew would reopen old wounds.

"How was leaving India for America different from leaving India for Kuwait?"

The silence itself that reached out to me through the phone lines wept. I didn't have to see my mother's face or her voice to know that the smile that seemed to live perpetually on her face had fled. In a low, pain-filled tone, Amma pushed the words towards me slowly, "I was young when I went to Kuwait. I didn't have to worry about you and your brother." I heard what she didn't say. There was no option for failure; she had to make it work, one way or another. And slowly, she told me how she made it happen, how she lived with a friend and her family, how she would wake up in the morning, take her friends' kids to school and then take the train to a job working under the table at a jewelry store, how she, a woman with a career in psychiatric nursing, babysat for money, something that I used to do while I was in college.

Eventually, she became a companion to an old woman and went to live with her. "She paid me well," Amma elaborated, "so I quit all my other jobs and studied while I worked for her. It was hard to study before. I passed my exam that summer. After that, I got a job, got an apartment,"—her tone was finally getting more upbeat—"and then you guys came over." Fifteen years after she brought us to NYC, my mother finally got around to applying for her own citizenship.

I took my mother's journey full circle, went back to India, to find my own answers. My road to U.S. citizenship was filled with blocks I placed for myself to prove what my features announced every time I looked in the mirror, what my brown skin color stated, what made most Americans of European descent ask the very hated and clichéd question, "But where are you really from?" As part of the 1.5 immigrant generation who grew up in the United States, I had developed my own set of issues, of having to prove that I was enough, both here and there, that I belonged, selfishly, in both places.

Searching for a place for my identity in this world, the U.S. citizenship wasn't just a practical process as it was for my first generation immigrant mother but more of an emotional journey for me as the daughter of the woman who had chosen to leave her home.

During my hiatus in India, my mother had joined me for a bit on a vacation of her own. My mother and I had gone shopping where I, with my short city haircut, attempted to blend in, pretend that I still belonged. My mother-tongue fell from my mouth, smooth, lyrical, just like my mother's voice, to prove that, in my blood, I was still Indian. Amma, however, replied in English, outing me, outing us, allowing the shoe salesman to jack up his rate a few hundred rupees once he realized he was dealing with people who earned in dollars instead of rupees. I snapped at my mother for that the entire evening, as if she had insulted me in my own home, when in fact it was the home she had grown up in.

Eventually, it was while I was spending time with my family in India that I understood what my mother had left. I had raised a few thorny family issues to which a family member had replied, "If your parents hadn't taken you to America, things would have been fine. You'd have been married by now with a couple of kids—and you'd have been fine." There are some that can accept that life and be happy; I don't judge them for it. However, I knew it wasn't for me and my decision was made. I could visit home but I could never live there. My mind, my interests, my life, my contributions to society, were in America.

In a roundabout way, tracing my mother's footsteps back, I came to the same conclusion my mother had come to: once you leave home, returning is never the same so it's best to just keep moving forward. But, unlike my mother's practicality, mine was spurred by the emotional nature of wanting to belong, to feel an unquestionable right to home somewhere. At the discovery of finding it neither here nor there, it was only practical to flinch at being marked as an outsider in both places, as so different as to be considered alien, unnatural. It is only practical to choose to be considered natural, normal, in the society I have grown up in by going through the naturalization process.

I tell myself this version of the truth to soothe the constriction in my chest as I apply for my glossy U.S. passport and look up the process to apply for a visa to visit my family in India. A hollow space in me attempts to wrap itself in comfort that isn't marred with resigned acceptance, a reminder of always being my mother's daughter.

rican War

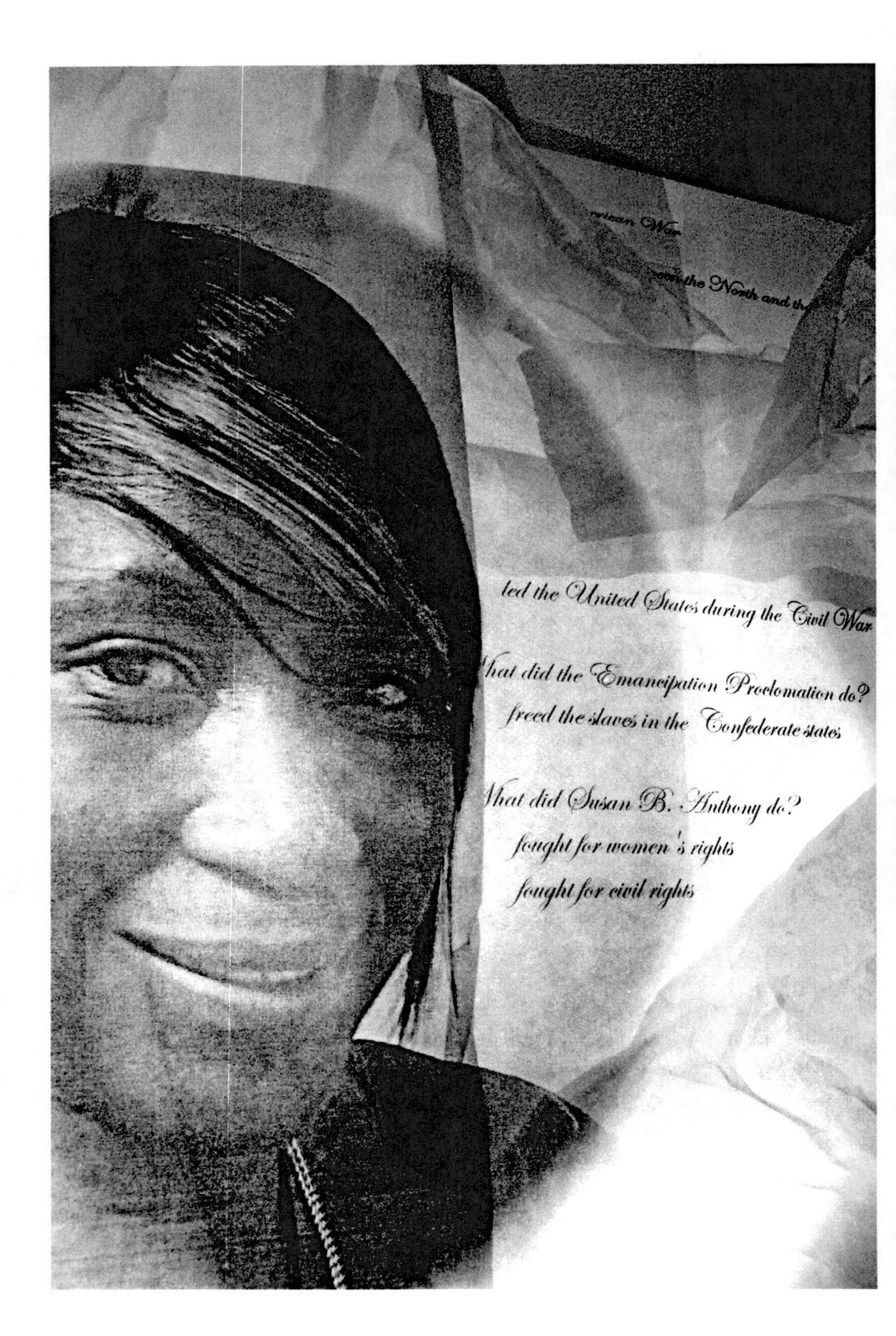

the North and th

led the United States during the Civil War

hat did the Emancipation Proclomation do?
freed the slaves in the Confederate states

hat did Susan B. Anthony do?
fought for women's rights
fought for civil rights

WHAT WE DO FOR OURSELVES

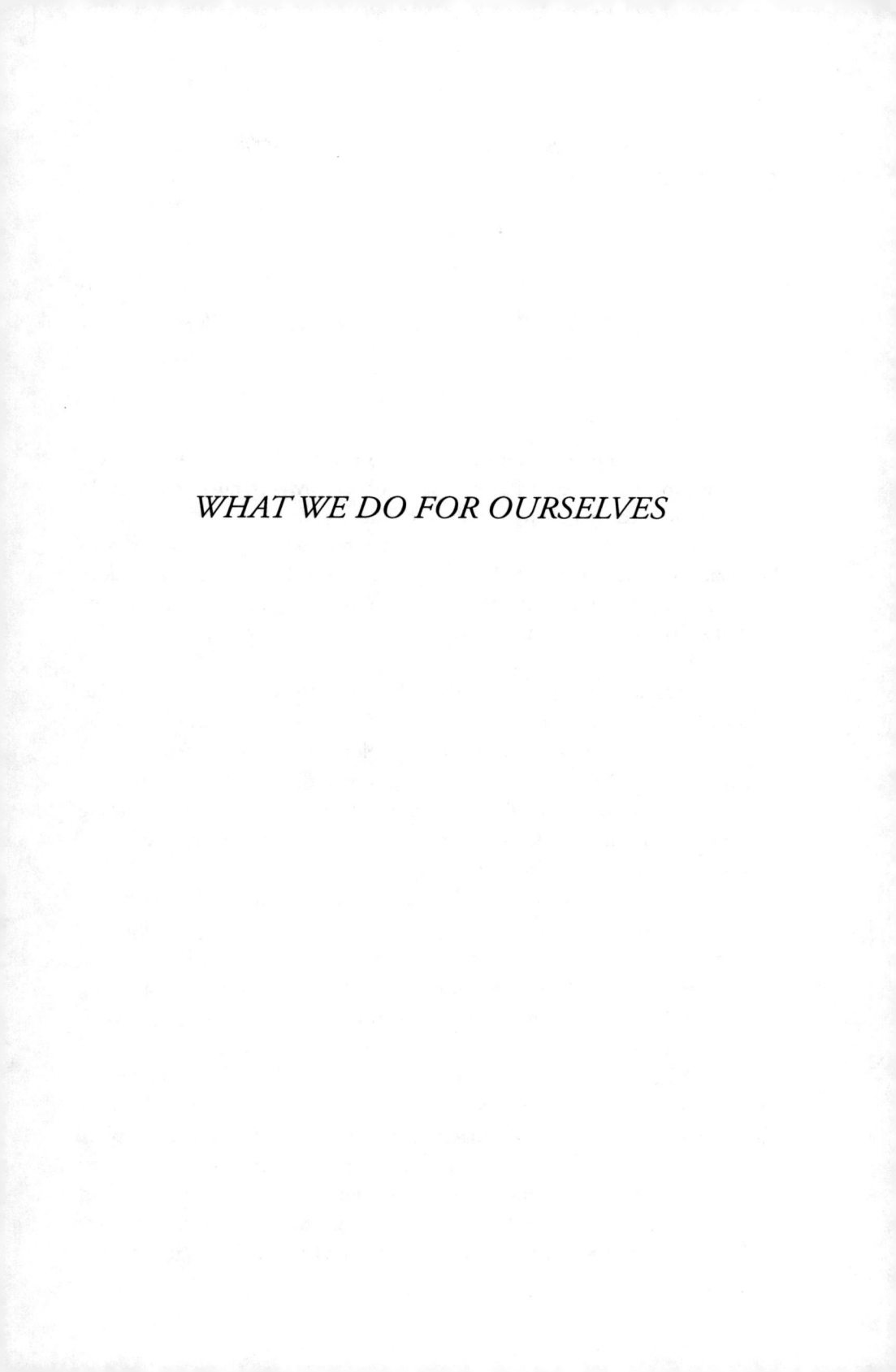

BORYANA ZEITZ

RUNNING AND CRYING IN AMERICA

I come from a line of men who ran towards the place they wanted to belong to, with everything they had in them. My grandfather, born in 1912, ran towards his country. Balkan conflicts had caused Bulgaria to lose territories and with that, his home remained outside of the newly redrawn borders. My father, born in 1952, ran towards America in pursuit of freedom and opportunity. But he had to give up halfway through the race because he couldn't leave me and my mother behind a wall that no one knew would one day turn into dust and German souvenirs.

I was born in 1976, early enough in history to experience a totalitarian regime, but late enough to not get damaged by it. As I was running in the sweltering streets of downtown Los Angeles towards my naturalization ceremony, I thought of these men, one long gone and one healthily flourishing in Bulgarian academia, and of my own journey here. My journey to becoming an American was not unlike that of many immigrants before and after me— part joy, part discovery, part heartbreak.

At eighteen, I flew across the world with one suitcase that contained my favorite books, a set of bed sheets and a sweater knitted by my grandmother. I came to the U.S. on an academic scholarship to attend a prestigious liberal arts college in upstate New York. It was my first time in an English-speaking country and my second time on a plane. I was the first girl in my family to leave home for another continent and a life that no one could imagine.

More importantly, it was my first time being identified as different from the rest. I was the only student who spoke with an accent in most of my classes at a preppy, largely non-diverse, wealthy college. I came from a place most people had never heard of (and some, much to my dismay, confused with Bolivia). I was without money, or parents who visited on weekends, or places to go during breaks. In turn, having grown up in communism and having lived through political and economic tumult, I thought that the obsessions of my peers—lukewarm beer and fraternity parties—were juvenile and boring. What we had in common, however, was both elemental and supremely important—we were learning, growing up, figuring it out.

My path after college took me to a job in New York City, the most vibrant place I had ever seen, then law school, then a big law firm job in Los Angeles. Along the way, I exchanged my student visa for a work one, the visa for a green card, and that for an American passport. I also confirmed what I had only suspected about America at eighteen—that it would greet me with open arms and give me education, opportunity without discrimination and the ability to achieve solely on the basis of my own merit.

America has also taught me about participating in the democratic process as a voting citizen and has made me realize that if you have a voice, silence is not an option. With every upcoming election (local, state or nationwide) I read, I discuss issues and candidates, I urge my friends to be fired up—even if fired up means voting for the opposing side. I tell them, having lived through the opposite, that being a part of a democracy is both an incredible privilege and incredible responsibility, and that we deserve the governments we tolerate.

I now realize that on my journey, with its American goals and destinations, I lost a piece of Bulgaria. For the most part, I speak Bulgarian only once a week on the phone with my parents. I reminisce about Bulgarian customs and holidays but seldom celebrate them. I visit Bulgaria but no longer think of it as home. The Bulgaria of my childhood, however, will always live through the fabric of my dreams and in my heart.

Tonight on my drive home from work, I listen to a story on NPR on the anniversary of September 11. A firefighter recalls digging through the rubble of the World Trade Center where I used to work a month before the attack. Through muffled tears, he describes looking for survivors and finding only body parts and carefully wrapping them in the American flag. I listen to the story and I start to cry as I can feel not only this man's pain, but the pain of every American who is seeing his people reduced to a handful of dust. Like most arrivals anywhere, mine, as a half-American, half-Bulgarian, is bittersweet.

NIKOLINA KULIDŽAN

BECOMING AMERICAN

My wipers on medium speed, I drive north on Highway 1 through the gloom that is Monterey Bay in July. The fields of artichokes stretch both east and west of the highway and the farm workers in bright yellow raincoats and red baskets strapped to their backs provide the only color in the gray, foggy landscape.

I navigate towards Elkhorn Slough Visitor Center more by instinct than by memory, singing along to Bruce Springsteen's rendition of "Old Dan Tucker." Of all the American music on my iPod, Springsteen's remake of the old folk songs seemed the most American, which is why I chose it as the soundtrack for this drive.

I follow the curvy, tree-lined street, hopeful that the entrance to the park will be obvious. A handful of protestors holding handmade signs and waving American flags make the gate hard to miss. "Sam Farr is a socialist," "Proud to be an American," and "Protect our borders," are among their messages. I slow down to read more of their posters but the cars start piling up behind me and I follow the parking attendant's instructions through the gate.

A persistent drizzle welcomes me as I walk out and I can't help but question the wisdom of an outdoor ceremony. Far worse has been endured to become an American citizen, I remind myself as I walk across the parking lot.

"Hey," I hear a loud, familiar voice. "Is there a 'Speak now or forever hold your peace' part to this ceremony?"

I turn around to see Andrei, my now-retired boss and a dear friend.

"I don't think so," I say and smile.

"Well, that is unfortunate. These fools don't know what they are doing." When we hug I know home is here too.

My relationship with America has always been a tumultuous one. Even as a teenager for whom a McDonald's milkshake was the epitome of gastronomical joy, I had somehow gathered that I was supposed to despise such blatant foreign encroachment on our Serbian soil and soul. So I did. But when my mom asked me if I was interested in spending my senior year of high school in the U.S., I didn't hesitate.

Although in my teens my future wasn't the highest of my concerns, one had to be blind not to notice the miserable way most people lived in Serbia. Middle-aged professionals sold smuggled gas and cigarettes on the streets, the elderly dug through the dumpsters and slept on the streets, the city buses were too packed to close their doors, and the students and teachers were too busy protesting various social injustices to spend any time in the classrooms. For those who knew how to capitalize on the state of near-anarchy, the times were ripe. For the rest, they were hopeless. On some instinctual level, I must have known that if I stayed in Serbia, I would join the latter group.

On top of that, there was also the fact that I had already been uprooted once when my family fled the civil war in Bosnia and Herzegovina several years earlier. Since then, I had become more like a moss, anchored to the ground with tiny threads, than like an oak, with strong, deep roots that don't survive transplanting. In some ways, Serbia was as much a new ground as the U.S. would be and since I had taken there well enough, I figured I could take elsewhere too.

That is why, in the summer of 1998, I bid my family and friends a farewell and traveled half-way across the world to try my luck. While the professed reason for my year-long visit to the States was to perfect my English, both my family and I knew that I would do my best to find a way to stay there. I can only guess how my parents felt sending the younger of their two children into the big, wide world, uncertain what it was they were sending her into or if she would ever return.

When I first arrived in Utah, I was too busy adjusting to a new life to ponder the fairness of the fact that I had to travel so far in search of a prosperous and dignified existence, which seemed reserved for only a small fraction of the world's population. Instead, I busied myself getting straight A's and surfing the web for a college scholarship, in hopes of one day becoming a part of the fortunate minority. Only occasionally, a vague pang of guilt reminded me that the sinking ship I was deserting was my country, which, despite its pitiful current state had provided me free education and healthcare, and was still home to everyone I loved.

I didn't wonder at the time if the phenomenon now widely known as 'brain drain' was only a less brutal version of the practice once known as 'blood tax.' Starting in the sixteenth century, every half dozen years, Ottoman emissaries swept through the conquered regions of the Balkans, taking young Christian boys away from their families, to convert to Islam and groom for service to the Sultan. Having received a top-notch education, the children grew up to become important religious, military and political figures, reaching the positions of power and wealth they could have only dreamed of had they stayed with their peasant Christian families.

Although I left the Balkans voluntarily, it seems to me now that my family paid an equally high price.

While we wait for Andrei's wife Sara to join us Andrei hands me a manila folder.

"I think you'll like it," he says.

Inside the folder is a photocopy of Andrei's naturalization certificate from more than forty years ago. The son of Russian World War II refugees, he was born in 1947 in a refugee camp in Germany, where he spent the first three years of his life before his family was permitted to emigrate to the U.S. His colorful and contradictory baby-boomer life included coming of age in Vietnam, becoming an impassioned, life-long anti-war protester, and retiring after thirty years of service as an Army civilian. Save for micromanaging me at work from time to time, Andrei has become one of my dearest friends and, more than three decades of age difference notwithstanding, the one who most closely shares my worldview. It somehow feels right that Sara and he are here with me now.

The three of us agree to meet up after the ceremony and I go to collect my Citizenship Tool Kit from the tables set up at the far end of the parking lot. Despite the unceasing drizzle, the ladies who work the tables are cheerful. Like the parking attendants and the rest of the ceremony organizers, they look at me like older siblings seeing their baby sister out on her first date—proud and patronizing at the same time.

In the sleeves of the glossy black folder I find a voter registration form, the words to the Oath of Allegiance I am soon to swear, a 3x5 American flag, a letter from President Barak Obama addressing me as a "Fellow American Citizen," and a few other educational pamphlets.

These materials in hand, I follow the crowd around the Visitor's Center and into a small open-air auditorium surrounded by trees. A dozen rows of benches are already half-filled by the time I get there. I scan the crowd of my soon-to-be fellow new citizens and feel hesitant to disappear in their midst. Andrei and Sara are in the back row, but as a participant I have to sit in the front. I find an aisle seat, put the folder on the damp wood, and sit down.

As I look around, I recognize a few colleagues. We exchange polite nods but nobody feels too talkative. Years of waiting and uncertainty, thousands of dollars in fees, the distant homelands to which we will soon swear off our allegiance, and lifetime's worth of gains and losses now balancing on scales visible only to us make this occasion one of deep contemplation rather than one of unqualified cheering.

As the benches fill up, the organizers and the media shuffle around. The red, white and blue pattern can be seen around the stage, in flowers, balloons and other decorations. The effort to make this feel like a special occasion is touching—it's clearly the result of the work of a few dedicated individuals rather than any large-scale government effort.

The program begins and several speakers take turns at the stage. As my hair grows damper, they praise Monterey weather, reminding us that it is over a hundred degrees on the other side of the hills. They also joke about the Tea Partiers assembled outside the gates, point out the importance of preserving our natural resources, and encourage us to vote and make this country what we want it to be. One sentiment is the leitmotif of the event, however. Each speaker is eager to welcome the fifty-three new immigrants to "the greatest nation on Earth."

The phrase has always grated on me and my impending citizenship does little to temper that. Tuning the speaker out for a moment, my mind tries to articulate the reasons for my negative gut reaction. I am not very successful. The best I can come up with is that the statement is utterly vague yet pretends to be so self-evident as to obviate the need for further debate or analysis. It robs an individual citizen of doing the hard but transformative work of defining for herself what it is that she loves about her country and what it is that she wishes to change. Besides, having ascertained America's status as the greatest, the statement seems to suggest that improvement is unnecessary.

It's only a few days later that I come across a quote which sums up my objections more succinctly. Speaking at a commencement ceremony at Dartmouth College in 1965, Stewart L. Udall said: "We have, I fear, confused power with greatness."

Only months into my American adventure, NATO announced its decision to use military force against Serbia if the Serbian government didn't agree to withdraw all its troops from Kosovo, the country's southernmost region and one with a majority Albanian population. For a while, I dismissed the threats as the usual political posturing, or even more cynically, as a White House-led effort to distract the public from the Monica Lewinsky scandal.

But this time the politicians meant what they said. Operation *Allied Force*, sinisterly nicknamed *Merciful Angel*, began on March 24, 1999 and lasted 78 straight days. In over 36,000 combat missions NATO forces dropped 23,000 bombs and missiles on a country the size of Kentucky, targeting everything from military installations to civilian bridges, telecommunications and factories, and causing upwards of five hundred civilian casualties. In his televised address, President Clinton stated that the war was not being waged against the Serbian people but against Milošević's evil regime. But as I watched the images of Belgrade in flames, and heard of bombs falling less than quarter of a mile from my family's home, it was difficult to see this intervention as anything but a double tragedy: an alleged attempt to avert a humanitarian catastrophe by causing another one.

Meanwhile, the people around me did all they could to provide me with comfort. My host parents came up with endless ideas for entertainment all specifically designed to divert my attention from the news. Teachers invited me to their classes to educate other students about the conflict (you can imagine what a fair and balanced education they received!). Kids I didn't know stopped me in the hallway to tell me they were sorry about what was happening in my country. And my journalism teacher, Ms. Perry, went one step further. Would it be OK, she asked me, if she started a fundraising campaign to send me to college? My own scholarship-search efforts had stalled as I questioned if this was the country I wanted to live in. But Ms. Parry's offer was so unusual I couldn't easily dismiss it.

"Really?" I wanted to ask her. "You want to spend *your* time asking other people for *their* money to send *me* to college?"

Apparently such things were done in America.

Over the next couple of months my story became the talk of the school. There were car washes, and instant photo booths, and kids carrying jars through the cafeteria at lunch time. I was spared the intimate details of Ms. Perry's money-making machine, but by June, as *Merciful Angel* was starting to run out of targets to lay its mercy upon, a small Utah community was completing its own mission—to send a random Serbian girl to college. They had raised $10,000 for someone most of them had never met.

Congressman Farr, the ceremony's keynote speaker, finally takes the stage. Hosting a Fourth of July Naturalization Ceremony has become his tradition and on this rainy day his speech wears marks of having become routine. Mr. Farr seems earnest, however, in his assurance that the diversity we bring to America is what makes this country great and he appeals to us to never lose our heritage. *E pluribus unum*, out of many one, is after all this country's motto, he reminds us.

Sixteen countries are represented in the crowd of fifty-three soon-to-be new citizens. When the congressman leaves the stage, the emcee tells us that she will call the countries alphabetically and when our country is called to stand up and remain standing until we say the Oath of Allegiance and thus conclude the Eucharist-like process of turning the non-Americans into Americans.

The first country to be called is Bosnia and Herzegovina. I turn around surprised to learn that there is a fellow compatriot in the midst. When no one stands up it occurs to me that this is me. With a slight sense of panic, I stand up. I am certain I had entered Serbia as the country of citizenship but apparently they go by the country of birth. Not that it would matter in most people's cases. People from Canada, Chile, China, Cuba, El Salvador, Great Britain, India, Iran, and Iraq all soon join me in standing. When the emcee calls Mexico, the majority of those still sitting stand up. A malice-free chuckle escapes from the crowd.

Once everyone is on their feet, we recite the prayer-like oath. I stand straight and solemn, my right hand raised as if to protect myself from a punch, and join the colorful choir in declaring "that I absolutely and entirely renounce and abjure all allegiance and fidelity to any foreign prince, potentate, state, or sovereignty of whom or which I have heretofore been a subject or citizen."

Rather than repeating these words I wish our task had been to write a thousand-word essay about what it is that we love about America and that makes us American. I would look at the people around me and draw my inspiration from the fact that we have all overcome tough odds to be where we are, and that what guided us was a common human drive to better our lives. That our luggage of stereotypes and preconceived notions was most certainly lighter now than it had been when we first arrived. That each and every one of us has been affected by the American fever of positivity and optimism, a prevailing sense that you can do it if you just set your mind to it. That through all the trials and tribulations, many of us have grown in our faith that people are basically well-intentioned, can be trusted, or at the very least, should not be feared.

But that is not our assignment today, so instead I conclude the oath by repeating: "I take this obligation freely without any mental reservation or purpose of evasion, so help me God." To seal the deal, I take the small American flag out of my packet and wave it towards Andrei and Sara. I smile and Andrei takes a picture of me. When I look at the photos later on, I see it's a very goofy smile.

The moment we are dismissed, the journalists surround us. I know it would be impossible for me to sum up my feelings in a quotable line so I do all I can to avoid eye contact. That doesn't stop a young man with a notebook from blocking my path. "I love it here," I later read my words in the paper. "I have a good life here."

On the way out, I pass the protesters again. They seem to have come prepared with different signs for before and after the ceremony. "Honk if you are proud to be an American," is the prominent one now. These folks are old and I imagine that having something to passionately believe in provides their lives with meaning. I give my horn a quick punch and I smile. A white-haired man wearing an Uncle Sam hat smiles back and waves at me. It's my effort for the day to do as I preach—to be tolerant.

If someone had told me that my first job out of college would be for the U.S. Army I would have called them crazy. Three years after the bombing, Serbia was still in ruins, my friends divided time into BB and AB, Before and After the Bombing, and I still refused to stand when the national anthem was played.

But aside from a short stint as a barista it was.

I ended up in Monterey by accident. My plan was to wait tables for a year while I applied to MFA programs around the country, going back to school being the surest way of extending my legal residence in the U.S. But this plan was wrought with uncertainty. For one, there was no guarantee that any school would take me. Despite my good GPA and a few awards and honors, my English was still wanting. And even if accepted, paying for another two years of school would have required a miracle beyond anything I had yet witnessed.

So when my fellow ex-Yugoslavs started dropping by the coffee shop where I worked to encourage me to apply to the military language school up on the hill, my resistance gradually crumbled. One day I decided to take someone's advice and call the Chair of the Serbo-Croatian Department. What I wanted was some sort of reassurance that working for this institute would not make me a traitor to my people or undo the fact that I was a Serb.

The man on the other line was Andrei. I don't remember much of what either of us said, but I remember that he was loud, direct, abrasively funny, and indignant towards authority, so much so in fact that I was surprised he didn't have a Serbian accent. As much as it's possible to do so in a five-minute telephone conversation, we connected.

A couple of months later I got the job. The letterhead spelled out the name of my employer: "Department of the Army." I shook my head as I looked at it. *Et tu, Brute?*

Whatever stereotypes I might have had about the type of people who enlisted in the military crumbled quickly upon my arrival. The students I taught ranged in age from eighteen to forty and were as different from one another as they were from me, but almost all of them shared a few traits—intelligence, wit, and curiosity. They brought to mind the line from Leonard Cohen's *Last Year's Man*: "And though I wear a uniform, I was not born to fight." Some of them had joined the military out of a nebulous sense of duty and service, some for the benefit of college education, but none, I am sure, from a desire to kill or destroy.

I taught for two years before Andrei, who had by then taken to endearingly calling me "Little Shit," asked me if I wanted to help him on a new project he was tasked with. Nearly six years later, with Andrei long retired, the office we started could hands down win any competition for the most harmoniously diverse workplace.

My new boss, Jiaying, came to the U.S. from China when she was in her twenties and has spent most of her life here. My officemate Jelena, a Croat from Dalmatia, came to the U.S. after she married an Army Major whom she met while working as a translator for the U.S. troops in Bosnia. Eileen, a Turk from Bulgaria, came to the U.S. on a college scholarship, and eleven years later, wears no trace of a foreign accent in her impressive English (one of six languages she speaks fluently). Emma, our bubbly and competent Admin Assistant is a second-generation Mexican. Vojin, our IT specialist and a Serb like me, has been in the U.S. for over twenty years, yet hasn't lost the habit of speaking at the eardrum busting volume his ancestors must have used to call across the Balkan highlands. The military side of our operations is no less diverse. CW2 Bokde was born in Argentina to an Indian father and an American mother; SFC Wilkins is an African American; while Cpl Brooks, the newest addition to our handpicked crew, is of Irish descent.

My colleagues and I don't see eye-to-eye on many issues, but the beauty of it is that we don't have to. We do our jobs, we are nice to each other, and we tolerate the differences even when we don't like them. It's pluralism at its best. It's what I love about this country when it works, and what I want to change about it when it fails.

A couple of weeks after the citizenship ceremony I throw a big party. On top of having turned American I am also turning thirty and I feel that neither of these occasions will mean much if I don't share them with the people I love. I send out invitations telling my friends to come dressed as anything American, and instead of gifts to bring me a phrase in English I might not know or something they had made themselves.

The party is a hoot. Emma and her husband come dressed as egg and bacon. Eileen is an American tourist, wearing a visor, Hawaiian shirt, calf-high white socks and sneakers. Jelena is a flapper girl. SFC Wilkins and Cpl Brooks are civilians, for a change. There is also a Marilyn Monroe, several cowgirls, and a Jedi. The party is in full swing when we start playing a drinking game (a uniquely American tradition). The rules are simple—each time I don't know a phrase someone has prepared for me, everybody has to take a drink. I learn things like "sloppy seconds," "bee's knees," and "half a bubble off." I would have no doubt learned more had I not taken so many sips.

As the game winds down and everybody is about to resume the wine drinking and dancing, Emma surprises me by taking the microphone. In her former Army Captain voice she addresses the crowd:

"May I have everyone's attention, please."

People quiet down and look at her but immediately shift their gaze to the side. Through the wide open door that leads into the hallway comes a voice I know well but have never heard sound so resolute.

To the sound of "One, two, one, two, one, two" my two colleagues, Eddie and Kevin who, while I wasn't looking, have transformed back into their doubles—SFC Wilkins and Cpl Brooks—are now marching out into the crowd each holding one corner of an American flag. In their uniforms, so tall and strong and reverent, they are the most beautiful sight I have seen in a long time. As they march in place, I feel a knot form in my stomach. SFC Wilkins issues the commands and they execute them as one. They hold the flag horizontally as if it was a sheet that needed shaking. Then, they bring the ends together, folding it in half. With surgical precision, they turn and fold the flag while the crowd watches them breathlessly. An occasional whisper is shushed immediately. When the flag is no wider than a foot, Cpl Brooks folds his end of it into a triangle. Taking small steps forward, he continues folding and refolding the flag until the stripes are subsumed by the stars and the flag is a pressed pyramid between his palms. As SFC Wilkins raises his stiffened hand in a dramatic slow-motion salute I am hardly even breathing any more. He takes the flag from Cpl Brooks, and Cpl Brooks repeats the salute. With the flag still in his hands, SFC Wilkins, my colleague of over four years, welcomes me to the ranks of those he serves and protects every day he wears his uniform.

"I tried to find a flag that was flown in Bosnia. But this is the best I could do. This one was in Kosovo," he says as he hands the flag to me.

Many thoughts compete in my mind. The guys must have gone through a lot of trouble to find a flag which could help bridge the gap between my two homelands. As touched as I am, though, I can't help thinking about the fact that flags are folded at funerals, that funerals are for soldiers who die in wars, that wars are waged by power-thirsty politicians, and that flags are a symbol they use to keep their power. To top it all, of course, I feel a dose of sourness at the fact that an American flag had ever flown in Kosovo.

But a surge of emotion overcomes all those thoughts. The two men standing sternly in front of me just gave me something from their hearts. And when I accept the flag from Eddie I accept it with my heart.

Navy of the
armed rebellion
government of the
necessary war

KAREN LEVY

AMERICANS

California, 1989
  I can tell my mother is nervous because she has the airport look on her face, the "don't speak unless you are spoken to, and let me do the talking" look. But this plan will only work for a brief period of time, until she and I are separated, and the man seated across the desk at the federal building will insist that I speak.

  The day of our citizenship test arrives, to determine if we are worthy of becoming Americans, and ready to give up our Israeli identities after years of traveling between our two homes. So far the immigration building and its officials have done their best to make us feel like outsiders, drab walls and unsmiling clerks unwelcoming to the handful of immigrants seated on hard plastic chairs in the waiting room. When our names are called my mother grimaces at the mispronunciation of both. Her Jolanta sounds like the Hispanic Yolanda, and my Caren sounds like Karen, her own fault for choosing to spell it that way. For a brief moment I wait for her voice to correct the speaker, set the clerk straight by pointing out her error. But it does not come. She must want what is promised behind that door more desperately than her need to prove the bored employee's ignorance.

  The man behind the desk is polite, but all business. Between questions about the number of stripes on the American flag and what the Fourth of July means, I try to read his face, but fail. My time in the United States and my exposure to its men has been too brief to help me decipher masked Anglo expressions. Mediterranean men hide nothing, their emotions writ large for all to see. Teachers yell their dissatisfaction, bus drivers growl their stops, and strangers flirt shamelessly, their dark eyes following a young woman's moves, desire licking at her heels like hungry flames. The blue-eyed official seems satisfied with my answers, making a few notes before surprising me by reaching across the desk to shake my hand, as he congratulates me for successfully responding.

Within days my mother and I are standing in a judge's chambers, our right hands over our hearts, about to pledge our allegiance to this country that has opened its doors and welcomed us in. In a few years' time, I will be almost indistinguishable from other citizens. My English will no longer be halting, my responses more natural, not scripted as I read passages I write out before making a simple phone call. I will learn to enjoy the quiet of a suburban afternoon, without neighbors peering into our windows, or showing up uninvited for coffee. I will remember to buy my swimsuit when the smell of snow still lingers in the air, quickly learning that the good ones are gone once summer sales arrive. One day I will sit on a grassy hill surrounded by other Americans, waiting for darkness to fall and fireworks to explode across the night sky. And I will feel the pride swelling inside me, understanding the words a roomful of newcomers are now repeating in various accents, some with tears in their eyes. I know it is good for us to finally be Americans. Our presence in this country will no longer be legally challenged, although my mother's thick accent will always earn her impatient looks from those claiming they cannot understand her. Yet I'm not certain I am prepared for the declaration we are all making—absolutely, and entirely renouncing all allegiance and fidelity to the place from which we came. "I take this obligation freely without any mental reservation—So help me God." But I *do* have reservations. And, *which* god? The one before whom old Jewish men in long black coats sway and rock, their prayers floating out the windows of the synagogue down our boulevard, while waiting children swing from the branches of the gnarled fig tree outside? Or the one all our American neighbors celebrate as they gather round twinkling, tinseled trees framed in windows of houses to which we have yet to be invited?

I'm not finished being me in the country I left; I haven't had enough time watching older Israeli girls to see if I want to be like them. Despite our frequent leave-taking, and my familiarity with the view of its receding shores from behind the thick window of a plane, I love my country with the fierceness and absoluteness of first love and youth. And now I am expected to be American, simply because our green cards expired and mother thinks the timing is right.

Not yet. Not when I still ache for the warmth of a Mediterranean beach under my bare feet, for the rosy sky of an Israeli sunrise as doves coo on my window's ledge, and for my best friend's laugh when I tell a joke in the language in which I still dream. Not when my father's absence is welling up and filling my own eyes here in this room during a ceremony he is not a part of, and never will be.

I don't know how to be American yet. Years still need to pass before I will adopt the easy banter and slightly drop the literary English with which so many non-native speakers give themselves away. It will be years before being referred to as "you guys" doesn't make me cringe and correct the waiter showing me to my seat. I refuse to use the word "cool," and the beautiful cowboy boots my American husband will buy me one day do not grace my closet yet. I still believe the clerk at the grocery store really wants to know when she asks how I'm doing. And when the friend I just met says she'll talk to me later, I wait for the phone to ring all afternoon before I realize I must have misunderstood.

In Israel I was a work in progress, watching others for clues to tell me who to be. Now I have a wardrobe filled with too many selves, and I don't know which one to wear.

GOING HOME

Israel, Morning, July 11, 2006
The Israeli airport official is young, her hair as curly as mine only darker, no gray snaking through it yet. The sun has barely had time to warm the day, and her face already shows all the signs of boredom and weariness. I smile warmly, a habit I have adopted from my American husband, a way to charm even the most disgruntled government employee. "Good morning!" I announce in my heaviest American accent, offering a fistful of American passports through the narrow opening in her glass cage. She eyes me suspiciously, mistrusting my early morning cheerfulness, thumbs through the paperwork, and stops so abruptly that I know she must have arrived at mine. I have been caught again, trying not to be me.

Your identity number, she commands, weariness gone from her tone. Now she is awake.

"What do you mean?" I ask innocently, still trying and rapidly failing to keep the Sabra tucked out of view, the daggers out of my eyes, the edge out of my voice, the anger I know is on its way out of the slight shaking in my knees. And I am seeing myself repeating a scene which has become a familiar dance between two countries, both claiming me as their own, yet one does so more aggressively, threateningly, not accustomed to losing her battles.

"Your identity number is in your Israeli passport" the clerk explains, impatience creeping into her voice, her eyes holding mine as if to say she's giving me one last chance.

"I don't have one," I lie, my expired Israeli passport pulsing slightly in my purse, trying to give me away. I clasp the bag a little closer to my side, as if the document inside could wiggle its way out and expose me, ruin the decision I had already made on the train ride to the airport. The clerk eyes me, contempt in her gaze, and turns to the phone hanging on the wall of her cubicle. I hold her eyes with mine as she switches to Hebrew and summons reinforcements for the problem standing before her. I dare a glance at my husband whose eyes are rolling at what he knows is sure to come. And as if on cue, a tall woman is rushing towards me, determination stamped on her tight-lipped face.

"Your identity number!" She practically yells in my face, as I straighten myself for some extra height.

"I still don't have one," I hiss back, "and you don't have to yell," I add, ignoring my husband's attempt to catch my attention and my children's wide-eyed stares.

"I'm not yelling," she yells. "But if you want to leave today I need your Israeli passport!"

I am just now beginning to notice the crowd behind us, staring intently at this early morning drama unfolding before them. The threat of detaining me has done away with my last attempt at polite American control, the thought of that plane leaving without me unbearable.

"I'm an American citizen and I don't live here," I declare. "I haven't lived here for over twenty years, and if you threaten me I won't be coming back!" I want to go home, the thought hitting me with clarity it has never had before.

"With this kind of behavior we don't WANT you here!" She retorts, and the hand I plunge into my purse has figured out what it has to do even before I have a chance to think this through, as I pull out the Israeli passport and throw it at the angry stranger in front of me.

"Take it. Keep it. I won't be needing it anymore." I have switched to Hebrew without even noticing, measuring out my words carefully so their meaning will not be lost on either one of us. I don't want to make a mistake in the language I no longer live, taking the official and myself by surprise as she stomps away with my claim to citizenship in her hand. I refuse to meet my husband's eyes, knowing all too well the disappointment I would see reflected there, the words that would be sure to follow if I gave him a chance to say them, which I don't. But I can hear them anyway as I stand facing the clerk whose eyes look almost regretful for the mess she could have avoided. "You're such an Israeli," my American husband is silently saying to my back, his favorite insult when I have misbehaved and slipped into my former self, the one I took so long to wake and don't really want to shove back into the genie's bottle. The one I allowed out in my father's garden the night before, when the sadness of the next day's good-byes spilled out using all the wrong words and turning into anger he translated as weakness. Anger he no longer needed once he had found his place in the world. But I was still searching, for the land that would feel like home, for the people who would remember what had been before it all changed, for the voice in which to say it all. And anger seemed to keep the tears at bay, and I could not afford tears right now.

The official has returned our documents in hand, and without a word she offers them back, my Israeli passport included just in case I change my mind. We're free to leave and I stride ahead, not looking back but trusting that my husband and children are in tow. The faster I walk the less chance that they will see the tears that are now coming hot and furious. I make my way to the gate where a tall man is wrapped and swaying in his prayer shawl. From a far corner cigarette smoke is pouring out of the smoking section where the door has been propped open for air by the very same people polluting it. "Idiots," I mutter as I throw myself into an empty seat, although I'm also grateful for the added cause for anger, which makes leaving that much easier. My husband and children have been following at a safe distance, he placing a hot cup of coffee in my hands, while they glue themselves to the large window to watch the planes. The coffee helps, warm liquid washing away tension that had been gathering for the last three weeks, even when I didn't know it. I thought I could do it, face old friends, old haunts, introduce the present to the past, not realizing that the past was present in every turn. Not just when I chose to bring the two together.

Despite my acceptance of Daniela, my good sense telling me that she made my father happy which he finally deserved to be, the little girl in me still found it difficult to see him as someone else's husband, father to another man's children. That past was in the handful of items I recognized on my father's shelves, a statue here, a vase there, bits and pieces from a past life taking me by surprise in new surroundings. The past was in the voice of my grandmother's oldest friend, even before she opened the door to let us in. "Karushka!" Her endearing name for me a sound I had almost forgotten. Still sharp, no nonsense like all the women her age who suffered more than any human should. I had to escape into her tiny kitchen when the phone rang and she switched to Polish. It was as if no time had passed and she could very well have been talking to my dead grandmother. Even the kitchen offered little refuge, everything about it reminding me of other kitchens. Old dish towels worn to bare threads, pots predating the war that brought their owners to this land. Everything saved by women who knew what not having meant. All these reminders were too sad, not because of what they represented, but because I had never been given the choice of saying goodbye, never allowed to decide what I wanted to be. Was I the Californian returning to her native land? The Israeli exile pretending to be American? A tourist bearing gifts for old friends, returning with Middle Eastern souvenirs to hang on her American walls?

And now, minutes before boarding would be announced, the tail ends of my anger evaporating around the corner of the terminal, I finally thought I knew. There would always be a place for me on this side of the world. A bed made in my father's new house. A plate filled at my best friend's table. People who would include me in their thoughts and hearts, missing me when I was gone. But I had become more visitor than resident, my camera at the ready to capture images I no longer assumed I'd see again. I now relied on photographs, on notes carefully recorded in a journal packed for the occasion. These tools would help me stop time, preserve it before people moved and strangers' faces looked out of familiar windows. Before loved ones died and their images danced away, and buildings in which I'd spent my childhood were torn down. Before change came and I'd forget while becoming someone else, joining that life I was waiting to begin while it had kept going without me. The balance had shifted, and when the plane touched down in San Francisco, the airport official checking my passport would welcome me home, and I'd be there.

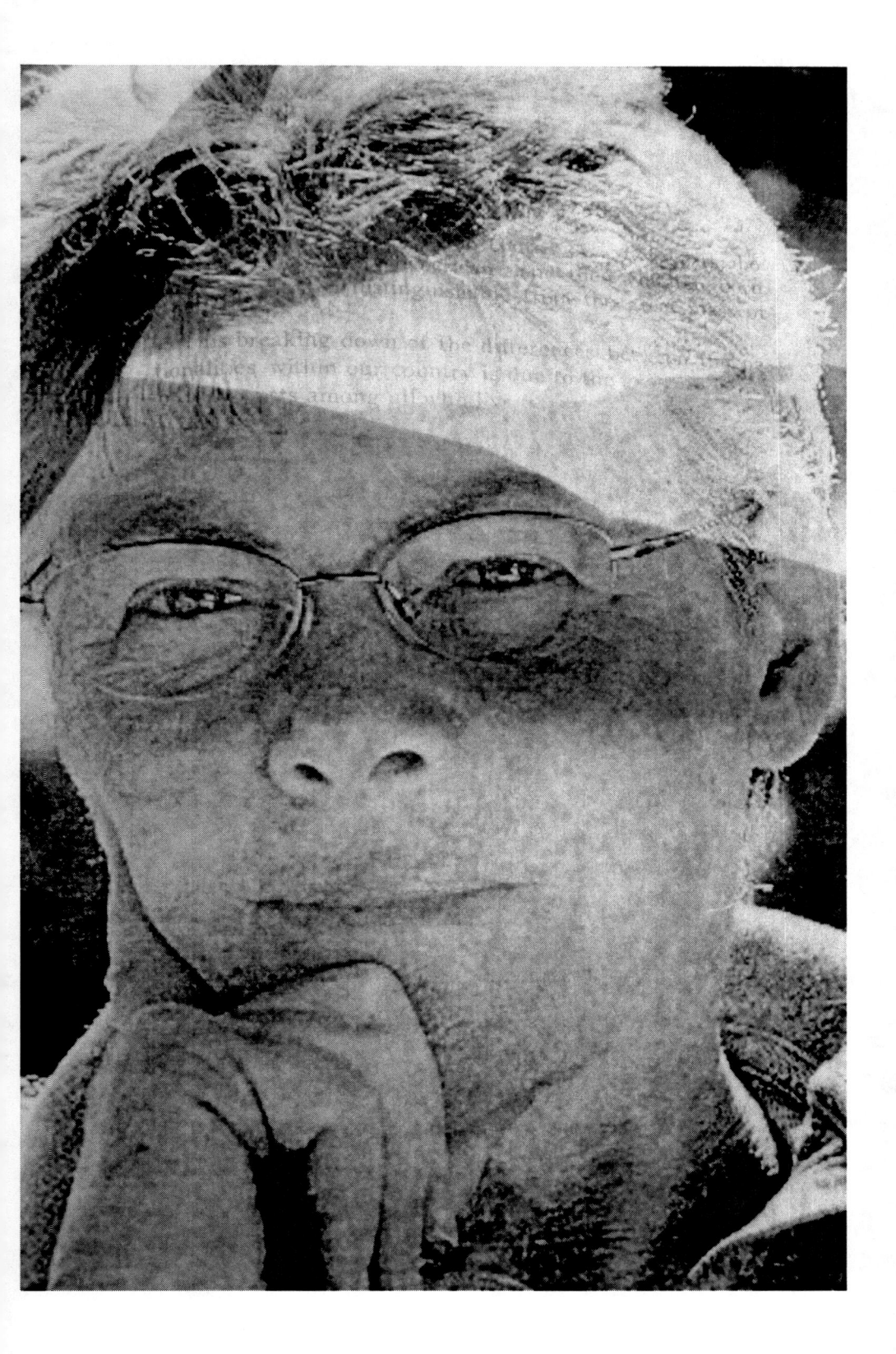

...breaking down of the differences between families within our countries is due to...
...among all...

ELIZABETH BERNAYS

LEARNING WITH POLLARDS

My large kitchen looks out onto a courtyard of green palms, shrubs and herbaceous perennials. On one wall is a poster of a painting by Vincent Van Gogh. It shows pollarded willows at sunset, the sun's low rays filling the sky and shining out at me over tall yellow grass and between the blue trunks of the gnarled trees, most of them leafless. It is a well-known painting—there are prints and reproductions of it available from hundreds of websites. Van Gogh paintings have a remarkable texture that is, of course, missing from my picture, but the reproduced painting is startling nonetheless. No other picture in my house emits such excitement and radiance.

Pollarding, a kind of pruning that is less frequently used today, was evidently common round Arles where Van Gogh painted. It encourages a close, rounded head of branches, and puts the foliage out of reach of deer. The custom was refined in formal manicured royal gardens of Europe for centuries, where the idea was to grow a durable tree to a fixed size and then maintain that tree at that same size forever.

The appeal of pollarding has waned but the practice is still carried out on old trees where it has been performed for years, and the particular garden or landscape would be much altered by leaving the trees to grow without pruning. Somehow, pollarded plane trees represented my life as I learned to become an American and spent time on the University of California Berkeley campus, where there are many such pruned trees. On my way home to a house on the hill above campus I often walked through Sproul Plaza where 'polka dot man' lay with legs in the air, 'orange man' walked in his green overalls as he carried paper oranges to tie onto trees, and older professors dreamed of the free speech movement in the sixties, still believing it was the only free-speech campus in the world.

I think also of pollards seen from the windows of Wellman Hall, the home of the Entomology Department, of which I was a member. One looked down into a square with pollarded plane trees in two rows, their knobby fists signaling upwards on winter mornings and their leafy heads shivering in summer breezes. Often I gazed out at them as I marveled at the strange fate of becoming a professor there. Wellman Hall was the memory of so much in Berkeley when I was a newly appointed professor, straight from a job as a scientist in the British Foreign Office. It was my first academic appointment, my first experience of the United States, my first exposure to the particular Berkeley culture, and exciting it was too. The dark corridors of Wellman Hall housed faculty, students, the Entomology office staff, the Essig collection of insects, a library and a teaching lab, and it was in Wellman that I attended meetings of the department at intervals and went to the chair of the department to complain.

My lab however, was three miles away, at a ten-acre site called the Gill Tract, because it was here that the Division of Biological Control had its headquarters, and as a researcher on plant-insect interactions I was to work on the biological control of weeds. At my interview I had been somewhat surprised at the rundown nature of the place, but in my excitement I looked on the bright side, imagined change, and was sure things would be fixed up for me if I were to get the job. In any case there were plenty of old rooms full of junk that could be cleared away.

When I arrived however, I was given three small rooms. They were totally empty. I was so surprised that it took me a few weeks to realize this was it! I was informed that I would get $10,000 in 'Hatch money,' but couldn't expect anything else. I realized that there was no point in getting mad, and that I should have negotiated. It was a brand new culture and I was a novice. No longer did an appointment automatically mean the provision of the wherewithal to do the work.

I used much of the limited funds to equip my lab from all the second-hand furniture and equipment places I could discover. I got a fine wooden chair made by prisoners at San Quentin jail (as determined by a plaque underneath the seat) and I cadged microscopes and lights from a professor nearing retirement. I was left completely to myself and in the absence of any project or money, I borrowed a video camera and tape recorder and embarked on something I had wanted to know for a while: can grasshoppers learn and thereby improve their foraging efficiency?

I did realize that my naiveté had been a problem, but I decided I would *show them*, and use all my ingenuity to demonstrate I could operate and do interesting research, even with almost no resources. And I would follow the topics that interested me before I embarked on biological control, especially after a more experienced expatriate in the department said to me, "You have tenure, you are a full professor, you can do anything you like. Just do something interesting and become famous and you will please higher levels at UC—that's all that matters!"

Others said, "You need to write grant proposals to get equipment," so I submitted three in the first month, after having several of my new colleagues read them. "Great," they said, "wonderful, excellent." And so I had some hope. Later, I discovered the proposals were ineffective by the accepted standards and that no one had honestly advised me, which was perhaps the hardest lesson for me in that first year. I was to make a fool of myself with the National Science Foundation and the United States Department of Agriculture review panels, all the reviewers, and even the administrative staff in Berkeley.

In time I did learn the tricks and obtained grant money—but not in those first years, and nothing was easy. First I managed to get money from a private foundation, on the advice of a good old friend on the east coast. Then I discovered one could get funds to improve unsafe working conditions and so started work on plant chemistry that required the use of toxic solvents. For this, I took my extraction apparatus out on a cart into the yard at the Gill Tract, so that I could write a report on the extreme situation of the conditions I had to work in. This got me money to roof in a space between two buildings, and make a new laboratory (without heating) where a fume hood was constructed to satisfy health and safety regulations. I was learning to be more resourceful.

But my lab remained minimal. I politely complained, but the Division of Biological Control had no money to distribute. I went up to the main campus, past the pollarded trees and into Wellman Hall to see the Chair of Entomology. His response was, "You are in Berkeley now, what more do you want?" I could have been angry, but at some level I enjoyed the challenge, and decided I would be damned if I couldn't get what I needed. Meanwhile I continued research that could be done with minimal equipment, and I hardened my resolve to work on whatever pleased me, never mind what my chairman might expect. I was learning to be an egotistical American and at the same time I was enjoying life in the Bay Area of California.

One day I had lunch with an elderly faculty member. He did no research himself, but he liked to pontificate. He said to me, "You don't want to collaborate with anyone—you need to make your own mark with single-author papers." I was aghast. It had always seemed that teamwork was the best way to do research. My experience as a government scientist in Britain involved much cooperative activity, but there had not been the fierce competition for money that was to be part of my career in the New World. However I understood his message and kept it in mind as I evolved my own research effort and worked around the problems—greenhouses with missing glass, environmental rooms and cabinets from a previous age that were all out of order, screen houses with torn screens, insect rearing rooms in disorder, inadequate quarantine facilities, leaking roofs, broken down trucks, rooms full of unlabeled insect materials from the good old days of biological control greats—Drs. Messenger, Van den Bosch and Huffaker. I had worked in several third world countries, and the Gill Tract was just like them.

Within the first few months I discovered that there was a kind of biocontrol religion. The central tenets included the following: too much theoretical work was counterproductive, biocontrol and intercropping were the only ways to deal with insect pests, chemicals of any kind were wicked, genetics was a load of baloney, molecular biology was evil and took all the money, Latin America was a good place, the other biologists including entomologists on campus were out to deprive the biological control faculty of money and facilities.

As a non-religious person, I found myself needing to go to the main campus more often. I wanted to enjoy all the seminars and journal clubs. I was exhilarated by the often-wild ideas, the wide-ranging discussions, and the novelty of getting outside the box that had been my training in England. Indeed, I was thrilled to find an environment so suited to the person I felt I was, where imagination mattered more than discipline. I bought a bike and cycled to and from the Gill Tract, chained my bike under the pollarded trees and found collaborators in the wider campus community. After my years as a government scientist in Britain I was finding out the joys of academic life, freedom, and American individualism.

One day I discovered that a newly hired young assistant professor was to be given over one hundred thousand dollars in startup funds, and I decided the time had come to make an appointment with the Provost to complain once more and request a dollar amount to complete my modest set up. She was sympathetic and immediately made available all the money that I asked for. It was a momentous occasion for I had learned to fight. I had learned to push for myself and to get what I wanted, instead of politely waiting for anyone to help me. I was learning a new culture.

I went to see the chairman of my department—after all I would be bringing money in and he would surely be pleased. Across the lawn I went, past the pollards, and up the steps of Wellman Hall two at a time, and into his office. When I told him my news he looked at me speechless. Eventually he said, "Because you are a woman I suppose!" I was too taken aback to reply, but I never forgot that jealous response. So much for liberal Berkeley, I thought.

Afterwards, sitting in Campanile Plaza, among rows of pollarded plane trees and pondering the novelty of being a professor in Berkeley, I realized that the symmetrical planting was somehow appropriate for the neoclassical architecture on parts of the campus. As I was thinking about the paradox of the 'liberal' institution with faculty who could remember the free speech movement of the sixties, and at the same time have limited ideals of equality, I was also examining the details of this lovely campus. Later, I read that the classical ideals expressed in designs by the École des Beaux-Arts began to appear on campus with John Galen Howard's Plan of 1914. He designed Wellman Hall and other buildings and organized plantings with architectural patterns in allees, bosques and hedges, and with them, the pollarded plane trees. Funny, I thought, how the trimmed trees represented a kind of tough discipline that had been my student training, while now I was really learning to branch out, but I still had much to learn.

The learning curve had already been steep though. I thought back to my interview and how incredibly naïve I was about anything to do with the university system, the Bay Area, and certainly, the United States. At my job interview I had a meeting with the Dean of the College of Natural Resources. My idea of a college was based on what I had known in London, where each college is effectively a small semi-independent university, or the system in the University of Oxford, where the colleges are independent of the academic departments. What was the College of Natural Resources I wondered, apart from the obvious fact that it included the Department of Entomology?

I kept my ignorance carefully to myself. At one point the dean remarked, "We are a land grant university."

"How wonderful," I replied, conjuring up the rich Californians that must give so much land to their famous institution.

"And we have the Experiment Station," he continued.

I was thrilled with this too. There must be some big farm or something for doing field experiments. Later, when I realized that the Experiment Station was not a place at all but an administrative structure relating to a federal government act in the late nineteenth century, I was somewhat dashed. But that was long afterwards, and it no longer seemed to matter. It wasn't for several years that I properly learned about the Hatch and Morrill Acts of the nineteenth century, allowing Congress to make regular appropriations for support of agricultural study, and land grants to make agricultural colleges within existing universities, or build new ones. Experiment Station meant Hatch money administered separately from the university budget, and research related to agriculture.

I thought back to my days in England and in the African and Asian countries where entomological work had taken me. And I thought back to my earlier college days in Queensland. Everything had been fun and interesting, and culturally it was easy to slip from one country to another. I was a British citizen, and before that, a citizen of a country that began as a colony of Britain. Coming to the United States was something altogether different. The transition had happened almost by chance, because I knew little about the big country across the Atlantic, and my European colleagues were mostly critical of it. "They kill one another," some said, or, "Think of the KKK for goodness sake." I had applied for the job in a moment of frustration with government red tape, was surprised when I was asked to come for an interview, and quite taken aback when the professorship was offered. But, adventurous by nature, I took the plunge without even thinking of what it would be like.

I was learning about individualism, a trait that is well developed in Americans and amply found in Berkeley. It has to do with that all-important independence, confidence, and much touted freedom, but also with the need to look after number one first. At least, that is how it looked to me. Confidence abounded among students and faculty, politicians and secretaries, shop assistants and street people. Richard Rodriguez writes, "(the American has) the confidence of an atomic bomb informing every gesture," and I found it catching and fun, even if it was sometimes confused with intelligence and even if it was often unwarranted. No more the rigor of strict rules or the need for anyone to give up anything to fit the overall expectations, or the community, or the institution. Replacing discipline and narrow projects, criticism of people and values, their research papers and faulty logic, their unusual beliefs and unconventional behavior, was an attitude of acceptance—a desire to include everything in the worldview. Terrorism had not yet struck.

No classified social system existed as far as I could tell, other than that of money, although there was an element of superiority about being associated with the University of California Berkeley. Joan Didion, in *Where I was From*, writes that at age thirteen she asked her mother to what class they belonged. Her mother replied, "It's not a word we use. It's not the way we think." It was this perhaps, that seemed most refreshing to me, coming from Europe, even though the class system in England was a lot subtler than Americans imagined. My New World friends like to point out that California may be different from other places in the United States, but Philip Roth had it right I believe when he summarized the difference between liberal America and more exacting Europe as "everything goes and nothing matters" versus "nothing goes and everything matters."

Now, more than twenty-five years after arriving in Berkeley, most of them spent in Tucson, Arizona, I look back with fondness to the California beginning, the home of my first six years in a new country. How I learned to be independent, more egotistical and demanding, yet accepting of others' ideas and lifestyles. Instead of the rigidity of rules that had generally made for smooth social interactions in English life, flexibility became the order of the day. Each individual had a say, and a story: a student could take an exam early if travel plans would be interrupted by waiting for the big day, a shopper at the store checkout had the right to discuss all manner of things with the cashier, even if there were a queue behind him. There were pros and cons, but I enjoyed the new life.

I became broader in my thinking, more flexible in my intellectual pursuits. I had to learn the rigors of writing convincing research grants and explaining why the work was important, a process that involved self-advertisement that had always been anathema to me yet ended up making me feel that I had a distinct place in the scientific world. The seminars and discussions, colleagues and students, took me into unknown places, brought me new ways to see theoretical problems, and ultimately made my work more rewarding and more visible to colleagues round the world. I began to actually feel the confidence that had seemed so unrelated to my life before I came to the United States.

And so, more than ever, I loved the green campus with the classical architecture, the groves of trees, the pollarded planes, the view across the

Bay to the Golden Gate Bridge enshrouded in fog. Those pollarded trees in the pale light, the western sun, the misty mornings, that couldn't be more different from the Sonoran desert where I live now, or the landscape of southern France, the willows painted by Van Gogh. The luminous picture in my kitchen, the brilliant colors, the excitement painted there on a few old pollards is a reason for standing still a while as I pass, for letting my eyes rest on a scene that at once is France and a particular painter, but is also at once for me the University of California Berkeley campus—all that happened there, and how much I learned about becoming an American.

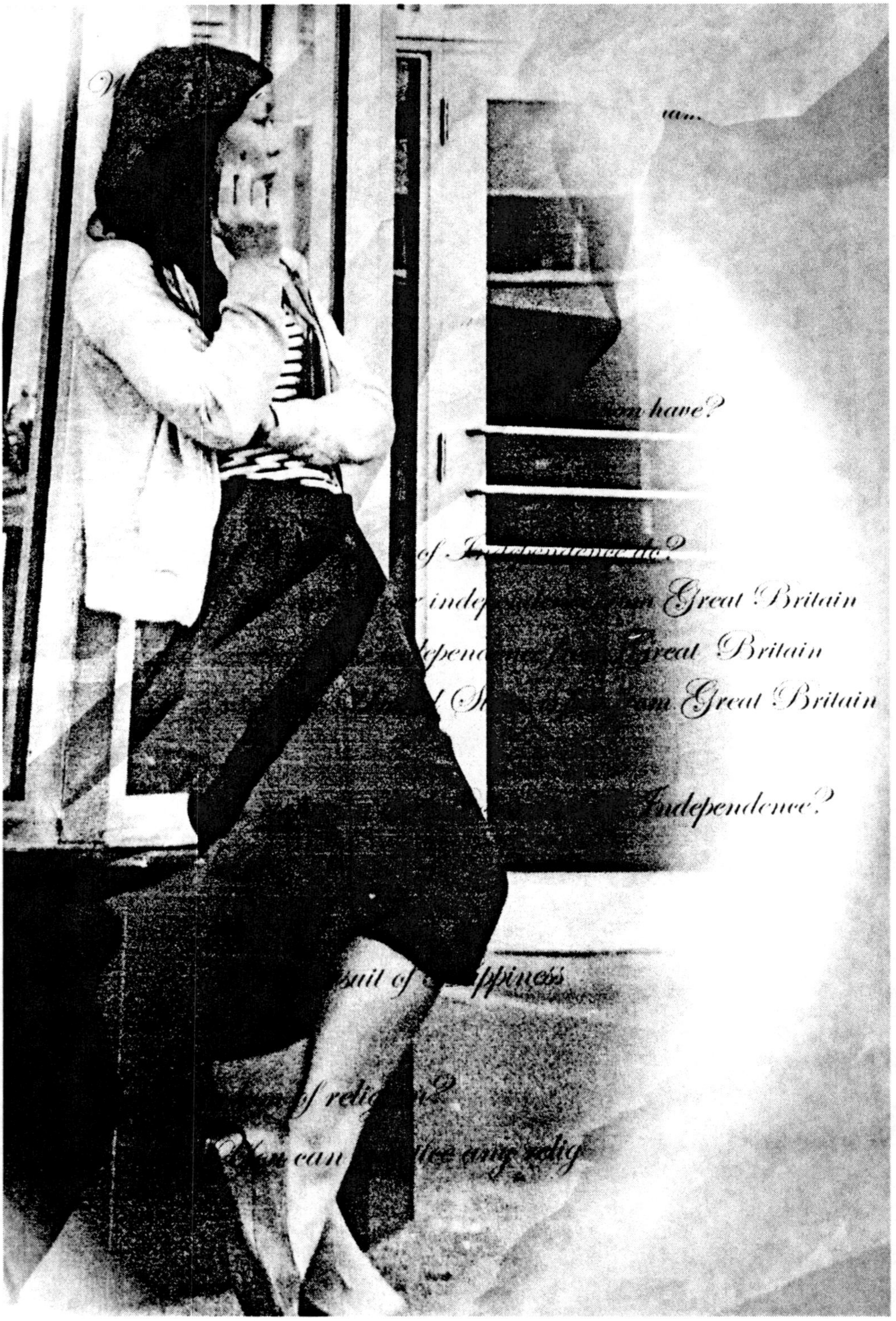

WEIHUA ZHANG

DAUGHTER OF THE MIDDLE KINGDOM

On January 31, 1989, I—a descendant of the dragon and the daughter of the Middle Kingdom—boarded a Boeing 737 at Beijing Capital International Airport on a transcontinental flight of twenty-three hours bound for the United States of America, my temporary home for the next six months. Little did I know that my journey would last twenty-two years and counting, that the United States of America would become my second home, my adopted country, and that my life would be changed forever.

The People's Republic of China of the 1980s was a hopeful place to live in. With the passing of the country's three founding fathers in 1976—Premier Zhou Enlai in January, General Zhu De in July, and Chairman Mao Zedong in September—the ten-year Cultural Revolution (1966-1976) came to an end. China slowly but surely achieved a state of normalcy. People were finally allowed to do what they did best: professors returned to classrooms to impart knowledge; factory workers churned out gadgets and gizmos to enrich people's lives; farmers reacquainted themselves with their crops; and soldiers resumed their solemn duty to safeguard the country. Gone were the days of sheer chaos and total destruction that paralyzed the entire country during the Cultural Revolution. Though our wounds were still fresh, Chinese people in all walks of life started the healing process. Once more, we were all members of a big family working for the common good of the country, the Middle Kingdom, the Center of the Earth, and the cradle of one of the world's ancient civilizations.

In 1989, I was not ready to make any big changes in my life. I had been teaching English (language and literature) at Nankai University in Tianjin, China since 1984 and married my college sweetheart that same year. Our daughter Feifei was born in 1986. Life was full of wonders. Change? I was not ready for it. I had a job for life and the respect of my colleagues and students alike. The trio of a handsome husband, an adorable daughter, and a blissful wife/mother formed a happy family. I was living in a country that was undergoing great transformations. What more would I want?

Growing up, my life had intertwined with the country's many upheavals and tragedies. I was born in 1957, the year that is forever linked to the Anti-Rightist Movement. Some 550,000 people were purged, ninety percent of them intellectuals. Punishments ranged from demotion, dismissal, forced labor camps, imprisonment, torture, and even death. This got too close to home: When I was just a month old, my mother was dismissed from her job for displaying 'rightist leaning tendency.' I was barely one when the country embarked on the Great Leap Forward (1958-59). A movement intended to modernize China, this groundless-unscientific-reckless pursuit proved a disaster that toppled the country's economic foundations. Furthering the miseries was the staggering death toll of the Great Famine (1959-1961): 15 million by the Chinese government's estimate (some western studies put the death toll at 30 million to 45 million), with millions more people displaced from their homes. Compared to my growing up years, China in 1989 was a paradise to me. I had to be out of my mind to trade this paradise for a sordid place like the United States of America, that decadent, capitalist country.

Yet, change was in the air, as evidenced by the exodus of Chinese going abroad to study, either on their own or thanks to their government's purse strings. I joined the crowd in 1989, courtesy of my university. I was sent to study at Swarthmore College, located in the suburbs of Philadelphia, as an exchange scholar for six months. What would that decadent country do to me? I did not have time to ponder. The exodus swept me away.

I arrived at Swarthmore on February 1, 1989, already two weeks late into the spring semester, yet I managed to enroll in Professor Kathryn Morgan's Folklore and Folklife class. A woman of medium height, who loved to wear colorful, robe-like garments, Professor Morgan was in her mid-fifties. Her hair was braided with an assortment of beads, and big earrings dangled from her earlobes. She was quite a contrast to the way professors looked back in China, including me. Professor Morgan was a light-skinned African American (these terms describing race and skin color were new to me). But her skin color did not shock me. After all, I had been exposed to African Americans in the past. When I was an English major at Northeast Normal University (1978-1982), Mr. John Brown—the first black person and first foreigner I had ever met—had been my English professor for three years. What shocked me or enlightened me was how Professor Morgan conducted her class. She would engage her students in critical thinking, which was a great departure from the spoon-fed and rote memorization method that had long dominated the Chinese educational system. She would bring in guest speakers of diverse backgrounds and viewpoints to enhance her students' learning experience. I recall one day when we had a guest speaker, a beautiful woman in her mid-thirties. She was a practicing witch in flesh and blood, married, with two kids! I remember asking myself: Wow, are there really witches on this planet?

But I soon grew to love Professor Morgan's class because she challenged us to think and speak our minds freely. This totally contradicted my educational experience in China. You see, I was not that far removed from a culture/country where the law of the land was to follow the leader, obey the authority, and march in unison. Our class assignments allowed me to try out this newfound academic freedom. In a paper discussing folklore's roles in the society, I used my daughter's favorite story, *The Big Gray Wolf*, to argue that folklore was alive and evolving. It was the storyteller who defined the characters (good and bad), not a bureaucratic organ that dictated the norm. In Feifei's story, the Big Gray Wolf is a benevolent character. He shares his candies with little kids and small creatures alike. He is not the evil Wolf in *Little Red Riding Hood*. I received an A for the assignment, my first taste of academic freedom! At the end of the semester, I gained a better understanding of the universality of folklore, a greater appreciation for cross-cultural differences, and a deeper respect for intellectual freedom. I was forced to admit that just like Chinese, Americans were genuine, smart, and reasonable human beings, not the 'foreign devils' we had called them in China. I also understood why we should not view people through tinted lenses. Whether we were Communist Chinese or Capitalist Americans, we were more alike than different. On the personal front, what followed was a natural progression: I developed a bond with Kathryn (sadly, Professor Morgan passed away in December 2010) and regarded her as my mentor and surrogate mother. Our friendship exemplifies what is possible for the peoples of China and America, countries on the opposite ends of cultural, social, and political spectrums: we can and must learn from each other. Together, we can build a better future for our two peoples.

While at Swarthmore, I also took an Honors English Seminar with Professor Peter Schmidt, who has remained my friend to this day. The course focused on the American modern period of 1900-1945 and challenged us to explore the literary texts in their cultural, historical, and social contexts.

In one session, we discussed some poems by H.D. (Hilda Doolittle), which proved too foreign to me. During the break, I approached Peter and pointed to a word I did not understand: 'deflower.'

Peter's fair complexion turned to crimson. "It means to lose one's virginity."

"Oh." I could feel the heat on my face as if I were on stage, with all the spotlights on me. To say I was embarrassed was an understatement, but honestly I had never encountered that word in my decade-long study of English. The Chinese saying 'never too humble to ask' was the driving force behind my question. In another session, we read Gertrude Stein's *Autobiography of Alice B. Toklas* and talked about their relationship (that was when I first heard the word 'lesbians'). One classmate also mentioned James Baldwin and how his book, *Giovanni's Room*, depicted a white American expatriate's struggle to come to terms with his homosexuality (another new word!). This was all foreign (no pun intended) to me, this discussion of homosexuality, gays and lesbians. We did not have homosexuals in China. Or so I thought.

"So what do homosexuals do?" I again raised my innocent question with Peter.

Looking back, many of my questions in those early days in the United States must have been downright rude or even offensive to some Americans. These questions exposed my ignorance and my lack of understanding of the western world, which had been compounded by China's isolation. When the People's Republic of China was founded on October 1, 1949, the West viewed the Communist takeover with hostility and severed all ties to the country. Between the economic and political sanctions of the West and its self-imposed isolation, China folded inward. The door did not crack open, however slightly, until the historic visit by the U.S. President Richard Nixon on February 21, 1972. So for a stretch of twenty-three years, China and the West had operated on two entirely different tracks. There had been little understanding between the two sides. Propaganda and misinformation had jammed the airwaves across a vast geographical and ideological divide.

But it gives me hope to think that ignorance can work both ways, and a mutual understanding can be bridged between China and the West. In my case, ignorance proved to be a blessing in disguise. After the initial culture shock I had encountered at Swarthmore, I became a sponge, absorbing as much as I could. Hence, when someone in class mentioned Toni Morrison's

Beloved, I couldn't wait to get my hands on the book, to figure out for myself why the house on 124 Bluestone Road was haunted (I would come to wonder later in 1998 why I bought a house that also had '124' as its street number). My experience in that Honors English Seminar led me back to Toni Morrison. Five years later in 1994, while a doctoral student at SUNY-Albany, I focused my dissertation on the works of contemporary African-American female novelists, such as Toni Morrison, Alice Walker, and Gloria Naylor. As a woman, I felt inevitably drawn to the powerful yet intricate works of these women writers. For the first time in my life, I faced the world as an unapologetic, unabashed woman. Coming from someone like me who had written a college paper on John Steinbeck, who had devoted her master's thesis to Ernest Hemingway's tragic heroes, who had been unfamiliar with the feminist movement and unexposed to works of African-American female (and male) writers before coming to the United States—this was *a big deal*.

The culture shock I encountered in America has forced me to examine my own beliefs and purpose in life. No one can change history, nor can I change my past or China's yesterday. I have, however, utilized the knowledge and perspectives gained in the United States to better understand the social issues and human matters that affect my country, my family, and my own life. A case in point is Betty Friedan's *The Feminine Mystique*. My mind was blown away when I first read it in 1990. I could never have imagined that in the paradise-on-earth that was the United States, across its affluent suburbs, there lived thousands of women whose very identity/existence hinged on the happiness/well-being of their husbands and children (I realize now what an oversimplification my reading had been; I was not in a position to fully understand her book at the time).

As a woman, daughter, wife, and mother, I found Friedan's book provocative, which led me to re-examine women's place in China. True, the modern Chinese society advocates for gender equality. Symbolically and significantly, China's Marriage Law (1950) was the first law the young country passed after its founding in 1949. The law gives women the right to inherit properties, bans arranged marriages, and prohibits human trafficking of women and children. Women in China have enjoyed voting rights with their male counterparts from day one. On paper, at least, Chinese women get equal pay for equal work. However, I also became keenly aware of the fact that I had been a victim of gender discrimination (another new concept). Upon graduating from the English Department of Nankai University in 1984, I had been assigned to teach at the Department of Tourism (less prestigious—teaching English to future tour guides and mid-level hotel management), and let go by the English Department (more prestigious—teaching literature to English majors). Why? I was a woman. In spite of my superior academic performance, the English Department selected my two male classmates over me. At least the department chair was frank: "You are a woman; you will get married and have a child soon; you will miss work when your child is sick; we need male teachers in this department." How ironic, the department chair was also a woman!

My scheduled six-month stay in the United States turned into one extension after another, coupled with my status change: started graduate study at SUNY-Albany in September 1990; became a green card holder in 1995; and in fall 1996, I began teaching fulltime at the Savannah College of Art and Design in Savannah, Georgia. All along, though, I clung to my Chinese citizenship and agonized over my next move. Finally, I chose to become a naturalized U.S. citizen and took the oath on January 2, 2002. When faced with the most difficult decision in my life, I simply resorted to one consideration that had been behind the decisions of millions of immigrants before me: my daughter's future. Feifei, a tenth grader at the time, would soon be applying for college admission and scholarships. As a naturalized citizen, she would be eligible for all scholarship opportunities, including those open only to American citizens. Didn't all immigrants come to this country—the beacon of hope—in search of a better life for their families?

In the post-Swarthmore years, I trudged along the journey to the West, to the discovery of a Self I did not know, to a Chinese-American identity that is a fusion of two divergent cultures, and to an artist/teacher who is committed to building a mutual understanding between her two peoples. As a Chinese American, I am no longer a transient but a contributing member of this great country. In July 2003, I put together a photography exhibition, *Take Root and Blossom: Chinese Immigrants in Savannah (1880s-1990s)—a Photographic Journey*, the first of its kind in Savannah, to draw attention to the contributions of early Chinese immigrants to the city. It marked the first conscious act of citizenship on my part: that I am a Chinese immigrant and these are my ancestors; that I can take root and blossom in this land of opportunity by standing tall on the shoulders of all immigrants before me.

With the great success of this exhibition, I found my niche. In October 2007, I staged a solo exhibition *Homebound*, which featured twenty-four black and white photographs selected from my trips to China in 2005 and 2006. Taken in several cities across China, these candid images provide the American viewers an intimate and unvarnished look at today's China: from playful children on their way to school to energetic elders exercising in the parks; from the hustle and bustle of a farmers' market to a happy family gathering on an eighty-five-year-old man's birthday (my father's); from a snow-covered corn stack in the northeastern city of Siping (hometown to my husband) to a giant Teapot King in the southern charm of Wuxi. This is a vibrant and multi-faceted China the West's photographers often either fail to capture or neglect to cover. Could it be that they, too, are looking at China through tinted lenses?

As a college professor, I see my classroom as a unique platform to advance a better understanding between my two peoples. My own cross-cultural perspective is certainly a big help. I am often compelled to share with my students the early culture shock I experienced so as to emphasize the importance of mutual understanding between China and the United States, between the East and West. Recognizing the need for diverse voices in American Literature course offerings in my college, I started teaching Asian-American Literature in 2006. This divergent yet remarkable body of literature has challenged my students to dig deeper into who we are as a country and as a people. It is gratifying to see what my students have been able to take away from the course: that America is a nation of immigrants, that people of Asian descent are an integral part of America, that literature opens our hearts and minds. Together, my students and I rebuilt the Transcontinental Railroad alongside the Chinese laborers; reclaimed our picture-bride foremothers from Japan; reacquainted ourselves with the Japanese Americans in the internment camps; relived the horrors of the Second World War, Korean War, and Vietnam; and reaffirmed our admiration for all the immigrants, from Asia and elsewhere, who have enriched our lives as well as their own.

Twenty-two years is just a tiny step in the long journey of the human race. But twenty-two years have added enough wrinkles to my face and gray strands to my hair that I can claim I am now an older and wiser woman. I am glad that my very first air travel twenty-two years ago took me to the United States of America. After the initial culture shock, the learning began and it has never stopped.

I will perform work
rtance under
d by the law; and
thout any mental
purpose of evasion; so h

MARIA SHOCKEY

ORAL HISTORIES: MEXICAN-AMERICAN VOICES

INTERVIEWEES

Interviewees' names were changed to protect their privacy.

Sandra Rocha, 36, is a divorcée and single mother currently living in Las Vegas, Nevada. She was born in the border town of Juarez, Mexico, and her family immigrated to New Orleans, Louisiana, when she was nine. She has been in the insurance business, in realty, and is currently in college. Sandra hopes to graduate with a nursing degree. Her interview was conducted in English.

Rosa Valdez, 78, was born on a small ranch in the town of Guasave, in the Mexican state of Sinaloa. She married in her late teens and settled on another ranch. The couple had ten children, and most of them were adults by the time she migrated to the United States at the age of sixty. Once in the U.S., the older couple lived with their daughter and her family. They have twenty-six grandchildren and twenty great-grandchildren—who live throughout the U.S. (mostly Los Angeles and Las Vegas) and northern Mexico. Her interview was conducted in Spanish. Her responses have been translated into English.

Lucero Gomez, 36, was born in Jalisco, Guadalajara, Mexico. She immigrated to the small town of Pahrump, Nevada in 1997. She is married with three children. She likes to work parttime as a cleaning lady because it allows her to contribute to the household income. Lucero graduated from high school in Mexico and plans to continue her education when her children are older. Lucero has not returned to Mexico since she immigrated to the U.S. Her interview was conducted mostly in Spanish. Some English was spoken.

Consuelo García, 43, moved to Nevada, in 1990. She is a housewife with three children, and her husband is a construction worker. She became a grandmother in 2008. She feels that it is not yet the time to work outside her home. Her two youngest children, ages sixteen and six, still need her. However, Erica has career aspirations. She hopes that someday soon she can begin taking nursing assistant courses at the local community college. This interview was conducted in Spanish.

Teresa Hernández, 44, was born in Chihuahua, Mexico. She immigrated to the United States in 1995 at the age of thirty. She is housewife and a mother of four. Her children's ages vary from one year to eighteen years of age. She has two grandchildren. This interview was conducted in Spanish.

Norma Alvarez, 42, was born in Mexicali, Mexico. She is the oldest of eight children. When she was sixteen years old, her family immigrated to the U.S. She is married to a traditional Mexican man, and they have two children. She married in her early twenties and became a housewife. After fifteen years of marriage, she began taking courses at the local college. Currently, she is a full-time medical assistant. Her interview was conducted in English.

Monica Anderson, 39, was born in Baja California, Mexico. Her family immigrated to the United States when she was thirteen years old. She is married to an Anglo American and has two children. She has worked as a language translator, sales representative, postal worker, and as a chiropractic assistant. Her interview was conducted in English.

Irma Martínez, 43, immigrated to the United States from Zacatecas, Mexico in 1973. She was seven years old at the time; she is married and has seven children. She works as a loan officer, and she was the first bilingual employee at her bank. Every semester, Irma helps Mexican-American children who have graduated from high school register at the local community college. This interview was conducted in English.

DEFINING ASSIMILATION

Sandra:

Assimilation means looking white. I wanted the 'American Dream.' You know? I wanted the big house, two cars, and my children in private school. I had to learn to hide who I was and try to lose everything that made me Mexican. I was a cultural chameleon. I could easily fool my co-workers into thinking that I was white. I had to learn when to use my Mexican accent, what to wear.... I even learned to use different vocabulary when at work. I was afraid of being labeled a particular way. I had to work harder than my co-workers to prove that I could be just as smart as them. It wasn't until my late twenties that I 'became white.' I started working at a firm and got a big house. I'm thirty-six now. . . . I don't believe the same way as I did in my twenties. I'm someone different. Once I got confidence and succeeded at my job, I felt like I could go back to being Mexican. 'Being white' put me in debt. I was in constant competition with my co-workers. Now, I'm happier. I've returned to my heritage.

Rosa:
I believe that assimilation means to have a good life here. Assimilation would have to include both American and Mexican cultures. English is important . . . learning the language is necessary. I don't know English, but my husband has to work. It is very useful to him. I'm just here in the house. I like it this way. I go to church and to the grocery store, too. This is where I come in contact with American society. Everyone smiles at me. I don't want to be a citizen or anything like that. . . . I just want to be close to my husband and my family. My husband wants to become a citizen, but I don't. This is why he's learning better English too. We don't have any education, but my husband was able to find employment in a casino. Financially, we are better off here than in Mexico. I don't want to return to the ranch I grew up in. I don't want to return to Mexico. This is my home.

When I lived in Mexico, I used to make fresh dough for tortillas every day. I used to make it from scratch. When my village became a bit larger, a grocery store used to sell readymade tortilla dough. My husband used to buy me the dough. It was easier on me. Now in Las Vegas, (laughs) I just go to the store and buy the tortillas already made. I just have to warm them up.

In Mexico, we didn't have electricity or inside plumbing. We didn't have air conditioning and the heat was almost unbearable. My body is used to having luxuries now. I never complained in Mexico because being hot or having to hassle over household luxuries was part of daily life on a ranch.

Lucero:
Assimilating into American society is a difficult experience to define. My response would be different than an American's. For a Mexican, if I had to leave my native culture just to become an American citizen, I would have

to say that I wouldn't want to assimilate or become American. If I had to combine both cultures . . . which parts of each culture would I lean to? This is my way of thinking. If I tried to become only American, then I would have to erase everything about me that makes me Mexican. No one can do this. Not even my children. They have Mexican blood in them. I believe that my children will think the same way. My children know Spanish, and they eat mostly Mexican food. If we had to choose cultures, I wouldn't want to be American because I couldn't leave my traditional customs. I'm raising my children with both cultures . . . Mexican and American. To be successful in America, we need both cultures. It is the same with language. Having two cultures and two languages will benefit the person. Being bilingual or even knowing many cultures makes an individual richer. I think knowing only one language is boring [laughs].

When we moved here, my husband was the only one who worked. Work is the first thing, I think, towards assimilating. My husband began working, and we began forming a home. We thought that there was no going back to Mexico. Our visas expired, but we had already established ourselves. Our children were in school. The same motive that made us move away from Mexico, kept us in the U.S.—work. Throughout the years, a friend of mine asked if I wanted to work cleaning houses. I told her that I was willing. I mostly clean houses for the Americans because Mexicans are pickier.

When we arrived in Nevada, we had family that spoke English very well. They helped us with everything . . . grocery shopping, doctors' appointments, etc. There came a time when I realized that it was time to learn English. A second step towards assimilating is learning the language. After a few years, my family forced me to learn it, and I did. My mentality was more advanced than when I had first immigrated. I had to study English through my kids' homework. I had a good experience learning English.

I have a life here. I feel safe here. Now, in Mexico there is too much crime. I don't wish to go back to live. It hurts to know that my native country has turned into a country of violence. There are good people and there are bad people. But . . . I would like to be able to trust a policeman if I was in trouble. In Mexico, I don't think I would be able to trust him. There's so much freedom in this country that I feel that I can put trust in everything. My husband and I are struggling for a better future for our children. The future is not for us—that time has passed. It's their future.

Consuelo:

I guess . . . combining Mexican and American cultures. In order to assimilate and triumph in American society, we don't have to lose all of our Mexican culture. We are still Mexicans. We don't have to lose our native language. We have to learn to do as Americans, but yet figure out a way to stay Mexican. It's possible to assimilate and combine two cultures. The first step in assimilating is learning the language. We need to force ourselves to have conversations outside our home. We need to learn to speak. I have experienced racism here . . . in the United States. In Nevada, there are many people who will yell at us for speaking Spanish in public. They will say "This is America. Speak English. . . ." This is discrimination. This is our land . . . at least it was. I should be able to speak Spanish if I want to.

There's a lot of racism in the school system too. My children had to deal with it. Their language tutors didn't stay with them for the allotted time . . . they didn't care much to teach them English.

We have to learn the ways of America. We have to assimilate . . . at least partly. We have to leave our home. I wanted to assimilate quickly. I wanted to learn English, and take some classes in college. I always dreamed of studying . . . continuing school. My husband didn't allow it. He wanted me to stay home to take care of the children. I didn't want to work, though, either. . . . I wanted to study. I wanted to do something with medicine . . . maybe a nurse's assistant. Even now, I want to study.

But then I had my first born, and I wanted to stay home with him. I was naïve. I had a little time, and I thought it was time to do something outside my home. Then, I found out I was pregnant with my second child. The cycle began again. Assimilation does not mean that we have to raise our kids the American way either.

When my first-born began kindergarten, I realized that I needed to assimilate more. It was necessary. Then my second child started school. I had to learn English. I could only read and write first . . . but I couldn't speak. My children suffered . . . they needed my help and I couldn't help them. I wish my children were less shy. I wish they would be more outspoken. My daughter says that it is my fault because I never learned English. I didn't have the capability to help them.

Teresa:

I think that assimilation means speaking the language of the country:

English. I didn't want to assimilate at first. I wanted to learn English and to prosper, yes . . . mostly because I want to be equal to everyone. . . . But I want to maintain my ethnicity. I don't want to change.

But I think it's better to have two cultures. We should continue being Mexican, but we should respect the American culture. We have to make ourselves a complete person . . . a person with two cultures. That's what I've been teaching my children. I don't want them to forget their family in Mexico. It hurts me when my children don't want to speak with their family. They're losing the connection. My children are Mexican, but they speak English great. I don't want them to forget their origins. I try to keep up with Mexican traditions . . . but I find it difficult. They just have a different mentality than I did. Everything outside the home is assimilation.

My girls are everything American outside our home. I have to understand that I have to meet them halfway. We both have to work to keep our connection: my children and us—my husband and me. For example, I try to incorporate both Mexican and American meals. Another example is the formal and informal manner of speaking Spanish. My children should speak to us using the formal Spanish . . . and they don't. I understand that they're not being disrespectful to us. It's just the way they're growing up in America. They've lost the ability to distinguish between using the '*tu*' and the '*usted*.'

We, my husband and I, have to follow the ways of the United States . . . or we lose our kids. Understanding this is a form of assimilating. My husband speaks English great. My older children are doing well . . . both have jobs. They're happy . . . and they have carried some traditions. My other two children are doing well in school.

Most Americans like Mexicans. There are people who are friendly and others who are not. It's just like Mexico. Most people have been wonderful . . . very friendly. But there's one incident . . . the laundromat. One day, I was putting my wet clothes in the dryer. A lady grabbed me and threw me against the wall. I didn't know what had happened. She just kept screaming at me. I ran out to try and find help. I just kept crying. A friend of mine was outside . . . and I told her about the lady. She called the owner and both went to calm the lady down. Apparently, she was on some form of drugs. She told the owner that she didn't want Mexicans drying their clothes where she did. I guess . . . this was what she kept screaming at me. I left my clothes at the laundromat. I went home. The owner and my friend picked up my clothes from the floor . . . where she had thrown them. They brought them to my home . . . still wet. I never went back to that laundromat. I have to use the one that's farther away.

I guess . . . part of me . . . from being in this country wants to have a little pocket money. I sometimes clean houses. I like to have money in my pocket . . . it's a form of independence . . . just a little pocket money. My husband doesn't like me to work . . . and he makes enough to where I don't have to, but I sell tamales and cakes. It also keeps me busy.

Norma:

A lot of work goes into assimilating into another culture. I didn't want to have to deal with American society. It was so difficult to do anything. I suppose . . . eventually, I had to. The first thing to do is to begin communication in any way possible . . . try really hard. Try to fit in . . . try to speak more . . . try to learn the ways of Americans . . . if you don't, you're left out. Learning the language meant becoming equals . . . with Americans. Another thing, I think, immigrants should do is learn the language . . . maybe not perfectly, but at least a little in order to feel part of society. I'm not saying to completely lose what makes you Mexican, though.

I can't stop being Mexican. I've encountered people who try to forget that they're Mexican. That's not me. I wouldn't even try. I think that as immigrants we have to combine the cultures. And I say combine the cultures in order to survive . . . but not abandon our ethnicity. It's possible to have some American and some Mexican customs.

The hardest thing I encountered in the U.S. . . . in an American school . . . the language was extremely hard. It was a different world. But if I have to think really hard . . . even more difficult than the language was losing my world—all that I had known. I had lost my life . . . the realization that I had to start again . . . it was a new way of being. Outsider is the word I'm looking for. I didn't know my way around. I didn't have the social tools that I had learned. I didn't feel incompetent or anything like that. . . . I just had to work so hard to accomplish so little. I wanted my life in Mexico back. It was familiar, and I could communicate.

Being a sixteen year old in Mexico is not like being a teenager in America. At sixteen, I was already an adult. Once in America, I was forced to become a child again. I didn't like that. Once here, I had to help my parents in any way I could find. I helped them work in the fields, and I cleaned houses in order to help support my younger siblings. I didn't have time or even want to deal with the usual teenage difficulties. I had duties . . . but America saw me as a child.

It took a long time for me to feel assimilated . . . about fifteen years . . . even longer . . . to feel like I was part of American society. It took longer for me than for me siblings because I married a traditional Mexican man. I married into his family, and they became my world . . . for a long time. It took longer for me to understand American ways. I had plans to continue school. . . . I hadn't planned getting married.

Monica:

The first thing towards assimilating, in my experience, was showing an interest. . . . I was very interested in everything . . . anything new. I had no fear of entering school. I think it's because I'm a very social person.

People would try to speak to me, and I would just stare at them. I learned to use hand gestures. My first memory of entering the eighth grade is of a clown. The principal used to dress up in a clown's suit for pep rallies and things like that. He approached me and gestured me to squeeze his nose. I had no idea where I was. . . . all I knew was that everything seemed funny and everyone was friendly. Later in the day . . . in another class, a teacher brought me over to his desk. He had three apples, and I think he wanted me to take them. He pushed the apples towards me, but I didn't take them. I was a bad eater. . . . I didn't want to waste food. I didn't want to begin eating something and not finish it. In my mind, wasting food was not a luxury.

I don't think that I've become part of America yet. I don't feel American, but I don't feel Mexican either. . . . I think I'm a bit lost . . . to the point where I don't know where I belong. When we first came here, I immediately tried to learn the language. . . . it was visual for me. I pointed; I poked . . . for example . . . eyes. Then, I would point at my eyes. *Ojos.* . . . I would point at their eyes. I felt like I was relearning the world.

My mother used to send me to English classes on Sundays. I never tried really hard at the writing aspect of the English language because I was a visual person. I wanted to communicate verbally . . . socially. I felt bad because I didn't try very hard, and she spent her money. The English classes did help some. . . . [laughs]

When we first moved to the United States, I didn't think our new home was a new culture. I was still a naïve child.

Irma:

First step, I think, is getting to know people and the environment. At least get to know one person . . . maybe at church . . . maybe find a friend. We were just dumped in places like at school. We didn't know anybody.

Crossing the border wasn't much. It wasn't until I was put in school and dealing with the new language that I began to feel alone. . . . I began to feel different. My sister cried. I felt like my mother abandoned us. The schools here are different from the schools in Mexico. In Mexico, school was just a huge room, and everyone—all ages in just one room. The schools here looked like a huge playground with large buildings.

We didn't know the language. Now . . . we were scared. What if my mother didn't come for us? We didn't know the land . . . we didn't know where we lived. We were lost . . . we couldn't understand the language.

I understood a lot of English after a year. I know that by third grade I was already speaking English . . . although I wasn't fluent. My mother still only speaks Spanish. My mother's life didn't change much after coming to the U.S. She was a housewife in Mexico, and she was a housewife here. Maybe how she went about her chores . . . was different. In Mexico, she washed dishes in a tub and boiled water on the stove. Here . . . she turned on the faucet . . . out came hot water.

I didn't want that kind of life for myself. I wanted kids, but I also wanted to work. I didn't want to end up only as a housewife. I'm more involved in my kids' lives. My mother really didn't have the time. I think that the reason why I wanted this is because I grew up in America.

My parents didn't know that education was the most important thing here. I wanted to go to college after high school. If I had wanted to drop out of high school at sixteen, it would've been fine. Education was not important especially for girls who had to stay home and learn housewife duties. To my parents, education ended after the sixth grade.

My parents looked at me and wanted me to follow Mexican customs . . . which I do. But I want what Americans have . . . what America offers . . . not so much for me, but for my kids. I don't want my daughters to only be housewives. Education is the way to survive in America.

Assimilating . . . mingling with the culture . . . don't be afraid. See what America is . . . the same thing with the American culture. They have to see us as we are. Hispanics are all about family.

My daughter is a freshman in college. Her way of thinking is

American. She wants to graduate from college, find a career, and have a family. She wants it all. I do believe that she has and will leave behind some Mexican customs. But . . . I don't want her to forget everything traditional. She is Mexican. She will never forget that. She does need to think American. If she thinks Mexican, she will not survive in America. Being bicultural is a good thing.

At my job, the Hispanic women including myself would socialize in Spanish. It wasn't intentional. It was just something we did. We got called in by the supervisor, and he told us that we couldn't speak Spanish because the other employees got offended. They said that we should speak only English. So, we still speak Spanish when we're alone.

CULTURAL GROUP AND SELF-IDENTIFICATION

Sandra:

I am Mexican . . . but I live here [America]. Being Mexican includes African, Portuguese, Spanish, and indigenous roots. I understand the limitations of Mexico, like the corrupt government. Yet, I appreciate having the freedoms the U.S. allows its citizens. I am not from here or from there. It's just a constant, stressful situation. It's like being in a state of limbo.

I used to fear that my daughters would reject me because I sounded Mexican. But I don't feel like I have to disguise my ethnicity anymore. I only want to be respected as a biracial individual . . . as I respect others. I don't want to use my minority status as a power tool nor do I want my ethnicity used against me. . . . I'm in a comfort zone. I no longer have to try and impress anyone. I can show love for both my countries. Just because someone has labeled me in a certain way, I don't have to believe it myself.

As a child living in El Paso, I knew being Mexican was bad. I wanted to be Anglo and succeed in American society because these feelings of inferiority were carried into my adulthood. I don't want my kids to deal with those kinds of feelings. I know that my siblings have lost their native culture. My sister doesn't teach my niece any of the Spanish language. It's almost like their native culture has been diluted by living in America.

My ex-husband defined himself as a Texan—Tejano—meaning he was a U.S. citizen. He didn't want his children to define themselves as Mexican. Tejanos are racist against native Mexicans, and I'm Mexican. So, he didn't want the girls to call themselves anything but Americans or Tejanas.

Rosa:

I'm Mexican, but I like America. I'm from there, but live here. I guess that makes me a Mexican American [laughs]. I might think this way because I was already older when I came over. I can tell that my grandchildren who live here think differently than when I was raising my children in Mexico. They have different ways of acting. They sometimes are too independent, and they talk back to their parents.

Lucero:

I'm Mexican. . . . But I live in the U.S. My children are Mexican American. The Mexican culture is a beautiful culture, but the country is not the same anymore. I know that I have lost some of my Spanish. My English is better. I don't realize sometimes that I switch languages. I just do. There are lots of things I have kept from my native culture . . . like making fresh tortillas. But there are other customs that I have lost: making salsas in blenders instead of the mortar, using a washer and dryer instead of hand washing . . . things like that.

It's hard to see that some people try to push us, Mexicans, to the side. If we think about it . . . this land used to be Mexico. The immigrants come to work hard and to succeed. It's the second generation who seems to lose its way. They don't want an education and get into trouble. They need to remember that this is our land. We belong here more than the Americans. Anglo America is afraid of the growing percentage of Latin people in America. They know they are the foreigners. It's difficult to argue your case because, of course, they are the dominant ones.

I'm becoming accustomed to life here—it's a collage. My ethnicity is disappearing a little every day.

Consuelo:

I always say that I'm Mexican. I am in this country, so I have to conform to this country's ideas and abide by the laws . . . simple as that. But I am Mexican. . . . I would not live in Mexico again . . . but I wouldn't want to lose my ancestral roots. My parents are still in Mexico. They're my connection to my native country.

My daughter was born here. She thinks differently than I did when I was her age [15]. I don't remember being confused about who I was. Maybe that's what being with two cultures means. I don't think of myself as being biracial—but I can see differences with my children. Their identity is different from mine.

My daughter is more American, I think, than Mexican. My oldest boy . . . he's more Mexican. It all depends which customs each child decides to adopt. My daughter is all American.

Teresa:

I can't say that I'm American because I'm not. I don't have the documents. I'm Mexican, but I love this country. I feel as if I'm part of this country now. . . . I do realize that my children will probably identify themselves as Mexican Americans.

Norma:

Identity. I have two children. I don't think that they would define themselves as I do. They didn't have my experience. They were born here . . . they're citizens. I tell them my stories, and there's no way that they could feel the same. But . . . they understand what I have been through.

I identify with Hispanic . . . and it's because that's what I was told to use. I'm not clear as to what it means exactly. To me, I guess Hispanic means to me that I am of the Latin group, that I speak Spanish, and that I live in the United States. I chose my identity from the categories that were offered to me. I am not American. I wasn't born here. I'm a citizen, but I'm not a natural born American. I don't consider myself a Chicana either . . . or a Tejana.

There's two countries inside of me. . . . I guess what I mean by Hispanic is Mexican American. This country has given me a lot, but I'll never forget my native country. I have heard other Mexicans say that they will never be American. I'm not like that either.

Monica:

I don't have a Mexican identity or an American one. I'm just a person. I think that my identity has more to do with my personality and not with my origins. If someone asks me about my ethnicity, and I tell them that I'm Mexican. . . . they automatically think that I'm stupid, lazy, or an alcoholic. They automatically think that they can flirt with me.

I visit Mexico, and Mexicans tell me that I don't act Mexican. Americans tell me I don't act American. I'm criticized in both countries . . . in both cultures. So, I end up being myself . . . the person I was meant to be. My parents are indigenous. . . . I am indigenous too. People often accuse me of looking Mexican but having 'white' ideas. I was born in Mexico, but I'm not sure where I belong. According to other people. . . . According to America, Latina is what America wants to call me.

If I have to choose an American term . . . I would choose to be identified as Hispanic or Latina. These are terms that America understands . . . words that help America define me. I am no different from a person of Colombia or a person from North Dakota. There are no borders . . . or boundaries. We are just people, and we share the world.

When I'm asked to check a box which defines who I am . . . I choose to leave it blank. My daughter always calls herself an American. . . . [laughs]. She sometimes jokes around and says that she's Canadian [laughs].

I am a U.S. citizen . . . I have my documents. It's really just a paper though. It defines me as an American citizen, but it doesn't define me as a person.

Irma:

I'm Mexican. I don't consider myself a Mexican American. I'm just a Mexican . . . who speaks English. I don't have identity issues. I want American things for my children. I'm Mexican, but I worked really hard to have what I have. I wanted to show my kids that they can have it all . . . just like American kids.

Hispanic is a good word. It is a word that means Latin. If I say I'm Mexican, then I'm from Mexico . . . but when I'm asked to fill out a questionnaire of some kind, Mexican is not an option. It's always Hispanic. So, I have to make a decision. Hispanic it is. . . . this is probably why I say Hispanic a lot.

KEEPING TRADITIONS ALIVE

Sandra:

I have two daughters: Alejandra, fourteen, and Gabriela Raquel, twelve. I always knew that I wanted my kids to have Mexican names. I hope they pass on Mexican traditions to their daughters like our food. . . . I hope that when they're adults, they decide what kind of people they want to be. My youngest told me that she didn't want to be Mexican, once—a while ago. I asked her what was so wrong with being Mexican. I told her that Mexicans are hard working and that her grandma was Mexican. I told her, too, that we would never be white. Both my daughters only needed to be educated because they love the Mexican culture. That is key—people need to be educated about diversity and ethnicity. It's up to my daughters how they want to be identified. As long as they make educated decisions, I'm comfortable with how they will identify themselves.

When I'm stable in my job, I want to spend whole summers in either El Paso or in Juarez . . . maybe even deeper south into Mexico. I want my kids to experience Mexico like I did. My grandpa and I used to walk to the market center to buy fresh vegetables every day. He would let me carry a small basket. Summers in Mexico would help my kids establish a bond with the country and its culture. I want my daughters to know about their native origins including the Spanish language. Today, Mexican kids living in America have lost and have even rejected the Spanish language—the language of their parents. My family never stayed in one place for too long. We went from Mexico, to Louisiana, then to Texas. As an adult, I moved from Texas to Las Vegas . . . although my mother is a strong influence in my life, there is something missing. I was brought up in a well-structured, loving family which included my grandparents.

Once they passed away, the feeling of home and security died with them. I don't have a connection to Mexico anymore. . . . I consider home to be where my family is . . . my daughters, brother and mother. I don't want to own a home at the moment. I lost my first home. I want to build a home in El Paso or Mexico proper (Guadalajara or Guanajuato), once my children have made their own way into American society.

Rosa:

My children, grandchildren, and all the rest have kept some traditions. We return to Mexico once a year. I won't let my children forget Mexico. I want them to have a connection to their native country. I want them to remember that Mexico is their true home. I want them to respect their parents. Mostly, I want my children and their children to respect their parents' land.

Lucero:

The most important part of our culture is the food. The flag, the government—we didn't worry too much about politics in Mexico, and it was because of our young age. So, now I think about how food could be a connection between me and my family. I carried it from home, and now I have it here. The only traditional, national, holiday we celebrate is September 16th*—I like to celebrate it very much. No other traditional holiday though.

Consuelo:

My children, I can tell, are losing our traditions. Native food, music, dancing, and traditional dress . . . I think . . . are the most important ones. Parties like *Cinco de Mayo* . . . they don't want to celebrate them anymore. They have lost much of the Spanish language. They understand and can speak some. My oldest doesn't even like to visit Mexico. He doesn't like it there because he's scared of the crime. For this reason, we haven't visited Mexico for three years. When I go to Mexico, I get so sad. There's so much poverty . . . people begging on the streets.

In American society, children usually leave the home at eighteen years of age. Mexican culture doesn't work that way. They can live with their parents until they feel it's time to move out. It's not that they're lazy, but our culture deals with extended families. I never liked my children to be left alone which is something American parents do. This is why I couldn't assimilate well into the American culture. I would rather be home and not succeed than lose my children to America.

Teresa:

The most important custom I want my children to follow is respect. My children are very respectful to elders . . . to their parents. I hope they keep this custom.

Irma:

The history of Mexico, the music . . . these are things that are not as important for me to pass on to my children. They are important, but I have to choose what I pass on. Most important is religion and family. The Catholic religion . . . and that family is everything. I have shown my children where I was born. . . . I wanted them to have a connection to their country by having a connection with family.

I do visit Mexico often, and my children go with me. I like to drive because I like for the kids to see the Mexican landscape. . . . I want them to see how people live . . . and I want them to realize that people there don't have opportunities like we have living in the U.S. No matter how poor we are in the U.S., we are not as poor as we would be in Mexico. They got to see why my parents decided to leave their country and why they brought their family here.

On September 16, 1810 Mexico gained independence from Spain. That date is a national holiday, Mexican Independence Day.

CLEMENTINA
Interviewed by Heather Tosteson

I WANT TO BE ONE, BUT I WONDER...

I was born in Freetown, Sierra Leone. I came to the United States on September 21, 2006. I will be able to become a citizen in September 2011. I have always wanted to be a citizen since I came. In June I can apply. Then I will have an interview, fingerprints, and take the test.

Womanhood

My mom taught me most about what it was to be a woman. I grew up with my mom and aunt and dad. I had a twin sister. In Africa, you are told what you can do at different ages. In Africa, fifty to sixty percent of women are housewives. Both my mom and my aunt were. As a girl if you're coming up the first thing your mom teaches you is that you will have menstruation and then you will have to defend yourselves against boys or you'll get pregnant.

In my tribe you need to be twenty-one before you can lose your virginity. In Sierra Leone there are twelve tribes. I am of the Krio tribe. We don't have female circumcision, so I can't tell you about it. But the rest of the tribes do. We're from the English tribe so we don't believe in that circumcision. In the other tribes, fifteen is the age of maturity. That is when you would be married and start having kids. But in our tribe twenty-one is the age at which you can become sexually active and have affairs. This allows women to have more education.

In Africa we raise our children strict so that children will stay in the same way all their lives. You can't start late, it won't stick. Even if you are in your thirties, your parents can whip the hell out of you if you do something wrong. For the parent, the kid is never grown to the parents. That independence doesn't apply in Africa. In Africa, you shouldn't look in people's eyes, especially your parents. Your hands should always be behind your back and your eyes down. In the U.S., I can hear children calling their mother, "Aye!" What way that be to talk to your mother? "Aye!"

My mom passed away in 1999 and my dad passed away in 1993. I just lost my twin sister on May 20, 2010. I had two sisters and two brothers. I was the oldest. My brothers and sister are in Freetown now. I was separated from my twin sister in 1999 and only got together with her again in 2007, so her death is very hard for me. I am helping her three daughters. They are two, eleven and fifteen. I want them to come and stay with me here. After I am a citizen that will be possible. Then, I will try and get my GED and go to college. But I have these responsibilities.

I would teach my nieces differently from the way I was taught if they were living here in the United States. Here I am going to be really really open because teenagers get involved in so many things here. Girls are wild here. Boys are more mature there in Sierra Leone before they approach girls because they are scared. If they approached a girl, the girl could prosecute them to the parents. If a boy came and talked with you, you would go to your mom and dad and they would go to the parents of the boy and complain. That's why it's safer over there than here for girls. In Sierra Leone people know each other. Everything starts from talking, so in Sierra Leone we didn't talk to boys.

I went to a mixed school in primary. In secondary I went to a girls school. Some parents prefer their boys to go to a boy's school so they can do well in school. I would want my nieces to be in an all-girls school here.

Civil War and Displacement

I was displaced from all my family in 1999 and only found my twin sister in 2007. I have found a brother but I have not seen him yet.

We were attacked in the night. We were sleeping and someone screamed, "House on fire. House on fire." Everyone ran in a different direction. I was running with my mother. My mother was shot and I had to leave her, I couldn't take her with me.

For two or three days after that, I was hiding in buildings. Then I ran to the seaside and I found people who were going to Guinea-Conakry in a canoe and I went too, traveling with them. I was in a refugee camp in Guinea-Conakry, the Famoriah Camp. People kept coming from Sierra Leone. I left the camp to go to the Sierra Leone embassy in Conakry to see if I could find my brothers and sisters. We were all displaced.

In 2000 there was a rebel war on the border of Guinea. People thought it was Sierra Leone and Libyan soldiers doing the fighting. The president of Guinea, President Lansana Conté, said all the refugees needed to leave the country. I was in Conakry near the embassy when he said this. The Guineans guards and Guineans, regular Guineans, they came and took us. This was not kidnap. This was all in the open in the daytime. They went to the houses of Sierra Leoneans and took all their things. These men took us women to a school and they locked us up and they beat us and kept us locked in there without food and water for four days. There were so many of them, so many women. It was dark. You couldn't see. I have a lot of bites on my back from fighting them. All this happened in a *schoolroom*.

A woman came to my rescue. She was a Sierra Leonean. A nurse. Her name was Maryam. All she heard was this screaming and crying in the school. She kept knocking on the door. She thought there were kids in there. She got the police to open the doors. It was just women. I was bleeding. She took me to the clinic and she took care of me. But I was sick. I didn't want to be in Guinea anymore. I could not be in that place. I was eighteen when all this happened.

The Guineans treated us as if we were rebels. I was not expecting them to turn against us. They were our neighbors. It was shameful and disgraceful. There were pictures of us. The president of Sierra Leone sent ferries for refugees to come back to Sierra Leone. Our brothers and sisters in Sierra Leone decided to take revenge on Guineans in Sierra Leone. But the president of Sierra Leone stopped that. The president of Guinea apologized. He said it wasn't Sierra Leonean and Liberians fighting, it was Guineans fighting themselves.

I could not stay in that place, so I went to the island of Guinea-Bissau. That was better. But the houses were all of bamboo and when the water rose it would come into the houses and all your things would wash away. So I got tired of it and I went to the city of Guinea Bissau. That was better. No water to wash into the houses. The city had no light, no electricity—you used candles or lamps. That was true of the city for a long period before. It had nothing to do with war.

In Guinea Bissau I met my late husband, Foday Kanu. He asked me to go to the UNHCR (United Nations High Commissioner for Refugees) for documents. He said he wanted to marry me. He was very kind to me. He was thirty-two. He left Sierra Leone before the war. He was running a business. He was moving to Brazil and back. We got married. We were together. He was a Muslim and I was a Christian. One time he went to Brazil to get the stuff for his business like he usually do. He came back from Brazil with a stomach ache and went to the hospital and passed away. That was October 6, 2005.

My husband's death was very unexpected. Back home it is not like in America, so there was not much you can do for him.

My husband was Muslim and I was Christian. In my tribe it was an issue, but at the war, you are looking for someone who can take care of you. At that time that was what everyone was looking for—someone who could care for you. There was no criticism any more.

I am married to another Muslim man now. I was married on November 7, 2009. He is also from Sierra Leone. We met in 2007 here in Georgia.

Coming to the United States

Since I went to Guinea Bissau, I got to register with the UNHCR. In 2005 when I lost my husband there was a resettlement program going on. They were interviewing refugees from Sierra Leone, Liberia, and Ivory Coast. The UNHCR was doing the interviews with the refugees. The president of the Sierra Leone Union was working at the UNHCR office, and the coordinator asked his wife to get me to the office to arrange an interview. They asked questions like you are asking now, how I came to be there. Then the coordinator said they wanted to take me to Senegal to be interviewed there. Senegal was where the resettlement interviews were taking place. So, the U.N. drove me to Senegal, to the UNHCR office there. They interviewed me. The lady who interviewed me was so nice to me. Her name was Yolande Ditewig. She said, "We want to resettle you, but we don't want you to go back to Guinea Bissau." I stayed at a refugee house. There was another interview. Then an immigration interview. Then a letter came that said I was accepted at the United States of America. I was not dreaming about America. I was looking for where I can be rescued in the first place.

I had lost my mom and my dad. I was displaced from my brothers and sisters. I had lost my husband. I didn't know if I would ever find my brothers and sisters. I said, "God, what have I done to deserve all this? It is really getting too much for me."

Sometimes I ask that now too. When I lost my twin sister. She is my only really really blood sister, the only one from the same mom and the same dad. That is why I feel so bad. We were identical twins. The voice, the face, the talking, everything was the same. Even my late dad, it was hard for him to differentiate. Even at school they had to put us in different classes because the teachers couldn't differentiate us. I only found her in 2007, so it was very hard to lose her again in 2010. We helped each other very much.

When I came to the States, I came straight to Georgia. I was stressed. I had no family, no relatives. That is when I started thinking back about the past. I was all alone. All by myself. I had no relatives, nothing but myself.

I began to feel connected when I started working. The refugee agency, it helps you only with hard labor jobs, your first job. I was working in a hotel. I met a Sierra Leonean woman there, and then I started connecting with other Sierra Leoneans. I had someone I could share my stress with. Her name was Haja. But before that I was really stressed. I started to take stress medicines.

Haja and I started working together. We would ride the MARTA together. We helped each other at work. It was hard labor at the hotel. Sometimes it was very hard for me. You had to clean more than fifteen rooms each day. Double beds. We helped each other at work. If she finished first, she would come to my floor and help me. If I finished early, I would go and help her. We would have lunch together. If you see her, you see me. Everyone knew we were a team. We were really so close until I met the man who became my husband. Haja and I still talk every day.

Marriage

I met him in 2007. We became friends. We would move in together, break up, come back, break up, come back. Three or four times. We moved into an apartment together with a one-year lease. Ash Grove Apartments. He moved out after the lease ended. Then we had another apartment together, Carriage Oak Apartments, and break up again. Then I was in La Carre Apartments. We get together again, break up, get together again before we married. Even now we're married, he moves out whenever he's upset. He's thirty-five, a big man.

He's a nice man. He has helped me a lot. He's taught me so many things. My husband left Sierra Leone in 2004. He's had many of the same experiences. He had been here long enough before me. He could teach me things. He's the one who force me to get my CNA, Certified Nursing Assistant. He helped me buy a car. He helped me achieve my goals, giving me advice. Standing by me too.

I've learned as a woman you need to be independent. I've been struggling by myself for so long, I can't depend on someone. What if someone disappoints me? If you do it for yourself, no one lets you down. When he is moving back and forth, how am I going to depend on him for a mortgage or to pay the bills? I have to do it again. But I must thank him as well. He helps me to become even more independent.

My husband went to a four-year college. He has a degree in political science. He says he wants to go on and get his B.A., no I think it is his M.A. He said when he met me and learned about what I'd been through, he felt passion for me. He wanted to help me. He does have a temper though. One time he was angry and I thought he would hit me and I called his sister to make a complaint, but she said, "You need to call the police. I don't even know why he is with you. He said he already had another woman in mind to marry." My husband asked her why she said that to me, why she just wanted to hurt me like that. He leaves when he gets angry. There's never any question of another woman, he just packs and goes to his friends and comes back when he's not angry anymore.

I do not mind now that he comes and leaves. We do not have children. I would like children, but if it happens, it happens. I'm not going to stress myself about that. I just want God's will to be done.

Citizenship Process

When you come as a refugee, right away you get a work permit and a Georgia ID. After a year, you receive a letter and then you need to apply for a green card. They will apply for you. I got my green card in 2009. At that time I was sure I wanted to become a citizen. Immediately I got here, I was open—there were many things I saw you have to be a citizen to do, so that helps me make up my mind.

I feel more like a Sierra Leonean in the U.S. I *do* want to be a citizen, but sometimes you do have a home fever—for your friends, your family. You go on Facebook and chat with friends. On Facebook you can meet people—

even from Africa. You can find people. (I was on Facebook but I closed it because there is a lot of gossip on Facebook.)

What will I do when I become a citizen? I will do the best I can to find me a suitable job. With refugee status, you can only do hard labor jobs. There are some easier jobs out there—but not for refugees. They only give them to citizens.

I want to see if I can apply for a loan and go back to school. I would like to work for the United Nations in Sierra Leone or Guinea. I would like to work out of the country, as a foreign citizen, so I can get paid more. If you get sent out to work, you make more money than if you work from inside. If I was asked to work for the U.S. embassy, that would be fine. I would be differentiated from the Sierra Leoneans.

Becoming a citizen means you can leave the country. Now I'm not authorized to go to Sierra Leone and Guinea. You go and come if you are a citizen. It doesn't hold you back from coming back here.

I would also be comfortable staying in the U.S.

To become a citizen, you must go and have the interview and get your fingerprints taken again. And then they give you a book and a CD with one hundred questions. You must know all these one hundred questions and answer six. You must pay $678. If you do not pass these one hundred questions, you must begin again. All that money again and you must still pay your bills and your mortgage. That is why people live here fifty years and do not become citizens. They do not dare. Sometimes it is the questions, sometimes it is the money, sometimes it is the language. There should be another way. People from Africa, about fifty percent are not educated. There should be a way when you go to the interview that people see someone is not educated and give them another test.

What do people give back as citizens? There are women here who have ten or fifteen children all born U.S. citizens. They are giving a lot. And people make businesses here. And there are many many home health agencies all made by Africans—that is giving something important back too.

Friendships, Family and Building a New Life

Most of my friends are from Sierra Leone. I do have American friends. I meet them at the park, or the zoo, or a restaurant. All those places are good for making friends. There is a large community from Sierra Leone here in Atlanta. There is a Sierra Leonean organization, and businesses and parties. You are lucky to meet people you haven't seen for fifteen years. You see them and say, "Like wow. I didn't know your life—"

My family was displaced and it took me time to find them. In 2007, soon after I came to Georgia I found my sister. I had friends in Guinea-Bissau. After I arrived in the States I called them and told them where I was. I did not tell them when I was in Senegal because I did not know where I was going, but when I arrived in the U.S. I called and gave them my information. They travelled often to Guinea-Conakry to buy merchandise and one time they were in the market and they saw my sister Carmina and thought she was me. They said, "Clementina what are you doing here? We heard that you were in America and here you are in Guinea." And my sister said, "I'm Carmina. I'm not Clementina. She is my twin." And my sister asked for information about me and that is how we got connected again.

In 2009, I was also lucky enough to meet my elder sister on my father's side. She had been here in the U.S. for twenty years but I did not know where. She was my godmother when I got christened but I had not seen her since then. I met her when I was getting ready to wed. A woman I had asked to be my godmother for the wedding was telling a friend of hers that she was going to do this and this friend (who turned out to be my sister Sylvia) asked, "Who are you going to be godmother for?" She said, "Her name is Clementina. She is from Sierra Leone." And then Sylvia said that she had a sister named Clementina. The woman said my last name was D_____ and Sylvia, who had another last name, said, "You don't know this but my middle name is D_____ too." The woman said, "She said her father was a brewery distributor in Kissey Road." My sister said, "But *my* father was the only brewery distributor in Kissey Road. Is she a twin?" And the woman I asked to be my godmother called and asked me and I said yes (that was before I lost my twin sister)—so that is how I met my sister Sylvia from my dad's side. Then I met her mother, my father's sister, and her daughter, who live in Maryland. And my sister then connected me with my brothers on my dad's side who live in London. There I was, getting married, feeling I had no family, I was just by myself. As soon as I met her, she felt familiar to me. She told me she was living in another state but then she and her husband moved to Atlanta, but when she got here they broke up. We see each other now.

I'm happy now. I met some very good people. Even Miss Mary I am working with. She is like my mom. She is really helpful to me. She helps me with advice. She is very sweet and nice. I've worked for her for three years now. I have worked for four different home health agencies. Miss Mary changes the agency but she keeps me. That is important. When I get another job, she can write a recommendation for me. The agency can only say how long you worked for them. The client can say you were a good worker.

Habitat for Humanity: Home Ownership

Miss Mary helped me get my Habitat house. Miss Mary had an interest in the Habitat houses so she called and asked about the rules. I was there when they called back and we listened as the man told us all about the application. Miss Mary and I both filled out the applications.

At first they rejected me. I was working double shifts then because Miss Mary didn't have anyone else, sixteen hours without stop, and they said I made too much money to qualify. I called the woman and told her this was not usual. I sent her my next pay stub and they called the agency and asked to see my records and when the agency sent them my usual records, they reinstated me. To have a Habitat house you cannot earn very much money for ten years. They tell you how much. After that you can earn more. The mortgage is in my name. That was one of the times when my husband had left again so it is in only my name. I am not dependent on him. If men think you are dependent on them for everything, they can act not right.

Aftermath of Sierra Leonean and Liberian Civil Wars

There are Sierra Leoneans here and Liberians here in Atlanta. The wars don't matter here. We don't hold each other responsible. The Liberians, they fled to our country. We fled to theirs. We are neighbors. What we had was a civil war. We fought our own brothers and sisters.

If we were to meet someone here who was in the war, a soldier, no, we wouldn't hold him responsible. It is the ones who cause the twelve year olds to pick up the rifle, the ones that give them drugs, that rub the drugs into their cuts so they are crazy and don't know what they're doing: They are the ones who we must hold responsible. They are the ones that make children kill their own mother or have sex with their own mother. Who in their right mind could do that?

We fought our own brothers and our own sisters. That is what we did. It was terrible.

Acculturation

I speak Krio, English, Susu (a language in Guinea-Conakry), French and Portugese Creole. If I go to any country, I always try to force myself to speak so I can communicate. The first thing I do is make friends with little kids—they always be correcting to help you. You can't learn from adults. They ridicule you. But children they just want you to be able to communicate. I like children. Wherever I go, I just sit myself down in the middle of them and I learn from them.

Some cultures I'm still trying to come out of them. My husband is from a different tribe. He had come out of some of the traditions before we met. He is mature in that way. My husband helped me. He told me, "*Look* at people. Stop putting your eyes on the floor. They will think you are afraid." A habit is like smoke—so you have to come out of it. He said to me, "Clementina, you can look in people's eyes." It was uncomfortable and a little scary, but my husband kept telling me, "No, to be an American you must act like this. You must come out of this village self. Otherwise people will be able to take advantage of you. You need to look like an American."

Now people don't know I'm African. When they learn I am, they want to learn from me. People ask me if I'm African because I speak English. They don't know in Africa people speak English. You can't be blind all the time. You need to learn. You need to come out of the smoke.

Living in the U.S.

Sometimes I think the only thing that helps me is my faith. When I first came to the U.S., that was not the end of my troubles. The first thing that happened to me here was I was hit by a car and it dragged me. I was hit and run. A woman came to help me and called the police. But I did not know who did it. I did not know you need to know the name and color of the car. I did not know you must remember the number on the license plate. No one told me. I was new to this country. I was blind. So the police could not help me. They took me to Grady Hospital and then I was sent home—and then the hospital sent me a bill for $1,700.

And then I was robbed. I was wanting to get a car and I had saved money and I was going to see it. I had the money to buy it in my bag. These boys came up to me and they hit me with a pistol and they took all my money—$4,500. They took it and my phone and my identification. I had to go to Grady again. They hit me on the side of my face and it was swollen way out here.

But that was not the end. Then they came to my house. I was not at work because I had just come from the hospital. My boyfriend (he was back again then) had given me his cellphone. I was expecting him back from work but not so soon so I went to the door and looked through the little window and I didn't see him. I saw those boys again, the ones who had robbed me and I was very afraid. I thought, They have a pistol and they already hit me with it. What shall I do? I called the police and I put the phone on speaker so they would hear and I was screaming and then they went away and the police came and they took me to the leasing office and had them put new locks on all the doors. And then I was safe.

America! That is what it means to be a citizen! I want to be one, but I wonder. . .

its
with

cessary
hat the
foreigner
be trans-
formed in
American

y must b
ns amo
elves,
nd

*WHAT DOES MARRIAGE
HAVE TO DO WITH IT?*

PATRICIA BARONE

THE WOMEN ACROSS THE STREET

For thirty-four years,
I've tended my perennials,
not seeing the women, Filipinas,
he ordered through the mail.

His next door neighbor used to greet
Chesa, the current one,
walking on our river road.

I must have passed her, only seeing
her dark glasses, reflecting back
the sun to me, leaving her in shade.

Now she never leaves
unless he's had his fill
of beating her,
and she scuttles to a neighbor
for help she never gets.

Police arrive
but she's still there,
her child-like brassiere
dripping on the line.

I met Molly, his first wife, once—
she lifted her cellar-white face
as I gave her the time of day,
but she looked through me.

I could have offered
something, a pot of daisies,
but I've kept myself
to myself.

I never knew
Molly, Tala,
Amihan. Now
I see Chesa.

CATHY ADAMS

CHUAN

Chuan was angry, so angry she forgot her English. She ran from her house thinking in her own tongue, not his, not when she was this angry. She was in a town where she couldn't get lost. Or rather, she shouldn't. It was dangerous to get angry and lost in a town that was his, the one he grew up in, his people, his country. Reaching a paved stone street, she slowed to a dragging walk. She put out her hand to steady herself against the board and batten wainscoting of the row of green houses extending like game pieces along a narrow sidewalk. She stood up straight, drawing in her breath and forcing herself to look confident as if she knew where she was going, but she did not. Since coming to America, she had been in town by herself only three times, and each time she had carried a map folded up small in her purse that she could open privately in a public restroom stall when she felt lost. Today she had not even brought her purse. She just ran out the door with the awful words they had spoken to one another still stinging the air around her ears.

"Next time I kill you with poison," she had shouted at him. Jack, her husband, shouted something back, but she couldn't make it out. She had already tuned out his language.

She hadn't meant it. Or maybe she did, just for a few seconds. She didn't even have any poison. She wouldn't know where to get it, or more importantly, how to ask for it. In China she could have gotten some poison if she asked very sweetly at the right place.

"I have rats, so many rats." And she would have gotten enough poison to kill a very big rat.

But in America everything was different. Every day she had to settle the things she saw into new categories in her brain. Penny loafers, silver polish, barbeque chips, press-on nails, property tax. Even their words sounded funny. These people did not push their words out in the right places. Consonants sat like gummy bread on their tongues, not crisp and undulating the way she was used to speaking them. The lady at the butcher shop at the end of her street said things Chuan could never understand, so she pointed and smiled a lot. The lady would not haggle either. Chuan had to pay the price marked on the plastic sticker, not a penny less. Her face hurt after talking to this lady. The second time Chuan had been in the store the lady asked Chuan if she was Vietnamese. "My son died over there. In Vietnam," she'd said when Chuan didn't answer. Chuan searched hard for her words and told her she was not Vietnamese.

Sometimes the woman gave her meat with bones when Chuan knew she had pointed at the boneless roast. The wrongness of it made her angry. And if the meat was not something he wanted for dinner, or if it was not cooked the way he liked, it was wrong.

"Tell her you want the lean pork roast. This is nothing but fat and gristle!" His face was pink when he yelled, pink like undercooked meat. Chuan knew how to buy meat, but she could not make the butcher shop lady listen.

On the upper end of the street was the Woolworth store. Once last summer, Chuan went there with the ladies from the Methodist church. They had ordered sodas and shakes. One of them ordered a strawberry drink for her and it had tasted so good, so sweet and cold. Thinking about it now eased some of her anger away until she remembered she had brought no money and could not buy one for herself now even if she could have remembered the name of it. Jack gave her a little money, pin money he called it. But she needed no pins and could not understand why he called it such a name. When she had asked for patio furniture he reminded her that he had paid the 'premium' price to bring her there. She knew full well the three levels men paid. Premium was the highest price. It cut the red tape by six months, he had said. She didn't know what red tape he was talking about. She'd never seen any, but he liked to remind her that there was always red tape to prevent her from getting something she wanted.

Chuan's feet throbbed in pain as the cold of the stone street penetrated her thin pumps. Kicking off a shoe, she rubbed the ball of her foot. Her big toe popped loudly, and she massaged her heel. She did the same with the other heel, and then flexed her foot in a circle.

Some of the women in China had been in the system for years answering letters from men who offered no serious hope. "You are a pretty one. You will find love fast," they had all said. Chuan had her picture made at the studio the way her friends told her to, except she insisted on sitting with her hands folded in her lap. And she did not wear the shoes the others brought for her to wear. She never wore such high heeled sandals with a dress. It made her look like the type of woman she was not. She ended up taking the shoes off and being photographed with bare feet. It was the bare feet that got Jack's attention when he looked through the photographs. He said in his letter that he could tell she was "poor and simple, but a real lady." After she arrived in America and he married her, he often insisted she go barefoot around the house. Once in summer he even took her shoes away so she would have to go barefoot everywhere. After a week he gave her shoes back, kissed her blistered feet, and told her she was beautiful.

She did as he asked. She had his meal ready each night when he came home. She washed and ironed his clothes. She even taught herself how to use the weed cutting machine that had so frightened her the first time she saw him crank it up and swing it back and forth cutting down all the weeds around the porch. She learned English fast, and she liked to watch TV and talk on the telephone to the neighbors so she could improve everyday. She learned to speak so well he sometimes told her not to.

"I hear customers yak at me everyday. I don't want to come home and hear it from you," he had said the week before.

She knew three neighbors well enough to speak to. The women back home had told her she was lucky. She would make friends fast, and she would have if he hadn't insisted she go places only when he could accompany her. "I don't want anything happening to you," he had said. He let her go to town with the church ladies only because they had teased him at the Wednesday service about keeping her locked up. He did not know about the other trips she took alone when he was at work.

"You are lucky, Chuan," the women at home had said. "You are a nurse. You can get a job in a big American hospital and make lots of money. You and your husband can travel. See Yellow Stone National Park." But they had not seen it. And she had no license to work as a nurse in the U.S.

"You have to pass a bunch of tests, and I'd have to sign a bunch of papers," Jack had told her. He tried to dismiss the subject, but Chuan got in front of the television. "I can pass tests. My English is better. You can sign papers."

This was the first time he'd gotten angry with her. He slammed his glass down on the coffee table and reminded her again that he had paid the 'premium' price and he deserved respect for that. "I didn't bring you over here to take off in some career. Family comes first. American women have forgotten that, but Chinese women are supposed to understand that if the husband says no work then that means no work!"

She went to bed angry that night. Her anger smoldered so long and so deep she could not sleep. She was as trapped as she'd been at home. Perhaps even more trapped. People knew her in her village. She could run to any house, and someone knew her. In his town the people kept their houses locked at night, and she could not get in if she tried, even the homes of the few people that she could call by name.

That morning he had been kinder. He waited patiently at the breakfast table for her to prepare his meal. She did it wordlessly. He took it for obedience and not the anger it was. He smiled as she slid the butter toward him. She did not return the smile. She kept her eyes on the floor the way she had done the first few weeks she had been there. He took it for modesty. She feared that if she looked at him she would fly into a rage and tear at his face with her hands.

"Shawn," he said. He'd never been able to hear the nuance in the pronunciation of her name—*Shoe on*—with the two halves pushed together and emphasis on the latter. So she had lost even her name. Everyone now called her Shawn. "Shawn, I brought you here to take care of you. And your job is to take care of me. This is the way the Lord means for things to be between men and women." They had prayed to this god in his church, but he was not her god, and the only place she heard that the Christian god wanted women to cook, iron, and clean all day was from the white men who went to his church.

She raised her face to his and her lips were white with anger. Everywhere was his. No one knew her who had not known him first. "This is your place," she hissed.

He raised his eyebrows in a condescending expression. Missing her point once again, he said, "That's right. And your place is right here at home." He pushed his plate away, shaking his head. "They said Asian women were demure. Said they don't bust your chops about stuff. I brought you here because I wanted a sweet, delicate woman who appreciates a man. But I swear, Shawn, you're not acting like you appreciate much of anything. I take off early every Thursday so I can take you to the beauty shop. My father didn't even do that much. My mama had to walk to the beauty shop." He flipped up the newspaper edges and began reading the sports page.

She searched for the words to tell him she was not so delicate as he wanted to think. She was strong and smart, and she knew respect meant more than a ride to the beauty parlor. "I cut off hurt man's arm. Doctor could not come. Sick babies kept him away. With a saw I cut. Like this." She made a sawing motion on her own arm with her hand. She smiled, proud at the memory.

Jack's face wrinkled in disgust and uncertainty. "What the hell are you talking about?"

"Am—Am—Amputation. I did this. I was good nurse. I save his life."

He put his paper down and looked at her a long time after she said this. She began to wonder if he had not understood what she was trying to tell him.

"Don't tell anybody you did that," he finally said.

"I save his life," Chuan repeated, frustrated that he was not impressed with her words.

"Just don't go telling people you cut some man's arm off. In America they put women in jail for doing things like that." Then he added, "For life."

She knew women got into trouble for cutting off men's body parts. She'd heard about it on *Hard Copy*. But it wasn't arms they were talking about. She smiled and he caught it from the corner of his eye.

"Clean up these dishes," he said.

"No." She stood firm.

He lowered the corner of his newspaper. "Now Shawn, let's not make a big stink out of this. Get these breakfast dishes cleaned up and tonight we'll go down to IHOP, and I'll buy you some pancakes." He resumed his newspaper reading.

"No pancakes."

"No?" He put the paper down on the table. "Are you saying no to me?"

"No, I say no."

He stood from the table and clenched his fists. He lowered his eyes to meet her upraised ones. "You'll say no to me in this house only once."

"I can speak my words," she said.

"You go acting like that and I can send you right back to where you came from." A little spray of spittle landed on her cheek. She took a step back, her voice faltering. "You can not. I am your wife. This is America."

He stepped closer and pointed a finger in her face. "You go talking about cutting off your husband's arms and I can divorce you, then you won't have anywhere to go."

Her pumps were by the door. She pushed past him and quickly slipped her feet inside. Taking her coat from the hook, she turned and screamed the words, "Next time I kill you with poison." And then she was gone, his threats fading behind her.

On the street Chuan held her shoe in her hand and rested her foot on her knee. Tears blinded her a moment and she shook her head quickly, determined to hold herself together. She slipped the shoe back on and looked around. The other end of the street did not look right. Suddenly she could not remember if she had come from the left or the right. She felt her throat closing up and a paralyzing fear overtook her that was so debilitating it choked out the rest of her anger.

"I can not get lost. I will be so alone," she thought, and she felt a heart-pounding homesickness for a place she knew, and more importantly, a place that knew her. These streets would open up at any second and swallow her down into darkness so thick all she would be able to do would be crawl on her hands and knees searching out any shape that she could put a name to. The fear rolled up her body and she gasped out loud.

"You okay, lady?" a voice called out. A man in a large gray coat turned back toward her as he kept walking past, sidestepping slowly, unsure of whether to keep going or not. She opened her mouth to answer, but the reply was a squeak. She turned from the man in the coat and ran in the direction of the Woolworth store. When she got to the store, she turned the corner and sideswiped a young couple carrying bags of bath towels. Holding her hands out in front of her in a terrified panic, she pushed past the other exiting shoppers. She kept running until she was across the street moving past a coffee shop, an upholstery shop, and a Sunbeam Thrift store. Then she spotted a fountain in a postage stamp sized park. Bundled in their warm coats, children played, and a few adults milled about trying to catch bits of sunlight through the crisp winter air. A white granite fountain blew a chilling gusher of water over a circle of cement swans. Their wings were laced in spikey ice crystals. Jack had brought her here last August, her first month in America. They had placed their hands one over the other atop the swan's dipping heads and let the water splash warm over their fingers. The gold on Chuan's finger sparkled under the crystal drops of water. Smiling, she had thrown her head back and said, "I am luckiest woman everywhere." He had laughed in delight and kissed her lightly on the lips.

Running toward the water, her arms out, her hands open, Chuan ignored the stares from the other park visitors. At the fountain she thrust her hands into the icy water and splashed her face over and over, washing away her wild tears until her shocked skin was red. She opened her eyes and looked down into the fountain, her eyelashes, lips, and nose dripping cold water.

"Ma'am, are you feeling all right?" an old woman asked, her hand reaching for Chuan's arm.

"I know this place," Chuan said, a light smile curving her lips. "I am in a place I know." And she held her left hand under the icy falling water until the red of her fingers outshone the gold.

YU-HAN CHAO

FROM FRENCH MAID TO CHINESE BRIDE

My first encounter with racism was when I was in first grade. My mother often made me wear a certain awful black polka dot dress with white fabric-and-lace overlay that made me look like a French maid.

"You need to wear it more before you grow out of it," she said, pulling it down over my head with superhuman force.

Oh, how I longed to grow out of that atrocious maid uniform. What she didn't know was that at school, I was being teased: "Chinese people are so poor, they have to wear the same clothes every day!"

The maid outfit (which I eventually outgrew) aside, I did consider myself American although I didn't land in this fair land until I was in kindergarten—and promptly left the country in fourth grade, yanked out of Turtle Rock Elementary by my freshly graduated graduate student parents. Held hostage in Taiwan for the next dozen years, I always talked about "going back to America" in a way that implied that was where I belonged, a place that defined an important part of my identity.

I did not actually make it back to post-9/11 U.S.A. until graduate school. As I passed through immigration inspection and customs, being fingerprinted, photographed, and questioned about whether I could afford tuition as a international student even on my fellowship, I realized that maybe I wasn't as American as I thought I was. To everyone here I was a little Asian girl who held a dull-green-covered Taiwanese passport bearing no shiny eagles, who remarkably and even suspiciously, spoke perfect English. So I didn't belong here after all. I would never be truly 'American,' would always be asked where I was from, why I had no accent.

After graduate school, I went from job to job begging for work visa sponsorship, which was difficult to get, but absolutely required if I wanted to work. Immigration had to approve it, too, but they usually did. It was horribly expensive to be an alien in this country, and opportunities, especially employment opportunities for a non-engineer-English-major-loser Asian like me, were limited. Besides teaching I'd done all sorts of little office jobs at Asian-owned companies that were willing to take on foreign employees—law firms, even a bridalwear manufacturer. All this time, I constantly thought to myself, if I get fed up or things get too bad, I'll just go back to Taiwan. My nostalgia for the place called 'home' had shifted from a distant and idealized U.S.A. to cozy old filthy, sunburnt, betelnut-juice-stained Taiwan.

A sudden twist in the story was my marriage, not approved by everybody in my family because he was, gasp, Mexican-American, but I was happy and stopped plotting my escape back to Taipei. After some terrifying and expensive blood tests, a painful tetanus shot, a strip search by a civil surgeon, and many forms and fees, I am on my way towards (fingers crossed) becoming a temporary permanent resident. Because I married an American, I should soon be able to work for any company or school I want without begging them for visa sponsorship and asking immigration for work permission first. After all those years of struggling in this country as the disadvantaged alien, I don't know if this is a happy ending. I feel like I caved, gave in to my oppressor. But I shall stop saying such things because I do want my status granted. . . .

untry,
their
kind of g
like ours,
upon u
America
ions of p
foreign
om. Others have come,
for political freedo

JULIJA SUPUT

A BOUQUET OF ROSES

After our love-making, my hands lazily explored my lover's spine, and my finger tips caressed each vertebra with the dedication of a scientist who hopes to make some sensational discovery. Time seemed to stand still on those hot summer afternoons of 1999, when the whole town on my small island took a collective siesta. The thought of having a lover who lived in the States did not bother me a bit. The summer would last forever, and we would repeat our love ritual every afternoon in my lover's rented studio. Afterwards, I would run home, my flip flops hardly touching the irregular stone pavers on the narrow passage between houses, and take my boys to the beach.

But the summer ended. Fifty thousand tourists I didn't care for, and my lover, whose soft skin I still desperately longed to touch, left. Sometimes, while I sat on the terrace of a coffee shop chatting with my colleagues about our students, I would see the silhouette of a man that reminded me of my summer lover. And my heart would beat faster. But I was not sure anymore whether my love story really happened or whether it was just my imagination.

Until my lover's phone call in November. Until his return in the middle of the winter. This time, I offered him my hospitality in my little run-down house, and the summer love suddenly acquired a different dimension. It seemed to have a future. A future in the United States, in California.

My knowledge about and interest in America was a loose patchwork of the best American movies I had seen in our small town theater. I mostly forgot the American authors I had zealously read in the seventies and eighties. I knew that there had been and perhaps still was an American dream, but it had never attracted my curiosity. I was a French and Italian teacher after all.

Nevertheless, when my lover had proposed marriage and asked me to come with him, it did not take me long to decide. I started imagining infinite possibilities for my young boys. All of a sudden the narrow streets of my town became too narrow for my feverish imagination, the familiar faces boring. I wanted a change. I wanted my boys to have a better life, although what exactly that would be, I was not sure.

My lover left for the second time. My boys and I would follow him as soon as my fiancée visa arrived. My friends and colleagues looked at me in disbelief while, with my hands dancing in the air, I talked about my plans. Their eyes told me what they didn't want to say. "You are too old for this big move. You are forty-six and you have kids. Where are you going? Are you crazy?" I was not scared. I was excited and curious.

With two of my boys I left on January 14, 2001. At the airport, I felt a lump in my throat while I hugged my oldest son who would not come with us. I was on the brink of tears when my mother hugged and held me tight, and wouldn't let me go. Then, the last call for all passengers flying to London.

"We will come back next summer," I told her and freed myself from her embrace.

I pushed my boys gently towards customs, holding three passports with visas stamped in them in my hand. I turned back one more time and tried to smile. I saw my mother crying, my oldest son hugging her; I breathed deeply.

It was midnight when we arrived at the San Jose Airport. My fiancé kissed me furtively on the cheek. He didn't embrace me.

My eyes were wide open in amazement as I carried my suitcase to our master bedroom. The house was huge with five bedrooms and three bathrooms, high ceilings, everything clean and new. Later, in bed, my hands wanted to reconnect with the lover I remembered from my island. But they could not. There was a barrier between my hands and my lover's skin, as though I were touching a knight in his armor. "Probably jetlag," I concluded as I sank into a dreamless sleep.

The next day, as we drove to Costco, my eyes searched for some sign of a real city, some tall buildings, some skyscrapers. In Costco, I felt dizzy from seeing so much food and so many people pushing their gigantic carts around. My fiancé hopped from one stand to another where ladies in red aprons and white hats offered samplings of different foods.

I soon learned that *free* was my fiancé's favorite word. When he saw it or heard it, his face lit up, acquiring an almost pious expression. *Expensive* and *destroy* were other buzz words for him. The expression I detected on his face when he uttered them was far from pious.

"It's expensive," he said with determination when, after spending a day at the beach, I suggested we stop for some coffee and ice cream.

"Your boys will destroy my house," he repeated so many times a day that my whole body hurt; it felt as though it were shrinking. His voice was still soft, but filled with fury.

We went to Reno to get married, one weekend in February when the Sierras were covered with the snow.

"The license is cheaper there," my fiancé said.

My boys stayed with the neighbors. I wanted them to come with us, but I didn't have a voice.

"We will have fun without them. Anyway, we are coming back tomorrow."

I could not have fun. I was worried about my boys. I didn't understand why we had to go to Reno. My fiancé took me to some dark motel on the outskirts. In the evening, he took me to a big hotel and we had dinner in a restaurant on the tenth floor where one can eat as much as he or she wants for only ten dollars. My fiancé was excited. I was on the brink of tears.

The air was crisp and the sky was icy blue in the morning when we walked downtown looking for a wedding chapel. In the chapel, the lady looked at us smiling and offered her service. My fiancé checked the price. The lady put us in front of a fireplace and we repeated vows after her. We didn't exchange rings.

From a gentle lover and impatient fiancé, my husband became a sulky man. I listened to the same complaints over and over. I explained, I tried, but it was not enough. He continued. Then I stopped talking. The dark circles under my eyes grew bigger, I felt trapped, I felt abused. Then, one afternoon, I snapped at him. I threatened to cut his carpet into small pieces before I left him. I shouted and I shouted. He looked at me. He was afraid and didn't move. I stopped hollering only when I lost my voice.

I started working and the work kept me sane. I met people. I confided in a colleague, but she didn't know what I should do. It was a complicated situation due to immigration policies. I needed a green card. We had not yet been scheduled for the first interview and the only thing I had was a Social Security number and a work permit.

For the next couple of months, my brain became foggier and foggier; I felt nothing but dullness. Then, we received a letter from the Immigration and Naturalization Service in San Jose with a date for the interview.

JULIJA SUPUT

My husband was in a bad mood, and with my boys in the back seats, he drove to San Jose in complete silence. But the silence was telling. He did not really want us. He wanted me, but not me as a human being but me as a slender body that he could reach for every night. He didn't want my boys. He was never kind to them.

The INS officer looked at the boys with surprise. The scheduled interview was only for the two of us, not for my boys as well. My husband needed to fill out an immigration package for each boy separately. He should have done it within three months of our arrival. The officer turned the pages of my immigration package and checked whether all documents had been submitted. The interview was short. My palms were sweaty.

There was little communication between us from then on. Even my boys stopped talking. In the evenings, when my husband would watch TV, his favorite and only pastime, I would glance at him wondering how I could have misjudged him so much. "Passion wears rose-colored glasses," my mother used to say. She was right. I flew across a half of the world to realize that the man lying on that bed was not a man with whom I wanted to spend the rest of my life. During the sleepless nights I thought about my friends back in my home country. I thought about my two older brothers. They had all doubted that my decision to leave my modest but sheltered life on my island was the best one. Mornings, as the first streaks of light came through closed shutters, I wondered whether they were right. I hoped my green card would soon arrive. I hoped that would bring some solution. The two yellow envelopes with immigration papers for my boys rested on the hallway table unopened.

The neighbors watched as a friend from work and her husband helped me load two mattresses on their truck and some of my few other belongings. My husband stood on the sidewalk as if not sure whether he wanted me to leave or not. I was sure, though. My mother, who had come to visit a month earlier, also helped. We moved to a small seaside town close to where I worked. I could afford a one-bedroom apartment in a very nice complex with a swimming pool. It was January 14, exactly one year after our arrival in America, and I had a green card granted for two years. My three female colleagues surprised me and bought me some kitchen utensils, a plastic table and chairs. I was grateful to them and I felt less lonely.

My colleagues at work, all with their own immigration stories, warned me that I could get in trouble because I had left my husband who, in the meantime, had already filed for divorce. I went to see an immigration lawyer, and she told me that I should be fine because I was earning enough money. I could take care of myself and my boys. I didn't have the opportunity to talk about the status of my boys. But I was not concerned. Nobody ever asked me about their green cards, and when I called the Immigration and Naturalization Service, a female voice told me that once I got my unconditional green card, I could apply for my boys. I didn't yet know that this information was incorrect and that my boys were illegal residents.

Reassured by the incorrect information, I focused on our every-day life. My boys went to high school and played sports. I liked the fact that their English became native-like and that they acculturated so quickly. I wanted them to live in the country which seemed to offer many more opportunities than they would have had in our native country. I also saw new opportunities for myself. I could again go to school and learn new skills; improve my English; widen my own horizons. Once I got out from my unfortunate marriage, the possibilities seemed endless. I felt as if I could breathe again.

I liked the fact that we lived close to the ocean. It reminded me of the sea that washes on the shores of my island. I liked the neighborhood's Victorian houses. When I met my first American friend, and took walks with her along the sandy beach wrapped in fog, I started loving fog, too.

My daily schedule was busy. I held a full-time day job, taught two evenings a week in the town's adult school, and went to school for my master's. I didn't have time to remember the life that I had left on my island. I couldn't go there to visit, but my mother came and spent six months with us. When my boys came home from school, hungry after sports practice, and I from work, a hot meal cooked by my mother was waiting for us.

Time passed. One day at work I confided in one of my colleagues. I told him that my boys did not have their green cards yet and that I would apply for them.

"You will not be able to apply for them, you are not a citizen," he told me.

"But a lady at the immigration office told me I could," I said.

"It's not true," he told me.

He thought I should do something. He warned me that my kids could get in trouble and never get green cards. He gave me the name of an immigration lawyer who had helped him. However, the lawyer couldn't do anything yet for us. My green card was still granted conditionally for two years.

"Call me once your conditional status is removed," he said, "then I will see what I can do."

I could not sleep at night. I was afraid for my kids, so I decided to go to the INS outreach. I drove there one Thursday afternoon. There were two officers in a small office. One started yelling at me; he told me that we were in big trouble. He made me write some statement and told me that he would take it to his boss and his boss would call me. As I drove home, my brain hurt, my whole body shook.

For months after that, nothing happened; nobody called. So I decided to go to the INS outreach one more time. There were a lot of people waiting in line. In one of the two small offices, I saw the same officer who had yelled at me; in the other, a female officer. When my turn came, I told her everything. I told her that I had left my husband, that I felt he abused me and my kids, and that I had to leave. I told her that he did not want to apply for green cards for my kids. She listened to me. But, like the officer who had yelled at me, she told me that I was in big trouble; she gave me a pass to go to the INS main branch office in San Jose to talk to somebody there.

In San Jose, I waited endlessly before I was called into a small office. The officer did not know how he could help, it was too complicated; he had not yet heard of a case like mine. So, he went to talk to his boss. My gaze was fixed at the door behind which he had disappeared. I waited and I waited. Finally, a woman called my name, and I followed her. She had my file on her desk.

"Your ex-husband still can adjust your kids' status," she said.

Her voice was like a storm. It shook me, but I was hopeful again.

At home, I called my ex-husband. He was not convinced. He was afraid my kids would cost him money and ruin him. I started begging him. I told him that my older boy wanted to go to Australia with his basketball team, but could not leave the country without a green card. I told him that it was not their fault that our marriage didn't work. He asked me to come back to him. When I told him I could not, he refused to help me.

I got mad, furious. I thought there must be some law that protected minors. There must be some law that would force my ex-husband to do what he was supposed to do in the first three months after our arrival in America. I called the lawyer again. He assured me that such a law didn't exist. This was not the answer I wanted, so I started to research on the Internet. What I found blew my mind away and made my heart race: Fifteen-year-old illegal immigrants waited for hearings in regular prisons for years. I could not believe what I read. I could not believe that it was happening in what I had been told was the most democratic country in the world.

My Italian students detected desperation on my face. They engaged me in animated discussions. One of my students decided he would write a letter to a bigwig in the Democratic Party. The other lady would talk to her husband who had a very important role in the local branch of the Republican Party. Time passed. It rained again. I received two phone calls.

"We are sorry, INS has its own laws," their voices echoed each other.

"Have a nice day," they wished me.

"How cruel they are," I thought.

Another friend told me about young illegal students who were protesting in Washington. Immigration reform would happen soon. My sons were seventeen and fifteen. Hopefully John Kerry would get elected.

"Anybody would be better than Bush," my American friend said.

I ignored my fatigue until, one day, I could not get out of my bed. I was sick, very sick. I got pills to manage my condition. I will have to take them every day for the rest of my life.

My older son didn't talk much. He played football and basketball. In the spring he tried track and field. One day, when I came to pick him up after his practice, he sat on the lawn and laughed. There was a girl sitting beside him. She talked and giggled. I waited. My son talked and giggled. I waited. Warmed by the sun, I enjoyed watching my son. A man came from the other side of the field and called to the girl. He was angry. The girl talked and giggled a little longer. Then she stood up and dragged her feet towards the gate where the man disappeared with her.

It was September when I saw the same girl and the man again. We were standing at the entrance of Trader Joe's. She was tanned and much prettier than I remembered her. She had grown up. She had spent a month in Europe with her dad at the seaside. I wanted to know whether she was still friendly with my son. She was taking two classes with him. She introduced me to her dad. He looked at me indifferently, swinging the bags in his hands.

A month later after I parked my car behind the adult school where I worked, I heard the girl's voice. She was talking to a janitor, a skateboard held up against her chest. I called out to her. I wanted to know about her and my son. She said they were friends, but she had other friends, too, and that she was very busy and had to go; she had to write an essay for tomorrow. I asked her about her mother as well. She only said she lived with her dad.

In a heavy January rain, my mother and I rushed from the car to the store and bumped into the girl again. "Happy New Year," we said, then kissed each other. Her dad and an older lady were there as well. The father's mother was visiting. The girl talked and giggled.

"It seems that my daughter has found a mother," he said, looking at me.

He suggested that we could get together sometimes, go for a walk with our mothers.

I waited three weeks for the rain to stop before I called him. We went to a state park. The clouds still lingered in the sky and the chill penetrated my bones. Our mothers connected right away. They laughed. The man and I walked side by side, and it felt awkward. I didn't know what to talk about other than my work and the illegal status of my boys. As we returned back to our town, I found out that it was the man's birthday. We were the same age.

Later, the man and his mother came to dinner at our house; then we went to dinner at theirs. We drank red wine and ate fish. The man knew a lot about music. My boys came, too. They ate in the living room at a small table with the girl. She talked and giggled.

My son was now a senior in high school. When his statistics teacher found out that he didn't have a green card, she offered to help. She and her husband took me to a lawyer, the same one I had called a couple of years before. He said the same things as the INS officer. The teacher's husband was confident, the lawyer was confident. They both called my ex-husband.

The man's mother left at the end of February. One Saturday he invited me and my mother to go to the beach. My mother declined the invitation. He and I walked and hiked to reach a beach where only birds come. Side by side, we bent over the rocks to look for abalone shells. Our bodies were close but they never touched; I was already madly in love.

I went to see the lawyer again. My son's teacher and her husband were there, too.

"What kind of man is he?" the teacher's husband inquired after my ex-husband had again refused to help.

"What if I get married now?" I said.

"Do you have somebody in mind?"

"Not really."

"Yes, that would be a solution."

No, I could not ask the man. We had just met. But one evening after a movie, as we walked to his car, I did ask him. He stood on the sidewalk, smoking a cigarette. He needed to think. The following morning he said he would marry me.

We met during our lunch break in a little wedding chapel in our town. He brought me a bouquet of roses. I did not have my driver's license with me, I did not have any form of I.D. The lady married us anyway, she knew some people from my work. At home that evening my mother waited for us with a special dinner. We celebrated our marriage and my younger son's birthday.

The lawyer filled out the immigration application forms ten days before my older son's eighteenth birthday. I felt nothing could go wrong anymore. The feeling of being stuck with illegal kids in America that had hovered over my head for four years dissipated in the embrace of my husband. I stopped having my recurring nightmare: My boys and I are back on the island; we want to return to our home in California, but I don't have visas for them. I panic. We cannot go back.

The longing to go back to my home country stayed, though. So I made a trip back to my island. At the airport, while I was waiting for my luggage, a man waved at me. Only when he smiled, did I recognize him as my brother. When I had left, his hair had been dark, his body slender. With him was my oldest son who had not come to the U.S. with me. We hugged and hugged. The weather was grim, the traffic dense and the streets so narrow. I walked the streets of my youth, meeting old friends whose lives were confined within the city limits. I visited my family. I traveled to the island I had left four years before. I met my friends, listened to them chat. But I missed my husband, I missed my two boys in the U.S., I missed my colleagues who had come from different parts of the world to live in America. Winter is a sad time on the island.

"This is my home now," I told my husband when he hugged me at the airport on my return to the U.S. He handed me a bouquet of roses.

In the oasis of our home, friends were welcomed. We discussed politics, read books, compared and criticized the world in which we live and the world we had left behind. I was changing. Having more than one choice and driving on the wide roads once overwhelmed me. Talking to a cashier about my private life was unimaginable; the concept of pot luck was a sign of not being hospitable; smiling to unknown people was a sign of weakness; laughing while talking about a dead person was the utmost lack of respect. All these behaviors that once had shocked me imperceptibly became a part of my own being.

And there was more. Although I was over fifty years old, I was going to school. Unimaginable in my country. I didn't have to serve my husband. Rare in my country. My husband saw me as his equal partner; we supported each other. When we went to the beach accompanied with our kids and our dog, and I looked at the sky, I wanted to fly. Yet, every year at the beginning of the summer, I felt nostalgic for my home country. I dreamt of the hot summer evenings there.

"I don't have two homes," my neighbor told me.

"You are lucky," I said.

I went to my home country again, and again the following year, and again. The scenario was always the same: a long flight, jet lag, family, friends and the urge to come back to my California home.

On a hot day in October 2007, I became a naturalized citizen. I didn't feel any different, until November 2, 2008, when, in the town community center, I stood in the line and waited for a lady with a little American flag pinned on her lapel, to find my name on the list and give me a ballot.

if ever one to help

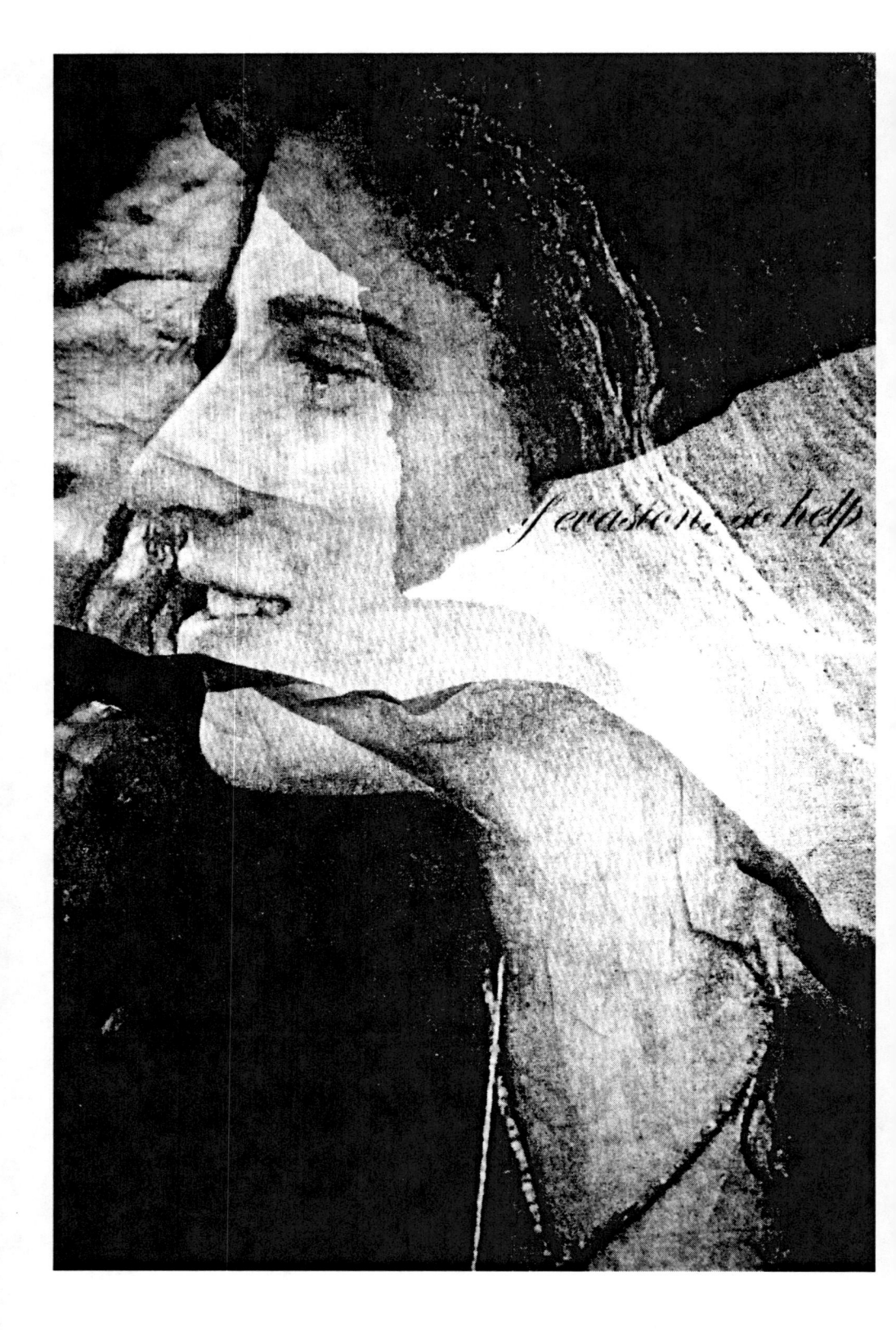

HOME IS WHERE . . .

MARIEL COEN

NOT FROM HERE, NI DE ALLA

I am
in certain moments—
like when I soak
sweet bread in black coffee
just like Maria Elena,
the servant,
with her stained face and
tired legs heavy with
engorged veins bulging
like patterns on tree bark.

I am
parts of
Fatima,
when I'm not looking
straight at myself
and someone registers my face—
recognizes a trace
now of instinctive elegance
acquired
in the way I learned
through infantile mimicry
to hold my chin slightly
up and out.

MARIEL COEN

I am
Giorgio,
the foreign blue-eyed man in search of
exotic adventures in tropical lands,
torn between the life he left half-eaten
and the one he sought to taste.
Though he never knew me,
he is the shadow that
walks beside me;
that lurks behind my actions—
and leaves me with questions
he'll never answer
of boats and oceans and why he came.

Sono italiana, o force averei potuto esserlo,
pero tambien, Chinandegana
aunque nunca vivi ahí.
I also carry with me
loud articulate echoes of
Mary Jane Doe
accented with a pitch I can't camouflage.
Je suis aussi le français appris,
mais j'en ai pris seulement ce que me fallait
selon moi.

I am Indian, native, but new to this land,
both conqueror and conquest.
I can sway my demeanor
my diction and conduct
depending on the meal set before me,
the shoes of my audience,
the tone of your voice.

I am princess and pauper,
adorned or stark naked,
a faithful missionary
who can steal meat during famine,
and host you impeccably at feasts.

*Je suis comme je suis,
parte tuya, toda mia,
e non c'è risposta nessuna,*
for you cannot solve me
by plopping an x in front of my whys.

I am a Guatemalan river that surges down
a Nicaraguan volcano
erupting on a Palm Beach golf course
atop a New York high rise
erected on a Tuscan field
with a fire exit door leading to London.

PALABRAS PROHIBIDAS

No se habla inglés en la casa
Mi mama no entiende.
This makes us want to speak it more
which makes her protest louder.

We learn quickly,
blend what we come from
with the world we're thrust into
acquiring a taste for rushed food
and rooted beer.

Our familiar *pinolillo*,
pulverized cornmeal and cacao,
replaced with *Coca-Cola Clásica*.

With practiced pronunciation
we perfect slang
to master it like natives.

We mend our broken English
with unpatriotic patchwork.
Liquando idiomas.
New words trail behind us
all the way back from school.
They invite themselves in
to battle against her
impulse to instill our culture
so it's not forgotten and replaced.

Palabras prohibidas always win
planting themselves proudly on
the tips of our tongues.

They stretch and swell on the surface,
threaten to jump on the dinner table in crooked
somersaults until landing in the
arroz aguado
causing a loud, linguistic leap into *castigo*.

They roam incessantly in our minds
like shiny new remote-control cars.
Sin control.

Before too long, these words start
to stake claim and set up their quaint
American dreams within us,
picket fences and all,
making our Mother's tongue wave
like a furious flag.
Mama, cómo se dice en español?

She fights harder, saying the words louder
as if her pitch will make them stick
to our minds *confundidas,*
finding a fuzzy frequency to tune out
the English intruders.
Los intenta silenciar.

Regularmente we nervously request
her to fill in the blanks of our
cracked conversations.
She is the saviour of our lazy lexicon.
Dios te salve María, llena eres de gracia.

The fight never ends between the words
either forgotten or forbidden,
but soon, with great regularity
she turns to us to clarify the *gringo*'s gabble,
and sometimes even asks us,
Cómo se dice en inglés?

...nprisoned lightning

L. Estes

ANGELIKA QUIRK

I AM FROM THE OTHER SIDE

I am from the birch, its bark white and grey
split in half, the one that stood
near Wacholder Park, from the wetlands
of the Baltic Sea, I am from the other side.

From the gatekeeper, the clock tower
ticking, watching hands slide
into the crevices of passing days.
I am from the dance of the hours
climbing up when the minutes decline.

I am from *Sauerbraten* and *Borsch*
and *Bienenstich* and Sunday walks,
wandering winds, and honey wax candles
lit on the fourth of Advent.

I am from the amethyst stone,
the feather bed, mulled wine,
and chamomile tea, from ice flowers
on windowpanes melting with my breath.

I am from the longing arc
and the gothic script,
the sentence without a period,

from hooded dreams worn thin
where stones and sculptures stand
peering across covered with lichen.

MY LIFE

Ten degrees below zero at birth,
a city in ruins,
that's what I called my home.

Reciting Rilke and Goethe
and Hermann Hesse,
I stumbled onto words and verses
and carried them with me.

I climbed mountains in the Alps,
the skirt of the *Queen of the Night*,
and at Christmas skated down
frozen rivers.

I rehearsed *Solveig* from *Peer Gynt*
and visited Sibelius' monument
with pipes whistling in the wind.

I still cook *Rindsrouladen*
and bake blackforest cake.
But now I only swear in German.

I pledge allegiance to two countries,
and when I travel across the ocean,
I yearn for the other side.

SWEARING-IN CEREMONY, MASONIC AUDITORIUM, APRIL 25, 2005

Afghanistan, Algeria, Argentina, Angola
           We stand up one by one
Belgium, Bulgaria, Cambodia
           like candles on a birthday cake.
Canada, Chile, China
           Guten Tag! Hola! Szia!
           Bonjour! Shalom!
           Konichiwa!
           We shake hands,
           each fingerprinted
           with a foreign touch.
Denmark, Dominica, Egypt
           Lingering doubts
           leap to twelve o'clock
           urgencies.
Finland, France, Germany
           I stand.
           Will I die on this land
           where the sun rises
           nine hours too late?
Ghana, Greece, Guatemala
           My right hand perspires.
           Held up high,
           it trembles in thin air.
Haiti, Honduras, Hungary
           My hand, a fledgling
           learning to fly.

India, Israel, Italy
        We carry our ancestries
        in the side pockets
        of our first arrivals,
Japan, Kenya, Lithuania
        packed tightly
        with terror of wars,
        homeland songs,
        claims of returns.
Mexico, Nicaragua, Nigeria
        Years linked like chains
        wrapped around our wrists,
        our neck
Oman, Poland, Portugal
        choking our voices,
        a tear,
        then another.
Russia, Serbia, Slovakia, Spain
        Refugees of foreign tongues,
        we belong
        neither here nor there,
Turkey, Turkmenistan
        but forever oscillate
        in-between.
Uganda, Ukraine, Uruguay
        Yet now we stand,
        now we swear.

Venezuela, Vietnam, Yugoslavia
        Nous jurons,
        giuriamo,
Zaire, Zambia, Zimbabwe
        wir schwoeren,
        wij zweren:

        one thousand
        four hundred
        fifty-one
        voices
        e pluribus unum.

        Cheers echo from rows
        to pews to the overhang
        accenting each word,
        each dream.

WHAT IS IT THAT'S CALLED YOUR COUNTRY?

Heimat, Homeland?
Witches' lures, creaky floors, and open flames?
Your place of birth, nine time zones away
where Snowhite's stepmother danced on ashes,
and your mother's eyes reflected the fear of rubble?

    Or is it where your children were born
    and don't understand your language?

Is it called *Dein Vaterland*?
Where the chimney sweep crossed
your street for good luck, and you thought
he would climb up his ladder
to wipe off soot and sorrows
stored under each roof and rafter.

    But now you live in a house
    with chimes and ceiling fans.

But remember the oak your forefathers planted?
Strong and stubborn branching
over your entrance. Didn't you learn from it?
Wasn't this what you called *Heimat*?

    Yet today you inhale the scent of lemon trees,
    and wait for magnolias to bloom.

Remember the chest in the attic,
hand-carved, of solid wood?
Inside your mother's wedding gown,
her womanhood hidden from soldiers
that plundered, and you held on
to your porcelain doll that could
open and close her eyes.

Yes, you were a survivor: fleeing west,
still restless like the cuckoo on your wall
punctually sticking out its beak
pecking:

    What is your country now?

SANDRA SOLI

HOW I LEARNED RESURRECTION

> *Explain that you live between two great darks,*
> *the first with an ending, the second without one.*
> —Mark Strand

I have seen harbors and ports of call:
New York, Liverpool, Bremerhaven, Le Havre
and the ships two-stackers or three,
their energy! Cunard liners above all
enticements to dance whistles, foghorns
a band playing, flapping flags and confetti,
it becomes a movie and people waving,
even those who don't know me, hey none
of them know me, why are they waving?

This burden of responsibility to enjoy everything!

Every crossing is the same.
Arrivals and departures are the same.
Souvenirs, customs and baggage tags.
Green-faced passengers in deck chairs are the same
and the ocean, keeping its foamy, interstitial clock.

Staterooms below the water line are the same
and dizzy corridors, smiling stewards,
second sitting bells, mothers who regret
their daughters & Titanic jokes at lifeboat drills,
all the same. Finally I recognize the chink
between the Atlantic and the otherworld and jump
like Hart Crane.

Suddenly nobody grows older, everyone has a ticket
and even in third class children are born over
and over again, these new lives
that come always to save us.

FOREIGNER: LEARNING THE LANGUAGE

Foreigner Foreigner Foreigner F
Outsider Outsider Outsider Outsi
Stranger Stranger Stranger   Stra
Alien Alien   Alien   Alien Alien
GobackwhereyoucamefromGoback
YouDon'tBelongHere. YouDon'tBe
You'llpay You'llpayYou'llpayPayPay
Interloper   Interloper
Saythatwordagain Say
Zed Zed Zed Zed Zed
Youtalkfunny Youtalk
Forenner Forenner F
RunnerRunnerRunner
Runfaster Runfaster Runfaster Run
Don'ttrytohide Don'ttrytohideDon't
Wait till after school   Wait till after
SticksandStones SticksandStones S
Seethisrock   Seethisrock   Seethis
Stuckup Stuckup Stuckup Stuckup
Nobodywillsaveyou Nobodywillsave
ThisIsTheEndOfYou
RenderRenderRender
FinderFinderFinderFi
AlleeAlleeOutsinFree
Shutup Shutup Shut
Ourplace   Ourplace
Private Private   Priv
Club Club ClubClub
GetoutGetoutGetout
AndDon'tComeBack
Crybaby CrybabyCry
Teachyou Teachyou
Stupidbitch   Stupid
Can'tYouTakeaJoke?

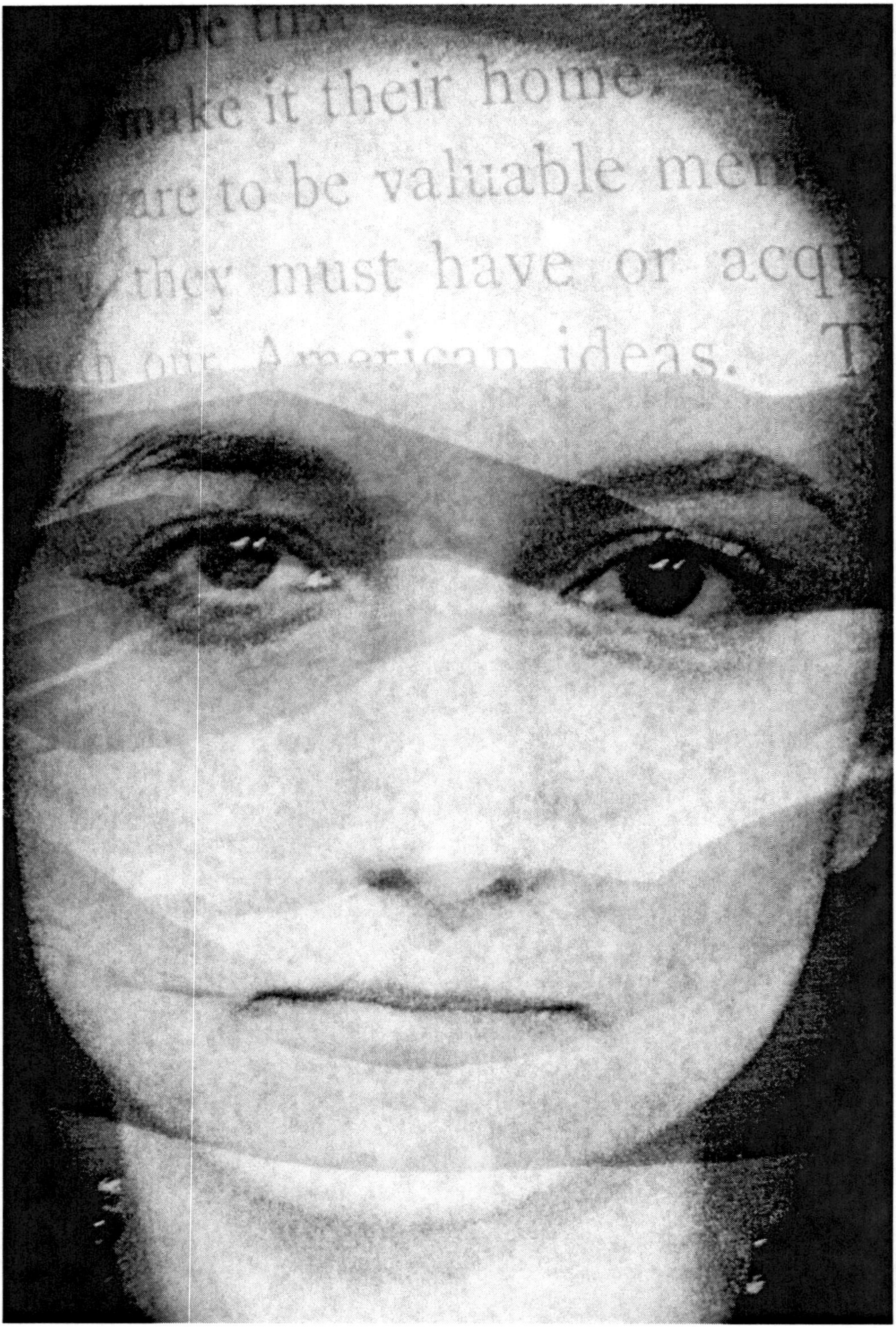
make it their home.
are to be valuable mem
they must have or acq
American ideas.

SONYA SABANAC

BILINGUAL

My two languages live like step-brothers,
sometimes they get along,
sometimes they hate each other.

I am the girl they both want.

"Give me the words!" I ask
and they compete
who would find the better ones.
They clash or complement,
interweave or whisper back and forth.
If one is a little slow,
the other jumps to respond.

Playful and witty,
the words they feed me with
are fresh and sweet as wild strawberries.

I take every one of them and before they melt,
I roll them in my mouth to learn their sound:

"Kroshnya,
Crown,
Dusha,
Illumination,
Passion"

Savoring their taste, I drift into a dream
in which I sail on two magnificent rivers at once,
and breathe the blossoms of their banks.

And just when I feel enriched
and ready to use the gift,
with no warning signs
the friendly duel erupts into a genuine fight.

The last I hear before my brain gets flat,
is that threatening sound of the Beethoven's Fifth,
a war to the very last word is on:
<u>Slavic vs. Anglo-Saxon!</u>

Each language wants to conquer
all the cells of my brain and
push the other out
of this gray and white land.

Serbian—my first everything:
books and loves, sins and stars,
my child's lullabies,
threatens:
"If you lose me—you will lose your soul."

English promises, coaxes:
"Don't look behind, I am the freedom
to express who you truly are."

An impossible choice! I am destitute,
left at no man's land.
I stumble for words, but I have no
language to speak!
I try to use one, but the other intrudes
with its soldiers, verbs and nouns,

putting in its own syntax to block the way.
My mind is cracking, this conflict
turns me into a schizophrenic!

I am about to explode.
Enough,
enough of this jealousy and war!

With a pretense of a smile
I give each of them a task:
From Serbian, I ask a fair translation of e.e. cummings
and from English, a justice for Dobrisa Cesaric.

Working on this assignment the step-brothers
give each other a hand
and realize how vain they were
and how much more there is to learn:
To unveil Truth and Beauty
is the task of a lifetime.
Humbled, they respond
to the noble cause,
and though from a different descent
true brothers they become
and pledge to faithfully serve me
on this long and uncertain road
to achieve this wondrous goal.

HOW I DECIDED TO GO A LITTLE CRAZY

Being a "little bit crazy" can go a long way. Before I explain that, let me tell you a joke:

"Father and son are on their way to America. At some point, son asks: 'Daddy, daddy, are we almost there?'

'Oh, be quiet my son and keep swimming.'"

Finding ourselves immigrants in America felt in many ways as if we were thrown into deep waters and the only way to survive was to be quiet and keep swimming. In order to establish ourselves in our new patria, we almost had to learn how to walk again. I am going to skip the part about how one actually starts out in the new country not knowing a living soul and endowed with a 'fortune' of $400. I have to admit that we did come with a certain degree of expectation that we would be recognized as newcomers and, as such, offered some help or at least guidance. False. We had to learn everything by ourselves; most of the time it felt as if we were blind, stretching out our hands in the dark, trying to find what we were looking for.

Even the people whose job it was to help refugees could not care less. I'll just mention the Armenian lady (an immigrant herself, but with longer 'years of service') from the International Rescue Committee who, instead of the customary $700 welcoming check, gave us only $400 with the indecipherable explanation as to why our check shrank. What could we do about it? Nothing, we were "silent and kept swimming." Furthermore, in order to be born administratively, we had to go to numerous windows of many governmental institutions at which we were met with the unexpected rudeness and shortness of those behind the windows. And, oh boy, did they exercise the power the State of California vested in its officials! They made us feel as if our lives were at their disposal. For instance at the immigration office, after long hours of waiting in uncertainty and suspense, when I was finally allowed to approach the window to submit the paperwork for the green card, a stern-looking official of Vietnamese background claimed that one of the papers was missing. In my naiveté, by putting a hand inside of his window with the intention of showing him where the 'missing' paper was, I endangered myself. It was like putting a hand in the lion's den. The guy literally slapped my hand. And what did I do? Beside withdrawing my hand immediately—nothing. I was "silent and kept swimming."

Next, the welfare office! Even more important! Again, long hours in deep anxiety, my husband and I biting our nails wondering: "Are they going to find us eligible for money support or not? Are we going to live before we could find work or are we going to die of starvation? Did we really have to come all the way here to die, why didn't we just stay in Bosnia and get killed by bullets? At least we would have had the benefit of a fast death." When our number was finally called, a lady with the longest nails we had ever seen gave us a look of suspicion under which we immediately felt guilty and the fear we came with escalated like boiling milk, not to mention the uneasiness in communicating with our school-knowledge of English. With apologetic smiles, I would say over and over: "Excuse me, pardon me, could you please repeat that? . . . Sorry, I did not understand. . . . Could you please speak slower?" Everything I said seemed to frustrate and irritate the welfare lady even more. Exiting the office in dismay and still not knowing what our fate would be, surprised by the offensiveness with which we were received, we almost wanted to run back and ask the lady: "Hey, do you know how much we cried watching Alex Haley's *Roots*?" We did nothing of the sort and by now you already know what we did do: we were "silent and kept swimming."

Two years into our immigrant life, we were fully aware of harsh reality. Nobody really cared about anyone else, immigrant or non-immigrant. We landed in Los Angeles, one of the harshest cities in the U.S.A. to survive; the city where people were preoccupied with themselves, their appearances and their success; after all this was a Hollywood state. It was also a city of vast contrasts and differences. We could not see the rich at close range since we did not belong to their world, but we could observe a lot of homeless people who constantly raised questions in our minds: "How is it possible in the richest country in the world? Could the same fate happen to us?" One out of many nights that I could not fall asleep, I turned on the television to try to soothe my anxiety and what did I come across? Oprah telling us that an average American is two paychecks away from being homeless. The message was clear: it was not just the 'privilege' of drug addicts or really crazy people. Oprah stepped out of the TV and was now standing in my living room and while I was trying to hide under the blanket, with only my eyes and nose peaking, she pointed her finger at me and said: "You too could become homeless!"

She scared me to death! In order to document what she was reporting, Oprah followed the story of a woman, I suppose that 'average American,' who became homeless due to an illness and excessive medical bills. I vividly remember that the woman was living in the forest. Oprah's crew filmed the woman for a year or two. At the end, the woman passed away, homeless and alone. Now I have to say that I was scared, not only because of the fact that in this day and age, those were possibilities for 'normal' people, but also by how merciless those in search of a 'good' story or 'good' news were. It reminded me of the biologists who for long periods of time would go into the wilderness to observe the wildlife, but in no way were allowed to interfere. On another occasion while watching TV, I observed a newswoman, who, upon hearing that a little boy was trapped in a laundry machine and lost a hand due to the accident, could not hide her 'journalist's excitement' and exclaim quite cheerily: "What great news!" At that point I realized I immigrated to another planet.

While we are on the subject of TV news, I have to tell you what my husband was half jokingly telling me all along about our relatives who asked us to help them join us as immigrants in the U.S.A.: "We should have them watch L.A. news for several hours and then if they still wanted to come, at least it would be at their own risk." He also wanted to add the film *Multiplicity* with Michael Keaton on the 'must-see-list before immigrating into the U.S.A.' We loved this movie because it entertainingly demonstrated the fast-paced way of life we happened to fall into.

Los Angeles indeed lives one hundred miles per hour and that leads me to the topic of the most common question asked: "How are you?" In order to explain the fundamental cultural differences with respect to this subject I have to digress a little and tell you a short story, so you will know where I am coming from. In one of his novels, the great Bosnian writer Mesa Selimovic went back in time when the distances between places were still measured by 'days of walking.' The hero of the story was walking long hours on a hot summer day and, at the moment when he thought he would no longer be able to continue his voyage, he came across a water fountain made of stone with the bench as an integral part of it. On the stone, there was engraving that said:" How are you?" The man was thrilled with the fact that not only he found cold water that revived him and the bench at which he rested his weary body, but also that he was greeted with those kind words: "How are you?"

He kept repeating those caring words. "Someone cares how I feel, someone is concerned about me, someone wishes me well," he thought. He had a good rest at this place and with the strength regained and joy in the heart, he was able to continue the trip and reach his destination. Yet, he did not forget the kindness of an unknown benefactor who helped him on his journey. Being a good man, he wanted to do the same for others. So, he built a similar water fountain on some other road and wanted to engrave a saying equally nice as: "How are you?" He was thinking and thinking for days, searching for the right words to express his care for the unknown travelers. Words such as "hello" and "be well" and "greetings" came to his mind, however all these words would come together in this simple question: "How are you?" At the end, our hero gave up his wish for originality since he could not find better words for his own water-fountain than those already written.

Back to my own story. The event I described happened long ago but the way I was taught to respect the "how are you" question remained intact. Now picture me, with this frame of mind, on Monday mornings when some of my co-workers would casually ask me the same question. With the warmest smile I could produce, I would start answering and soon enough I would find myself talking into thin air. I would then stop in the middle of the word with my mouth open creating a picture of a perfect idiot! Once, allowing myself to be irritated both with me and that colleague of mine, I went after her and asked why bother posing a question if she did not care for the answer. She put a hand on my hand and, as though she was talking to a five year old, said that she "just wanted to be polite." "It was rude" I thought, but finally learned the proper way: If someone asked how you were, simply say that you were fine, no matter what. It won't make a difference; no one has time to care about you anyway. Keep your worries or joys to yourself.

Since I was married (for better or worse) I could share with my husband all the peculiarities I encountered in my daily struggle to become an American. For my daughter it was really hard. Being an only child, she was deprived of the companionship of a sibling and like any other child, she wanted to belong. Don't we all? The feeling of belonging is a whole new subject about which I could say a lot, but in this text I have to stick to my title to which I am slowly coming.

When my daughter was about to start high school, I asked her school counselor to put her into the dancing class and insisted that he give me some kind of written evidence that this would be done. (As you can see, I was moving forward, becoming a little bit more demanding.) The counselor assured me that no written proof was necessary and that my daughter would be in that class. As always, I kept silent knowing that I had no other option but to rely on the promises that were given. The last two years showed me that most things were not in my hands; I was simply not in control. Also, I felt at odds even with the people who spoke the same language as I did. As if I had become a species of my own, I had no tribe to belong to. As my life seemed to be sinking into hardship, loneliness and unfulfilled dreams, but there was one dream I could not give up on, the dream that my daughter would have the opportunity to do something big and important with her life. I was bargaining with God, asking Him to open the doors for her and that would make up for all the bad and wrongs in my life: the loss of my baby boy, the loneliness, the feeling of misplacement, the longing for the life I knew, the hardship, the estrangement that stood between me and everybody else.

Dancing was my daughter's thing. I not only wished that she would do what she was good at, but also hoped that dancing would do that magic trick of giving her a sense of belonging. I was still bursting with pride remembering my daughter's performance with her own choreography a few years before and how popular she was in our small community of Bosnian refugees in Denmark, not to mention the future success only a mother's heart could so vividly imagine: *"I am sitting in the darkness of Carnegie Hall, sharing with others that unique theatrical anticipation, waiting for the curtains to lift, something magical is about to happen and we are all here to witness it. So, the curtains are slowly lifting, music of Ravel's Bolero fills the air and my daughter appears on the stage, dancing gracefully like a snowflake under the street lamp . . ."*

Well, back to reality. When I called the school just before the class was about to start to make sure that my daughter was enrolled in it, the indifferent, falsely-polite voice of my daughter's counselor simply said:

"I'm sorry m'am, this class is full."

"But you promised me," I said with just a hint of desperation in the voice.

"I'm sorry m'am, but this class is already full."

"But you promised me, you said there would be no problem!" This time, despair was ringing loudly in my voice.

Irritated, the counselor, trying to get rid of me and forcing himself to keep his voice at a 'professional' level, said for the third time, very slowly with accentuation of every word: "As-I-told-you,-m'am,-this-class-is-full.-There-is-nothing-I-can-do-about-it."

What he actually said to me was: "Woman, you are either crazy, deaf or do not understand English."

I have to confess that something extraordinary happened to me at that moment; since I was not deaf and by that time understood English quite well, I decided to claim craziness!

All of a sudden, different shapes and forms of lucidity managed to surface into my memory. "Praise the Foolishness," said Dutch philosopher and writer Erasmus of Rotterdam back in the sixteenth century and for a reason. Then the image of my friend from high school came to my mind; every time her parents had a disagreement, she would have one of her famous attacks of hysteria and could not stand to see her parents for a while. As a convenient solution, she would move in with me and my family. Momentarily, she would become her old self—no signs of any hysteria—and we would enjoy some of the privileges we would not have otherwise, one of them being going out on a weekday night. During this 'intermission,' her parents would get a lesson and, driven by guilt, would try to win her over with all sorts of gifts and promises. And I can say, overall, my friend had multiple benefits from her 'hysteria attacks.'

In this beautiful revelation of craziness, I felt a relief like never before in my entire life. The 'good-manners' burden that my mother had built up in me for years all of a sudden fell down, as the expression goes, like 'a castle made from playing cards.' LIBERATION! I finally felt like I did not have to behave myself at all. No rules apply to craziness. Not only could I say whatever was on my mind, in any given moment, but I could also do whatever I felt like doing. For instance, I could finally sit the way I felt suited me for the moment, not the way my mother considered appropriate for a person of the female sex. Do any of you remember how boring it was sitting at the table during a long meal or family gathering when you were forced to be still, sit and do nothing? It was not in my nature to be still, so as a little girl I invented a 'chair dance.' I would sit in a chair with my legs open, hanging in the air, since I was too short to touch the floor. With some melody playing in my mind, I would swing my legs according to that rhythm: back and forth, left and right, forth and back, right and left until my little chair dance would be abruptly stopped by my mother's scolding voice:

"For God's sake Sonya, sit in this chair properly and do not dangle your legs." (Apparently she did not realize that I was dancing.)

"What?"

"Sit properly," she would say. "Straighten your back, otherwise you will have a hunchback for the rest of your life. Keep your legs closed, be still and eat your food."

"But why do I have to keep my legs closed?"

"Because this is how nice girls sit."

"How is that so?" I would insist. Irritated by my need for some logical explanation, she would end our discussion with the tone of voice I would not dare to object: "Because I told you so."

There are numerous examples of how I was taught to behave. For instance, every time we were preparing for a formal visit (actually all the visits with my parents were formal), my mother would warn me: "Sonya, you can take one cake and no more. When they ask you to take more, just say: 'no thank you.'"

"Why?" I would ask with disappointment. "I love cakes."

My mother would answer with a question of her own, the one that was supposed to get me worried: "What will they think of you?!"

Once I broke the 'one cake only' rule. (I was only five and still learning.) The hostess insisted that I take another piece. Hard to resist a plate full of cakes right in front of my nose, but still wanted to be polite I said giving in:

"Mama told me to say that I cannot eat more, but I can." Everybody laughed, however later at home I had to learn another very important rule: "Never, ever, under any circumstances I was to disclose anything that was said in the privacy of our home."

Manners, manners, manners! All my life I had to take good care of what other people would think of me. When I was little, it was about the way I sat and ate; when I got older it was how I behaved at school and much later all about boys. There was a code that I was supposed to respect, but that would better fit in another story. There are also many examples of certain crazy streaks I had that would, from time to time, surface in my childhood and youth, however, I was more or less an obedient child. Later, I became an obedient wife and, generally speaking, I was an obedient person in every aspect of my life.

Now back to my daughter's school counselor and his attempts to dismiss me and my demand. He had no idea that what he has said unleashed my craziness, that I traveled great distances in between two single breaths. No more "think what other people would think about you," no more "be silent and keep swimming." After years of swimming I finally reached firm ground. I was a changed person, crazy person, and as such I had no worries at all. Not only did I not care what he would think of me, to the contrary, I wanted him to consider me crazy. My voice was joyful, almost singing when I addressed him:

"I want my daughter in a dancing class and I do understand there are no openings today. No problem! I will call you tomorrow to see if something has changed. If the situation is still the same, I will call you the day after tomorrow and then the next day and the next day. . . ."

The counselor interrupted stating that the situation would be the same and that I did not have to lose my time.

"No worries" I said imitating a cheerful mode. "I have time and I am going to call you e-v-e-r-y day." (I released some lunatic determination in the word 'every.') And I did call the next day. You may be guessing what happened on the third day? I did not have to call, instead he called me "happy to inform me that there was just-one-opening and he placed my daughter in it."

So, this is how I became a little bit crazy; what politeness could not do, the craziness did. (Too bad that my mother is suffering from dementia and I am not able to prove to her that good manners do not work all the time.)

Since then I've pulled my craziness many times. It works both in the benevolent and serious situation, out in the world and inside of your own home. I am getting so good at it, it seems I could write the commercial about craziness! For example:

If I wanted to wiggle out of whatever situation or discussion I am having with my husband that is not to my liking, I would say something like this:

"Wait, wait, wait, we are not going any further until you explain that look to me. What was that suppose to mean?"

"What look?" he would ask.

"You know, I've seen it. Explain yourself!"

"What look, what are you talking about? Are you are crazy?"

Of course, I would not admit, it would not work. As a rule, crazy people do not acknowledge their own craziness, their mind target other people's mind. After making such or similar "scenes" to various members of my family whenever they were becoming too demanding, they started to respect my craziness: "Oh, do not start with her, leave her alone." Finally! It took me good forty years to learn!

I can positively say that craziness is saving my sanity. (Is this statement an oxymoron?) I also learned that craziness can help inwardly. It can loosen you up, so generally speaking it is good for your health. Do not drink or smoke grass, get crazy. Unleash your mind, at least once a week, forget about being smart. Tell those who bother you exactly what you think of them or how you feel. Sometimes, it is like having a second pair of eyes that makes you see the funny side in any situation.

I feel I should make some kind of conclusion to this story. What happened to all of us? My daughter did not become a dancer, but is doing very well and I feel that God fulfilled His side of our bargain. He also made me remember what I loved before that lost and confused immigrant took over and pushed away all I was before. The world of words once again opened for me and luckily I just happened to be in the right city. Los Angeles is heavily populated with poets and writers, and believe it or not, some of them are way more crazy than I. In that way, my story has a happy ending. I finally found my tribe!

Not to mislead you, life is still a suspense movie and I keep swimming, but this time around, I am making as much noise along the way as I possible can.

secure these rights

LOURDES ROSALES-GUEVARA
Interviewed by Heather Tosteson

MY LOVE FOR THE U.S. CAME LATER

I was born in Baire, Oriente, Cuba in 1951 and came to the United States on April 5, 1968. I turned seventeen three weeks later. My son was born in 1983 and I became a U.S. citizen in 1987. It was not a happy day. I remember not being happy. I was already divorced or separated and my son was about four.

Becoming a citizen was a process of convenience. My mother, father, sister, and brother had already been citizens for awhile. I went to medical school in Spain as a permanent resident with a re-entry permit. Everyone told me it would be easier to practice medicine if I was a citizen. I can't say that I was proud to become a citizen. My love for the United States came later.

I did feel I would be renouncing something. I would be renouncing being Cuban—even though when we left Cuba they stamped our passports *apatrida*, without a country. My favorite cousin went with me to Immigration for the citizenship papers and I told him, "I am having a hard time with changing citizenship even though Cuba says it doesn't want me to be Cuban."

Developing Identity as a Woman

Even when we came to the States, I was treated as a child. I think of myself in Cuba as a child, and also in high school. I was so nostalgic for Cuba, darling. The feeling of womanhood didn't come until I went to Spain at twenty-one. It was the first time I was separated from my family. In Spain, college and medical school are together. These responsibilities were so great, that is when I began to understand myself as a woman, not as a child.

I received a call from the United States about my younger brother having an accident. My feelings were different from everything I'd ever felt before. I left Cuba as a girl, but now, in 1972, I was hurting as a woman. This grief I was feeling about my brother was different from crying for a boyfriend in Cuba or for my grandfather. When I heard about my brother, I left the party I was at and went to the Catholic church across the street to pray for him. I had a boyfriend in Spain. (There was only hand-holding in my culture even abroad alone—being boyfriend and girlfriend was only this.) My boyfriend told me, "That made a big impression on me—your going to the church to pray." I didn't know how to answer. I think it is my destiny to be apart from people I love when important things happen in their life or mine.

My relationship with my mother and my sister was not close. My mother was close to my brother. I was closer to my father then. I love them unconditionally but not as if I *belonged* in that family. I belonged with my grandfather and my aunt. I was always referred to as different.

My mother, who was born in 1924 like my father, led a very private life. She was a teacher in Cuba. She had her three kids. I never saw her really involved with us, the girls.

My aunt was single, a *solterona*, most of her life. She married in her fifties—when we were in the U.S. She was *the* special person in my life. I follow more her pattern. She had gone to university and gotten a PhD in pharmacy. Everything I learned about justice, honesty, and everything good was from her and my grandfather. My father was like a prince, a little spoiled, and my mother was passive.

My aunt was very intelligent, petite, a nice lady. Competent. My aunt married an old friend of the family who had become a widower. They told us he was looking for someone to care for him. They never left Cuba. I hear from other members of the family.

My grandfather was spectacular. Everything that has to do with goodness I learned from him. He was very successful in business, but when there was a hurricane, he'd go to the poorest in the town to help. My whole idea of how I could practice medicine came from my grandfather and how he behaved. He and my aunt were *good* people, he had a great sense of humor.

Our houses, my parents and that of my grandfather, communicated through their backyards and patios, so I spent many nights in my grandparent's house. After Castro, we all would eat together so the food would look like more, so we were at least eating breakfast, lunch and dinner there every day. They would let me sleep with my aunt in her bedroom many times. Even for

Christmas and *Tres Reyes Magos,* we would share our presents there.

Early Experiences in Cuba

My parents originally thought Castro was a liberator. My father and the Castro brothers went to the same boarding school. My father shared his treats with them because they always had the same thing: guava paste and cheese.

In 1959, when I was eight, one night they woke us up and took us to my father's cousin's house, where Castro had made a stop on his walk of *"freedom"* through the island. I felt so privileged. I wouldn't wash my cheek after Castro kissed it.

A couple of years later everything turned. My father said we would have to leave.

I do remember the fighting, when the *mau-maus* would come down from the mountains. I remember that for thirty days and nights there was no electricity. We ate catfish and rice, the only things that would preserve.

My grandfather owned two beautiful farms outside town. There was a manager and many employees. One of my grandfather's brothers lived on the farm. The revolution was worse outside of town, so my grandfather brought his brother and his family and every single employee to his house. We all slept on the floor. It was dangerous to sleep in beds because of gun shots.

My most revered image of my grandfather is that he brought *all* these people to town. I don't know if other people did that. I felt my grandfather was a hero. I felt privileged that they could do this.

Developing National Identity

How was I taught to be a Cuban, darling? During the fight to free Cuba from Spain, the citizens in my mother's city, Bayamo, which is a *Monumento Nacional,* would rather have their city burn than go back to Spain. I remember studying patriots, being enamored of José Martí's poetry. I remember having admiration for this city.

The town where my father and I were born is the town where prior to the Independence War, a group of Cubans decided to rebel from Spain. They call this *El Grito de Baire*. In my city, there were monuments to Martí and also to a local family with many patriots.

All of that had a lot of importance for me. Now when I think about it—I haven't remembered it for a long time, but I remember it now—in Bayamo, my maternal grandmother as a widow lived with a daughter who had not married yet. The previous owner of the house had left a locked armoire in the bedroom of my aunt. I was always curious about what was inside the armoire. They told us the family who lived there were parents to a woman who was engaged to Manzanita, which was the nickname of a young patriot who was a student at the university in Havana. During the Castro revolution, Batista's police entered the university in Havana (Castro was in the mountains) and shot a lot of people, including Manzanita, who became a martyr for the revolution. One day I opened the doors of the armoire. There were many letters from Manzanita to his girlfriend. I couldn't tell anyone about those beautiful letters. The girlfriend's family was one of the first who later abandoned Cuba because of the Castro regime. I was so impressed by these letters, the history.

Acculturation and Attachment in U.S.

When we got to Miami in 1968, Miami was in chaos because of riots after the death of Martin Luther King. My family were all separated and sent to different friends for six days. They gave us a box with sandwiches and we were immunized when we arrived, but the minute we were out of immigration, we saw an African-American man driving a police car with dogs in the back seat and two African-American men bleeding and running. The people with me said, "This policeman has a problem. He is African American and has to catch those other African-American men."

I said, "We left Cuba for this? This is what you made us leave Cuba for?"

I am a Cuban who has only visited Miami twice in forty years. Part of my anger comes from that introduction.

But my affection for the U.S. grew soon after I came. I began to work in the summers for money and I began to understand my parents saying we needed to go to the U.S. to provide us with an education. My brother was in a private school. I was able to go and study abroad through a federal loan. I could study medicine and enter the world of my dreams. I thought this was great.

When we came from Cuba, I was looking for a way to belong. In 1971, I joined a Cuban-American group, only Cubans. We were college students who thought that we could overthrow Castro. It was a proud group because there was no connection with past governments. Its name was Abdala, the name of the first epic poem by José Martí. We would get together and discuss politics, we would be appalled by the conditions in which political prisoners in Cuba were kept. We were a group of educated and idealistic young Cubans trying to recuperate our own country. There was nothing about bearing arms. We would meet in New York. We would write newspapers and propaganda against Castro.

One young man said, "I am Cuban not only by birth but also by conviction." I thought about this and realized this was true of me. We all talked for hours and asked, What is a country? The soil? The Constitution? Family?

I remember in March 1971, we went on a hunger strike at the United Nations while some members of the group Abdala tied themselves to desks in the United Nations with handcuffs that couldn't be unlocked with a key. This wasn't terrorism. These were people against Castro protesting the state of political prisoners in Cuba. I was not one of the handcuffed. The police came and had to break the handcuffs with a huge scissor-like instrument; they took everyone to jail that night.

Around midnight, I called home. My father said to my mother, "Don't continue dressing to go out. She hasn't been put in prison." Then he told me, "We saw a girl who looked like you being put in a police car, but I told your mother not to worry because you would be in an *American* prison."

Two of my cousins did go and handcuff themselves. But one is a consul now and the other a commissioner of education.

The next morning the newspapers said seventeen Cuban troublemakers spoiled the perfect record of the U.N. Inspector General. The students handcuffed themselves to different seats of different nations' representatives, but everything was orderly.

In Spain, where I went to school as a U.S. resident, I had to go to the Spanish police every six months because I was not an American citizen. We continued the Abdala group in Spain. With this group I got the sense of being Cuban. We had respect for this country that was accepting us and educating us, but *passion* for Cuba.

My father asked me not to belong in Spain because Spain was not the U.S.—this was the time of Franco—but I didn't promise. I lost two years of medical school because I was so involved with Abdala. It was so chaotic, and I thought my father would kill me. I had to repeat the exams. But my father didn't get angry. I guess he thought I would end up doing the right thing.

I remember my first year in Spain, a Puerto Rican student saying, "I'm flying to my *islita* for Christmas." This was in 1973. I thought, "I'm flying to the U.S., but not to my *islita*."

They allowed us to celebrate May 20th, the date of Cuba's independence from Spain, with a demonstration by this group. I wanted to print a Cuban flag but printers wouldn't let us make prints of a communist flag. They would not accept our explanation that we were politically exiled Cubans against Castro. There was a mimeograph machine we used in the middle of the night so no one would know we were printing some propaganda against Castro.

One day, there was a man in a suit who asked if I was Lourdes Rosales Guevara. He was a policeman from Madrid in charge of following all foreigners studying in Spain. That man spent several days in Saragossa, where I was studying. He met with us several times. He showed us pictures of ourselves in the U.S. demonstrating. We got really scared. His presence became like a ghost. It was not easy to do things against Castro in Spain. We were clearly not going back to our *islita*.

After that, everything settled. It felt *good* to be back in the U.S.

As I said, I became a citizen after I married and divorced. It was when I started working in a community health center for underprivileged children in Connecticut that I started to think I couldn't do this anywhere else. I began to see my father's point of view—that the U.S. gives opportunities. (As long as you don't mention the Kennedys to him. He still feels they would have sold Cuba to Khrushchev during the Bay of Pigs.) My father feels *very* American. His car and house both have American flags. He is Cuban to the core and American to the core. He has amazing respect for this country—and now I have the same.

My mother always said if the Castro regime fell, she would be on the first boat back to Cuba. She died here. People ask me the same—but I wouldn't go back. Everyone has died. My father's parents and sisters have died. I can't imagine going back without my grandfather and aunt.

Son's Cultural Identity

My son was born and lives in the U.S. My family is here. I was able because of my schooling to give my son an Ivy League education possible only here.

My son, when he was little, when people asked him what he was, he'd say, "Cuban." He spoke only Spanish and ate only Cuban food until he was five and a half. When he started kindergarten, he asked for cereal all the time to be like the other children.

He is bilingual. He reads, writes and speaks Spanish (with an American accent). He is an attorney and loves the Constitution. He is married to a very patriotic woman. He likes to do pro bono work. In high school, he wanted to visit Cuba but his father said no and he didn't pursue it.

My son likes Cubans—the food, the music—but sees us as a little wacky. One time he and my father were out and the car broke down and they called AAA. The man who came said *coño* when he saw the flat tire. (This is not a nice word in Spanish, darling.) My son came back and said, "Mami, it is amazing. My grandfather can tell with one word if a person is Cuban." He used it when he was a boy with one of the men I worked with in Atlanta, a man who also comes from Cuba. He thought it was OK to say it among Cubans. (He is almost right.)

Voting

My son says votes don't count, it's electoral votes that count. But I think my vote counts. I intend to vote the day after tomorrow. It's my privilege and my responsibility and I take it very seriously.

Value Conflicts

It might sound strange, but the ideal that I find most important here is the American ideal of the family. In Cuba we live more on the outside. My father used to go out with his friends. One thing I like about America, people come home after work and stay with the family. I was able to do this with my son even raising him alone.

The values from Cuba were imposed on me, and I imposed them on my son. I didn't object to them. Raising my son, I based it on Cuban values. In Cuba, we keep kids at home until they marry. Eighteen doesn't mean anything to us. They still have to follow the rules of the home. We say, "I don't care how old you are, you have to respect your mother. As long as you live here you have to follow the house rules."

I left home to go to school. When I came back at twenty-eight, I went back to my parents' house and followed the rules until I left at thirty to marry. My brother had an apartment in New York, but also a room in the house. I moved back with my parents when I divorced because I was finishing residency. I left their house forever when I got my first job as a doctor.

My son went to boarding school in Princeton when I went to work at CDC so he could stay close to my parents and his father. Then he went to college in New Hampshire and law school in Indiana, but always came back home.

Sometime I feel teenagers are feared by their parents in the United States. I can't swallow that. There was no question that my son had to do what was expected. My son felt the same way. There was a respect for authority, for age. My father was a difficult man but we didn't argue with him because he was the father.

EEO Lawsuit

A very big experience for me was when I filed an EEO complaint against CDC. I sued my division director, the deputy division director and my branch chief. I sued for discrimination on the basis of national origin and age and also for retaliation and a hostile work environment. I won twice. This is one of the wonders of this country. You can sue for your job. This was also the loneliest part of my life. I was abandoned by my peers. I didn't tell my son or my parents. I think my mother would have been in shock. We were never the kind of people to get into a lawsuit.

I felt empowered. I never doubted that my father brought us here for freedom. In my mind, in the way I was raised, I could not allow anyone to step on me. I couldn't do it any other way. It was hard, very hard. It lasted four years. But I never doubted I would win, even when EEO didn't support me. I felt the EEO person assigned to my case did not believe me, she was biased and unsupportive so I talked to her supervisor. She was no help either, so I called *her* supervisor, an attorney from Washington, D.C. He was half Cuban and half Puerto Rican and he believed me. The EEO binder they prepared was eight inches thick and it had all the proof they needed.

This all started when I was called into the office of my division director and told to sit down and shut up. She said that if I said anything at all, action would be taken against me. She read me a letter of reprimand based on strange complaints by my supervisor: contentious behavior, anger issues, stalking, shadowing, calling her a liar. I was told the letter would remain in my file for two years. I didn't know what to do. What they said was not true. I learned that an African-American toxicologist had received an almost identical letter. He was a very meek man.

From that point on I would not trust my own shadow. That woman had said things that were untrue. I didn't know how to defend myself. I called an attorney. He told me that the burden of proof was on them. That they needed to provide proof of what they were saying. But they had no proof. I had kept all the emails, all the copies of my work. Two years after the lawsuit was over, one day I heard this click, click, click on my computer and it was a sound to alert me that a message had been received, all those 32 emails my supervisor had said she never received were finally being accessed and deleted without reading. In court, she kept saying to the judge I did not do the work she had assigned me, but here all my work was still on her computer two years after the lawsuit was over.

At the first hearing, the judge allowed a certain amount of hearsay. This was when they said most of their lies, and because of that I felt, for the first time, that I could lose. The deputy division director, my supervisor and my division director all came. I was called incompetent. They said I knew nothing of pediatrics. They said that a previous director who was a physician herself favored physicians and gave physicians like me undeservedly high ratings. I saw the devil in front of me.

The judge asked them questions. I don't remember if my lawyer asked them any questions or only of me. What my lawyer would say was, "Judge, if you can refer to page x in the book. . . ." He said that many many times.

There was a moment when it all turned. The judge was reading through that big file we had given her. My lawyer looked like he was asleep. The division director took the stand and said, "I am so tired of all the paperwork and meetings Dr. Rosales is making us go through." The judge didn't look up. I felt terrible. I thought, oh, the judge is just reading and my lawyer is asleep and no one is going to say anything. But then the judge stopped reading and said, "Are you saying that it bothers you that Dr. Rosales is appealing to her rights under federal law?"

My lawyer, his head back, his eyes closed, said, "Yep."

The judge was female, petite, very white skin and red hair and blue eyes. She said she couldn't prove discrimination on the basis of national origin or age but that there was a clear pattern of retaliation. She said, "The system is there to protect the employee. We need to see that when an employee sees something wrong, they are free to report it otherwise the system doesn't work."

I wasn't suing for money. Maybe that impressed the judge. My lawyer asked that his attorney fee be paid. The judge asked if he had his bill and he did and she thought the amount was reasonable. I said I wanted an apology from these people, but the judge said, "The CDC doesn't apologize." I thought I was suing these three individuals but the suit was Lourdes Rosales Guevara vs. Tommy Thomson (Director of Health and Human Services at that time) and CDC. That brought tears to my eyes because I always looked up to CDC. I thought I was suing three people, not an institution.

My lawyer asked that a memo be posted that would say that retaliation had been committed in this agency and that these were the people who had done it. The judge said they couldn't list the people because the suit was against CDC but that a memo could list CDC and announce the results of the lawsuit and be posted on all the bulletin boards at CDC. When I saw the poster, I saw it didn't have my name on it either. People were reading it and asking, "Who could this be?"

I called my lawyer and sent a copy to him. I was so disappointed that it didn't include my name or their names. I told him, "I have a question. Can I put one of those posters on my office door—with my name and their names?"

He said, "You won this case and you can do what you want. You aren't under any gag order."

By then I was working in another division. I am respectful of the order of command, so I went to my new branch chief and told him I wanted to put the notice on my door and I wanted to put their names and my name on it."

He said, "I'd rather you didn't."

I said, "I need vindication and my lawyer said I could do it."

So, I put it on my door. People started stopping in my office, saying, "I didn't know it was you. You are my hero." From being so alone, now I was a hero. The word spread. I received many calls.

One woman said, "Luly, that was you? And I thought you were a nice lady."

I said, "It is because I am a very nice lady that I have to do this. So it doesn't happen to anyone else." Just the other day, I reminded her of this, and she asked, "Did I really say that?"

That was the first case I won. The second case shouldn't have gone to the judge. It was related to the first case and was also about retaliation. Since I had won the first case, the second case should had automatically been granted a win, but they didn't withdraw it. By that time, my lawyer was slacking off. I noticed he was complaining about the work. When I asked him how it was coming, he told me "Your paper is at the bottom of the pile but it is making its way closer to the top." I got tired of his attitude and wrote him a note, "You have work to do on this case. Do your job." He sent me a certified letter firing me as his client. I could have taken him to the bar. It is not right to abandon your client in the middle of a case. But I didn't do that. (We made up later, and he came to see me after my mother died. He was very different from me. An unadulterated product of the South. Republican. We never saw eye to eye. When I saw him on Facebook, I read he admired George Bush. I was so surprised. I was always talking about Hilary Clinton.)

When my lawyer fired me, I called a friend in New York and she called some friends and they helped me find another lawyer. He was young and very tall, 6 feet 5 inches. He came to my house and noticed my books on Cuba and said his wife was Cuban. This created a bond. My son was there. He was studying government at Dartmouth. Now that I had won the first lawsuit, I had told him what had happened. The lawyer asked us whether we wanted to pay him a flat fee or go on a contingency basis. My son and I decided to give him a flat fee.

I said, "We didn't sue for money before."

He said, "We're suing for money now and we have a deadline. Meet me at my office."

I went once. It was an impressive building. He asked a few questions of me. He took me in a black beautiful Mercedes to the hearing. The attorney for CDC was a young lady. The judge was not the same one. This one was African American. She had impressive jewelry and short hair, very attractive.

My lawyer informed them that I was getting compensation this time. The CDC attorney said, "We're not authorized."

My lawyer said, "The division director and the supervisor didn't stop their retaliation even after my client won the lawsuit. I want to ask for money for my client because CDC doesn't like to pay and it is a moral debt."

He said to the CDC lawyer, "Call your boss." He pushed four papers over to her. She looked at them and said, "I guess I'll call." She came back with a figure. He said, "I guess you didn't see this," and slid the paper over again. We received a financial settlement this time.

It made me cry and that made me mad because I'd kept my cool all this time.

When I came home and my son heard I'd won again, he lifted all my 180 pounds and said, "You have taught me determination. I've never been so proud of you as I am now."

I am a different person after this experience. During the first lawsuit, I was moved to another division. The branch chief was someone I was friends with, but now he was my boss. When I went in, he had us both sit on a sofa in his office. He said, "Congratulations. I hear you won. She was an idiot."

I told him, "I am not the same person I was. I am damaged merchandise."

He said, "The only thing there is no cure for is stupidity. The rest we can fix."

Now, I have heard from others that my previous branch chief had told other people she heard voices, so I think this person who I thought was so evil may have had mental illness. But that did not explain the behavior of the woman above her, the division director. In her career, she had made enemies. That helped me. My new branch chief was one of them. I knew for him to have me in his branch was a way of getting back at her. I'm not stupid.

He negotiated that I come, but only bringing my own full-time position (FTE). There were long negotiations, very antagonistic ones, but he got the FTE.

After those four years, darling, I felt I was a unicellular organism, like an amoeba. My branch chief helped nursed me back to health. I had a very serious time with depression. I made new friends who were good to me, gave me positive feedback.

They sent me to Pennsylvania to work with the EPA on lead contamination. There were very high levels of lead in soil and it was my job to talk with the community. I clicked with the EPA representatives and the people from the Department of Health. I had my own table. It was always full. Parents wanted to talk with me. Children wanted to talk with me. For me it was very natural, the closest thing to clinical practice.

When I came back, my branch chief asked me, "How did it go in Pennsylvania?"

I told him I thought it went pretty well.

He said, "That's all? Come and listen."

He played his answering machine. It was a message from the state agency representative: "What can I tell you? I didn't want you to send Dr. Rosales. But Dr. Rosales stole the show. Everyone revolved around her. She was a hit."

My branch chief said, "You don't get it. At first he said he didn't want you but at the end he admitted you were the hit of the whole show."

Even now, years later, I am on anti-depressants. I don't think I will ever be off them. I ask myself, can an event like what happened to me change my brain chemistry so I will always need medication?

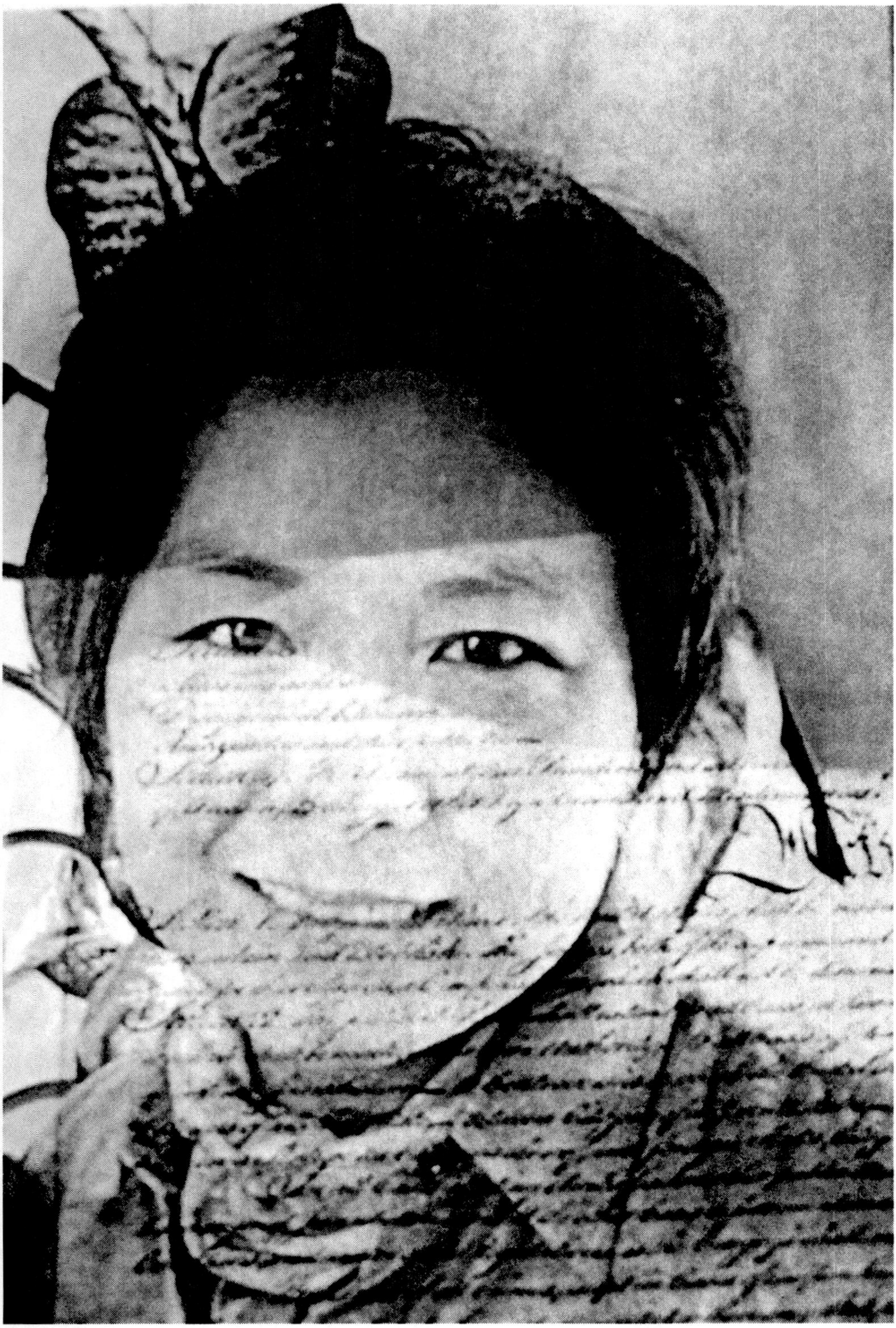

JIAN DONG SAKAKEENY
Interviewed by Kerry Langan

TODAY, I DON'T FEEL LIMITED BY ANY BORDERS

I'll begin my story by telling you about my mother, Jinghua, who was born in Baoding in 1934. When just a few days old, her parents sold her to a family that owned a lot of land, as well as a brothel and an opera house. Many girls had been sold to this family, and they all began doing chores as soon as they could walk. My mother refers to her position there as 'one of their daughters.' At a certain age, the girls began to train as singers. This involved lots of physical training. In Chinese opera, women play the male parts and men play the female parts. A performer has to learn accurate movements and gestures. The training was rigorous and brutal. The movie *Farewell, My Concubine* is an accurate portrayal of what it was like to grow up in an opera house. The children were beaten constantly as they struggled to learn to sing.

Each of the girls was assigned a surrogate mother, an older girl who would mentor her. My mother clearly remembers her opera mother, a very kind and protective young woman who worked as a singer and as a prostitute. She was beautiful with big eyes. My mom still remembers those big eyes staring at her when she misbehaved. One day she came to say goodbye to my mom. My mom never saw her again. She heard that the surrogate mother was found to be an underground communist and was buried alive by the nationalists.

My mother was fifteen when the communists came to power in 1949. She was then training to become a prostitute, but, fortunately, Mao outlawed prostitution. My mother will always be grateful to Mao for saving her from that life.

The communists assigned my mother a job in the Peking Opera, and she performed with them for six years, until she gave birth to my older sister. By that time, she was attracting attention in the world of opera because of her precise and superior enunciation. She had fans, one of whom she remembers clearly was a gentleman sitting in the same seat in the front of the opera house every night. My mom quit singing when my grandfather was relocated to Luoyang, Henan Province by his company and the whole family moved with him. At that time she was pregnant with my older sister.

My mom never regretted giving up her opera career. She said it's a hard life especially if one is a woman. She mentioned that the director of the opera house slept around with the singers a lot. That was how he decided whom he would promote to be a leading role. When I was growing up, I always wanted to be an actress or a musician. But she would say that women should never work in the entertainment industry.

My grandparents didn't stay in Luoyang long and moved back to Beijing as my grandmother kept getting sick in Luoyang for some reason. When they left, they took my sister with them. My parents stayed and got trained to be tractor factory workers at Luoyang Tractor Factory.

Four years later, my brother was born, and I followed a few years afterward. We remained in Luoyang with our parents, but we took trips to Beijing to visit my sister and grandparents.

Life was difficult in Luoyang. It was an eight-hour train ride from Beijing, a medium-sized city with millions of people, but vastly different in terms of sophistication and cultural opportunities. We lived in a one-room home and there was little money. Each month, my parents had to borrow money from the neighbors to buy food and make ends meet. My parents would repay the money at the start of each month only to have to borrow again a few weeks later. My mother often commented on the 'railway money,' the money we had to spend to take the train to Beijing to visit my grandparents.

One of my greatest joys today is being a gourmet cook, having the money to cook all different kinds of ethnic foods for family and friends. It is a much different situation from my childhood when we lived from paycheck to paycheck.

I was a very quiet, obedient child. Each day after school, I did my homework and then cleaned our one-room apartment. I cleaned up the tea set and swept the floor covered with the cigarette butts, I made the beds, and then I started cooking dinner. These chores did not fall upon me because I was a girl. My parents never forced me to do anything, but my mother often remarked, "My daughter knows exactly what to do. She sees what needs to be done and just does it." I was prone to sickness when I was young. My parents would save pennies to be able to buy me a small piece of meat to help me recover. They were very loving and made me feel like a little princess.

My grandparents' household was a matriarchy. My grandmother made all the decisions and was the authority to be feared and obeyed. Her husband was my father's stepfather. My biological grandfather was captured by the Japanese when they invaded China and was never heard from again. I inherited my Chinese surname, Dong, from my step-grandfather. He was very kind to me and would not allow my older siblings to bully me. He also tried to protect me from my grandmother's wrath. She was so domineering, however, that he could barely protect himself from her tyranny. Fortunately, he worked for a bus company located far from their home and was only able to return to Beijing every two weeks. Spending time in my grandparents' home impressed upon me that women are not inferior to men, that they can dominate them. My own parents had equal status; they worked and provided for the family together. I have never been in a domestic situation where women were considered less than equal to men.

My grandmother accused my parents of favoring me over my brother. She preferred boys. Boys carried the bloodline and the family name. My grandmother always wanted her grandson in Beijing with them. He visited them often and lived with them every summer and part of the school year. My grandmother used to fret that he was too thin and overfed him. Because he spent so much time in Beijing, I was essentially raised as an only child. Gender didn't matter to my parents. In fact, my mother became pregnant a fourth time with a boy, but she had an abortion. She didn't want too many children; life was already very hard with little food to go around.

From a very early age, I had a strong intuition that I would leave China. One of my early, if not earliest, memories was walking on a crowded street in Beijing with my family. We came upon a group of tourists (I assume they were Russian), and one of them picked me up and smiled, exclaiming over me in a foreign voice. I was perhaps only two-and-a-half, but I remember being drawn to the tourists, thinking I would one day go to the land where that language was spoken. I knew I would one day live my life overseas. I have always felt that I am a world citizen. I knew the path to travel was education, and I pushed myself to study hard, especially English. My parents were uneducated and that was a blessing in disguise. They didn't know about the typical mores and customs of raising children, how they should and shouldn't behave. Living with my grandparents, my sister was raised with lots of rules about what she should and should not do. Basically, I was left to my own devices and that allowed me to explore different life paths and different spiritual paths. I had the chance to figure everything out for myself instead of being told what to believe. I didn't regurgitate something I was told; I had nothing to regurgitate. I learned to rely on myself, to find inner strength. As a child and young adult, I chose to study very hard. My parents were very proud of me, but they didn't push me. That was my choice and I became a lifelong learner.

My brother and his friends found studying English boring, but I was always fascinated with learning English. I became passionate about learning it and eventually needed lessons beyond what my school offered. My father was very mechanically inclined and bartered English lessons from one of the English teachers at my school, an overseas Chinese from Indonesia, in exchange for fixing her television. She started teaching me college level English. Also, through a connection, my father managed to get me a set of BBC Lingaphone English Course with Records that I listened to over and over. When I first came to America, I had a British accent.

My life in Luoyang province was routine except for our trips to Beijing. Life became busier when Madame Mao wanted her operas performed around the country. Workers who had previously performed in opera houses were asked to join troupes and tour. My mother and many of her fellow factory workers began performing. When I was four or five years old, our whole family traveled with the troupe. I loved being immersed in music. My mother started training girls and young women to sing. No higher education existed at the time. After high school, you were expected to go to the countryside and become a laborer. To avoid going to the countryside, boys were encouraged to go into the army. Girls who could sing could become military entertainers. Young women were constantly coming to my house to train with my mother, so I was constantly surrounded by music.

My mother never trained me personally, though, because she did not want me to pursue a career in entertainment. She never forgot her experience at the Peking Opera House and cautioned me about men who took advantage of female entertainers. Still, music was very important to me and would play an important part of my life in later years.

My school life offered no opportunities for art or music, but I excelled at academic subjects. When I recited English in class, the room became very quiet because everyone wanted to hear me speak. My high school classmates questioned me about why I studied so hard. At the time, China had an employment policy where a child could inherit a job from a parent. My parents worked at a tractor manufacturing plant, and a job was readily available to me, but I wanted to escape poverty and I wanted to go to college.

It was an interesting set of circumstances that enabled me to go to college. Schools of higher education were closed during the Cultural Revolution. My older brother had no college to attend. The schools finally reopened in 1979, and I graduated from high school in 1980. I got accepted at Henan University, the first person in my family to do so. I majored in English and graduated at the top of my class.

Afterward, I moved to Beijing and worked for four years as an English teacher in a management college affiliated with the Chinese Academy of Sciences. It was an eye-opening experience. I realized that the people in the capitol city were quite knowledgeable and well read. They were much more sophisticated than people from Henan Province. For the first time in my life, my confidence faltered. My colleagues, while friendly, were also at times condescending, telling me how naïve I was about many matters. I was often quiet while hanging out with them, interested in what they were saying, but shy to contribute, and I realized I had to study more, learn more, and become more fluent in English. Every moment I wasn't teaching, I was studying. I worked there for four years.

During that time, I learned how to apply to graduate schools abroad. I studied hard to prepare for TOEFL and looked up schools in *Peterson's Guide to Graduate Studies*. I applied to eighty graduate programs in the United States and Canada during a three-year period. Because I was poor, I asked them to waive the application fees. I didn't get in the first year, I didn't get in the second year, and by the third year, my mother was concerned. She said, "Jian, if you don't go abroad this year, you should consider getting a boyfriend and getting married." I was twenty-six and she was worried for me. There's a saying that you get discouraged once, defeated twice, and the third time, you're a total failure. For me, though, it was just the opposite. I became more and more determined to go abroad. Finally, I got a letter from Southern Illinois University at Edwardsville telling me I was accepted and offered me a teaching assistantship in Philosophy and Women's Studies. I had no idea what that involved; I had applied to study those subjects because

I thought my background in English was good preparation, better than, say, for economics or other quantitative subjects. When I boarded the airplane to come to America, I didn't look back.

But when I arrived in the United States, my confidence faltered again. I had thought my English was very good, but when I went to school in Illinois, I realized I had much to learn. As a teaching assistant in the Philosophy department, I taught Symbolic Logic. I had to educate myself about the most basic tenets of philosophy in order to teach the course. I took some undergraduate courses to help me prepare. Writing papers was very hard. I had never really learned writing skills while growing up. I had a lot of catching up to do, so once again I studied and studied.

For a while I was feeling depressed. To lift my spirits, I decided to spend most of my savings on a flute. I had played a little while in high school and began to take lessons with the flute professor at SIUE. I realized how happy I felt while playing the flute and how much I missed being surrounded by music.

I completed my coursework in Philosophy and Women's Studies in two years and received mostly A grades. My advisor and my teachers thought that as a Chinese woman, I should write my thesis on problems facing Chinese women. I did exhaustive research, but my heart wasn't in it. The key issues everyone was talking about were so inapplicable to me and also, I felt, to Chinese women in general. I never felt that my status was lower than men. Women are in every way equal to men.

In America, abortion is a major political issue, but in China, everyone just accepts it. Yes, that's because the government is your parent and you do what your parents tells you. Americans see that as political, but abortion is genuinely not an issue in China. I see how much time the politicians in this country spend arguing about it. People devote their lives to defending or protesting abortions in America. People have lost their lives over abortion here. It's hard for me to understand why it's such a controversial issue. I couldn't pretend to have strong feelings about a topic that isn't an issue for me. I decided not to write the thesis and instead pursued another interest, instructional technology. It was a relief to study an educational, rather than a political, subject.

Music came back into my life full force when I met my husband, George, a bassoonist. He visited my campus to give a performance and it wasn't long before I joined him in Oberlin where he was employed at the Oberlin

Conservatory. George had been previously married to a Japanese woman and has a great appreciation for Asian cultures. We share many interests, especially an appreciation for international travel. I continued studying Instructional Technology and spent an academic year completing my master's degree at Rochester Institute of Technology. I returned to Oberlin and George and I married a month later. I attended performances of classical music and opera and also began studying art. Eventually, I began working for the Allen Art Museum. After years of studying English, I also learned French and Latin, and began studying Japanese.

When I became pregnant, I didn't care whether our baby was a boy or a girl. Gender didn't matter to George or to my parents either. We were thrilled to have a son, Nicholas, but we had a girl's name ready, Lucia, in the event that we had a daughter. As a parent, I allow my son to follow his interests and advise him to do what makes him happy. He's a musician because he loves it, not because he has to play piano or percussion instruments. Although also born in the Year of the Tiger, I am the opposite of Amy Chua. Many people are talking about her book, *Battle Hymn of the Tiger Mother*. I have seen what such parenting produces, children who seem accomplished on the surface, but who are actually automatons. She says "Rote repetition is undervalued in America" but that type of strict education, with no time off for creativity or time with friends, results in socially awkward students who know how to perform or recite, but nothing else.

My son and I have been students together. We took an independent French class together, and I received permission to share an art table with him at his high school. Sharing his learning has helped my parenting and it has created a very special bond between us. Nicholas sees that I am a life-long learner and I have no doubt he will be as well.

Many people have asked me about the one-child policy in China. I think the abandonment of baby girls is ridiculous because women are every bit as strong and capable as men. When I was in college in China, I knew a woman two years younger than myself, incredibly smart, who was the oldest child in her family. She was stronger than her brother and the only child in the family able to pull a big cart of coal. Her father worked in the city and she single-handedly did all the physical labor at home. Girls can work every bit as hard as boys. Some people cling to old feudal ideas about gender, but they're outdated.

I became a U.S. citizen in 1997, three years after marrying. I didn't want to rush into it because traveling back to China with a green card is very easy. As an American citizen, I have to deal with visa issues when I go there now. My Chinese family, however, were very eager for me to become a citizen and petition for my parents to come to America. My brother and sister-in-law were living in California and expecting a child. They wanted my mother to live with them and take care of their child. Every member of my family pressured me to become a citizen as soon as possible. To end the family drama, I became a U.S. citizen sooner rather than later.

I appreciate the freedoms I have as a citizen. Americans can speak out about social injustice and work to change things. My favorite aspect of citizenship is voting. I consider myself a Democrat. Perhaps in one hundred years, there'll be a voting system in China. Right now, one-party officials think they can do whatever they want, and no one can vote them out of office. The rich people in China are the government officials. Regardless of what's printed on their paychecks, they have much more money than everyone else. As an American citizen, I feel more or less protected when I visit China.

Today, I don't feel limited by any borders. Wherever I go, I feel comfortable. I'm not limited by nationality. I feel more comfortable in the United States than I do in China. I feel fine when I visit there, but I've never felt like I want to retire back in China. I feel I'm a world citizen. I think it has to do with the freedom I have always felt because of my upbringing. Nothing was ever imposed on me the way it is with other children in China. I was allowed to figure things out for myself and so learned what truly made me happy. When I was growing up, my mother said, "I have two daughters. One is a realist, the other is a surrealist." I'm grateful she allowed me to be a surrealist. It led to a wonderful life.

DONNA PORTER
Interviewed by Heather Tosteson

IT'S ONLY ONE WORLD. LIVE IT UP!

I was born in Ndola, Zambia, a town about four hours from the capital. I came to the United States twice, as a child for three years and again to go to college in 1991. I've lived here in the States ever since. I got my permanent residency in 2002 and became a citizen in 2009. I have dual citizenship.

First Exposure to the U.S.
The first time we came was after my parents were political prisoners in Malawi. My parents were imprisoned there in 1975. My mom was from Malawi. We had gone to Malawi to visit my mother's mother. They thought my father was the man who was running against the dictator there because he had the same name as that man. They would not believe that he was not that person. They were political prisoners for about a year. I was about three years old when this happened. I was in jail with my parents for a few weeks, then my aunt came and got us. My younger sister was born in jail. After that, my parents returned to Zambia where my father was a successful businessman.

In 1978, my father was jailed again, this time in Zambia by the Zambian government. They thought he was a traitor, that he was doing business with South Africa. He did have a business in South Africa but he wasn't a traitor. Afterwards, he was cleared and it was said to be false imprisonment. But after that, my dad said we were leaving Africa. So, in 1979, we left. He had a cousin in Connecticut who invited us over. We stayed until 1982.

I was in school in Connecticut. I remember the cold. In Zambia the official language is English, straight British English, not Creole, so language was not a problem for us. At that age, in school, I had a sense of being African, not necessarily from Zambia, but something different and exciting.

Our intention at that time was to stay. My parents were working on their green cards.

Then my parents had their own issues, and my mom separated and brought us all back. Really, we ran away. We went back to Malawi to her family. Malawi was very different from the United States. We were under all these rules. We couldn't wear pants or shorts or dresses above our knees. There were no television stations. We missed TV, but Malawi was a new place for us and there was lots to see. We had cousins we were meeting for the first time.

In a month, my dad came and joined us, and he and my mom must have worked something out because we all went back to Zambia together. (I have one brother and two sisters. I'm the oldest.) There was more freedom in Zambia than in Malawi. We got back into school. We began making friends.

But we didn't think we would stay there permanently. We thought we could go back to the States. We started coming back to the States every Christmas in 1982 and 1983. We were hooked to the U.S. at that point. I was comparing everything. Oh, there's no school bus here! Oh, there's no Toy-R-Us! No snow!

Holding Pattern in Zambia

I stayed in Zambia until I went to college, but I always intended to go to college in the States. In 1986, my parents took to me to London to have open-heart surgery. The heart problems didn't really affect me. I was very athletic. I was thirteen when I had my surgery. London felt smaller than the U.S. to me. I didn't like it as much. We were there for six weeks. My parents rented an apartment. It was just me, Mom and Dad. I felt like an only child and had a mix of emotions. I loved the attention but I missed the whole family.

For a long time, my dad said he just had a few things to work out and then we were going to move back to the States. We all thought we were temporarily in Zambia. We'd say, "Dad, this isn't fair. You said—" We kept visiting Connecticut every Christmas through 1985. We stopped after my heart surgery. So in 1986 and 1987, my dream was fading. When we came to the States people would say, "You don't have an accent." That was because we learned so early.

I tried to come back earlier to finish high school in the States but my father and mother thought I was too young. I ended up going to boarding school in my hometown, about forty minutes from home. A holding pattern, that's what it felt like. But going to boarding school was prestigious. I started there in eighth grade. I got great grades. By tenth grade, I said, "This is too much. We have to get out of here. You've said since fifth grade we were going—"

I was *so* determined to leave. I remember sitting with my siblings outside in our yard looking up at the stars and saying, "Take us out of here. I want to go back to New York." My brother and sisters, we all shared that feeling. We kept it alive with each other and would gang up on our parents. There was no Facebook or Internet, but we'd write our cousins and call. We kept that dream alive.

Then my cousins came to visit when I was in tenth grade and I had a secret conference with my aunt. "You've got to get me out of here," I told her. I brought her my report card to show my good grades. And my aunt took it on. She found colleges for me to apply to and sent me the application forms. It was good that my mom was all for education. There were big reservations about my going by myself. They said boarding school was a test of my maturity.

Coming to the States was a proof of adulthood. But it wasn't a rebellion against my family. In private school, it was prestigious to have brothers and sisters abroad. I felt it was bringing honor to my family. I had no fears initially. I made a secret promise to my siblings. They said, "You can't forget about us. You've got to get us out of here too."

My parents had a strong African orientation themselves but they encouraged our identification with the U.S.—in the movies we watched, in how we would all talk together about our experiences there. My dad bought a Caprice (we called it 'the boat') because it reminded him of the U.S.

College in Kentucky

I finally returned to the States in 1991 to go to Berea College in Kentucky. It was very different. I was awarded a full four-year scholarship. That was awesome. I don't think I cared where the college was. I didn't know where Kentucky was. I was clueless about where, but just happy I could go and that my parents agreed and that my aunt agreed to be my legal guardian.

But it was a shock. In my mind, the U.S. was New York. And we got to this little airport and this small town where the biggest thing was a Wal-Mart. My boarding school was in the bush too, I reminded myself. In my mind I thought I was going to a UGA (University of Georgia) type of campus. But this was a small college.

It had advantages. There was nothing to do, so you studied more and the distractions were less. There was nothing to get you in trouble. You had to do work-study. I worked ten hours a week. It was quite different from Zambian life, but fine. There were many foreign students—from Tibet, Liberia, Greece, India. Most of my friends were foreign students. There was a lot of adjusting at Berea: the foreign students, and the work-study program, and also meeting kids from all over the U.S., and trying to fit in and also trying to emphasize your Africanness.

There was one other girl from Zambia. Her younger sister and I had gone to boarding school together, but I didn't know she had a sister in the States (although I knew she had a sister in London). Meeting someone from Zambia there was a relief for me. I thought, here is someone who knows where I'm from. We can relate. We went to school there together for two years. We're good friends still. She's still in Kentucky, in Lexington. There was another guy from Zambia, a senior, but he hadn't been in Zambia for a long time. I think he spoke more French, oh yes, he'd lived in Belgium. I speak English, Tumbuka, Nganga (which is similar), and Bemba.

Some people wanted to correct you. In the first year, a girl came up to me and asked, "Are you gay? You *touch* a lot. In America we care a lot about our personal space."

Initially, I was taken aback. I felt as if I was chastised. For me touching was normal. So when someone approached me like that, I felt odd. But then I thought, I have to look at what I'm doing. I *am* in a new environment. Other people told me not to worry about it. They wanted to learn about me—my food, dress, the country. That made it all exciting again.

And I began learning a lot. I began learning about the Hood. I told a friend, "I've never been to the Hood." So we had our first Hood sighting. She was from D.C. and I went to visit with her one summer (the college encouraged foreign students to do that). I was trying to talk Hood. "Stop," my friend said. "It's not working for you. You're too polite."

"What?" I said. "I'm *down*."

But the truth was that I was coming from successful affluent parents and an affluent neighborhood. Many of the African-American students at the school were not. There were tensions about white and black music. I'd never had to choose before. In Africa, it was just music. We divided music by type, not by the race of the musicians. This was a re-education. I felt I was forced to choose one type of music, and I had to choose the African-American crowd if I was going to be in with the hip crowd. You should see my pictures!

It was a two-way street. I was also telling them about me.

"You don't belong here," one girl told me. "You are a *rich* kid." I was talking about BMWs, Mercedes, drivers. "Is your dad a king or something?" she asked.

The African-American students *were* poor. They were on scholarships. They came from real Hoods. There was a big group from Alabama. I thought I was coming here for the family mentality. We had watched Bill Cosby and we could relate to that—the four kids. That's what I thought I was in for.

They would ask me to do really basic things and I would say, "My maid used to do that. I don't know how."

Some people got offended.

"You Africans come here—you're kings and queens where you're from. You come and get our scholarships and then get to go back to be kings and queens again and we stay here in this racist fricking country." I guess they thought we had a bright future—that we were going to become great leaders.

I felt they just really didn't understand. It was very different for us. Many of the African students had lives similar to mine back home. My parents gave me $10,000 a semester spending allowance in college. It wasn't until I began to work and I had $400 a week that I thought oh, what do I *do*. We were at Berea and doing work-study and we would ask ourselves, what are we doing here? We could be back home and comfortable.

It *is* important to know where people come from, the culture they come from, what they are comparing things to. I meet people here and, like me, they went away to school—to England or the U.S. or to South Africa or Australia. And our lives have been quite similar. It affects what you think is success. For example, if I were to move into a little ranch house here, that would not feel like success. For someone else it would be a very big improvement. To understand someone you need to know what they are comparing.

But I also learned other things at Berea. There were students from Liberia who had to run away. They came from countries at war. That was not my experience. There is a woman I know who went to boarding school with my sister in Kentucky (I kept my promise to my siblings)—and her family had to run away from Liberia because of the war. They had to come here as refugees. Then her father went back and became president there. They were refugees and then he was the president. I met him. He was a nice man. Now he is on trial at The Hague but she lives here, just normal. She is my sister's best friend.

Marriage and Acculturation in Atlanta

My intention was always to stay in the States. I came to Atlanta after college because my best friend's brother used to live here, and I came once in college and liked it. Compared to Kentucky, it was a big city. It had more cosmopolitan appeal and gave me some independence from my family in New Jersey.

I knew what work I wanted to do. I was premed with a biology degree. I thought I could work at CDC (Centers for Disease Control)—but I couldn't because I wasn't a citizen. I worked at Macy's as a sales associate. When I first came, my parents helped me financially and then they stopped.

My sisters had already come to the States by then and were going to a boarding school in Kentucky. I didn't mentor them. They came so much younger, thirteen and fourteen years old, ninth and tenth grade, that I found myself needing to be a mom, not a sister. They had different expectations. They were into the high school thing—proms and things. I was never into that.

What was the shocking part of being on my own? Lots. The paycheck. The lifestyle—the difference between the one I was accustomed to and the one I could afford. I didn't want to go back to Zambia.

In Berea I was assigned to be a dental assistant to the college dentist for my work study, ten hours a week. After I worked for two years in sales, I decided to use the skills I'd learned at Berea and to see if I could get back into the health field that way. I wanted to see if I wanted to go back to school. So I started working here with Dr. Goettl. Eventually, I did end up going back to school, but that was after I was married and had kids.

I met my husband in 1998, we married the next year and I had my son in 1999. He's twelve now. I also have a daughter who is seven. I married someone born and raised here in Atlanta. It was a big culture shift. Being from the South, he could relate to the importance of family. But the cultural differences in our backgrounds were great. He didn't come from an elite background. He didn't understand my background for awhile, and then, when he did, he said, "Oh, you're a spoiled little African woman."

He was young, twenty-one, and still living with his mom. He didn't finish high school. I didn't want to tell my parents about us for the longest time. Not until I was pregnant. My parents said, "He's a security guard!"

I liked a lot about him. He has a good heart. He was a good friend. He was there for me. He showed me around, shared my goals. He helped trying to finish school. Initially we talked about it, and I thought he would do it. Then I understood his values for education were very different than mine, so we started clashing.

There were other issues as well. I am the first born, so it is natural my parents would come and stay with me when they come to the States. "How long are they staying?" he would ask. "I need my privacy."

"I haven't seen them in two years. They're staying six months," I would answer.

I was used to having my family around. Later my siblings followed me here to Atlanta. I don't know if this is a question of culture or just my family. We all go to church together. There isn't a week when we don't get together. "Who's cooking?" we ask and then we go there.

Or we'll just call up and ask, "What are you doing?"

"Nothing."

"We'll come over."

A month ago, we were at my sister's and after a big lunch, there we all were—my sister and my sister's husband and my other sister and my brother and his wife and me—all lying on the big bed watching movies with the kids jumping up and down all over us. That's just how we are. If you're not open to having people around, you'd have a difficult time.

I come from a household with ten cars. The keys were just hanging on hooks. You'd just pick up the keys and take whatever car that was. We still do that here.

My husband would ask, "Where is your car?"

"I don't know. I think my brother took it."

"You just change out your cars like that?"

I'm coming from a unit. What's mine is yours. I go to my sister's house and just open the refrigerator. I don't ask. It's just how *we* are as a unit. That's how *my* family is. Like my sister borrowed my other car—like back last summer. I haven't thought about it. But you know, now gas is going up and the Mercedes is getting expensive and it just occurred to me I have another car, a Corolla, and maybe it would be better to use it. So I told her, and soon it will be coming back.

"You are all like *Coming to America*," my husband once told me when my dad came to visit. My dad was with the president of Zambia. "Is your dad a king or something?" My dad gave me $10,000 just like that and my husband, I think he thought all Africans live in huts. He kept telling people, "Her dad was here with the *president*. He handed her $10,000 as if it was nothing."

My husband dropped out of school in ninth grade because he had a son and he needed to support him. My parents offered to pay for his education—but his priorities were different. This was when he began to see that there was a difference in the expectations of my family as a unit. There wasn't so much tension for me at the beginning because when I married him, I thought he was going to rise in status. Then I realized he wasn't, that he didn't have the same priorities. That was when it didn't work anymore.

Citizenship

I didn't become a citizen when I first came to the States. At first I was on a student visa. I couldn't get a visa through my husband because he had a bad work ethic. He had to prove he had a job and could support us and he couldn't. I always wanted to be a citizen.

I was out of status for a couple of years. It was worrisome to me. Maybe not for fear of Immigration, but because I've always liked to travel and I couldn't. If I left, I couldn't come back. It didn't affect what I wanted to do—except graduate school. I needed papers to go as an international student.

I got permanent residency in 2002, but because I applied for it as a single person, I had to wait for five years to apply for citizenship. It was more significant for me to become a permanent resident. It meant I could travel, go to school, apply for jobs. Before that it was more difficult to apply for *some* jobs. I always have this problem: In Africa, I don't have an African accent. In English, I don't have an accent, so people don't know I came from Africa, they just assume I am a citizen. That helped with some jobs because people didn't ask.

During that period, it didn't matter. I was in a holding pattern. I was here with Dr. Goettl. I came to work here as a dental assistant when my son had just turned one. When there were problems, Dr. Goettl would just say, "I don't want to lose you. What can I do to help?"

My brothers and sisters hadn't become citizens yet. They didn't worry about it. They all came as international students. We all had student visas, they had them for high school and then college. They traveled. I could have too if I'd maintained that status.

My husband didn't understand the immigration system, but when he heard they could kick me out, he said, "What do I have to do?"

"Keep a job." But he couldn't.

The process of becoming a citizen was not a big deal. At the actual interview process, they assume your English isn't that great. They ask you to write something like "I'm having a great day." They ask you, "What day is it?" They give you a DVD with 200 questions. What do the stars mean? What are the branches of the government? Where does the President live? Then of all that they only ask you three or four of them. When they tell you if you passed the test, you have to have your ceremony the next day. They put it up on a monitor. What your privileges are. What your responsibilities are. The ones I remember are that your privileges are freedom of speech and movement and your responsibility is to stand up for your country.

I brought my family to the ceremony. They took pictures. My kids asked, "So, Mom, are you are a real *African* American now?"

I said, "You're absolutely right. I was an African and now I'll become an American. Now I'm both."

Cross Currents

I am a dual citizen. I haven't thought about it that much. It just worked out that way.

My son and daughter are just U.S. citizens. My son feels like he is half Zambian. It's a girl-magnet point for him at twelve. He went to visit there when he was four. I'm taking them after school this year. My daughter is seven. I want them to stay for a year. I'm going to put them in an international school there. I would have done it a long time ago if I could. I feel there is a big disconnect in the school system here, and with the amount of help I know they need, it will be cheaper to send them to my parents than put them in a private school here. I think it is best if they go early. They will get a good foundation there.

It will be a big shift for all of us. I am finishing my master's degree next month and will begin a job hunt. Who knows where I'll end up. It will be more stable for them with their grandparents, and less stress on me as well.

My kids love to travel. We had a test run last year; I took them to London to my cousin's. I'm taking them to the U.S. Virgin Islands for their spring break. And then they're going to Africa. They think they're going only for the summer. When I did my research about college, I saw that grades don't really matter until ninth grade. My son is in sixth and my daughter is in first.

No, this doesn't bother me. With my upbringing I don't have an issue. I was in boarding school myself for four years. I tell people, "I'm not sending them to the bush. I'm sending them to the people who raised me and to the school I went to." I want my kids to be independent. They have no trouble going on trips with their aunts and friends. They just say, "See you later."

I have an MBA and I'm completing a Masters in Project Management. I want to transition into healthcare management. I wouldn't mind staying in the Atlanta area. I like Atlanta, but I'm open. I'll go to Dubai. Whatever. It's only one world. Live it up.

My brother and sisters followed me here, but I know they wouldn't follow me to Alaska. Nowhere near Sarah Palin. But everybody is grown now, with kids of their own. They'd think twice about moving. My brother and sisters all married Americans, but my parents continue to live in Zambia. I don't think they'd ever come here full time. Four to six months, maybe.

I'm in a new relationship with a man from Ghana. But he's not a good example of an African either. He came to the U.S. young—in high school. He is not traditional, more from New York.

I haven't voted yet—I missed the cut off. I'm learning how to get into all that. I didn't know about registering. I thought you just went in and voted. But I'm going to do it next time.

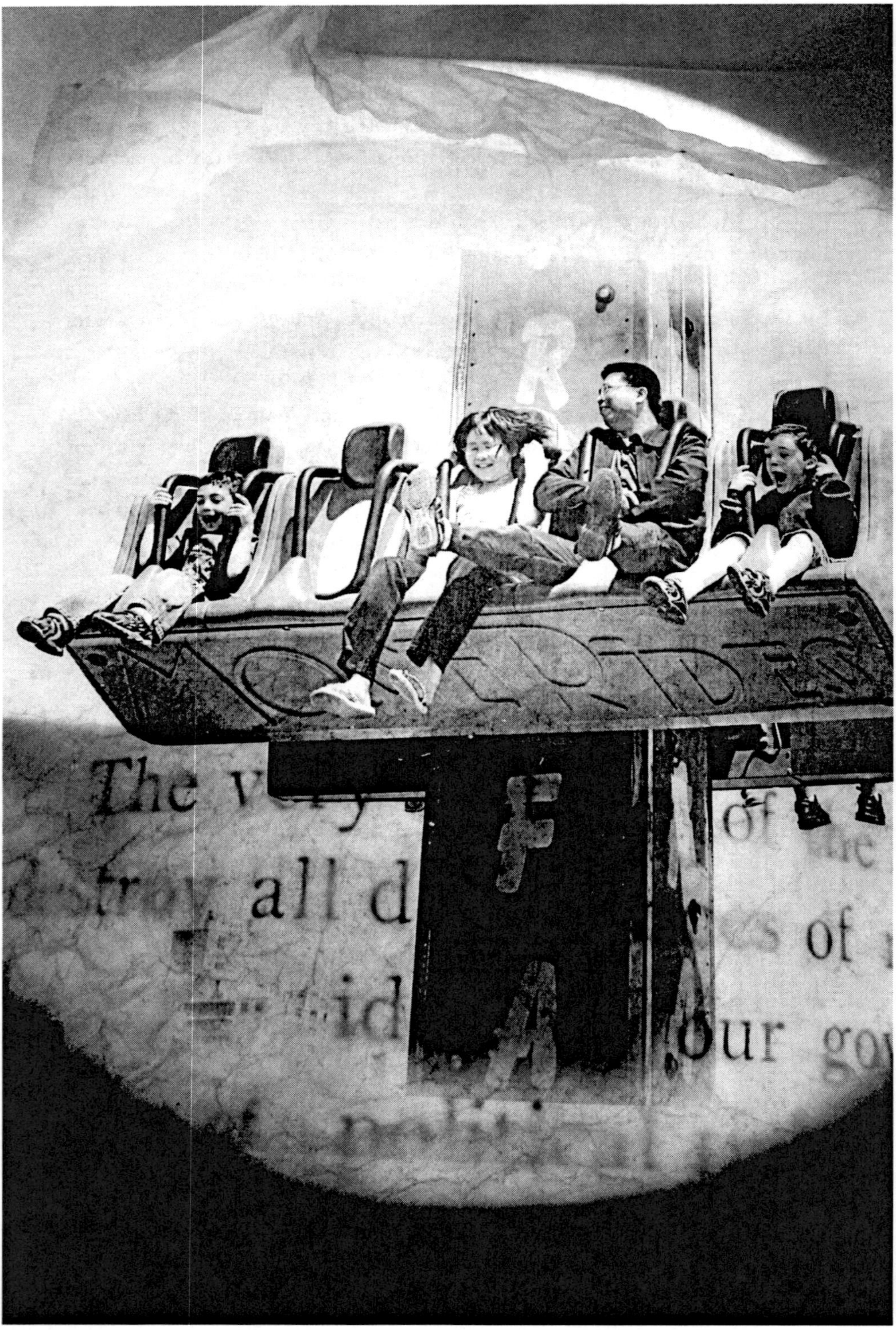

SELECT BIBLIOGRAPHY

Berger, Roni. *Immigrant Women Tell Their Stories.* New York: Haworth 2004.

Bloemraad, Irene. *Becoming a Citizen: Incorporating Immigrants and Refugees in the United States and Canada.* Berkeley: University of California Press, 2006.

Coates, David, and Peter Siavelis, eds. *Getting Immigration Right: What Every American Needs To Know.* Washington, D.C.: Potomac Books, 2009.

Foner, Nancy. "The Immigrant Family: Cultural Legacies and Cultural Changes." *The Handbook of International Migration: The American Experience.* Eds. Charles Hirschman, Philip Kasinitz and Josh DeWind. New York: Russell Sage Foundation, 1999. 257-64.

Gabaccia, Donna R. *From the Other Side: Women, Gender, and Immigrant Life in the U.S., 1820-1990.* Bloomington: Indiana University Press, 1994.

Graham Jr., Otis L. *Unguarded Gates: A History of America's Immigration Crisis.* Lanham, MD: Rowman & Littlefield, 2004.

Huntington, Samuel P. *Who Are We? The Challenges to America's National Identity.* New York: Simon & Schuster, 2004.

Pessar, Patricia R. "The Role of Gender, Households, and Social Networks in the Migration Process: A Review and Appraisal." *The Handbook of International Migration: The American Experience.* Eds. Charles Hirschman, Philip Kasinitz and Josh DeWind. New York: Russell Sage Foundation, 1999. 53-70.

Pickus, Noah M. J. *Immigration and Citizenship in the Twenty-First Century.* New York: Rowman & Littlefield, 1998.

Renshon, Stanley A. *The 50% American: Immigration and National Identity in an Age of Terror.* Washington, D.C.: Georgetown University Press, 2005.

Riley, Jason L. *Let Them In: The Case for Open Borders.* New York: Gotham Books, 2008.

Schlesinger Jr., Arthur M. *The Disuniting of America: Reflections on a Multicultural Society, Rev Ed.* New York: Norton, 1998.

Schuck, Peter H. *Citizens, Strangers, and in-Betweens: Essays on Immigration and Citizenship.* Boulder: Westview Press, 1998.

———. *Diversity in America: Keeping Government at a Safe Distance.* Cambridge: Harvard University Press, 2003.

Carol M. Swain, ed. *Debating Immigration.* New York: Cambridge University Press, 2008.

U.S. Citizenship and Immigration Services, http://www.welcometousa.gov

U. S. Commission on Immigration Reform. "Becoming an American: Immigrant and Immigration Policy." 1997. Web. 3 Apr. 2011.

ACKNOWLEDGEMENTS

Jennifer Bao Yu Jue-Steuck's "Goodnight Moon, Goodnight Mom" was first published in the anthology *From Home to Homeland: What Adoptive Families Need to Know Before Making a Return Trip to China*. Ed. Debra Jacobs, Iris Chin Ponte and Leslie Kim Wang (Yeong & Yeong, 2010).

Mariette Landry's "Immigrant Home Movie, 1963" was first published in *Compost*.

Karen Levy's "Americans" was first published in *Mused*.

Diane Raptosh's "The Mother of Her Second Daughter" was published in her book of poems *Parents From a Different Alphabet* (Guernica Editions, 2008).

Maria Shockey's "Oral Histories" is based on the third section of her MA thesis, "The Effects of American Assimilation on Chicanas."

Alexandrina Sergio's "Immigrant" is from her book *My Daughter Is Drummer in the Rock 'n Roll Band* (Antrim House, 2009).

Portions of Azadeh Shahshahani's "Reflections" have previously been published by the *Atlanta Journal Constitution*.

Sandra Soli's "How I Learned Resurrection" previously appeared in her book *What Trees Know* (Greystone Press, 2007) while "Foreigner: Learning the Language" was published in *Cross Timbers*.

Photographs by Heather Tosteson—who thanks all those, including contributors, friends, and family, who so generously donated images of themselves to art with no idea what words or ideas they would be brought into association with. A special thanks to photographer Alexander Devora. Texts come from questions for the U.S. Citizenship test, the Citizenship Oath, the *Declaration of Independence*, the *Emancipation Proclamation*, and *Civics: The Community and the Citizen* by Arthur William Dunn (California State Series, 1910).

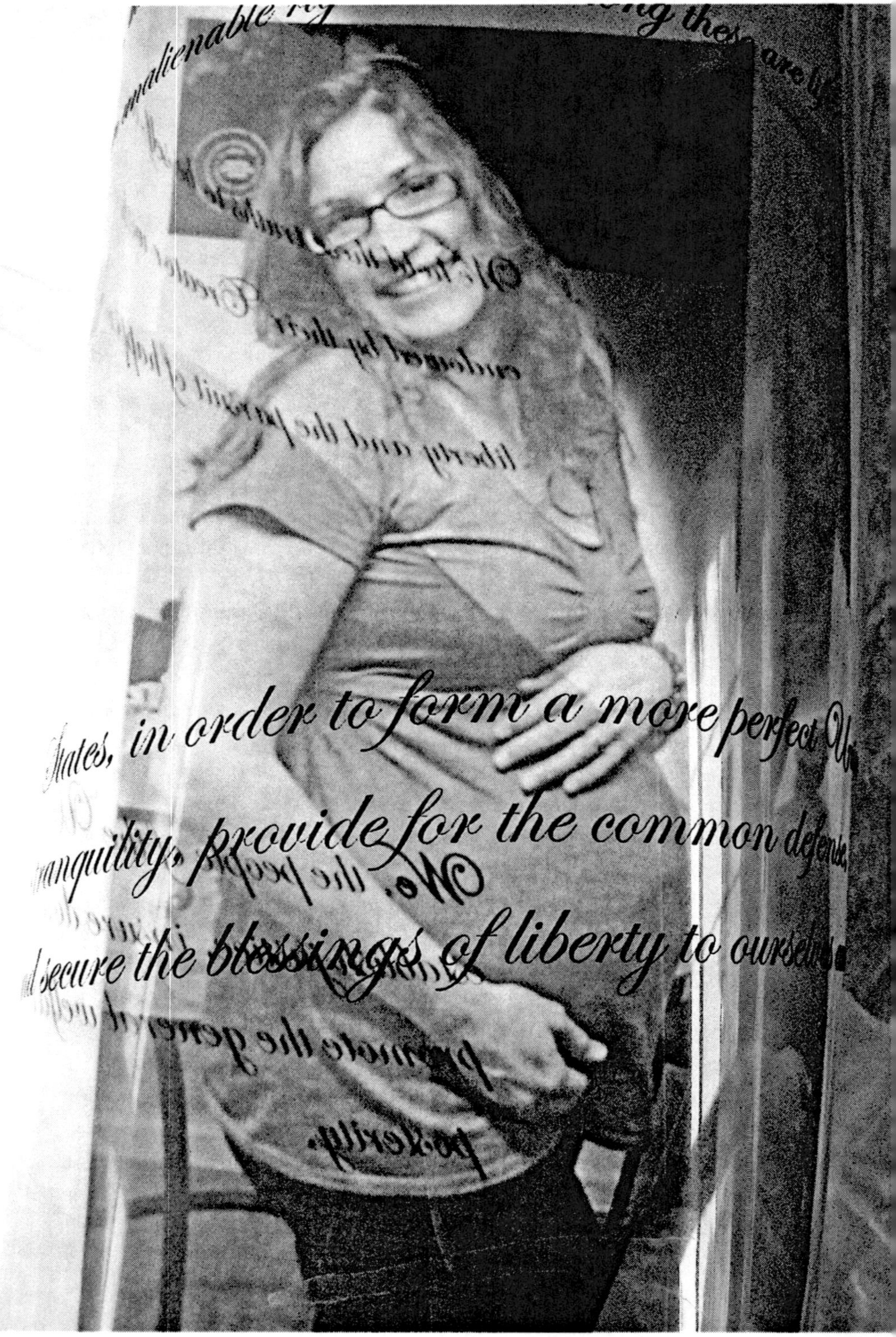

DISCUSSION GUIDE

I. THE HOLDING ENVIRONMENT

1. What are some of the most significant experiences you have had with naturalized citizens? Have they made you understand the importance of immigration differently? The importance of citizenship? Do you feel free to share these insights with foreign-born citizens? With birthright citizens? Why or why not?

2. If you are a naturalized citizen, how many conversations have you had with native-born citizens about their journeys to citizenship-by-conviction? Have you shared your own journey to citizenship with them? Why or why not?

3. If you are a birthright citizen, do you have a close relative who is a naturalized citizen? Do you think he or she is as much of a citizen as you? Why?

4. Do you have a strong ethnic identification that makes you feel like a hyphenated American—for examples, Vietnamese-, Korean-, Irish-, Serbian-, or Cuban-American? In which order would you put the identifications, for example, do you feel more American than Korean? Would you consider moving back to the country on the other side of the hyphen and becoming a citizen there? Why or why not?

5. In your lifetime, do you feel that the population of foreign-born residents has risen dramatically in your neighborhood? City? In the country at large? What do you base your impression on? Do you think other people share your impression?

II. CHINESE DAUGHTERS: ALL-AMERICAN GIRLS

6. What are the advantages you see for the baby girls given by the Chinese government to U.S. families for adoption? Do you think they lose something by being raised in the U.S. instead of China? Why or why not?

7. Some of the American mothers sharing their stories here feel a strong imaginative bond with the birth mothers of the babies and toddlers they adopt, one which, sometimes, extends to Chinese culture. Other mothers have a stronger feminist orientation that considers the babies in need of saving both from the culture and the government policy. How do you think these different attitudes may influence how their daughters understand their rights, privileges and responsibilities as U.S. citizens? Global citizens?

8. After reading these stories, especially the questions and answers of the teenagers, when you see a Chinese girl with Caucasian parents, do you think you will have different questions you would like to ask her? If you see an Asian teenager without her parents, will your assumptions about her and about her parents be different than they were before?

9. If you are a birthright citizen, how would you feel about having to make a citizenship oath for your baby that is far more explicit than anything you have been asked to make yourself?

10. Do you feel a child naturalized through adoption before the age of five should be able to be President? Why or why not?

III. NATURAL WOMEN: NATURALIZED CITIZENS

11. Heather Tosteson suggests that questions about attachment and interdependence are the source of some of the greatest concerns on both sides of the immigration question, in particular how well we can hold in consciousness that, on both sides, there is choice. How do these questions of attachment, interdependence and choice resonate in the stories in this collection? How do they resonate with your own experiences of acculturation?

12. Do you have a relative you know personally who came here as an immigrant? If so, what stories has your family built up around them? How do these stories reflect your own concerns about American culture?

13. Is it easy for you to identify with the aspirations of the mothers in these stories? Are their aspirations for their children, including citizenship, any different from those of the American mothers for their Chinese daughters?

14. The idea of going to college to improve future generations—often at a high emotional cost such as leaving family behind—appears in many stories in this collection. Can these stories offer hope to young students in America today who are often looking at fewer educational possibilities than their parents did?

15. Natalia Treviño worries that her mother may not pass her citizenship test because she has received only a third-grade education; Azadeh Shahshahani sees that her father can't tolerate the loss in status he experiences as a physician in the U.S.; Amita Rao, in her teenage disparagement of her mother, fails to see her mother's strengths. How many of these attitudes are amplified by the surrounding American culture? In what directions?

16. What are some of the gifts that the women writing here bring to U.S. society?

17. How important do you think age at time of immigration is to how successfully people integrate into U.S. society? Which of the women you are reading here feel most 'American' to you?

18. When she comes to any country, Clementina immediately takes on the task of learning the language. The Mexican-born women in Maria Shockey's interviews all stress the importance of learning English. Sonya Sabanac describes her languages as step-brothers, but for Mariel Coen, they sometimes feel like different outfits she can don to fit an occasion. Do you speak a second language fluently? Was it easy for you to learn? Do you ever feel, speaking it, as if you are a slightly different person? Does this experience help you empathize with the challenges immigrants face adjusting to a different society?

19. Did any of the attitudes toward the U.S. of the different writers surprise you or make you uncomfortable—for example, some of the adjectives Bernays uses to describe American culture and character, or Kulidžan's observation that Americans confuse power and greatness, or the comment that parts of the U.S. really belong to Mexico? If someone were to say these things to you, how would you feel? Would you say anything directly? Would your opinion of the other person, in particular of their patriotism, shift? How?

20. A number of women are in marriages that either facilitate or make it more difficult for them to become naturalized citizens. Is becoming a naturalized citizen an expression of allegiance to the relationship—or independence from it? How do you feel about a woman becoming a citizen out of loyalty to a spouse? How do you feel about a woman getting married in order to become a citizen?

21. In her story, "Goodnight Moon, Goodnight, Mom," Jennifer Bao Yu Jue-Steuck says, "the homeland trip is—in essence—a lifetime journey, one that varies as much as the vicissitudes and veracities of each individual human spirit." How is Sonya Sabanac's idea of "going crazy" also a lifetime journey that allows her to embrace and expand her idea of homeland while learning how to live in the United States?

22. Yearning—for both sides—is a pattern woven through many of the stories in this collection, including Angela Quirk's poem, "I Am from the Other Side," and Julija Suput's "A Bouquet of Roses." Many of these stories tell a tale of loss associated with the journey to the United States. What keeps people in America when the costs are so high and the yearning is so strong? What are the values America offers "on this side" that unify so many foreign-born residents and naturalized citizens with native-born citizens?

23. Sometimes, our cultural identity unfolds before our eyes in a surprising place or time. Born and raised partly in Cuba, Lourdes Rosales-Guevara describes how her sense of identity as a Cuban developed in the U.S. and in Spain, and how her identity as an American developed later. Heather Tosteson describes how living in Mexico paradoxically consolidated her identity as an American. Can we only discover a sense of identity by, however briefly, stepping out of the world in which it was created—whether that world is family, culture, or country?

24. Nostalgia is powerful in the works in this book, but so is resilient realism. How do we feel, as citizens, about some of these situations that demand that resilience from immigrants: for examples, the xenophobia described in Soli's poem "Foreigner," Kulidžan's description of the protesters at her nationalization ceremony, Clementina's experience with crime, Rosales-Guevara's experience of workplace discrimination? Are these dimensions

of choosing to become American that we factor into our understanding of cultural attachment?

25. In these works, women see themselves clearly in others, as Jue-Steuck does in the little Chinese girl she sees in Spain—and sometimes only vaguely recognize themselves in their own reflections, like the Bulgarian narrator in Sergio's poem, "Immigrant." In both experiences, there is mystery, questioning, and an accepted, but powerful, uncertainty. Many of the voices in this collection document the discomfort of uncertainty. How might accepting uncertainty influence the story of our becoming a citizen with a complex identity or allegiance?

26. The complex journeys in these stories, essays, interviews, and poems can be compared to the changing seasons, so much new growth, so much promise, patience, sacrifice, and loss. How does a particularly powerful story you read fit into the paradoxes of these seasons? In which season do you see yourself now? In which season do you see your own family's history of acculturation in their native country or birth country? Which season helps you understand your journey in cultural awareness and identity?

GENERAL QUESTIONS

The following more general questions are ones you would more commonly find in a discussion of immigration and citizenship. We invite you to think about how reading and identifying with the stories in this anthology and reflecting on how they resonate with your own experiences may have changed how you respond to some of these questions. We also invite you to reflect on how explicitly grounding your responses in personal experience—your own and others—might change something in the quality of your response, making you surer on some points and permitting doubt or even a radical revision of opinion on others.

ACCULTURATION

1. Which aspects of U.S. culture do you personally find most valuable? Which aspects do you find most distasteful? Why?

2. If foreign born, which aspects of your original culture did you most value,

and which did you find most troubling, before you immigrated? Now? How important has it been to you to continue with traditions from your original culture? Which ones? Why?

3. The culture of the United States came about from a composite of the many cultures of people who first migrated to America. Should American culture continue to change to incorporate aspects of the cultures that new citizens bring to the country or should new citizens be expected to adapt to the established culture? What personal experiences influence your opinion?

4. What are some of the most important cultural gains you see for the U.S. from the diversity brought by immigration?

5. What should all American citizens have in common? Do you think there are core characteristics of the U.S. culture that all naturalized citizens should be expected to embrace? All long-time residents, even if they have no intention of becoming citizens? If so, what are these characteristics?

6. Some immigrants come from cultures that allow females far less freedom than men. Do you know immigrants from such cultures? Do you feel immigrants from such cultures should be expected to change? If so, how rapidly? How does the right of privacy granted to all citizens allow for a variety of gender roles whether or not these agree with the American understanding of equality?

7. What responsibilities does the larger society have to immigrants to help them to adapt to their new life in this country? Are they greater if the person is a refugee? What responsibilities do individual Americans have?

CITIZENSHIP

8. What to you are the most important responsibilities of the citizen? To the government? To each other?

9. How good of a citizen are you? How do you define this? Patriotic feeling? Voting? Political action? Civic action? Private behavior?

10. What do you see as the most important advantages to you of U.S. citizenship? What to you are the most important rights of the U.S. citizen?

11. Do you think that there are certain privileges and rights that should be reserved to U.S. citizens and not made available to others living in the United States? Why?

12. How important do you think English literacy should be for gaining U.S. citizenship? What level of speaking, writing, and reading should be required, if at all? Should voting instructions be made available in languages other than English? Why?

13. What relationship or loyalty do you feel is appropriate to have with one's birth country after becoming a naturalized American citizen? Why?

14. Does it bother you that some immigrants might live in the U.S. for many years with no desire to become a citizen? Why or why not? Do you know any permanent residents who have made the decision not to become citizens? Do their reasons make sense to you? Would you expect Americans living in France or Senegal to make similar decisions?

15. What responsibilities, if any, do you think permanent residents with no intention of seeking citizenship have to their country of residency? Would your answer be different for American citizens living as permanent residents in other countries?

the _____ th_____
of hap_____

_____ ese rights, governments are

_____ stituted among women, deriving their _____

powers from the consent of the governed,

_____ that whenever any form of government _____

_____ _____ these ends, it is _____

_____ to insti_____

AUTHORS

Cathy Adams' short stories and essays have been published in *Utne*, *The Philosophical Mother*, *Ghoti Magazine*, *Heliotrope*, and *WNCWoman*, among others. Her writing awards include the Mona Schreiber Award for Fiction, a National League of Pen Women's Prize, and a National Public Radio News Director's award. Her work has been aired on Georgia Peachstate Public Radio and on Isothermal public radio.

Anna Mae Anhalt was born in Hefei, China and raised in Wisconsin, USA. She's grateful for being raised by a mother and father who love her so much. She has passion for photography, traveling the world, shopping, and learning everything there is to learn in life, and at sixteen, is more eager than ever to move out and head to college as far away from home as possible.

Patricia Barone has published a book of poetry, *Handmade Paper*, and a novella, *The Wind*, with New Rivers Press. Her poetry and short stories have appeared in anthologies such as *Bless Me Father* (Plume/Penguin), *One Parish Over: Irish-American Writing* (New Rivers Press), and *View from the Bed, View from the Bedside*; and in periodicals including *New Verse News*, *An Sionnach*, *The Shop*, *Pleiades*, *Commonweal*, *The Seattle Review*, *Visions International*, and *Widener Review*. She has received a Loft-McKnight Award of Distinction in poetry.

Elizabeth Bernays grew up in Australia and worked as an entomologist for the British government. She came to the United States as a professor at the University of California at Berkeley in 1983. Later she became Regents' Professor at the University of Arizona where she also obtained a Master of Fine Arts. She has published thirty essays in literary journals such as *Snowy Egret*, *Antipodes*, *Driftwood*, *Copper Nickel* and *Stone Table Review*. She has won several awards including the XJ Kennedy award for nonfiction.

Lisa Chan grew up playing around in her parents' Chinese restaurant kitchen. After pursuing a career in interior design, she traded her colored pencils for colored sugar. She now spends her days in a French pastry kitchen, designing desserts. She is working on a collection of recipes for living well and eating well.

Yu-Han (Eugenia) Chao was born and grew up in Taipei, Taiwan. She received her MFA from Penn State and currently lives in northern California. The Backwaters Press published her poetry book, *We Grow Old*, in 2008.

Clementina is the pseudonym for a young woman who arrived from Sierra Leone as a refugee in 2006. She works as a Certified Nursing Assistant and will be applying for citizenship this year.

Mariel Coen is an MFA student in Creative Writing with an emphasis in Writing Poetry at Kingston University in the United Kingdom. She is originally from Nicaragua, was raised in the United States and Guatemala and currently lives in London where she plans to study a PhD in English Literature and Creative Writing. Mariel writes in three languages and is currently working on a bilingual Spanish/English poetry collection.

Linda D'Arcy is working on a collection of essays and is a student at the Writing Institute at Sarah Lawrence College. She is the mother of four daughters and lives in Mt. Vernon, NY.

Madeline Geitz was born in Hefei, China, and has since spent her time undergoing commonly-accepted metabolic processes at the expense of other biological constructs. Madeline's favorite things include literature, history, science, mathematics, community service, social interaction, and her phenomenal mom, dad, and sister, Anna. She is currently a sophomore at Oberlin High School in Oberlin, Ohio.

Jennifer *Bao Yu* "Precious Jade" Jue-Steuck's birthmother is a native of Jiangsu Province, China. Adopted from Taipei by Americans from Los Angeles, she is the proud older sister of Chris, her brother (adopted from Seoul, South Korea). Jennifer grew up in Laguna Beach, Orange County, California. She is a graduate of New York University's Tisch School of the Arts and Harvard University, where she was a Bill & Melinda Gates Scholar.

Alicia Karls was adopted from Hefei, China when she was seven months old. She grew up in Rochester, MN and has an amazing mother. She is a sophomore at John Marshall Senior High School and is on the Competitive Dance Team (which is a sport). Dance is her life. She is planning on going to the University of Minnesota to get a special education teaching degree.

Nikolina Kulidžan's fiction, nonfiction and poetry have appeared in *The Sun Magazine, Best New Writing 2010, Exquisite Corpse, Reed*, and others. Her short story "Belgrade Motion Pictures" was nominated for a Pushcart Prize. She is currently at work on her first novel.

Mariette Landry has published poems and short fiction in literary magazines including *North American Review* and *Narrative,* and in the anthologies *Microfiction* (Norton) *Brevity & Echo* (Rose Metal Press), and *View From the Bed, View From the Bedside* (Wising Up Press). She teaches in the English Department and the Options Through Education program at Boston College.

Karen Levy is an American-Israeli writer whose themes focus on the need to find home and voice from an immigrant's perspective. Her most recent publications include excerpts of her memoir, *My Father's Gardens,* in two recent issues of *Blue Moon Literary & Art Review,* as well as in *So to Speak.*

Karen Loeb writes and teaches in Wisconsin where she and her husband raise their daughter, now thirteen, adopted from China when she was three. More poems about the adoption are in *Spillway* 15 and *Terra Cotta Typewriter*, an online journal devoted to everything China.

John Manesis is a retired physician. His poetry has appeared in over sixty literary magazines and journals, including *Wisconsin Review, Measure, California State Poetry Quarterly, Zone 3, North Dakota Quarterly* and *Charioteer*. His first book of poetry, *With All My Breath,* was published in 2003 and the second, *Other Candle Lights,* in 2008. His most recent book, *Consider If You Will* (2010), is a collection of sonnets that takes another look at nursery rhymes, children's stories and classic myths.

Katherine D. Perry has recently published poetry in *Melusine, Southern Women's Review, Poetry Quarterly, Bloodroot Literary Magazine, Sleet Magazine,* and *Women's Studies: An Interdisciplinary Journal.* She is an Assistant Professor of English at Georgia Perimeter College.

Donna Porter, a native of Zambia, is now a naturalized U.S. citizen. A graduate of Berea College, she has also completed her MBA and is currently studying for a Masters in Project Management. She lives in Atlanta with her two children.

Angelika Quirk was born and raised in Hamburg, Germany. At the age of eighteen she immigrated to the United States, graduating from U. C. Berkeley with a BA in German Literature. She has written and published poetry since 1990 in various literary magazines and anthologies, with ten of her poems appearing in *Parallel Verses* (2007). She was a member of the board of directors of the Marin Poetry Center for six years. She is in the process of publishing *After Sirens*, a book of poems summarizing her childhood experiences.

Amita Rao has had her prose and poetry published in *Papercuts*, a South Asian literary magazine. With a Bachelor's in English and Economics from Wellesley College, she previously worked in the corporate sector as a recruiter and currently does outreach and volunteer management for a nonprofit; she often mulls over the benefits of becoming a hermit writer. She is currently located in Atlanta, GA.

Diane Raptosh teaches literature and creative writing at the College of Idaho. She has published three collections of poems with Guernica Editions, *Just West of Now* (1992), *Labor Songs* (1999), and *Parents from a Different Alphabet: Prose Poems* (2008). She has published widely in journals such as *The Los Angeles Review, Michigan Quarterly Review*, and *Women's Studies Quarterly* and anthologies. She has won three fellowships in literature through competitions sponsored by the Idaho Commission on the Arts.

Lourdes Rosales-Guevara came from Cuba at the age of sixteen. Her family arrived in Miami on April 5th, 1968 and requested political asylum. After she completed high school, she studied medicine in Zaragoza, Spain. When she graduated, she returned to the U.S., took the necessary examinations for a residency in Pediatrics, and has practiced medicine and public health since then. She has a son who practices law in Washington, D.C.

Sonya Sabanac was born in Sarajevo, former Yugoslavia. She graduated from a law school in her native Sarajevo and in spite of working in the legal field all her life, her heart belongs to art. She considers herself to be a late bloomer. A passionate reader since childhood, she only started writing in her late forties. Her poems have been published in *San Gabriel Valley Poetry Quarterly*, *Magnapoets* and Poetic *Diversity*.

Jian Dong Sakakeeny was born in 1962 in Beijing, China. She holds a BA in English from Henan University and an MS in Instructional Technology from the Rochester Institute of Technology. She studied reflexology at the TCM (Traditional Chinese Medicine) School of China Reflexology Association. Jian is employed at the Allen Art Museum in Oberlin, Ohio where she has worked in a variety of capacities and is currently a Collection Management Assistant.

Alexandrina Sergio's poems have appeared in *Long River Run*, *Caduceus*, *Connecticut River Review*, *Encore*, *Wisdom of Our Mothers* (Familia Books), *Love After 70*, *Double Lives*, *Reinvention & Those We Leave Behind* and in a collected volume published by Antrim House. Her work has been performed by a professional stage company. Awards include first place, 2007 Connecticut Senior Poetry Contest, and second place, 2008 NFSPS Dorman John Grace Contest.

Azadeh Shahshahani is the Director of the National Security/Immigrants' Rights Project at the ACLU of Georgia. A 2004 graduate of the University of Michigan Law School, she currently serves as Co-Chair of the American Bar Association Committee on the Rights of Immigrants (of the Individual Rights and Responsibilities Section); Chair of Refugee Women's Network; and Chair of Georgia Detention Watch. She was born in Iran and moved to the United States at age sixteen.

Maria Shockey has a BA in English and an MA in Cultural Studies. Her thesis focused on Chicano Literature, specifically Chicanas and their path to assimilation. She currently resides in Los Angeles, California and is working on a book about the Chicana experience.

Sandra Soli entered the U.S. through Ellis Island. She received a 2008 Oklahoma Book Award, the Eyster Poetry Prize, and two nominations for the Pushcart Prize. A former magazine columnist/editor, she continues teaching and editorial assignments by special arrangement. Her poetry and short fiction appear widely, most recently in *Ain't Nobody That Can Sing Like Me: New Oklahoma Writing* (Mongrel Empire Press, 2010) and *Broken Circles* (Cave Moon Press, 2011).

Julija Suput has been a translator, foreign language teacher and foreign language educator for over twenty-five years. She holds both a BA in French Language and Literature with a minor in Italian Language and an MA in Teaching Foreign Language. Her first published work, "A Bouquet of Roses," is part of a book-length memoir in progress in which she chronicles in detail the first four years of her American life.

Natalia O. Treviño's fiction appears in Curbstone Press's *Mirrors Beneath the Earth*, and her poetry has appeared in a variety of electronic and print journals such as *Bordersenses, Borderlands Texas Poetry Review, Houston Literary Review, The Sugar House Review, Voices de la Luna,* and *Inheritance of Light*. She has received several awards for her work including The Alfredo Moral de Cisneros Award for Emerging Writers and the Dorothy Sargent Rosenberg Poetry Prize. She is married and has one child. She holds a MA in English and a MFA. Her first collection of poetry, *Eight Marry Wives*, is forthcoming from Pecan Grove Press.

Boryana Zeitz is a lawyer living in Los Angeles. She is working on a short story collection and on her first novel, a gossip thriller about European expatriates conquering lalaland.

Weihua Zhang received a PhD in Humanistic Studies from SUNY Albany in 1996. She teaches composition and literature classes at the Savannah College of Art and Design in Savannah, Georgia. She has written articles on Asian- and African-American literatures, exhibited her photographs in Savannah area galleries, published poetry and creative nonfictions in *People's Daily, Overseas Edition* (China's leading newspaper), *offcourse: A Literary Journal*, and *hopscotch: an online magazine for and by women*. She is currently working on her memoir.

Mother of Exiles.

GUEST EDITORS

KERRY LANGAN was born in Buffalo, New York, and completed her undergraduate and graduate education there. She had a career as an academic librarian before becoming a fiction writer. Her short stories have appeared in dozens of literary magazines in the United States, Canada and Hong Kong and have been anthologized often. Her non-fiction has appeared in *Working Mother*. She is the author of *Only Beautiful & Other Stories*. She lives in Oberlin, Ohio, with her husband and daughters.

DEBRA GINGERICH is the author of *Where We Start,* a collection of poems published by Cascadia Publishing House. She completed her undergraduate studies at Eastern Mennonite University and received an MFA in Writing from Vermont College. Her poems and essays have appeared in *Mochila Review, MARGIE: The American Journal of Poetry, Whiskey Island Magazine, The Writer's Chronicle* and others. She was awarded a John Ringling Towers Individual Artist Fellowship in 2007. She lives in Sarasota, FL where she works as the Web communications and publications manager for State College of Florida, Manatee-Sarasota.

EDITORS/PUBLISHERS

HEATHER TOSTESON is the author of *The Sanctity of the Moment: Poems from Four Decades, Visible Signs, Hearts as Big as Fists* and *God Speaks My Language, Can You?* She has worked as executive editor of two public health journals and in health communications with a focus on comunication across professional disciplines, racism, social trust, and how belief systems develop and change. She holds a MFA in Creative Writing (UNC-Greensboro) and PhD in English and Creative Writing (Ohio University). She is founder, with Charles Brockett, of Universal Table and Wising Up Press.

CHARLES BROCKETT, as a scholar of both U.S. and Latin American politics, has taught about immigration issues for over three decades. He has written two well-received books on Central America, *Land, Power, and Poverty* and *Political Movements and Violence*, and numerous social science journal articles. A political science professor, he is a recipient of several Fulbright and National Endowment for the Humanities awards. His PhD is from UNC-Chapel Hill. He lives in Atlanta.

See our booklist and calls for submissions for new anthologies
www.universaltable.org
wisingup@universaltable.org

tired, your poor,